Gardening with Woodland Plants

Gardening with Woodland Plants

Karan Junker

To my children.
To Greta—may your cycling ambitions be fulfilled.
To Torsten—may your love of nature never wane.

Published in 2007 by
Timber Press, Inc.
The Haseltine Building
133 S.W. Second Avenue, Suite 450
Portland, Oregon 97204-3527, U.S.A.
www.timberpress.com
For contact information regarding editorial, marketing, sales, and
distribution in the United Kingdom, see www.timberpress.co.uk.

ISBN-13: 978-0-88192-821-1

Design by Dick Malt
Printed in China

Library of Congress Cataloging-in-Publication Data
Junker, Karan.
  Gardening with woodland plants / Karan Junker.
     p. cm.
  Includes bibliographical references and index.
  ISBN-13: 978-0-88192-821-1
  1. Woodland gardening. 2. Woodland garden plants. I. Title.
  SB439.6.J86 2007
  635.9'67--dc22
                                2006013713

A catalogue record for this book is also available from the
British Library.

Frontispiece: Guaranteed to make a statement in any
woodland garden, *Acer palmatum* cultivars are beautiful at
any time, but their forte has to be their autumn colours.

Contents

Foreword

One of my father's many interests was trees, from the humble moorland birch to the giant Douglas fir that grew at the top of the garden. He had a great passion for them, and when as a boy I went out on walks with him, that passion and knowledge were transferred to me. It was this small beginning that brought me into horticulture as a profession, and therefore as soon as I became a student I was drawn into the world of plants, particularly those plants that grew in the woodland garden at Dartington Hall.

Karan Junker's enthusiastic love of woodland plants, and the practical knowledge she has developed by working with these special plants, has allowed her to write this book in such an informative way so as to make easy reading for the amateur gardener or for professional horticulturalists alike. Her enthusiastic writing takes me back to the time when I started helping to create the Garden in the Wood at Knightshayes, in Devon, in the early 1960s. The idea of forming borders and raised beds in an English woodland setting was relatively new at the time and the owners of Knightshayes, Sir John and Lady Heathcoat Amory, had first conceived the idea in the late 1940s. Initially they carried out the project themselves, developing the borders and setting out the plants without the aid of gardeners to help them.

Many years later, it was at Knightshayes that I first met Karan and her husband, Nick, when they were thinking of creating a garden of their own in Somerset. I have subsequently had the privilege to watch it develop and grow. Their selection of plants, be it choice bulbs, the natural woodland ferns, herbaceous plants, or the range of shrubs and trees that they have planted, has provided firsthand experience for Karan to enable her to write this excellent book.

The plants that she has chosen, whether the North American erythroniums or trilliums, or the Japanese maples, are all mouth watering. Memories for me flood back when I am reminded of great drifts of early spring woodland bulbs growing under the swelling buds of the numerous shrubs that prefer the canopy shade of their larger cousins. Further reminders are in the book for the many herbaceous treasures that thrive in dappled shade and all the plants that give those brilliant autumn colours that subsequently light up the arena at the end of the year. I have been lucky enough to be able to grow so many of the plants described in this book, while there are several which are new to me. If only such a book had been available when I first started, it would have been such a great help to my colleagues and myself to have been able to refer to Karan's hands-on knowledge.

For me and for many other gardeners, growing plants and gardening within a wood-land setting has given so much pleasure and satisfaction. When traditional gardens have produced beautifully planted herbaceous borders in full sun, it has always been a fasci-nation for me to grow a wonderful range of herbaceous plants beneath the trees or on the edge of a woodland clearing. This book has brought together all the best available plants for creating a "garden in the wood" so that there is now no need to spend unnec-essary hours searching through nursery catalogues looking for likely plant subjects that will thrive in a woodland. I am sure that once this book is part of a gardener's library it will be used so frequently that it will become the best bedtime reading.

Michael Hickson
Member, Royal Horticultural Society AGM Selection Committee and NCCPG
National Committee; former Head Gardener, Knightshayes Garden, Devon England

Preface and Acknowledgements

Woodlands are such magical places, with the ghostly winter structures, the riotous colours of spring, the cool oasis of summer tranquillity, and the exuberant magnificence of autumn. In these pages, I share my enthusiasm for the plants which thrive in their protective embrace. I discuss how a woodland can be created from scratch, no matter how small the scale. I explore the bewildering array of beautiful plants adapted to woodland life. I hope to inspire everyone to make the most of the environment which they have, to show how easy and rewarding it is to enhance natural woodland.

Acknowledgements

Gardeners are wonderful people, prepared to give of their time, wisdom, and gardens unconditionally. Without them, the world would be a poorer place.

I am grateful to the National Collection holders who shared their specialist knowledge, with particular thanks to the following who allowed us to enjoy and photograph their plants and woodlands: Mark Flanagan, Savill Garden, Windsor, Berkshire; Bleddyn and Sue Wynn-Jones, Crûg Farm Plants, Caernarfon, Gwynedd; John Lanyon, Knightshayes Court, Tiverton, Devon; Kenneth Ashburner, Stone Lane Gardens, Chagford, Devon; Jane Kimber, Littlecourt, Taunton, Somerset; Lady Christine Skelmersdale, Broadleigh Gardens, Taunton, Somerset; Sir John and Lady Quicke, Sherwood, Exeter, Devon; John Massey, Ashwood Nurseries Ltd., Kingswinford, West Midlands; and Christopher Ireland-Jones, Avon Bulbs, South Petherton, Somerset.

The balance of the photographs were taken in our own gardens and nursery.

I would also like to express my appreciation to Michael Hickson, former head gardener at Knightshayes Court. The woodland garden there has been a source of personal inspiration for a great many years.

I am indebted to my husband, Nick, for his help with proofreading and most of the photographs. I am delighted that I was also able to use some photographs taken by my young son, Torsten. His enthusiasm is a joy. Thanks also to Tordis and Geoff Pagotto, at Fototek, for their technical assistance.

Most of all, I am eternally grateful to my mother, from whom I inherited my love of gardening. Without her encouragement during my childhood, none of this would have happened. This project would not have been possible without the patience and support of my family. Thank you.

Galanthus nivalis carpets this natural woodland to be followed by *Narcissus*, one species succeeding the next almost to the exclusion of all else.

Japanese maples such as this specimen, resplendent in its autumn colour, are perfect additions within a natural woodland to create the middle canopy.

The bare woodland floor is transformed when a wonderful, informal riot of colour—here including *Cyclamen repandum*, *Epimedium*, *Scilla*, *Anemone*, and *Ranunculus ficaria*—follows on from native snowdrops.

CHAPTER 1

The Magic of Woodlands

Woodlands are magical places at any time of year, and the many different types of woodlands provide unique experiences. Completely natural woodlands may have a wild abundance of vegetation or almost nothing between the tall trees and the bare soil. Woodlands within gardens may also include predominantly natural flora, or they may consist of a carefully cultivated collection of eclectic shade-loving plants. Perhaps the best solution is a wonderful compromise, where the innate exuberance of the wild plants is supplemented with a seemingly limitless array of exciting woodlanders originating from all corners of the globe.

A woodland can be to any scale; of course, the larger it is the more scope available for additional planting, but careful plant selection can bring a woodland atmosphere to any garden. Within a woodland, plants are layered, growing one beneath another to make maximum use of not only the area, but of the special micro-climate created within it. In the woodland garden, we can manipulate nature to develop these layers, encourage the juxtaposition of numerous species, and create different textural and colour combinations. Weaving a lovingly planted carpet of native and cultivated species beneath beautiful trees creates a unique and rewarding gardening experience.

Veiled woodland opportunities are abundant in so many gardens. These need not be large areas; just a few trees planted at the end of the lawn, or a large and mature specimen, can be perfect starting points. There is exciting potential to develop the natural woodland character of such features while simultaneously bringing them into the garden. Even a utilitarian mixed deciduous hedge can become an area of beauty. It is equally feasible to transform a single old fruit tree or a whole orchard (although care should be taken not to reduce light and air movement around the fruit trees); careful consideration of seasonal growth patterns need not even affect the harvest. Indeed, a woodland effect can be achieved without any trees at all—perhaps utilising a shady wall of the house or another building, or an area along a damp and shaded passageway. There is no better solution to those dark and difficult corners, all becoming magical opportunities for experimentation with woodland plants.

A multicoloured carpet, with *Anemone nemorosa*, *Cyclamen repandum*, and *Scilla bithynica*, takes time to develop under modest sized trees that create the canopy in smaller woodland gardens.

Woodland Layers

I have divided my dream woodland conceptually into three different levels. The upper canopy are the large trees, the mature woodland giants towering majestically over the middle canopy beneath. The middle canopy can be chosen from an almost limitless range of smaller trees and larger shrubs, but it is this layer which is so often missing from truly wild woodlands. Continuing to diminish in size, the lowest canopy is to be found on the woodland floor, where herbaceous perennials and bulbs can gloriously intermingle to form a carpet of colour. Such is the diversity of wild woodland that sometimes all three may merge to become a jungle-like whole, but more often the middle layer will be almost absent. The lower two layers are thus present to varying degrees, determined, as we shall see, by the character of the upper canopy.

Each layer makes its own contribution to the success of the woodland as a whole, but the selection of canopy plants should be influenced by the size of the woodland, so that within a small garden everything needs to be scaled down. The same type of tree that becomes the middle canopy in a large woodland would in a smaller garden actually provide the canopy itself. It is important to match the trees with the site, in terms of sun tolerance and speed of establishment. Fundamentally, the more resilient middle canopy trees will be perfect to provide the smaller scale canopy in their own right. No matter the scale of the canopy, the principle is still the same; the biggest plants provide the protection and shelter to allow others to flourish beneath and around them.

Upper canopy

In an existing mature woodland, the upper canopy is already in place. However, if it is sparse, it may be appropriate to supplement it with additional trees to develop the canopy further; if it is dense, it may be necessary to remove some to increase the amount of light reaching the woodland floor. If space permits, this upper canopy can comprise some truly big trees, though it will take many years before the ultimate height of the new additions is achieved. A number of aesthetically pleasing trees will augment the natural woodland feel. These need to be tough enough to withstand the elements and to attain substantial proportions as fast as possible to provide protection for the lower layers.

The sugar maple, *Acer saccharum*, is the source of delicious maple syrup, though for my woodland planting I am more interested in its cultivars with pretty divided leaves and wonderful autumn colours. Another North American native is *A. rubrum*, whose common name of red maple aptly describes its fantastic autumn colour. All the many named selections of these are worthy of inclusion for their magical autumn displays. I can think of few trees which are as undemanding, yet pleasing, on our heavy clay soil as *A. campestre*, the humble English field maple. Inevitably cultivars are available, but this is one occasion when I am content to enjoy the simplicity of the species.

Colourful additions for foliage, flower, and bark

Often confused with *Acer* is *Liquidambar*, also grown primarily for its outstanding autumn colour, which varies from the deepest, darkest burgundy to brighter, more fiery shades of red, orange, and yellow. The simplest way of differentiating between these two aesthetically similar genera is to look at the arrangement of the buds. In *Acer* buds are paired, or opposite, while in *Liquidambar* they are alternate. It is noticeable how late *Liquidambar* come into leaf, giving plenty of opportunity for spring light to warm the woodland floor beneath them, encouraging early bulbs to burst into life. Happily, they change colour later in the year, too. In fact, they are often still clothed with their autumnal leaves after Christmas where I live, so it is rather useful having them out of synchronisation with everything else.

The brilliant autumn colours of *Acer rubrum* 'Somerset'

Magnolias are classic trees. Some are grandiose enough to take their place in this upper canopy, though modern breeding has developed numerous cultivars which do not become quite so large but which flower from a young age. It may be more appropriate, dependent on the scale of the planting, to consider some of the aristocratic big

Liquidambar styraciflua 'Worplesdon' in all its autumn splendour

Opposite: Deciduous magnolias illuminate the upper canopy when they burst into flower, such as this modern hybrid blooming at a young age.

magnolias. Long associated with the great plant-hunters exploring China at the turn of the twentieth century, the great drawback of these awe-inspiring species is that they can take many years to flower; certainly 15 or more is common. Utterly spectacular for a few weeks in the spring, they quietly merge into the canopy through the summer. *Magnolia campbellii* is beyond comparison in the Cornish gardens, but it performs best in sheltered locations on acidic soil. Though still benefiting enormously from the woodland environment, I am relieved that other majestic species are more easily pleased.

We have planted a great many *Betula* because they are so easy to grow, even on our heavy clay. They rapidly gain height and substance, so a canopy can be achieved with deceptive speed and ease. Their one drawback is that they are shallow rooted, so thoughtful underplanting is needed. It is easier to introduce carpeting plants with relatively newly planted *Betula* than it is to add them beneath mature plants whose roots have become established, as they can develop together. I cannot dispute the beauty of the many named forms of the glistening white-barked classic silver birch, *Betula utilis*, but other selections have different bark colour, even deep orange-mahogany. Indeed there can be few more inspiring sights at almost any time of year than a shaft of sunlight sparkling on their bark. It takes a few years for the wood to mature to reveal its true characteristics, but it is always worth the wait. My personal favourites are the smoky pink colours of the *B. albosinensis* cultivars. These trees give me pleasure through every season. In spring, the new foliage is so fresh and clean while the vertical accent of the different bark colours adds another dimension to the verdant summer woodland. Yellow autumn colour gives a hint of the beauty to come as I eagerly anticipate the unencumbered view of the gorgeous peeling bark, radiant in the winter sun.

Handsome ferns overcome this birch's shallow root system.

Some trees are not ideal

Unfortunately, some trees do not lend themselves to underplanting and are not welcome additions to the woodland garden. Although acers are an obsession for me, sycamores (*Acer pseudoplatanus*) are to be avoided—in fact, they are often considered to be weed trees in forestry situations. There is discussion that the sycamore problem is worsening with global warming, that they are adapting to take advantage of the milder winters faster than other trees. Thus they are coming into leaf earlier in the spring and achieving more growth in a season, making them grow even faster. They form a dense canopy which will let little light through and have an aggressive root system; they also set copious seed which germinates very readily so they spread prodigiously. Although it is possible, with a great deal of effort, to underplant sycamores surprisingly effectively, many more amenable and attractive alternatives are suitable for this upper canopy.

Aesculus can also be thugs, as they have aggressive root systems, taking up lots of water to support the huge canopy. An almost greater problem is caused by the leaves that drop; they are large and decay slowly, thus potentially smothering the more fragile plants on which they land. Indeed this is something to consider when planting trees. Even magnolia, which are spectacular and eminently suitable woodland trees, have large leaves that will overwhelm smaller plants beneath which are still active in the autumn. I restrict my underplanting in these areas to spring performers who will happily push up through the protective remains of the leafy autumn blanket.

An existing sycamore canopy can be extensively underplanted with woodland plants such as *Tellima grandiflora* by adding topsoil and mulching generously. Middle canopy trees and shrubs will, however, struggle to compete.

Ornamental cherries are some of the most popular garden trees, and admittedly many are spectacular in spring while in flower, but they also have aggressive root systems, which are actually very shallow. This is troublesome for underplanting since they are in direct competition for the same moisture. The deeper rooted plants take their water from a much lower layer, which need not have such an impact on the shallow-rooted woodlanders. Cherries are also notoriously vulnerable to an astonishingly wide range of diseases, being unsightly until such time as they kill the tree.

Conifers can be difficult to underplant, too, although they are a valuable asset for winter interest and protection. With their shaggy, needle-clad branches against the comparative roundness of most deciduous foliage, gnarled mature pines can be magnificent and are rarely a problem. By contrast, the ubiquitous Leyland cypress, so often used for rapid hedging, is so dense and greedy that little will thrive beneath it. Most other conifers are worth salvaging and many can beneficially be added, though the majority are slow growing so will take a long time to achieve the desired effect. Nevertheless, the winter shelter which they bring to all levels of the woodland is sufficiently valuable that it is worth the effort.

Middle canopy

When chosen well, the upper canopy will act both as shelter and backdrop to some wonderful shrubs and smaller trees. High canopy can allow good light to reach beneath it, while protecting the lower plants from the sun's full intensity, thus increasing the range of plants which can be grown. Exciting choice plants that would struggle in more open areas of the garden will thrive in this more sheltered environment. Enhancing mature woodland creates so many exciting possibilities, and while bulbs are often added beneath existing trees, the middle canopy is frequently forgotten. This is an opportunity which is seldom exploited to its full potential.

Providing a dramatic focal point at the end of a vista, *Cornus controversa* 'Variegata' is a perfect choice, particularly in a clearing, where it catches the light through the trees.

My preference is usually to choose plants in harmony with nature that also have interesting characteristics during a particular season, but I cannot resist including some plants with coloured foliage. It can be fun to include the occasional variegated plant for real impact, to brighten up a dark corner or to create a surprise, feature, or talking point. Variegated plants lack chlorophyll in the paler areas of the leaf. This reduces their ability to generate energy, consequently reducing their vigour and increasing their vulnerability to scorch. Thus this group benefits greatly from a shady site and also increases the colour and interest within the woodland throughout more of the year. Clearly this is particularly important in a small garden, where each plant must earn its place.

Acer is one of my favourite genera. It includes a bewildering number of species, some of which are definitely more suitable than others, with those that I have recommended for the upper canopy generally being too large for the middle canopy. However, many of the slower, smaller Japanese maples are perfect. A mystical aurora of impossibility and unsuitability surrounds their culture, and indeed they can be notoriously difficult to establish in the open garden in full exposure to sun and wind, but this makes the woodland setting absolutely perfect for them; after all, that is their natural environment. They are shallow rooting and can therefore be happily introduced among deep-rooted mature trees, since they will not be competing for moisture at the same levels; nor will they preclude woodland floor planting below them. *Acer palmatum* is my archetypal Japanese maple, but within this species, the choice becomes bewildering in its magnitude since literally hundreds of cultivars are available. Too many, in reality, as a number of them are very similar. However, some do stand out and others can be grouped by characteristics. Some are at their best in spring, many also have distinctive bark to give winter interest, while autumn colour is clearly their most famous feature. Indeed, the diversity of colours all through the year has completely captivated me, making them unique and unrivalled in a woodland setting.

Winter colour

Once the psychedelic displays of autumn have ended, the temptation is to retreat indoors and plan for next year. Yet I try to savour the harsher months to the full, as it can be a dramatic time in the winter garden, when its structure is revealed in all its naked and architectural glory. Some of the stars of my winter woodland are the snake-bark maples, so-named due to the dramatic white striations on the bark that resemble the skin of a snake. These markings are particularly noticeable in winter, when the spectacular colour intensity and contrast peak, ranging from pink-orange to deep purple. Such is their versatility that many have wonderful autumn colours as well as prolific winged seedpods, with a surprising diversity of shape and size. I like to grow them multi-stemmed, which maximises their glorious bark at eye level, where it contrasts against a dark background rather than being lost against a murky grey sky. Their inclusion in the middle canopy can greatly lengthen the season of interest, to make winter as colourful as spring and autumn.

There are so many ways of making the woodland exciting in winter. *Acer griseum* from China is one of my "must-have" trees; having been in cultivation for more than 100 years, it may be well known but is still highly prized. It is called the paperbark maple on account of the wonderful cinnamon-coloured bark which peels to reveal a richly coloured underlayer. It is a magical sight when the winter sun slips between the bare branches to caress the richly coloured curls of exfoliating bark. Much less well known is *A. triflorum*. The bark appeal may be a little more subtle, but it more than matches its close relative for autumn colour, with the added benefit of being more vigorous when young. I cannot resist planting these trees in groups of three, which compensates a little for the slower growth of *A. griseum* while maximising their impact in the winter woodland landscape.

Autumn sun streams through the foliage of *Acer palmatum* 'Ōsakasuki', exposing its inner structure.

Acer pensylvanicum 'Erythrocladum' is lit by the low winter sun. Note the effectiveness of the evergreen middle canopy behind it.

The bark appeal of *Acer griseum* is unquestionable.

Top: *Cornus kousa* var. *chinensis* 'China Girl' in full glory in mid-June

Above: *Cornus sanguinea* 'Midwinter Fire' looks spectacular against a dark background.

The diversity of dogwoods

Though I make no apology for my obsession with its beauty, *Acer* is not the only option for this middle canopy, for the flowering dogwoods are also glorious additions. Of these, the most suitable species for woodland gardening is *Cornus kousa*, which, along with its derivatives, are extremely tolerant of dappled shade and maritime climates. In our frost pocket on heavy soil, they benefit from the protection afforded by the surrounding planting, which shields them from desiccating winds in spring and summer. These are fascinating plants; closer inspection reveals that the gorgeous white blooms which cover their branches in early summer are not flowers, but bracts surrounding a central boss of tiny true flowers. These bracts are actually modified leaves, so they last much longer than true petals, having evolved to attract pollinators to the insignificant little flowers. Autumn colours can be gorgeous if conditions are right, while many cultivars produce large strawberry-like fruit which are edible, though not especially tasty. Developing very fibrous root systems, they will survive in a relatively shallow depth of good soil. Indeed their cultural requirements are similar to those of the Japanese maple—not too wet in winter and not too dry in summer. Without a doubt, if that balance of soil moisture retention and drainage can be achieved, there is almost no limit to what can be grown.

Even where conditions are tougher, *C. mas* will thrive, tolerating much greater extremes of exposure and moisture levels. Easily cultivated, it will eventually become a small tree that makes a wonderful small-scale canopy plant and contributes valuable winter flower to the middle canopy. The cultivars of Cornelian cherry are true multi-season plants, starting their display in late winter when petal-less staminoid yellow flowers adorn the bare stems, before producing a huge crop of edible, large, cherrylike fruit beloved of the wildlife.

Also *Cornus*, but completely different, are the incredibly resilient shrubs grown for their vibrant winter stems. Their cultivars provide a mesmerising colour range, with further choice of foliar interest. Some have also been selected for prolific fruiting, while most develop tremendous autumn colours. Aesthetically very pleasing, but also jolly useful, they will act as a lower level windbreak, sheltering more delicate neighbours from wind funnelling along the woodland floor beneath the main canopy. I enjoy them planted among *Betula*, against a backdrop of tall grasses—not the most likely of woodland combinations perhaps, but the winter effect is delightful as the dried flowerheads shimmer in the breeze or the frost adorns the coloured stems.

Hidden beauty
Tremendous possibilities open up if the appropriate soil structure can be achieved. Hamamelidaceae is traditionally associated with acid soils, and although they dislike too much lime, they are vastly more tolerant of pH than is often realised. For me, there can be few more uplifting experiences in the grey depths of winter than the sight and smell of *Hamamelis* in full glory. Although yellow is the traditional colour and my favourite for illuminating a gloomy winter corner, breeding and selection has resulted in a riot of golds, oranges, and reds, potentially perfuming the woodland from early winter to spring, such is the succession of flower. These distinctively lack petals, being fundamentally a bunch of overdeveloped stamens, using their scent rather than showy petals to attract pollinators. I remember walking through a woodland one summer's day and passing under what I took to be a large hazel shrub. When I returned a few months later in winter, I was astounded to find a fountain of yellow catching the ethereal winter sunshine, emitting a fragrance worthy of bottling. It was in fact a witch hazel, but I was so impressed with how naturally it fit into the landscape, biding its time before amazing us all with its beauty and perfume.

Parrotia persica is a less familiar member of that same family, which makes a wonderful gnarled feature, eventually becoming wider than tall. It is notoriously slow growing and long-lived, hence my inclusion in the middle canopy. It disappears into the natural landscape through summer, merging perfectly with the hazels before bursting into colour in autumn, progressing spectacularly through reds and oranges to golds and yellows.

In the spring, this area is a complete carpet of gorgeous *Erythronium*, but I can envisage *Hamamelis* or *Corylopsis* glowing here in the warming rays of Mother Nature's spotlight.

Another genus more tolerant of alkaline conditions than literature often suggests is *Corylopsis*, natural in its leaf shape and glorious autumn tints. The subtly perfumed, yellow, bell-like flowers hang in bunches, glowing in the early sunshine as it filters through the leafless canopy, until the emerging foliage hides their final fling and hazel-like foliage blends into the natural vegetation once again. In the normal garden environment, they can be vulnerable to damage in the spring from late frosts and chill winds; but they thrive in the light shade and protection of the woodland setting, rewarding the gardener with their delicate beauty early in the season.

The influence of soil structure

I cannot overemphasise the importance of soil structure. By achieving a balance of moisture retention and drainage in an area that is lightly shaded and protected from the worst of the weather, a veritable treasure-trove of plants can be enjoyed.

Most of the modern hybrids and cultivars of *Magnolia*, which are vulnerable to damage from late frosts when grown alone, benefit from the protection of the woodland setting. More modest in size and exhibiting greater tolerance in terms of soil requirements than the species from which they are derived, modern magnolias are bred to flower at an early age, with a multitude of colours to dazzle in the spring, from the purity of white, to the delicately flushed creamy pinks and rich purples. The yellow-flowered cultivars bloom later, thus extending the season as well as combating tiresome frosts. Some have huge flowers—great goblets of colour—while others are smaller and altogether more refined. So many of our spring-blooming magnolias are spoilt by the frost that I have become quite besotted with those which flower in midsummer. Having white flowers with a prominent boss of bright red or orange stamens in the centre, it is unfortunate that they are all so similar, but they are lovely and some are exquisitely scented.

Left: *Magnolia* 'Susan' merges into the middle canopy behind the steely silver birch trunks.

Above: *Euonymus hamiltonianus* 'Indian Summer'

They tend to be multi-stemmed and rather shrublike in their habit, which I find particularly pleasing in the middle canopy.

Where soil conditions are irreparably difficult, interesting variants of indigenous plants are valuable. Looking at what thrives in adjacent hedgerows is an excellent indication of what can be expected to grow with minimal effort. Here in southwest England, on an area of heavy clay soil, *Euonymus* is the perfect example. The wild *E. europaeus* can have attractive autumn colour and fruit, but it tends to become straggly and untidy. Named forms and alternative species, such as *E. hamiltonianus* and its cultivars, are much more exciting and fit well into the woodland environment. Some of these produce larger fruit or even white capsules instead of the usual pink, contrasting dramatically with the orange seeds which hang within. To my mind, deciduous *Euonymus* are woefully underused, although they offer some of the most outstanding autumn hues, including fluorescent pinks and the colours of vintage claret.

Woodland floor

Having perhaps the greatest potential for experimentation and variety, the woodland floor is the area which gardeners have most readily embraced. Hugely influenced by soil and moisture levels, the right plant for the particular position is an important choice.

A classic English woodland would be carpeted in spring with snowdrops, primroses, and bluebells. Few plants can be so aptly named as the snowdrop. For me, the moment when the first glistening white bud opens to a pristine bell truly heralds the imminent arrival of spring. Bizarrely, some snowdrops flower in late autumn, November here, which while rather fun when they appear through a carpet of fallen autumn foliage, somehow never seems to me to be quite right. In recent years, the snowdrop has earned an almost cultish reputation with Galanthophiles, oblivious of the late winter cold, gathering to examine the minute differences in the flowers of the various individuals. I find the simplicity of a woodland floor covered purely in *Galanthus nivalis* to be such a treat. Sometimes, there is no need to improve on Nature herself, but adding other plants to

Woodlands carpeted with snowdrops are an evocative sight but have sadly become rarer.

Above: In May, bluebells are the last of the spring bulbs to flower, here intermingling charmingly through a pale geranium beneath the glistening new leaves of a beech tree.

Above right: Sympathetic companion planting of the white-flowered form of the common bluebell makes the blue of *Anemone blanda* seem all the more intense.

frame the purity of their display and to succeed them as spring progresses is certainly worthwhile.

The humble English bluebell, *Hyacinthoides non-scripta*, was recently elected to be a British national symbol, so it is worrying for naturalists that the integrity of our native species is being threatened by *H. hispanica*. The Spanish bluebell is at first glance attractive, with larger, more open flowers of blue, white, or even pink, but the leaves are also larger and coarser with a tendency to swamp everything as they flop after flowering. It is proving to be vigorous and adaptable to the point of being invasive, so careful consideration should be given to its use.

If the area is too restricted to accommodate a bluebell carpet, many other smaller blue-flowered spring bulbs, such as *Scilla* and *Chionodoxa*, can be used for their rich blue or pale violet starry flowers. So often I am disappointed by blue flowers, as many

Narcissus cyclamineus may be a meadow plant in its native habitat, but it is perfectly adapted to life in the woodland and is the ideal stature to naturalise beneath a small tree like this *Acer palmatum* var. *dissectum*.

are in reality closer to purple, so I delight in these bulbs, as well as certain anemones, combining them with acid greens and yellows, perhaps punctuated with a little white.

Even the least green-fingered city dweller must be familiar with the ubiquitous daffodil. Full size *Narcissus* will stand their ground among long grass, but I prefer the simplicity and apparent delicacy of the species which are more appropriate to naturalising. However, I do find a number of classy hybrids derived from dwarf species quite irresistible. My favourite species which, although feared close to extinction in the wild, thrives in dappled woodland cultivation is *N. cyclamineus* with its typical swept-back petals, a trait often seen in its hybrid progeny.

It is incredible that *Fritillaria meleagris alba* can find enough sustenance in and around this mature crown of *Osmunda regalis*.

Although many *Fritillaria* need true alpine house conditions, a number are suited to cultivation in the more open areas of the woodland garden. With many reports of how these should be grown, confusingly, accounts differ. Water meadows are the traditional English home for the pink or white-chequered bells of *F. meleagris*, but some say that heavy clay is best, while other authorities insist on sharp drainage. Clearly these seemingly delicate beauties are much more adaptable than we give them credit for.

Looking further afield

Exquisite variations on local native flora harmonise with the natural woodland setting and, the more thought I give to the alternative ways of planting the woodland floor, the more excited I become at the extent of the choices. New plants are discovered in the wild and introduced to eager gardeners every year. China covers such a vast area that it is little wonder that its floral gems have gone unnoticed for so long. One genus that has come to the fore in recent years is *Epimedium*, with an incredible number of new species being introduced to cultivation. The foliage of this genus can be every bit as attractive as the flowers, particularly the richly marbled young growth.

Different styles can be used in planting *Epimedium* across the woodland floor (this principle applies to many herbaceous perennials). Sometimes I plant in large drifts for serious impact, or I may scatter a number of the same species across an area for a naturalistic appearance, interspersing them with other plants of similar vigour. Some will colonise quite rapidly by underground rhizomes, and I use these in the less conducive sites, saving the more sedate spreaders for the choicer positions.

Evergreen *Epimedium rhizomatosum* create a lovely carpet, even in winter.

The relationship among plants is a complex issue, but it never fails to amuse me that *Epimedium* is in the same family as *Berberis*. Another member of Berberidaceae is *Podophyllum*, lesser known than its illustrious brethren, but a fascinating genus which mesmerises my son, who has converted me with his infectious enthusiasm. Evoking images of primeval mushrooms as they emerge in the spring, they open as great leafy umbrellas, sometimes hexagonal or almost square, and beautifully marked or with wonderful wavy edges. The flower usually hides beneath, as if sheltering from the weather, often giving rise to large, egg-shaped fruit. *Podophyllum peltatum* grows wild throughout North American woodlands, with colonies of 1000 or more shoots not uncommon, in much the same way as snowdrops or bluebells do in the woods near my home. (I still struggle with the concept that a plant which I nurture in my garden and celebrate each spring could be considered a weed in another country.)

Above left: *Podophyllum peltatum*

Above: *Arisaema ciliatum*

Left: *Trillium* jostles among other classic spring woodlanders including *Erythronium* and ferns.

My son has an affinity for plants that could be described as weird and wonderful, and a plethora of them inhabit the woodland floor—*Arisaema*, for example. Emerging late in the spring or even early summer, the great divided leaves are usually held singly, often on tall, slender stalks. These do not have conventional flowers; rather they produce a curious, reptilian hooded tubular spathe. Spikes of fleshy red fruits are all that remain come autumn. Some are fully hardy and rewarding, while others are distinctly more tricky.

It is strange how even plants can be subject to the vagaries of fashion. One genus to capture the attention of both media and gardener of late is *Trillium*. At first glance a fairly humble little plant, yet as with so many, once you get to know them they are utterly captivating, even if their nomenclature seems to be a minefield of confusion and mistaken identity. Yet they are collected and cultivated with a relentless passion bordering on obsession.

Inspirational gems

Most *Erythronium* have similar cultural requirements but have not attracted the same attention. One of my favourite genera, with utterly charming Turk's cap flowers, their diversity of natural habitat results in a wider range of specific needs, so it is important to choose the right plant for the site. They may not be the easiest plants to grow, but once established, large colonies can develop. One of my earliest gardening memories and an inspiration to this day is the drift of pink *E. revolutum* 'Knightshayes Pink' at Knightshayes Court in Devon.

Arguably the ultimate spring woodlander, the carpet of *Erythronium revolutum* 'Knightshayes Pink' at Knightshayes Court, Devon, is a truly inspirational sight.

Erythronium will freely hybridise, though supposedly only with another species from the same continent. Sometimes I find it difficult to decide whether I prefer the delicacy of nature or the extravagant excess of breeding. The potential of the shy-flowering, pure yellow *E. tuolumnense* has been unleashed in several pale yellow hybrids which are free flowering and easy to grow. Their size and robustness gives them presence on the woodland floor, but their heavy leaves need disguising or ignoring as they die down. If I am honest, I do prefer the more delicate species which will naturalise surprisingly readily when happily positioned.

I have become completely besotted by *Erythronium* and suffer from the resultant need to collect as many different species and forms as I can find. I keep the new, the few, and the downright fussy in frames, under careful control. The easier species will happily naturalise in my woodland, and to preserve the integrity of their gene pool, I try to ensure that I have at least a small area of each species planted out in isolation, to

The stature of *Erythronium* 'Pagoda' allows it to compete successfully with more vigorous plants on the woodland floor, pretty here with *Muscari* and *Cyclamen repandum*.

allow the collection of true seed. In other areas I can release them to run riot and hybridise as they will. The toughest will survive, the weak will be overcome, and the resultant offspring will pop up among their neighbours; maybe one day I will find something special.

As with so many spring-flowering woodlanders, their ephemeral nature leaves a gap in the woodland carpet as spring turns into summer. I associate them with late emergers and summer-flowering *Tricyrtis* or accept the space they leave, casting my attention elsewhere. I find that they combine perfectly with small evergreen ferns, which protect the delicate flowers from the ravages of early spring winds.

Heuchera and its allies are in vogue at present. Similar in foliar effect, but from a most unexpected, though related, genus is a Japanese species, *Saxifraga fortunei*.

The soft fronds of *Polystichum setiferum* complement an array of dwarf spring bulbs like blue *Scilla bithynica* and *Narcissus cyclamineus*.

Traditionally associated with alpine gardens, this type of saxifrage is quite different, having been first introduced to European cultivation as long ago as the 1860s. The scalloped leaves, though deciduous, are highly ornamental and occur in a rich range of colours from deepest purple through green to brightly variegated. The pink or white flowers held in clouds above the leaves are delightful, but the best part is that they bloom late in the growing season. The earliest cultivars will commence their display in early autumn, while others will resist the first frosts even into early winter.

It is tempting to concentrate on the vast array of flowering treasures so well suited to growing in this environment, but one last group of plants so vital to my woodland floor are ferns. The new fronds unfurl in the spring, adding to the luxuriance of summer with their textures, and they supplement the colours of autumn as they decay, while some are even evergreen to enhance the structure of winter. In fact, the colour range is not restricted to green and includes rich reds, muted browns, and steely blues. The leaf shapes can be thick and green and tongue-like, soft and delicate, or even bizarre, crested, and crisped until they remind me more of parsley for the kitchen than a fern for the woodland.

Seasonal Interest

Bulbs play a vital and classic role in the spring woodland, but by careful selection and planting one can extend this beauty through much of the year. Too many woodland gardens are inspirational in spring but then decline as if exhausted by their efforts, to disappoint for the rest of the year. Gardening is a personal experience; I look for plants that blend well into a natural setting and add interest year-round. Woodland plantings should harmonise with nature, not conflict with it. The plants should be vigorous enough to make an impact in the landscape, naturalising to form a carpet where appropriate. Bulbs are natural opportunists and will find niches which suit them. Many plants will demonstrate their contentment by setting seeds and gently spreading around. The skill is to choose plants which will achieve this at just the right rate. I find it frustrating to have just one lonely clump which refuses to develop into a proper colony. Yet it is clearly not helpful when something grows so vigorously and energetically that it spreads bullishly to swamp its more polite neighbours. I need to achieve a happy medium.

Spring and summer
It is easy to create swathes of colour through the dazzling displays of spring, when each new day brings yet more excitement as fresh life bursts from beneath the warming soil. Native spring bulbs may already be present in an established woodland, while many classic woodlanders can be easily cultivated among them; others can be just as dramatic and effective but are perhaps not quite so obvious. They may be newly discovered or introduced, rare because they are difficult to propagate, or they may have simply fallen from fashionable grace. I find it stimulating to seek out plants which will offer their

A delightful mixture of spring bulbs, including *Erythronium*, *Narcissus*, *Anemone*, and *Muscari*, are perfectly proportioned to grow together.

Hosta foliage mingles with the contrasting ferns, but they can also be remarkably effective as flowering plants.

Handsome, but thirsty, large-leaved perennials create a verdure with an exotic tropical feel.

moment of glory later in the season when the spring divas have faded. The canopy is needed in summer, as the leaves provide vital shade and protection to plants below. On a hot day it can be a relief to escape the bright light and the vivid colours of the borders to the tranquillity and peace of the green oasis beneath the trees. It even smells different.

Hostas may be archetypal woodland plants, and for good reason. Some have quite tiny leaves while others are simply huge and need plenty of space, which can be easy to underestimate if planting a dormant crown. I like to fill the surrounding area, which in summer will be suppressed by the leaves, with spring bulbs which will have flowered before the hostas wake up, dying down long before the great leaves reach their zenith.

Somehow flowers are superfluous in summer, perhaps because so much colour appears elsewhere in the garden. I am soothed by the greenness of the summer woodland and eager to create an area which oozes with a feeling of luxuriant tropical abundance. This is difficult to achieve without a naturally moisture-retentive soil (or an efficient irrigation system), yet the woodland is the perfect place to experiment. The shade will reduce water requirements while the shelter of the middle canopy will protect those great leaves from being damaged by the wind. Yet sometimes it is fun to introduce another colour among all those shades of green. The creams and yellows of variegated plants add a dynamic splash among the green, but I particularly appreciate the more subtle sparkle of the silvers.

Autumn and winter

The precise colour tones of the autumn garden are influenced by light levels, but autumn colours are triggered by a combination of the reduction in both light levels and temperature as summer draws to a reluctant close. As the plant starts to shut down for the winter, the sap retreats from its leaves, resulting in the magical displays which make autumn such an exciting time in the woodland garden. Sunny sites offer more reds in their kaleidoscope of autumn colour, while yellows tend to dominate in shady places. But it is never quite that simple, because some cultivars have a greater predisposition to a certain spectrum of colour; in the case of Japanese maples, those purple in summer mostly turn red in autumn while the greens will often progress through a whole sequence of colours, before erupting into a final fountain of glory. With the benefit of woodland protection, many trees keep their leaves for longer as they are sheltered from the worst ravages of approaching winter.

Autumn is such an exhilarating time of year in the woodland garden that beneath a canopy of blazing leaves, the woodland floor is sometimes overlooked. Yet autumn bulbs will push their precious heads up through the colourful carpet of fallen leaves. Crocus are famed for their suitability to naturalise in short grass, but many species will happily colonise a woodland grove, provided that the squirrels can be persuaded to concentrate on the hazelnuts rather than eating the crocus corms. The autumn species are often dominated by their spring cousins, but I find them particularly effective planted among *Cyclamen*, whose foliage gives support to the slightly taller stems.

Plants which flower and grow during the winter must be able to tolerate the worst

A delightful example of the new generation of hellebores, *Helleborus ×hybridus* Ashwood Garden hybrids

that winter can, and often does, throw at them. So many times have I seen the gorgeous hellebore flowers, several to a stem, lying limp and apparently lifeless following a night of hard frost. Yet later in the day, when temperatures rise to a more sociable level, they again stand tall. Planted en masse, hellebores provide an unequalled winter spectacle, embracing everything which is endemic to growing woodland plants. No garden, however big or small, should be without them, for their beauty is beyond question and they will thrive in a wide range of conditions. In my garden, some flower buds are visible and showing colour even before Christmas, yet they will still be in full glory in March. Some gorgeous selections line the path between the house and the nursery, and they never fail to lift my spirits on even the grimmest winter's day. If the seedpods are left on the plants, they will spread, with the potential to colonise a large area in no time at all. Of course, the offspring will vary, and none will exactly replicate their parent, but this infinite variety is part of their thrill. Seedpods could be removed, prior to maturity, from plants in confined spaces, but the seeds need not be wasted; they can always be sprinkled elsewhere.

The Value of Evergreens

I have mentioned the benefits of preserving any large conifers already contributing to the upper canopy, but I like to add some evergreens within the woodland, particularly on the windward side. At Knightshayes Court in Devon, the development of the evergreens is such that it is sometimes difficult in January to realise that it is not the middle of summer. Aesthetically, they provide body and structure to the woodland even in the depths of winter; but more importantly, on a practical level, they prevent the wind howling through the area, which is particularly valuable early in the spring when soft young growth in the middle canopy is at its most vulnerable. Strategically placed evergreens can divide the woodland into "rooms", to allow a continually new focus of excitement as we wander through it, but they can also show off the winter-flowering plants to their best, particularly if we can skilfully position the latter to catch those elusive shafts of low winter sunlight.

I find it frustrating that so many evergreens are slow growing, particularly the more desirable ones; indeed an annoying number are acid-loving, so unattainable in my garden. Happily, easily grown alternative possibilities, such as a number of *Viburnum*, can be used. *Buxus sempervirens*, so familiar when clipped into submissive obedience around parterres and formal gardens, is naturally a woodland plant. I love the more open habit which it develops when left unpruned in a shady site, partly because it reminds me of a favourite family walk in France, where it grows among evergreen oaks and *Ruscus aculeatus* on a rocky hillside. I have incorporated these *Quercus coccifera* to good effect adjacent to the rock garden, where their prickly glaucous leaves, with almost furry white undersides, sparkle in the sunlight while protecting the tiny treasures below. Our growing conditions are much moister than those of its native habitat, so I will need to keep an eye on its size. *Quercus ilex* is similar, in time becoming a massive tree, but it is incredibly tolerant of windy sites, making it a fantastic first line of defence where space permits. I had always thought of it as being a British native, but although it has been cultivated here since the sixteenth century, it comes from southwest Europe and the Mediterranean basin.

The presence of some large evergreen shrubs transforms an open woodland, enabling a much wider range of choice middle canopy trees, such as magnolia, to be grown.

When considering evergreens, hollies are a natural choice, with the archetypal species for me being *Ilex aquifolium*. The annual search for holly adorned with succulent red berries to decorate the Christmas table was an integral part of my childhood. Its cultivars are exceptionally useful in a woodland setting, as they are tolerant of dry shade, arguably the most challenging of woodland combinations. However, there is no need to consign these evocative beauties only to the most difficult of sites where they will struggle to fulfil their potential. They can be interspersed among newly planted middle canopy trees to grow up with them, offering protection as they develop. They offer myriad options of foliage colour and shape with every combination of variegation and red or yellow berries, but I cannot ignore the elegant simplicity of those deepest green leaves punctuated with vivid scarlet berries. Most plants cross the Atlantic quite happily, but hollies seem to be the exception. Unfortunately, my valued English holly rarely thrives in that more continental climate, while many of its North American equivalents are acid loving or extremely difficult to grow in the British maritime climate. However, *I. vomitoria* and *I. opaca* selections are popular in the United States, along with numerous hybrids.

When the going gets really tough, I confess that I resort to *Prunus laurocerasus*, although it is sometimes considered to be a "thug", having naturalised in many places. Laurel may be large and green and, frankly, boring, but I plant it not for its beauty but for its supreme tolerance. I want it to grow in places where little else will thrive, in heavy shade and beneath the drip of overhanging trees on heavy clay soil. I need it to grow rapidly but be easily pruned, to be cheap but expendable when it has outstayed its welcome. And it does all that with consummate ease. It makes a wonderful backdrop to the glistening whites of the silver birch or my more cherished *Hamamelis*, creating an almost instant windbreak and supporting many birds' nests. For something a little more refined, a number of named forms can develop large and elegant symmetrical silhouettes, or much smaller selections provide protection for woodland floor plants. Some offer extravagant white spikes of spring flowers; variegated forms can be useful to lighten a particularly dark corner.

Low-level protection

Any winter vegetation, whether evergreen carpeters such as *Epimedium* or even as seemingly flat as *Cyclamen hederifolium* foliage, will help trap the fallen leaves, preventing the wind from whisking them away, leaving them instead to rot down and contribute to the natural woodsy mulch. Yet many woodlanders that flower early in the season when the weather is potentially at its cruellest are delicate, if only due to their small stature and vulnerability at what is often the harshest time of year. To increase the protection and add structure, I intermingle evergreen woody plants, even at this lowest level, though careful positioning is needed to ensure that shelter is achieved without obliterating the view of the beauties being protected.

Ruscus aculeatus is a fascinating plant and incredibly tolerant of even dry shade, forming neat erect thickets. Another small evergreen prolific in its berrying abilities is

The protective softness of low-growing evergreen ferns, here *Adiantum venustum*, creates an attractive mix of texture and colour against the vertical accent of emerging crocus.

Sarcococca. This is a fantastic genus of winter-flowering shrubs, with the earliest starting here in November and the latest still performing in March. They are superbly scented, filling the air with perfume from their pretty white flowers. Berries will be red or black, and they pick well, too, unfailingly adding decoration to our Christmas table.

Some *Daphne* are inappropriate scree-loving alpines, but other species will revel in woodland conditions. The shade provided by the canopy will offer them vital protection in summer, while they in turn protect their more delicate neighbours in winter. In my garden, an unnamed hybrid between *Daphne pontica* and *D. laureola*, with wonderful

Daphne bholua is naturally a woodland plant and thrives among the deciduous middle canopy.

glossy green foliage, creates a surprisingly verdant feeling in summer. Much larger is the aristocrat of the genus, *D. bholua*. These magnificent winter-flowering shrubs are among the most beautiful and exquisitely scented of all woody plants. Too often pampered in a sunny site, they are natural woodlanders and perform to perfection in that environment.

So much choice, so much opportunity, so much scope for making the woodland garden into a special area where something new will be appearing on an almost daily basis. There is no better place in which to sit quietly and watch the passage of the seasons.

CHAPTER 2

Preparing and Maintaining Enhanced Woodland Areas

Before starting work in an established woodland, one must analyse the existing planting to determine the level of canopy and the nature of the soil, as this will indicate where enhancement is appropriate. Monitor an area for a full growing season to gain complete understanding of what plants are already present and to learn which areas remain the wettest and which may dry out the most. This helps make the most of the existing features and helps one to avoid some costly mistakes.

The finished result should reflect each gardener's personal taste, as there is rarely a "right way" or "wrong way" to do any of this, but some basic principles can be of help in any woodland planting. Three fundamental factors must be carefully considered before work begins; each is important, but they interact to determine the type of planting which can be done. These are scale, light levels, and soil conditions.

Think about the dimensions of the woodland, along with the nature of the existing trees. Clearly, a large woodland has scope to support all three canopy layers, whereas a small woodland bed would require small trees with associated underplanting. If large and mature trees create high canopy, having developed tall trunks devoid of side branches, the potential of lower level trees can be maximised, because plenty of light is able to reach the smaller shrubs and plants below them. However, if the existing planting is densely branched and bushy, it would be impossible to introduce middle and lower canopy plants without some degree of pruning. The same issues apply when underplanting a small copse of hazel, for example. If little light is able to penetrate the canopy, then beneath them one may be restricted to introducing opportunist spring performers, which get on with their business before the trees come into leaf. The alternative is to thin and prune to increase the light.

Every woodland gardener must decide whether to adapt the planting to suit the site or manipulate the site (within sensible limits) to accommodate a certain range of plants. The amount of light filtering through the leaves can determine the nature of the underplanting, or the canopy can be adjusted according to the proposed type of planting. Certain plants require more light in order to thrive than others. Soil characteristics will also influence the type of plants that can be grown. It is usually easier to work within existing parameters, but it is possible to adjust the soil to accommodate a wider range of plants, dramatically increasing the planting possibilities.

Opposite: At the foot of a large tree, *Eranthis hyemalis* and *Galanthus nivalis* make an irresistible display in the winter gloom. Red-berried *Ruscus aculeatus* are also effective.

The natural woodland prior to enhancement

Paths through the woodland garden allow it to be enjoyed throughout the year without causing damage. This new path will be edged on the downhill side to prevent the substrate washing away.

Clearing away scrubby undergrowth reveals dense carpets of wildflowers, revelling in their new-found light exposure. This is the time to plant middle canopy trees and evergreens.

If space is allowed for carpeters to colonise, initially the woodland floor will appear sparse. Perhaps some clump-forming rather than running infill can be included, to be removed as the permanent carpet develops.

Preparing the Canopy

If the leafy spread of the existing trees is such that they are almost touching, then Nature has created the canopy. Provided that the trees are in good heart, nothing more is required. It is important, however, that any potentially dangerous trees are dealt with appropriately, but dead wood (trees still standing as well as those on the ground) supports

so much insect life, which in turn is a vital food source for woodpeckers and other birds, that it is valuable to the wildlife not to clear all of it. It is fundamental to the ecological balance of nature that a certain amount is left undisturbed.

Checking for fungal bracts at the base of a tree in autumn and examining the foliage in summer will reveal the health of a tree. If leaves are sparse or drop very early in the autumn, it could be an indicator of problems to come. If in doubt, it is a good investment to have trees checked by a competent tree surgeon (arborist) prior to developing the woodland garden. If any are to be removed, it is best done at the beginning of the project, since such work could influence how the area develops. Similarly, if the area is too crowded, it is useful to thin out the least desirable trees: the future "thugs", the poorly shaped or weak individuals, or simply those in the wrong place. Trees, like all living things, inevitably will at some point reach the end of their time. I view that as an opportunity to plant something else, perhaps something more interesting or that elusive specimen for which there was previously inadequate space.

Where trees are to be removed, it is useful for the stump to be ground out at the same time. Once the resultant cavity is refilled with soil, it will be much easier for replanting, of course, but the removal of the stump will reduce the amount of dead wood available for fungus growth. The soil of any area of mature trees will naturally contain fungus which lives on dead roots, but little is gained by encouraging them. However, in most cases, young, strong-growing plants will be able to grow faster than any fungus may be eating the roots, so no detriment will be visible. *Armillaria* is a group

Dead wood is a part of the natural woodland environment, adding character as well as food and retreat for wildlife, as demonstrated by this decaying fallen tree among *Narcissus pseudonarcissus* 'Lobularis'.

Opposite: Winter brings to the fore things hidden in the leafy exuberance of summer, such as gorgeous lichen in a damp corner. However, the presence of too much lichen indicates a lack of air circulation and that insufficient light is penetrating the canopy.

Left: Many ferns are tolerant of heavy shade cast by low tree branches, but raising the canopy to allow more light to reach the woodland floor will dramatically increase the planting options.

Grassy drifts among birch trees demonstrate where adequate light and moisture are retained through summer to support herbaceous perennials or middle canopy shrubs, while closer to the trunks, growth is suppressed. A path may wind near these trees, releasing the more open areas for planting.

of severe root fungus organisms. Some plants are more resistant to it than others, and lists of these can be obtained on the Internet. But still the same principle applies; a senescent plant which is surviving rather than actively growing will be significantly more vulnerable than a vigorous youngster, particularly after a period of stress caused by extreme weather conditions.

It is valuable to retain as many of the existing trees as possible, since the canopy of a mature individual will inevitably take many years to replace. Unfortunately, some species are eminently more suitable for underplanting than others. Any tree with an aggressive root system will extract a great deal of moisture and nutrient from the soil.

Some of this nutrient is replaced each year as the leaves fall and decay, so it is useful not to interrupt the natural balance of the woodland by being too enthusiastic over leaf clearance in the autumn. It is a shame to waste valuable leaf-mould by removing rotting leaves, as the whole character of the woodland floor and the plants which thrive there has evolved due to this annual natural mulch.

Determining Light Levels

The amount of light filtering through the canopy in summer is an important factor in determining how much can be grown beneath it. Light penetration is difficult to judge in winter when trees are dormant; it is better to consider the situation in the summer once trees are in full leaf. At this stage, try to project how the canopy will develop over the next few years. If it is already fairly full, it is likely to become excessively dense as it continues to grow. It may be easier therefore to thin it prior to planting, rather than having that worry in the not too distant future once the new planting has become established. Canopy height is also relevant—that is, whether side branches occur low down on the trunks or are not present at all on tall, mature trees. In the latter case, the trees can be much closer together and sufficient light will penetrate beneath to support a wide range of plants. If, however, the trees are clothed to the ground, raising the canopy by removing the lower side branches may be necessary to let more light reach the woodland floor. It is always possible to remove limbs later as necessary, but it is clearly easier to do this before planting delicate plants beneath them.

Purple-foliaged plants generally need more light to display their best leaf colour, though good light does not necessarily equate to full sun. If light levels are inadequate for gold- and yellow-leaved plants, they will not exhibit their true potential, being more of a lime-green. However, this group needs care because too much sun will quickly result in unsightly scorch. If the canopy is high, light levels can be adequate without involving direct sun, a scenario which is perfect for woodland plants.

A solid canopy will limit the range able to survive in its shadow. Gaps in that canopy can be opportunities to plant trees which will subsequently fill that void, but clearings within the woodland can be stimulating features, being ideally suited to those plants needing more summer light. Clearings make the woodland a more varied environment, less predictable, and aesthetically more exciting, while giving the plantaholic an enticingly broader scope.

The fun begins when the woodland floor is ready for planting, though it is not quite as simple as just selecting a range of small, pretty plants which like shade. Light levels are inexorably linked with moisture levels and soil structure. Plants can be divided into groups appropriate to environmental conditions based upon their growth cycles to determine which type of plant will thrive in which area of the woodland.

Seasonal growth and moisture levels

Spring bulbs flowering early in the year are in leaf from late winter until early summer. At that time, most of the meagre winter light can reach them on the woodland floor through the naked deciduous canopy. Bulbs should be allowed to retain their leaves for as long as possible. The bulb equates to a food storage organ, and most of this food is used to produce flowers. To generate the energy to flower again the following year, photosynthesis through the leaves is necessary. Thus, if the leaves are removed immediately after flowering, the bulb will be severely weakened and may not flower or even survive for future seasons. However, flopping leaves can look increasingly messy once the flowers have faded. It is a relief when I deem the daffodils in the lawn to have had enough time to replace their lost energy so they can be safely trimmed away.

Bulbs also need enough space so that as the leaves collapse, their neighbours are not smothered. I prefer bulbs with finer foliage, avoiding the larger leaves inherent of so many modern hybrids. I have concluded that by planting something to flower at this stage, adjacent, but not too close, the eye is drawn away to something more pleasing.

It is easy to create interest at all times of year when space is plentiful, because almost by definition, when one plant is flowering, another is dying back. Spring bulbs are often ephemeral, but all will go dormant through the summer and autumn, which is why they are so well suited to growing in a woodland situation. They tolerate dry shade around trees because their main growth is finished before the trees come into leaf. While the trees are taking maximum moisture from the soil through the main part of the growing season, the bulbs are dormant. Thus they will do no harm planted close to the base of trees where little else will thrive, saving the choicer patches of ground for more demanding residents.

Summer-flowering bulbs—lilies, for example—are in growth from late spring to early autumn, which coincides with the growth cycle of the trees. These bulbs should be planted in glades where the soil retains enough moisture to support both the trees and the bulbs, and where adequate light penetrates the canopy to reach the foliage below, farther from the base of the trees in a more open area. If their position is too shady, the stems will grow tall and thin as they forlornly search for light, and fewer, smaller flowers will result. The soil must be adequately free draining during their dormant phase since they will not tolerate a heavy wet site while inactive.

Herbaceous perennials follow a similar growth cycle. Woodlanders are adapted to this shady environment, provided that adequate moisture is available to them through the summer. Some will grow satisfactorily even in heavy shade; but if light levels are too low for any plant, it will respond by becoming taller and leggier, more etiolated than is ideal, and with fewer flowers. It is therefore important that the canopy is not too dense or low; there is a balance between this density and height of canopy, where denser tree cover can usually be accommodated if it is high. Lower branches will need to be much sparser to allow this group of plants to thrive.

Autumn-flowering bulbs are a welcome sight when so much else looks tired and sadly bare, blooming prior to their leaves emerging in late winter and early spring. Thus the bulbs are replenished while the canopy of deciduous trees is dormant. However, the flowers can be delicate and easily damaged by cold wind in winter, so protected niches may be required. This shelter is easily achieved with skilful positioning of some low-growing evergreens.

Assessing Soil Conditions

It is realistically impossible to acidify an alkaline soil to the point where it will support rhododendrons and other ericaceous plants. For this reason, I do not cover these plants within these pages. Some people apply proprietary products to individual plants in their garden to prevent chlorosis, the yellowing of the leaves of these plants when grown on an alkaline soil. This is simply not practical on a woodland scale. However, a vast range of plants often thought to be acid-loving can be grown on almost any soil if a little care is taken, particularly with the extra protection of the woodland environment—*Acer*, *Magnolia*, *Halesia*, and an enticing host of others. Of course, they will thrive in acid soil, but it is not the pH (the measure of acidity/alkalinity) which is critical so much as the structure of the soil. This group of plants prefers a friable soil into which they can easily root; they hate to be too wet in winter but equally dislike drying out in summer. Thus, if the soil can be enhanced, a whole new world of planting opportunities opens up.

Overcoming heavy soil

Heavy clay is notorious. Clay particles are essentially flat platelets which, as they settle one on top of the next, become a solid layer. This remains very wet in winter and dries out on the surface in summer, becoming so hard that more delicate roots physically struggle to penetrate into it. I have described it as porridge or concrete and rarely in between. The problem in the existing woodland is how to introduce additional plants. If they are simply planted into the clay, some will survive but few will thrive, particularly if they have been grown in a peat-based compost, since the contrast is too great. Clay soils limit the choice to tough customers, cultivars of plants which would naturally grow there. Hazel, hawthorn, and oaks will all survive, but they will grow only slowly. Fortunately, we can do better than that; the whole area can be enhanced to make it more interesting over a longer period of the year.

From experience, I know that the worst possible procedure is to dig a lavish planting pit. We removed a barrowful of horrid, sticky clay and replaced it with friable and nutritious compost. Unfortunately, most of the plants failed, because we effectively dug a sump, a bucket which filled with water in winter, which then could not drain because of the heaviness of the surrounding soil. My solution is to plant on mounds. This has to be done sympathetically within an existing woodland, since it is important not to change the water level too much around existing trees. Adding extra topsoil, along with some grit and organic matter (well-rotted leaf-mould is ideal), and mixing it into the topsoil without disturbing the clay pan gives a good depth of soil for starting the plants. If, with time, plants do root down into the clay, that is even better because deep down the clay is naturally water retentive.

Although we are careful to sweep levels down to existing trees, often a big tree will appear to have almost risen a little out of the ground as buttressing roots develop, allowing a surprising amount of extra soil to be added around it. If the mixture introduced there is gritty and free-draining, it should not adversely affect the tree. This gives adequate depth of suitable soil across the woodland for some exciting planting. Carpeting herbaceous plants need little depth, but they require that the soil be adequately moisture-retentive in summer. Where there is a slight dip in the ground, we add a greater amount of soil, locating more demanding plants in those positions. As a basic rule, the bigger the plant becomes eventually, the greater the depth of soil it will require. However, some large trees (such as *Quercus*) are naturally deep rooting, even into heavy soil, while others (such as *Betula*) are shallow rooting whatever the soil. It takes the addition of only the thinnest layer to enable small carpeters such as *Anemone nemorosa* cultivars to thrive.

Controlling Weeds

Weed control is a contentious issue. In an established woodland, weeds will be present. If an area has become overgrown, it is vitally important that vegetation no longer required be removed before new plants are added. It is no use just hacking back the undergrowth to plant new treasures in the gaps, since the weeds will grow more rapidly, almost immediately swamping the new additions. This process is both expensive and demoralising. It is tempting when embarking on a new project to skimp on the time-consuming task of preparation, as the creative juices flow and the desire to enjoy the finished project overcomes common sense. However, patience is imperative. Careful weed control is possible around trees and many shrubs, but it is not worth planting the herbaceous elements of the woodland floor until the perennial weeds are vanquished.

Although potentially painful, nettles and brambles are relatively easily dug out. The problem comes with pernicious perennials such as ground elder and bindweed. It is virtually impossible to remove enough of the root by digging to eradicate them completely. Some people swear by smothering the ground with old carpets or black plastic, and indeed this will prevent germination of new seedlings (until it is removed), while the light deprivation will gradually kill most normal weeds or grass, but it will take forever to deal with these perennial problems. Much as I dislike the principle, I see no viable alternative to chemical treatment and strive to do the job properly in the first place, with a systemic weed-killer. This is absorbed through the leaves and travels through the plant to kill the roots. It is usually possible to spot-treat the offenders rather than treating the entire area. A contact weed-killer is adequate for grass and annual weeds, but for perennials it is no better than pulling the tops off as it does not kill the roots. Later on, when

Betula utilis var. *jacquemontii* were originally planted in rough grass. By improving our heavy clay soil, we can establish beautiful woodland floor plants.

the planting is done, newly germinated annuals may be easily removed by hand, but it is impossible to control the likes of ground elder among these carpeting woodland plants. These perennial weeds must be dealt with before attempting to plant the woodland floor. I might compromise by starting with spring bulbs, for these will soar into life in early spring, flower exuberantly, and gently die down for the summer. Thus, by the time the annoying weeds have gained momentum, the bulbs will be safely asleep below the ground again, and the weeds can then be sprayed with confidence—but of course they still cannot be dug up because of the bulbs beneath.

The benefits of mulching

After the weeds have been cleared, the opportunity arises to apply a thick mulch to the area, which is much easier to do when no tiny plants need to be avoided. Mulching is invaluable for many reasons: to reduce the ability of the weed seeds beneath to germinate, while making it easier to pull out any annuals which do arrive; to facilitate planting; to maintain moisture levels in summer; and to improve the soil. Adding a generous layer of quality organic mulch replicates the natural woodland litter—in an instant the woodland floor gains the equivalent of generations of leaf deposit. Indeed, many of the smallest carpeters will be happy to live in the mulch alone.

I cannot overstate the benefits of mulching. By covering the soil, evaporation is greatly reduced, thus keeping the roots of the plants both moist and cool. However, it is preferable to apply the mulch while the ground is moist, because it can take an awful lot of rain to subsequently soak through it, particularly on the woodland floor in the rain shadow of the trees. I avoid walking on the soil if it is extremely wet, as that can compact and spoil its structure. Sometimes this is unavoidable, since the growth-cycle of the plants may not give any choice of timing. In which case, working from a plank may be a bother, but it does help to spread the weight and protect the ground.

Many mulching materials are available, and the selection will vary with the scale and budget of the project. A quality chipped bark is the most aesthetically pleasing, but it is expensive, although it will remain effective for several years before needing replenishing. Cheaper mulches are not wasted, though; whether the soil is heavy or light, the worms will draw it down in as it decays, improving the soil structure to achieve improved drainage in winter and moisture-retention in summer.

Mushroom compost is an economical product, but one of its most important ingredients is lime. This is useful on a clay soil to help break it down, but it will do nothing to help the pH of an alkaline soil (that is, it will increase the alkalinity). This compost must not touch the collar of a plant, as the lime can be caustic and burn the stem. I avoid banking an organic mulch around a plant as it will tend to stay very wet in winter and can cause collar rot. Another potential problem can come from tree surgeon's chipped waste. This I find frustrating because it is cheaply and readily available and environmentally sound. However, it can harbour all manner of fungal infections which are not ideal on the woodland floor. English local authorities and waste disposal companies are tackling the issue of appropriate clearance of domestic garden waste by collecting and processing it to produce a garden mulch which is extremely cost-effective when bought in bulk. Although it varies according to what was in the original rubbish, it is generally excellent value and almost entirely free of weed seed as a result of professional composting techniques. Other substrates I have considered include coir, which is a by-product from coconuts. I think it is generally accepted now that peat is inappropriate and unnecessary to use in this manner.

Unfortunately, my desire for interest in the garden throughout the year will negate any dormant spell when mulching work can be carried out. Therefore, in the early days of woodland enhancement I may develop seasonal areas. While some part of the area is taking centre stage, maintenance can be carried out elsewhere. As the initial planting develops, it is always possible to introduce new plants to extend that season of excitement; after all, part of my pleasure in gardening is having justification for searching for fresh inspiration, while continually finding homes for new treasures. Once the area is completely clear of perennial weeds, it is easier to keep on top of annual invaders each summer. I can then carry out further planting with confidence.

A woodland can become the ultimate low-maintenance garden, needing little more work than the application of an annual layer of mulch and occasional pruning or tidying. My woodland is an enhanced natural area, not a manicured garden, but that choice is entirely flexible and personal. The problem in a normal border is that routine hoeing actually makes work; regularly disturbing the surface as the weeds are rigorously attended to simply results in further germination, which then need hoeing again, and so the cycle continues. Furthermore, the disturbance increases the rate at which the soil dries out. The presence of a carpet of woodlanders precludes hoeing and forking over, so thorough mulching therefore makes complete sense in all respects.

Planting

For me, the most exciting part of either enhancing an existing woodland or creating a new one is the planting. Most nurseries grow their perennials and shrubs in containers, so theoretically it is possible to plant year-round, but I prefer to establish woody plants in early autumn. The plants are still active but the wood is ripening; the soil is still warm from the summer, but it is reasonable to expect some rain. This allows some root establishment prior to dormancy, helping them overwinter; but more importantly, it will speed them on their way in the spring. The problem with waiting until the spring to plant is the unpredictability of the weather—the possibility of damaging late frosts or an early dry spell. Either can be detrimental to new planting. This is even more important under an existing canopy, since it allows establishment to begin while the canopy plants have least water requirement.

Herbaceous plants, however, often establish well in spring, just as they start into growth, and bulbs need to be planted when dormant so that as little as possible of their precious energy reserve is wasted; the timing will vary according to their growth cycle. Planting summer-dormant bulbs at the appropriate time can be difficult if the ground is really dry; it may be best to pot them up to plant out as soon as conditions permit rather than leaving them exposed for any longer than is necessary. Although labelling can look unsightly in a garden situation, I find it useful at least while planting is still underway, particularly if not all work is done in a single flurry. Little is more frustrating than digging a hole for a new plant to find one's spade driving through a patch of precious dormant bulbs.

Mass-harvesting of plants from the wild is now illegal, but it is sad that areas in so many parts of the world have been stripped of their floral treasures by thoughtless people, either for financial reward or in their efforts to take home a souvenir. When buying bulbs and orchids especially, ensure that they have come from a commercial source, not gathered from the wild. In some countries, individuals are granted special licences to remove plants from sites prior to development, so it is good to know that rarities will not be lost to the bulldozer. Awareness of the precarious position of the world's scarcest flora and fauna is not a recent thing; discussions commenced as long ago as 1960, culminating in 1975 with the implementation of a worldwide resolution known as CITES (Convention on International Trade in Endangered Species of Wild Fauna and Flora). This international agreement regulates the movement of endangered species around the world and amazingly includes 28,000 species of plants. It is encouraging that since CITES came into force, none of the species protected by it has been rendered extinct as a result of trade.

One principle to which I do strongly adhere when considering trees and shrubs for the middle canopy is the preference for planting cultivars rather than species. Species are the simplest forms of plants as they occur in the wild. These are by nature variable. Where flowers are their desirable attribute, these may take some years to be produced

These seed-grown examples of *Betula albosinensis* illustrate some of the variation in bark colour beyond the archetypal white silver birch.

on a tree grown from seed. Where an established woodland is to be developed, the over-all appearance can be enhanced by planting spectacular small trees within it. Any tree can be argued to be attractive, but named cultivars will optimise the particular beauty of the species. These cultivars have been selected for a particular feature—an improvement upon or change from the original species. Perhaps a tree is grown primarily for its fabulous autumn colour; a named form gives assurance that it will reliably perform well and that the exact colour will be especially good. In other cases, a particular trait might differ from the species; it might have purple foliage instead of the usual green, or pink flowers rather than the usual white.

Cultivars are produced by vegetative propagation; in the case of a cutting, a small length of shoot is removed from an adult plant and is treated in such a manner that it develops roots and grows into a new plant. Where rooting is not possible, it may be grafted or budded onto an existing rootstock. Tissue culture is a laboratory-based solution that rapidly achieves large quantities; it is particularly applicable to new introductions of woodland floor plants that will be planted in drifts rather than individually. It is important to choose the right cultivar for the job. Constraints of a particular site might dictate the requirement for a smaller growing selection, for example.

CHAPTER 3

Developing New Woodland Areas

Not every garden includes an area that lends itself to developing into a woodland feature. However, an apparently "full" garden often provides the perfect woodland opportunity because the existing vegetation offers that all important canopy and protection. I find it extremely satisfying to lift the crown on an overgrown, shapeless large shrub, thin out the twiggy side growth to reveal an often surprisingly attractive stem structure, and create space and light for woodlanders at its feet. To me, no garden will ever be "finished"; there will always be an area that is past its best or that perhaps never really worked. It can be helpful to look at a difficult area from a different perspective, to see it not as a problem but as an opportunity for something new.

Inevitably, it may be necessary or desirable to start from scratch. Without a doubt, establishing a fully fledged woodland canopy will take many years, as well as requiring lots of space. In a garden situation it is probably more appropriate to work to a more modest scale. How this is achieved will be influenced by the style of the garden and any limitations of the site and soil.

Constructing a completely new bed allows total flexibility; as much of this involves personal taste, I will provide some tips as well as established principles, since the detail will vary with every planting according to the conditions and the desired result. Once again I emphasise my belief that there is no "right" and "wrong". A beautiful woodland can be achieved within any gardener's budget, ability, and taste. The principles considered in Chapters 1 and 2 are equally relevant here, just scaled down as appropriate.

Opposite: A new woodland glade with the paths edged with branches will look spectacular when planted up. Huge trees need not be a nightmare; they present an opportunity to achieve a special area.

Woodland Bed

Whether rural or urban, a woodland bed can be an attractive addition even to a small garden, much along the principle of the real thing, but to a more modest scale. It could take the form of an island bed in the lawn or against a boundary; perhaps it borrows the canopy from a tree in an adjacent garden to make the new woodland bed appear part of the wider landscape rather than a discrete feature.

The gardener's first job is to decide on the position, the shape, and the size of the

new bed. I find it effective to lay out a garden hose to manipulate the outline until I am perfectly happy. Then I drizzle a line of sand to make a more immovable marker, or I use aerosol cans of paint, such as that suitable for marking out playing fields. Whether existing vegetation needs to be dealt with depends on the location of the bed; the job may simply be a matter of skimming off the turf. The organic matter can be incorporated into the soil, or it can be piled upside-down in a corner to rot down and await a future project. (Perennial weeds, however, need to be dealt with properly before planting commences.)

Having established the position and outline of the new bed, I can add further topsoil, as that extra depth will never be wasted. Some organic matter can then be worked into the existing soil to achieve the moisture-retentive but free-draining mix important to woodland plants. Initially, the shade provided by the young canopy will be limited, and with changing and unpredictable weather patterns, it may be worthwhile to install an irrigation system during construction. In its simplest form, this can consist of a "leaky pipe" (or soaker hose) laid under the final mulch, to which a hosepipe is attached when irrigation is needed. This can help the new planting to establish, but with irrigation becoming an environmentally sensitive issue, it is perhaps better to choose suitable plants which will thrive by themselves in the long term rather than requiring constant irrigation. I have also found it effective to incorporate some water-retaining crystals (such as those popular for hanging baskets) into the final topsoil; these initially resemble salt crystals but absorb up to 40 times their volume of water to become reminiscent of frog spawn. This water store is then accessible to the plants as required.

Proportions and design

The most important consideration is to maintain the scale of the planting in proportion to the size of the bed. Perhaps a single tree will be planted in the middle, with lower, shrubby plants radiating out from it to continue the canopy without dominating the bed. Thus the structure of the bed is effectively cone shaped. Another idea is to plant a taller tree at one end, so the height decreases down the bed's length. Factors which may influence the decision include the desired symmetry of the bed and whether it is to be viewed equally from all sides or predominantly from one area. I sometimes locate the taller trees at the front, where they can be seen through and under to the mid-height shrubs behind. It may seem illogical to decrease in height from front to back, but this actually can make it easier to see the entire bed, allowing the woodland plants to extend all the way to the rear of the bed rather than being restricted to the front edge. This does potentially make the planting more exposed, however. A new bed, particularly in the middle of an open area such as a lawn, will be vulnerable to the wind rushing through it. It is useful therefore to interplant with some evergreens of appropriate size to create more protected pockets.

A simple trio of silver birch can constitute a miniature woodland when the space between them is carpeted, here with snowdrops. *Cornus* stems glow in the background.

Another possibility is to plant a group of several of the same plant. Conventional wisdom dictates that an odd number of plants be included; for a small bed, three is usually adequate. *Betula* and *Acer* are obvious choices, but in theory the effect can be achieved with almost any plant, according to taste and scale. I like to feature *Amelanchier* if the soil is adequately moisture retentive. Otherwise, *Cornus mas*, *Staphyllea*, and *Euonymus* cultivars are all resplendently suitable.

In small-scale planting, only a limited number of plants will fit into the space. With so many wonderful selections from which to choose, it can be difficult to avoid "dotty" planting. Sometimes I restrict my options by choosing a particular theme for the bed, whether to restrict it to a certain colour or perhaps to achieve maximum interest over a single season. This latter option makes maintenance easier, too, as it all dies back together.

Spring bulbs are an obvious solution when the size of a woodland bed limits its scope.

If space is severely restricted, the size of the canopy planting needs to reflect the size of the bed. A single tree or small shrubs can be used, with dwarf bulbs and carpeters at their feet. Every garden has room for at least a piece of woodland.

Raised Bed

If the soil is inappropriate for whatever reason, my solution is to create a raised bed, taking the concept of mound planting one step further. As always, there is no end to the possibilities. Less physically-able gardeners often appreciate the easier accessibility of raised beds, while they can be utilised to link areas of the garden on different levels. They can even stand in their own right as an eye-catching feature.

I allow a shallow raised bed to phase out into the lawn, but greater depth will need retaining. Edging the raised bed can be accomplished in many ways, while achieving a satisfactory depth of soil in which to plant appropriate canopy plants as well as the treasures of the woodland floor. The type of edging dictates the formality of the planting. I have found dry stone walling to be a therapeutic solution but slow to construct. Railway sleepers (railroad ties) are a popular choice as they are substantial, but old ones are best avoided due to the chemicals used in their preservation. Peat blocks are

Below: *Betula utilis* var. *jacquemontii* 'Jermyns' resides within this raised bed edged by dry stone walling.

Above right: *Daphne acutiloba* 'Fragrant Cloud' enjoys the improved drainage achieved with this raised bed, retained with wooden fencing rails.

Right: A purple-leaved selection of *Acer palmatum* var. *dissectum* is thriving on a raised bed. Imagine some large-leaved woodlanders planted around it, such as *Beesia*, green *Heuchera*, or *Saxifraga*, to show off its finely cut foliage.

environmentally inappropriate these days. I have satisfactorily used fencing rails held in place by some vertical posts; they are inexpensive but most useable where straight edges are acceptable.

Raising the bed resolves any tendency to winter wet, but care should be taken to prevent the soil from drying out in summer. The choice of tree needs to reflect this likelihood, particularly in full exposure, rendering *Acer palmatum* cultivars a risky option to establish, unless the new bed is itself shaded by existing canopy. The type of root system should also be considered. *Betula*, for example, are very shallow rooted. Although they are aesthetically perfect for this scenario, their roots may compromise the retaining edge in time. Underplanting can then be undertaken in the usual manner. Individual raised beds provide an opportunity to isolate batches of plants such as *Erythronium* or *Trillium*, which naturally hybridise freely, allowing one to maintain a true gene pool of a single species.

Woodland Rock Garden

My inspiration for the woodland rock garden came from walking through beautiful countryside along local coast paths and in the Austrian Tyrol. In the wooded areas, rocky outcrops provided unique conditions for a range of plants that were quite different from those in the surrounding area. I imagined what fun it would be to build a rock garden in a shady site, perhaps under some overhanging trees or against a wall of the house or a fence. In its simplest form, it creates some height, being in principle a raised bed retaining the additional soil behind rocks. A rock garden provides a unique opportunity to position some of the smaller, more precious plants in a more controlled environment where they can be fully appreciated.

The woodland rockery creates such an exciting opportunity that it seems a shame to waste it on the easy classics.

Traditionally, English rockeries were constructed by spreading a token layer of top-soil over a heap of rubble, scattering a few rocks on top. This certainly achieves winter drainage, but woodland plants will require considerably more water retention in summer, so it is better to construct it in much the same manner as the raised bed. Working from the bottom, an appropriate soil mix should be backfilled against the first row of rocks before the second layer is then positioned on a solid base. As always, the scale will vary, but I derive huge satisfaction in making it appear as strata of rock emerging from the soil, and our sloping site lends itself admirably to this.

A quite different planting opportunity presents itself here, since I can utilise the rocks to provide that all-important protection, regretfully absent from other newly constructed areas. These will shelter vulnerable plants, becoming the ideal location in which to nurture my precious treasures—those that are too small, too slow, or too pretty to disappear into the wider landscape. I include eclectic *Scoliopus* and tiny *Trillium*, though I am also mesmerised by *Hepatica* and *Ourisia*. Small evergreens, including dwarf ferns, add valuable foliage and winter structure.

Sometimes an existing rockery can become overshadowed as surrounding vegetation develops. Rather than struggling with maintenance, I see this as an opportunity for a revamp, to change the style of planting to exploit this unique and exciting environment.

Hedgerow

The foot of a hedgerow or hedge is often considered to be an impossible place to maintain, let alone actually enjoy. Too often, only nettles and brambles thrive and gardening activities consist of little more than an annual application of weed killer or physical control of the offending vegetation. But that need not be the case, though as always it is important to ensure that no perennial weeds are present before planting. Hedges present a distinctly different environment as compared with the woodland itself, though some plants will enjoy both.

Although a hedgerow position will benefit from the same seasonal dryness, it may receive more light. In this respect, the direction that the hedge faces is a consideration. One side of the hedge may be heavily shaded and therefore limited in its options, but the other side is potentially sunnier, dependent on the amount of overhang. If the hedge is big and wide, it is possible that no direct sun will reach the base, though light levels are potentially good, replicating the woodland itself. The opposite extreme is a more formal clipped hedge where conditions at the base will be very dry and impoverished, with every stage in between. These principles apply to deciduous hedges, whether natural, formal, or ornamental. A clipped conifer hedge would be difficult to underplant, though some bulbs and *Cyclamen* would be worth trying.

As always, I start by thinking about the scale of the planting, considering the size of the hedge and how far the planting is to extend from its base. It could be literally just at the bottom, or if the hedge has a broad canopy, a wider woodland bed could be created.

Overgrown hedges can be cleared of brambles to create woodland areas of manageable size. Crooked and even broken trees add so much character.

The plants could be individuals to be admired from close up or a drift to be enjoyed from a distance. It is crucial to establish these principles at the start, and then the rest can slip easily into place.

Learning from nature

There is never a better method of deciding what will grow in certain conditions than to examine what grows there naturally. In many cases, cultivated forms and hybrids of native plants can be used to provide extra interest and excitement, to change the area from ordinary wild woodland into something special. A little caution is, of course, required. I still shudder at the sight of variegated ground elder for sale, and I am not convinced by cream-flowered dandelions. However, *Lamium* is a definite possibility. This rather vigorous plant with a distinctive square cross section to the stem will thrive in even the most testing of our woodland situations. Flowers can be yellow or pink, and variegated options can be found. Another possibility is the humble wild iris of English hedges. I tend to overlook *Iris foetidissima* when in flower, yet summer passes and it comes to life in autumn and winter, with breathtaking displays of bright orange berries. Other iris with more showy flowers are deep rooting yet benefit from the protection and warmth found on the sunny side of the hedge.

I love to see *Cyclamen hederifolium* jostling vigorously through the camouflage of native *Hedera helix* at the bases of our natural hedges. It is the hardiest species and so rewarding. Its name, meaning leaves like ivy, says it all, as no two plants of *C. hederifolium* have the same foliage, and it can be difficult to distinguish them from the ivy, until the pink or white flowers are produced in early autumn. This cyclamen is so easily grown that I am almost loathe to waste the protection of the woodland on it, though white-flowered forms look superlative beneath trees with vivid autumn colours. The

Iris foetidissima grows along an old track between two hedgerows, which provide a haven for wildlife, so it would be a shame to tidy it up too much.

The banks of this pretty stream already support colonies of primrose, bluebell, and wild iris, with exciting potential for additional planting.

foliage remains into late spring, so it can give double value as a dramatic backdrop to spring-flowering bulbs.

If the hedge is old with craggy root buttresses, little plants can be placed within the roots. *Cyclamen* spring immediately to my mind, but many other plants also benefit from summer dryness. It is even possible to add some extra leaf-mould–enriched soil to these pockets, perhaps retaining it with carefully positioned branches where necessary to maintain the natural appearance. These pockets are the perfect place to show off some precious plants which particularly benefit from a controlled environment; though I either need to choose plants which do not mind very dry summer conditions or take steps to ensure that these pockets do not dry out too much. The exact composition of the extra soil can be tailored to an individual's specific requirement, with the addition of appropriate amounts of leaf-mould and sand. I find ferns particularly effective in this situation, as I can develop a natural theme, supplementing the wild ferns already there. Even the introduction of a number of humble primroses and snowdrops will transform a messy area into one of beauty.

Crocus are incredibly tolerant, growing in the shallowest layer of soil, and they can happily colonise the base of even the biggest tree.

Single Tree

It makes sense to restrict the lawn immediately around the base of a tree, both for the tree's health and to facilitate mowing. These areas are perfect for bulbs, which can complement rather than detract from the character of the trunk. Spring-flowering bulbs are classics at the base of mature trees, because their growth cycle is out of step with that of the tree. *Crocus* and *Cyclamen* are obvious choices, but just the tip of the iceberg if a little soil can be added. I cannot resist the multicoloured clones of *Anemone blanda* and the smaller *A. nemorosa* which are so delightful in spring. Perhaps the pale yellow *A. ×lipsiensis* is my favourite, for its delightful flowers are never as delicate as they appear.

Trees with shallow roots can be a real menace in the lawn. *Prunus* and *Betula* are examples, whose roots push themselves out of the soil causing havoc with the mower. Nothing can be done to change it; it is their nature. The chances are that the grass is hardly worth cutting anyway, since the tree will be taking all the moisture. I have abandoned efforts at grass in areas like this and introduced a carpet of bulbs. Summer-active herbaceous plants are unlikely to thrive if even grass was struggling, but bulbs that are summer dormant are perfect. A coating of bark mulch after planting completes the

Root buttresses are a fantastic feature of mature trees. I would not want to conceal them, nor risk damage to the tree, by adding too much soil, but a gritty mix added to the pockets would support ferns or tiny bulbs.

scene, but I like to leave those troublesome roots visible to give the area character, both while the bulbs are flowering and through the summer when they disappear.

Sometimes an old tree can have seemingly pushed itself out of the ground; it was probably originally planted on a bank that was removed or eroded, leaving wonderful craggy roots exposed around it. These can be exploited in the same way as in the base of the hedgerow, but even old trees planted normally will often tolerate a thin layer of soil around the base of the trunk. This can be perfectly acceptable provided that the substrate is added in moderation and is very gritty and freely draining. This then gives the ideal home for some new acquisitions. Some of the smaller *Fritillaria* species are worth a try, as many of these love to bake in summer. Soil levels should not be altered too much, though, as this will disturb the water table and could damage the tree.

An unexpected success story here is with iris, though extremely tough conditions could prove too much for them; it would be easier to establish them around a middle-aged tree rather than a fully grown monster. I was astonished the first time I saw *Iris* Californian hybrids used in this manner, but they are perfect, spreading slowly and gaining little height. Transplanting these fleshy-rhizomed plants is an exercise in caution, as they never seem to have the same true dormancy as a bulb. The spring seems the most successful time for us, as they immediately grow into their new site. Careful watering is necessary until they are established, but their display is wonderful. An extensive range of colours includes peachy apricots, but dusky pinks, pale lilacs, and all manner of combinations can be found.

Adding colour in the canopy

An excellent way of adding an extra dimension to existing large trees is to train a climber up into the canopy, utilising the structure of the tree as a natural trellis.

Climbers have evolved to wind their way upward in their search for the sunlight that is unable to penetrate the tree's canopy. This limits their effectiveness in mature or dense woodland. However, climbers can be supremely effective as a means of gaining flower though an otherwise leafy but dull specimen tree or hedge.

My first awareness of this possibility was created at the Savill Garden, Windsor, where *Wisteria* cascades from the broad limbs of a majestic oak. Similarly, I love to see *Clematis* rambling through the canopy to provide splashes of colour all summer, while *Lonicera* (honeysuckle) adds its exquisite fragrance to the mature natural hedgerows around our garden. *Vitis* could even touch up the autumn colours, should they be lacking.

The most difficult part is persuading the plant to establish. I have already alluded to the problems of establishing new plants adjacent to mature trees, whose root systems have first call on the moisture. Indeed, it may be physically impossible to dig a hole adjacent to a large tree. The answer is to plant the climber away from the trunk and train it up into the canopy. Planting in the autumn will allow it opportunity for establishment before it has to compete with the tree through the summer. A rope tied to a stake in the ground is perhaps the best way of starting it on its journey, though it might require a tree surgeon to secure the other end up in the tree. A climbing plant will naturally wind its way up and soon continue beyond the rope. It is important that the vigour of the climber is in proportion to the size of the tree. Wisteria can be vigorous and heavy and could demolish too small or fragile a tree. Conversely, a delicate clematis that needs careful pruning each year is less suitable than a *Clematis montana* cultivar, for example, which can safely be planted and left alone, rewarding with an abundance of flowers each spring. Despite the perils of establishment, it is definitely preferable to introduce the climber to an existing mature tree. The danger in planting the climber at the foot of a new young tree is that the climber is likely to grow considerably more rapidly than the tree and will distort the tree's shape to the point of suppression and death.

Ivy has a bad reputation in connection with growing in trees, despite the wonderful habitat and food source that it provides for wildlife. Indeed, the heavy evergreen blanket in which it can shroud its host tree will potentially suppress the tree, but more worryingly it can conceal a problem, such as a dead branch. Ivy will also become heavy in time, and its weight can cause the host tree to topple or disintegrate in severe weather. English ivy is invasive in the US and best avoided there, but I like a carpet of ivy across the woodland floor in a more natural or difficult area. It suppresses the weeds and provides a glossy, dark green backdrop through which more colourful plants can emerge. It rarely remains on the ground for long, though, soon winding its way up the trunks to develop the arborescent (woody) growth that allows it to flower and fruit. For that reason, I carefully monitor ivy, allowing it to maintain a presence for the sake of the wildlife, but not allowing it to run riot.

CHAPTER 4

Plant Directory

With an almost limitless number of plants from which to choose, enhancing or developing an area of woodland is an exciting project. So many habitats are available that it is crucial to choose the right plant for the job or the correct site for the plant. Knowledge of a its native habitat can facilitate appropriately positioning a newly acquired plant.

Some gardeners have little time for complicated plant names; the plant itself is everything. However, I believe that a fundamental understanding of the basic principles behind plant naming can help gardeners make good selections and avoid costly mistakes. Most plants have a common name, which can be derived from a translation of the Latin name, from a reference to the appearance or habitat of the plant, or from a traditional use for it. The problem is that the common name can be localised, certainly varying from one country to another. Thus, if an American were to discuss a wood anemone with an English gardener, the two might be using the same words, but talking about two different plants. Fortunately, all plants have a Latin name, which can be understood by gardeners all over the world to apply to a specific plant, so using this name avoids confusion.

Take the name *Acer palmatum* 'Katsura', for example. The word *Acer* is the genus, but there are lots of acers. Sycamore is an acer, but a thug, so we need to look further into the name to know more about it. The next word, *palmatum*, is the species. This specific name is just that—it specifies the type of *Acer*, just this one type of wild tree. *Acer palmatum* is famed for its autumn colour. Over the years, plant hunters have explored the world, nurserymen have cross-pollinated, and gardeners have kept a watchful eye for new plants. These selected individuals have been given cultivar names—in this example, 'Katsura'. Naming rules have been established to determine what these names can and cannot contain, but the important thing to understand is that all parts of the name are needed to identify a particular plant. Just calling it 'Katsura' could refer to the plant that has the common name katsura tree, whose Latin name is *Cercidiphyllum japonicum*; this is quite different from our *Acer palmatum* 'Katsura' cultivar.

The next principle is propagation—that is, how new plants are made from an existing one. The species is how the plant occurs in the wild and can be grown from seed. A cultivar is a selected form of that species. If seed is collected from a cultivar, it will not grow into exactly the same plant. It will be similar, because it will be the same species,

Opposite: *Cornus alternifolia* 'Argentea'

but it will not be identical. To ensure that the progeny is identical to the parent plant, it needs to be propagated vegetatively, or cloned. This can be done in several ways, depending on the nature of the plant. For herbaceous perennials, the easiest technique is to divide the plant, which can be done at any time while dormant. Woody plants are propagated from cuttings: a shoot is removed in summer and treated in such a manner that new roots are formed. Sometimes this is impossible, as some plants will not root; these need to be grafted. A shoot is removed from the parent plant and effectively attached to the side of a young plant of the same species that already has its own root system.

This is all relevant because sometimes it is best to use a cultivar, but at other times the species is preferable. Some species offer more natural variation than others; sometimes all plants appear identical, and nobody has found or bred one of a different colour or a different shape. In these cases, no cultivars exist—there is no choice beyond the species. However, some plants have a huge gene pool, and when lots of them occur together, that gene pool is effectively stirred, so there is scope for variation in the next generation. Thus, over the years and around the world, literally hundreds of cultivars of *Acer palmatum* have been selected and named, with tremendous variations in their summer foliage colour. The species is green, but oranges or purples are available, or even pink and white–leaved selections. Leaf shape varies, too, as well as the eventual height and shape of the plant. Perhaps the woodland is natural and the simple requirement is for lovely autumn colour. Since the species is variable, some have better autumn colour than others, so it is better to select a cultivar that is known to be spectacular rather than leaving it to chance.

Sometimes plants can take many years to achieve the maturity to flower. Buying a grafted plant reduces that time. Couple this with the ability to choose its features—even if it is just the assurance that it is going to be good—and it makes much more sense to buy a named grafted plant than a seedling, even if the latter is usually less expensive. Good examples of this are *Magnolia* and *Cornus kousa*.

Despite the variety available with cultivars, sometimes it is in fact better to plant the species. It is frequently desirable to be able to make cultivar choices when only a single specimen of a particular species is required. However, in the woodland, particularly at the carpeting level, plants often need to naturalise, to look as if Mother Nature put them there. In many cases, clonal plants do not set seed as readily as the species; this can reduce their ability to naturalise, as with erythroniums, while viburnums need a pollinator to produce their ornamental berries. A natural drift will be quicker and cheaper to achieve using the species than by spending extra money on clonal plants. Sometimes a compromise is necessary: the quality of the named plants is desirable, because selection and breeding has developed a wonderful range of colours, but they need to spread. The solution is to plant a collection of different named forms; this achieves a quality gene pool. Although wild hellebores are delightful, for example, some gorgeous colours and forms of *Helleborus* ×*hybridus* are available. Initial plants can be selected when in flower. Not all the subsequent seedlings will be exactly the same, of course, but some might be better!

Another thing to consider is that species have evolved to thrive in particular locations. Improving on those conditions can result in too much growth. Sometimes the species apparently most suited to a site could actually become too successful and swamp its more delicate neighbours. Usually, an alternative species or geographical variant is available which will have a similar effect but will not be quite so invasive.

The final detail is that some species vary, perhaps from one locality to another. These are called a variety or a form and are signified by the characters *var.* and *f.*, as in *Lilium martagon* var. *album*. The variety *album* is white, while *Lilium martagon* itself is a lovely reddish purple. If it were a cultivar, seed from the white plants would be most unlikely to produce white-flowering offspring. Yet forms and varieties should be stable, meaning that a clump of white *L. martagon* var. *album* will set seed and spread. Of course, it is also very effective to mix the colours, but that is where it starts to get personal.

The nomenclature used here is based on the Royal Horticultural Society's *Plant Finder*, Vertrees's *Japanese Maples* (2001), and other reliable sources.

Directory Organisation

Genera are listed in alphabetical order. After the genus name, the family to which it belongs appears; this is the next rung up the nomenclature ladder. This information can be useful when guessing what conditions a plant may need or how it may grow, since genera within the same family often share characteristics.

My selection of species suited to woodland situations, along with a range of cultivars, follows a brief résumé of the genus. Most genera and species are diverse, so I have included a representative assortment, including personal favourites, worthy old campaigners, and new pretenders. Usually, the whole genus is suitable for the same area—for example, *Epimedium* are all small plants for the woodland floor. Occasionally a genus is sufficiently diverse to have members appropriate to different levels. Take *Cornus*, which includes trees, shrubs, and low carpeters; clearly, knowing how each grows and where it is best planted is of utmost importance.

In the larger genera, for example, *Clematis* and *Narcissus*, the cultivars are subdivided into formally recognised groups in which members have similar characteristics and cultural requirements. Some genera are not formally subdivided in this way, but where knowledge of a species facilitates appropriate selection and positioning of its derivatives, I have listed the cultivars immediately below the species to which they are most closely related (see *Saxifraga*). Many genera include cultivars that are of unknown origin. In the case of *Hosta*, for example, the breeding line is so complicated that cultivars cannot be assigned to any particular species. In these circumstances, all unattributed cultivars are listed at the end of their generic entry.

For most plants, disease is rare when the plant is happy but prevalent in conditions which cause it to struggle. For example, some plants develop powdery mildew during late summer, a sign that conditions are too dry for them (which may be indicative of the site or simply the recent weather). Ideally, woodland glades evolve into moist, shady places beloved of so many plants, but they are also the preferred habitat of slugs and snails which will inevitably feast on the succulent young spring growth of precious woodland carpeters. Mollusc control is an emotive issue. If woodland gardening on a small scale, some precautions may be appropriate; larger areas are more able to develop a natural balance. That is a personal issue to be addressed by each gardener. However, research has shown that throwing the creatures over the garden fence does not work; they simply walk home.

I have also indicated whether a plant is known to be toxic. I firmly believe that it would be an enormous pity to elect not to grow such plants as a result. It is a fact of life that many plants contain toxic compounds; it is always best to avoid handling or ingesting plants unless they are cultivated specifically for human consumption. A great many plants have been utilised for medicinal or culinary purposes in the past, and it is interesting to discover these anecdotes. However, this does not imply that their use is safe or appropriate.

Opposite: *Acer palmatum* cultivars often colour early in the autumn. Here, an outstanding specimen dramatically punctuates the calm. *Cyclamen hederifolium* flowers beneath the big tree in the background, protected by low evergreens.

I make little direct reference to hardiness. All the plants included are fundamentally winter-cold hardy to –15°C (5°F) or so. The problem is that standard hardiness zones are based almost entirely on minimum temperatures, which is only part of the equation. Whether or not a plant will survive the winter depends on the interaction of a number of factors in addition to the temperature—a combination of soil, location, and weather. Winter wet and late spring frosts are often bigger killers than cold. Mulching insulates winter-dormant plants, providing considerable protection; equally, an organic mulch gathered too close around the base of a vulnerable woody plant can cause the plant to rot at the collar. Many plants will tolerate lower winter temperatures if they have stored lots of sugars during exposure to heat and light during the previous summer. Thus plants in shady sites can be more vulnerable—though the woodland itself provides considerable protection from biting winds. This helps protect the evergreens in winter as well as the delicate new foliage emerging in the spring. Many woodland plants prefer cooler summer conditions, so in extreme cases, high summer temperatures can damage them rather than cold winters.

None of the plants listed here are tender; none need to be lifted and overwintered under protection in normal conditions. Do not be fooled by the fact that I live in the southwest of England. We regularly endure winter temperatures below –10°C (14°F). In especially cold or wet climates, it may be wise to plant just one of something to see how it fares before spending a lot of money on large quantities. Experimentation is part of the fun of gardening.

A to Z Plant Directory

Acer (Aceraceae)

This genus is so huge that there really is an *Acer* for every eventuality. I offer only a guide to establish a few principles.

The bigger, easy to grow trees make fantastic additions to the upper canopy, growing satisfyingly rapidly, while the middle canopy can include the Japanese maples. Where the canopy is high, taller forms can be accommodated. I am often asked how big a certain tree will grow, and it is rarely easy to answer simply. With this genus, it is even more difficult to answer because they are so influenced by their environment. Establishment is crucial, but once they are settled, they tend to grow within the parameters of the site. If the soil is nutrient rich and moisture retentive, they will potentially grow much more vigorously than a plant at the opposite end of the cultural spectrum on light, rapidly draining, sandy soil in full sun. In such a case, establishment will be difficult and the growth short and twiggy, with smaller leaves. The ideal soil would be free draining in winter, yet adequately moisture retentive in summer. Relatively low nutrient levels will result in firmer wood and a healthier plant, since very soft, lush growth will be more vulnerable to fluctuations in weather conditions. Acers are traditionally considered to be acid loving; however, soil structure is much more important than the exact pH, although they do well on soils of low pH. Mulching is of immense benefit to help maintain moisture levels in summer.

Where garden conditions are appropriate, the toughest of the middle canopy trees can perfectly create the framework for a smaller scale woodland. The amount of exposure they will tolerate is influenced by the moisture retentiveness of the soil, their level of establishment (as their root system develops, they will be able to react faster to weather changes), and their degree of ornamentation. Vigorous green-leaved cultivars similar to the species are the most resilient, while a brightly coloured dwarf form would be the most vulnerable, with every stage in between.

Acers are long lived but often slow-growing trees, taking many years to mature. Sometimes it is appropriate to plant for posterity, but often the desired effect is required within a certain timespan. If the area is large enough, it may offer scope for both. If instant gratification is required, it may be at the expense of long-term suitability, but such is the case with living plants. They will change and grow. By definition, it is impossible to have the perfect size immediately that will still be perfect in five, ten, and even fifty years. However, acers are extremely tolerant of being moved, so it is satisfactory to plant a large specimen should circumstances dictate. Alternatively, consider your timescale and choose the tree to fit.

Guaranteed to brighten any dismal autumn day with their fiery display of psychedelic autumn colours, many acers' spring flowers are surprisingly pretty, while the subsequent winged samaras (seedpods) are most attractive. These trees have it all.

Acer campestre

Field maples are a common sight along English hedges. An excellent choice for structural planting to create the upper canopy in smaller scale woodlands, it is easily pleased and very weather tolerant, with lovely orange and yellow autumn colours.

'**Pulverulentum**' An old cultivar from 1859, with interesting cream-flecked and splashed leaves and a rather shrubby habit. Extremely sun tolerant, despite the variegation. 4–5m.

'**Red Shine**' New growth opens rich reddish purple, becoming greener as the season progresses. 'Royal Ruby' is similar. 5m.

'**Silver Celebration**' This rather handsome sport occurred in our nursery on *A. campestre* 'Carnival'. The variegation is much more subtle; a narrower margin of cream on otherwise greyish green leaves is an excellent compromise. More interesting than plain green but tougher and less "gardeny" than 'Carnival'. 4–6m.

Acer circinatum

This vine maple is visually allied to the Japanese maples, yet it comes from the Pacific coast of North America. Of handsome shrubby habit with multi-season interest, its pretty flowers appear with the foliage in spring while young leaves are flushed with reds and orange, contrasting with the green of summer, before spectacular riots of colour in autumn. Even through winter the reddish orange bare stems are attractive. These shade lovers are superb middle canopy candidates but are suitable for upper canopy use only where adequate moisture is retained through summer to prevent stress and mildew. The named cultivars are beautiful additions to the middle canopy, where their greater delicacy and smaller stature can be gently protected. 5m.

'**Monroe**' Deeply incised leaves.

'**Pacific Fire**' Amazing recent selection with intense coral-red stems through winter.

'**Sunglow**' Gorgeous orange summer glow to the leaves.

Acer ×conspicuum

This hybrid snakebark group displays spectacular bark. Arguably, their autumn colours are less remarkable than *A. davidii* and its cultivars, generally changing earlier and for a shorter duration.

Acer ×conspicuum
'Phoenix' in early autumn

'**Elephant's Ear**' Vigorous and upright with massive leaves. 8–10m.

'**Phoenix**' Incredible Dutch selection with surreal bark. Delicate orange in late autumn, by the time this cultivar is completely dormant, the colour will have intensified to pink; it is always striated by characteristic white stripes. 3–4m. *Acer pensylvanicum* 'Erythrocladum' is similar.

'**Silver Vein**' One of the best in the group, being robust with magnificent purple and white–striped bark. 10m.

Acer davidii

This classic Chinese species epitomises the snakebark maple ethos, characterised by long vertical stripes marking the bark which may otherwise be green to purple. Although not liking to dry out in summer, some forms particularly dislike winter wet and can be prone to fungal problems in mild, damp winters. However, they do have everything: pretty spring flowers, some of the best autumn colours, and of course the distinctive winter bark.

> **'Ernest Wilson'** and **'George Forrest'** These wild selections were named at the Edinburgh Royal Botanic Gardens in honour of two of our most respected plant-hunters. 8–10m.

> **'Karmen'** Typical V-shaped habit but wonderful chocolate-coloured young leaves, with green and white–striped bark. 10m.

> **'Rosalie'** Pretty selection with early, frost-resistant young leaves, flushed reddish brown when young. Green and white summer bark richens to purple and white in winter. 12–15m.

> **'Serpentine'** Quite different habit; shrubby and rather arching, with much smaller leaves. Particularly free fruiting. 4–5m.

Acer griseum

The Chinese paperbark maple has distinctive cinnamon-coloured bark which peels off in flakes to reveal a wonderful shiny underlayer. A stand of these to underplant would be the most superlative investment a gardener could make. Although slow when young, after less than 20 years our first plant is a magnificent sight at a statuesque 5m. Reliable rich autumn colours seemingly encompass all the fiery shades of scarlet and orange.

Acer japonicum

Closely related to *A. palmatum* and equivalent in its requirements, it is slow growing with supremely beautiful autumn colour.

'**Aconitifolium**' Deeply divided leaves.

'**Vitifolium**' Larger leaves.

Acer palmatum

First described by a visiting Swedish botanist in 1784, it was not introduced to the West from Japan (it also grows in other parts of Asia) for another 50 years, when it caused great excitement. Though other acers come from Japan, this is the archetypal Japanese maple. Yet the variation within the species is huge; one can find an *A. palmatum* to suit every conceivable taste and situation.

Light levels can influence the exact colour of the foliage in many cultivars. Acers with purple leaves need good light levels to display their foliage colour to best effect. However, good light need not necessarily mean full sun; indeed, in good light, but out of full sun, is the ideal position for a Japanese maple, and such can often be found under a high canopy. If light levels are inadequate, the purple colour can diminish to a rather dirty looking green. However, within the vast range of purple selections of *A. palmatum*, some are known for their ability to hold their colour well. Although they enjoy the protection of the woodland setting, Japanese maples dislike to be too enclosed; they will object to a very dark overhung site, becoming suppressed in summer, while stagnant air in winter will inevitably result in fungal problems (particularly if the soil is heavy and has a tendency to be too wet).

For many gardeners, the ultimate Japanese maple is *A. palmatum* var. *dissectum*; the usually seven-lobed leaves are further divided and the lobes serrated to give a delicate effect enhanced by their wonderfully architectural, cascading habit, which makes them best underplanted with tiny early bulbs and low carpeters. This group of maples particularly benefit from the protection within the woodland setting.

Japanese maples can provide year-round interest, with vivid colours in the spring as new growth commences and delightful effects through summer before their unsurpassed autumn displays. Some also have surprisingly lovely bark, while their architectural structure makes them a pleasure to behold even in the stark bareness of winter. Many are similar, so this is a representative collection of more robust individuals. Only a few cultivars are included, but literally hundreds are available and a number of specialist books can enlighten further.

'**Aoyagi**' Spring growth is a vivid lime green, toning down a little through the summer before turning yellow to orange in autumn. Green willow is an apt name, as bright, light green stems light up the winter woodland. 3–4m.

'**Ariadne**' This recent Dutch introduction was named after the raiser's granddaughter. The deeply cut, but not lacy, purple leaves are vividly marked with pink and white with conspicuous veining. Not variegated (the effect is much more subtle),

Above: *Acer palmatum* 'Ariadne' autumn colours

Right: *Acer palmatum* 'Shinobuga oka', autumn colours just starting

the exact colours will be determined by light levels. Attractive grey bark with noticeable white striations and broad arching habit to 2m in all directions.

'Autumn Showers' The name says it all. Fabulous autumn colours and graceful, gently cascading habit.

'Beni ōtake' The Linearilobum group is characterised by thin, threadlike lobes. This purple-leaved form is not the narrowest, so it has more vigour. It is a favourite, with bright red colour in spring and again in autumn. 2–3m. Green-leaved members of this group include 'Shinobuga oka'.

'Bloodgood' This classic remains the standard purple cultivar against which all others are compared. Upright in habit to 5m and well-behaved. I also like the slightly redder 'Ō kagami'. The many purple cultivars vary in leaf shape and overall appearance; some, like 'Burgundy Lace', have deeply divided leaves with serrated lobes and a more arching habit.

'Chishio Improved' The Seigen group produces seemingly unreal fluorescent pinky red spring growth which matures to reddish green, then purples, reds, and oranges in autumn. Also in this group is 'Shin deshōjō'.

'Chitose yama' The beauty of this maple comes from its subtlety. The leaf colour seems to change constantly and is influenced by light levels. Initially bright red, it

Below: *Acer palmatum* 'Chishio Improved' autumn colours
Right: Snowdrops thrive beneath a low mound of *Acer palmatum* var. *dissectum.*

fades to purple-flushed shades of green before displaying spectacular autumn colours. Wonderful almost layered habit.

'Crimson Queen' A popular purple-leaved selection from *A. palmatum* var. *dissectum* Atropurpurea Group which holds its rich, deep colour well. Other good purples with equally lacy leaves include 'Inaba shidare' and 'Tamuke yama'.

var. *dissectum* Lacy green leaves and an arching mushroom-shaped habit characterise this slow grower. Many selections have been made to emphasise these features, including numerous with purple leaves derived from *A. palmatum* var. *dissectum* Atropurpurea Group. 1–2m.

'Emerald Lace' This recently named green selection from *A. palmatum* var. *dissectum* is particularly strong growing and robust.

'Flavescens' A traditionally shaped form of *A. palmatum* var. *dissectum*, the green summer colour brightens any woodland glade. 'Waterfall' and 'Viridis' are similar classics.

'Hōgyoku' Green summer colour develops superlative oranges and golds in autumn. 5m.

'Katsura' Early into leaf with vivid orange spring colour, becoming a more muted burnt-orange in summer before the fiery reds and oranges of autumn. 4–5m.

'Mimaye' Dense leafy habit within an upright silhouette. Summer greens change to the brightest yellow autumn colours late in the season. 3–4m.

'Mirte' The hybrids between closely related *A. palmatum* and *A. shirasawanum* inherited the latter's increased leaf size and durability, with the elegance and beauty of the former. This one has chocolate-coloured new leaves marked with green veining and a soft pubescence. 'Yasemin', by contrast, is a unique glossy purple in colour, with delicately serrated leaf lobes. 5m.

'Nishiki gawa' Sometimes known as the pine bark maple in recognition of its furrowed, corky bark. Perfect in natural surroundings, being upright and vigorous. Superb autumn colours. 5m.

'Ōsakazuki' Such a classic maple yet still one of the best, forming a broad, small tree with relatively large leaves; opens reddish purple but quickly matures to olive green. Fiery autumn displays go through orange before scarlets and crimsons dominate. 'Ichigyōji' is often considered a yellow equivalent. 6m.

'Sango kaku' The coral-bark maples are famed for their winter bark colour. Bronzy new leaves mellow to green through summer

Acer palmatum 'Ōsakazuki'

Acer palmatum 'Sango kaku' in autumn

before erupting into fiery shades in autumn. 'Eddisbury' is a more recent selection in the same group with even more intense orange-red winter bark. 5m.

'Seiryū' Although exhibiting the lacy, deeply divided leaves of *A. palmatum* var. *dissectum*, this cultivar stands out due to its upright and more treelike habit. Superb red and orange autumn colour.

'Shigitatsu sawa' (syn. 'Reticulatum') Green veins are prominent against silvery or yellow-green interspaces. This reticulate leaf pattern is typical of this group, though colouration varies between cultivars.

'Watnong' An Australian cultivar derived from *A. palmatum* var. *dissectum* which shares that dainty foliage and habit. Green leaves with contrasting red sepals are beautifully flushed with bronze-orange. 'Chantilly Lace' is an excellent alternative.

Acer pseudosieboldianum

This Korean species is remarkably similar to the more familiar Japanese equivalents, developing an open structure. Young shoots remain orange-red in winter following superb autumn colours. A good choice for structural planting because it is remarkably resilient. 8m.

Acer rubrum

Given time, the North American red maple makes a large tree of 30m. The little red flowers in early spring are quaintly attractive, but its forte is undoubtedly its autumn colour. It enjoys a damp site. With many named clones, the differences in form and colour are subtle.

'Firedance' Exceptionally cold-hardy with brilliant red autumn colour.

'October Glory' Pyramidal crown loses its leaves later than some, thus extending the autumn display.

'**Scanlon**' More compact and upright habit.

'**Somerset**' Deepest red autumn colour and attractive red stems.

Acer rufinerve

This shade-loving, but drought-tolerant understorey snakebark maple from Japan has typically spectacular autumn colours, often augmented by purple and white striated winter bark.

'**Erythrocladum**' Not be confused with the *A. pensylvanicum* cultivar of the same name, this 1953 English selection is incredible. The winter bark is amber-coloured, with a soft white bloom giving a ghostly appearance. Definitely more fragile than its relatives, the protection of the woodland environment is paramount.

'**Hatsuyuki**' (syn. 'Albolimbatum') Pretty white-flecked foliage develops spectacular autumn colours. Greener bark and smaller, shrubbier habit. 6–8m.

'**Winter Gold**' This cultivar is sufficiently similar to *A. rufinerve* 'Erythrocladum' that it may simply be a more commercial name for the same plant.

Acer saccharum

Including six subspecies, the drought-tolerant sugar maple is widely distributed and popular throughout the United States, where it performs best in warmer conditions, becoming surprisingly deep rooted. Less enthusiastic about maritime climates, it will have shallower roots and the potentially outstanding autumn colours may not reach their full potential. However, I still value this easily grown tree in the upper canopy, particularly enjoying the cut-leaved forms.

'**Brocade**' Smaller growing with deeply divided leaves.

'**Fiddlers Creek**' Even more divided foliage.

Left: *Acer rufinerve* 'Hatsuyuki'

Above: Winter bark of *Acer rufinerve* 'Winter Gold'

Acer shirasawanum

The characteristics of this lovely small tree are typical of its Japanese cousins, but it is stockier in growth habit.

'Aureum' Arguably one of the most spectacular of all maples, the vivid golden young growth matures to a lovely yellow or lime green, dependent on light levels, before fiery oranges erupt in autumn. A "must-have" for the middle canopy since shade is required; slow growing.

'Palmatifolium' This more resilient green-leaved cultivar is of exceptional merit for smaller scale structural planting, with gorgeous early autumn orange colours and a lovely architectural, eventually open structure.

Acer tataricum subsp. ginnala

Previously a species in its own right, this is a tremendous bushy tree. Extremely early into leaf in spring yet remarkably frost tolerant, the small leaves create a dense canopy which glows with a kaleidoscope of bonfire colours in autumn. Potentially 12m tall by 5m wide after a very long time.

'Fire' Just a baby at 3–4m tall, scarlet autumn colour is held for the longest time.

'Flame' The most widely available form is hardy and reliable but the leaves drop sooner than 'Fire'. 4–5m.

Above: *Acer tataricum* subsp. *ginnala* 'Flame'

Right: *Acer tegmentosum* 'White Tigress'

Acer tegmentosum

The Asian equivalent of *A. pensylvanicum*, this snakebark maple tends towards paler green and white–striped bark, overlain with a subtle white bloom (giving way to temptation to caress the inviting stems rubs it off).

'White Tigress' The exact colour of the bark can vary according to light exposure and the nutrient/mineral levels in the soil. For us it is one of the most spectacular; the striated bark is more purple than that of the species.

Acer triflorum

Related to *A. griseum*, it is more rapid in growth and even more extravagantly coloured in autumn, though with slightly more modest bark.

Achlys (Berberidaceae)

Achlys triphylla

Some of my favourite woodland floor plants belong in this diverse family.

Achlys triphylla

Native of one of the world's richest sources of woodland floor plants, western North America, *Achlys triphylla* is grown for its foliage more than its short bottlebrush–like flowers. This species is one of the least common but is surprisingly drought tolerant, surviving close to established trees. Spreading by virtue of slender rhizomes, the large peltate leaves (the stem appears to grow out of the middle of the leaf, like an umbrella handle), on stems to 40cm, are divided into three large lobes, creating a lovely leafy carpet through which other upright woodlanders can emerge—the arching stems of *Polygonatum* perhaps. Although the fresh leaves have no fragrance, when picked, dried, and crushed, they release a strong aroma of vanilla (hence the common name vanilla leaf).

> **var. *japonica*** This geographical variant from Japan is extremely similar, though some authorities treat it as a separate species (*A. japonica*). Smaller growing, with proportionally smaller leaves. 20cm.

Acis (Amaryllidaceae)

Research carried out in 2004 at the Royal Botanic Gardens, Kew, has established that a number of bulbs previously classified as *Leucojum* should revert to *Acis*, a genus originally established in 1807. Essentially, *Acis* encompasses the smaller-growing species with unmarked, bell-like flowers that are perfectly proportioned for a place on the woodland rock garden.

Acis autumnalis

(previously *Leucojum autumnale*) This dainty Mediterranean species will flower its heart out from late summer to late autumn. The tiny white flowers are often delicately flushed with pink. Good drainage is necessary when dormant in spring, but it will tolerate moisture at other times. 15cm.

Acis nicaeensis

(previously *Leucojum nicaeense*) From France, this species flowers in mid to late spring, with a green flush to the tiny white bells. Although needing good drainage when dormant in summer, it does not need to bake completely. 18cm.

Actaea (Ranunculaceae)

Until recently, elements of this genus were known as *Cimicifuga*. However, we must move with the times, although I still do not find the species originally classified as *Actaea* nearly as ornamental as those recently transferred from *Cimicifuga*. These latter species form leafy clumps of attractively divided leaves from which emerge tall spikes clothed in small, creamy white flowers at the end of summer. Flowers of some species can be a little sparse, while others become plume-like. They all have a very high moisture requirement through the summer, so an appropriate area of the woodland floor should be chosen. The green-leaved forms will thrive in very heavy shade, but some lovely purple-leaved selections will give best colour in a more open position, where adequate light can filter through the canopy. All parts of these plants are toxic, which is of particular concern due to their tempting berries.

Actaea arizonica

The Arizona desert is not where you would expect to find a shade- and moisture-loving plant, but that is exactly where these originate—albeit in exactly those conditions at the bottom of a deep canyon. Gently colonising rhizomes form leafy clumps of maple-shaped leaves, from which rise narrow spikes of white flowers in late summer to early autumn. 1–1.2m.

Actaea biternata

The value of this Asian species is its greater tolerance of hotter, drier conditions. Otherwise it is typical of that which I think of as *Cimicifuga*. Very elegant, slender flower spikes with staminate (lacking true petals) white or pinkish white fragrant flowers. 100cm.

Actaea dahurica

Debatably the most floriferous species, it is not widely cultivated, which is a shame. This species is dioecious (male or female plants), with male plants being considerably more showy. 2m.

Actaea japonica

Luxuriant foliage through the summer makes an excellent foil for earlier bloomers and brightly coloured hostas. Then, just as so much else is looking tired, it erupts into bloom with upright stems of scented bottlebrush–like flowers in late summer/early autumn.

Actaea matsumarae

This is a pretty, floriferous species (sometimes included as a variety of *A. simplex*), but for sheer "flower power" track down the cultivar 'White Pearl'.

> **'White Pearl'** The great, thick bottlebrush flower spikes are awe-inspiring. In fact, they are so heavy and dense that they could be said to detract from the grace of the plant.

Actaea pachypoda

(syn. *A. alba*) From eastern North America, this original *Actaea* species is grown for its berries, not flowers. The latter are held in white pompoms above leafy mounds of elder-like foliage in late spring/early summer, developing into remarkable white berries marked with a black eye; affectionately known as doll's eyes.

> **f. *rubrocarpa*** Red berries.

Actaea rubra

Aesthetically a red-berried equivalent of *A. pachypoda*, the berries being held on more slender stalks. *A. asiatica* has black berries held on contrasting vivid pinky red stalks.

> **f. *neglecta*** Confusingly, a white-berried form.

Actaea rubra

Actaea simplex

This is my favourite species, though it does need plenty of moisture. Many named selections have been chosen for their flower or foliage colour. All are sweetly scented.

> **'Hillside Black Beauty'** The best purple-leaved selection; so dark it is almost black, combining beautifully with pink-flushed flowers.

'**Pink Spire**' Wonderful pink flowers clothe the many spikes rising from dark green foliage, suffused with bronze-purple where light levels are high. The flowers attract butterflies, so position this one at the edge of the woodland to gain full benefit.

Adiantum (Adiantaceae)

Of more than 200 species, known affectionately as maidenhair ferns, few are hardy. However, those that are hardy make delightful little deciduous clumps of graceful, airy fronds with fan-shaped, tiny leaflets. The bright green fronds contrast with the black stems to create a two-tone effect, which can be enhanced by planting among black-leaved *Ophiopogon*, but these gorgeous ferns look good with almost anything. In favourable conditions, the most vigorous forms can grow as much as 75cm in all directions. The woodland floor is home for these ferns, which will tolerate a very dry site if supplementary water can be provided to aid establishment. The foliage actually sheds water, giving rise to the name *Adiantum*, which means unwetted.

Below: *Adiantum aleuticum* 'Miss Sharples'

Right: Twisty trunks of an ancient *Osmanthus delavayi* rise from a bed of leafy *Adiantum venustum*.

Adiantum aleuticum

From western North America, it is sometimes classified as a variety of *A. pedatum*.

'**Japonicum**' Young fronds are delicately flushed with apricot-pink. Gorgeous. 40cm.

'**Miss Sharples**' The delightful fronds are suffused with gold, particularly when young.

'**Subpumilum**' Dwarf form to 15cm, originally from Vancouver, Canada.

Adiantum pedatum

This is the equivalent species from eastern North America, and probably the one more usually cultivated in Britain. Smaller in habit, it makes elegant clumps to little more than 30cm in all directions. A notable characteristic is the semicircular leaf arrangement.

Adiantum venustum

This evergreen Himalayan species creeps along the ground, forming a wonderful soft winter carpet in surprisingly dry sites. 30cm.

Ainsliaea (Asteraceae)

These recently introduced, still scarce plants from Japan and Korea are hardy in mild areas. They grow naturally in woodland floor conditions and are tolerant of relatively heavy shade, even under conifers.

Ainsliaea acerifolia

Glossy clumps of pinnate leaves, each to 20cm across, cover the ground. Tiny, long, narrow tubular flowers, white with purple tips, are held in a panicle on a tall flower spike, high above the foliage. 80cm.

Ainsliaea fragrans var. integrifolia

This Japanese plant is quite different. The oval leaves are silver-grey with dark veins while the fragrant white starry flowers are held on tall, slender stalks.

Ajuga (Lamiaceae)

At first glance this is such a humble little plant, yet it is amazing how effective and versatile it can be. Forty species include annuals and perennials, most of which are grassland plants. Those enjoying the shaded woodland floor need some moisture to be maintained through the summer. It is in the mint family, which perhaps provides a more familiar picture of its habit and structure. *Ajuga* is rhizomatous, creeping along the ground, rooting as it goes, to form rosettes of leaves with short, erect spikes of flowers in spring and early summer. Often these flower spikes are still quite leafy, with flowers and leaves in alternating layers. The flowers are usually purple, to make a dramatic contrast with the chartreuse of euphorbias, small hostas, or dainty white-flowered spring bulbs. These subtle carpeters can fill the gaps between larger plants, while newer cultivars with coloured leaves can be flamboyant performers in their own right.

Ajuga incisa

This Japanese native is unusual for this genus in that it is deciduous. Almost heart-shaped, deep green leaves and bluish purple flowers in spring, often before the foliage. 30cm.

'**Bikun**' It will quickly become apparent that I am not a great lover of variegated plants, yet this one is rather spectacular. Originally released as 'Frosted Jade', it has broad, creamy leaf margins that set off violet-purple flowers.

'**Blue Enigma**' Introduced by the esteemed English plantsman Roy Lancaster, this selection has bright blue flowers which continue for six weeks.

Ajuga reptans

This classic species has a wide natural distribution. With so many named cultivars, the species itself has almost disappeared from cultivation. All have purple-blue flowers unless stated.

f. *albiflora* '**Alba**' White flowers contrast with the dark green, ground-hugging foliage. Plant among dwarf blue bulbs such as *Scilla* and *Chionodoxa*.

'**Arctic Fox**' This newer green and white–variegated cultivar takes over the mantle of popularity from the more vigorous 'Silver Beauty'. It is small and slow as a result of its strong variegation. A pretty combination with its purple-blue flowers to brighten up a dull corner.

'**Atropurpurea**' Perhaps the oldest cultivar, it is certainly the standard against which all new ones are measured. Blue-purple flowers sit above bronzy purple foliage.

'**Braunherz**' Even richer, coppery purple foliage.

'**Catlin's Giant**' Purple flushed when young, the enormous leaves will rise to 30cm; considerably more imposing than the others.

'**Golden Beauty**' Not yet widely available, golden foliage contrasts with purple flowers. The exact foliage colour will vary with light levels, but even in heavy shade where the gold tones will change to a lime green, it will be just as effective. 15cm.

'**Pink Elf**' Not particularly elfin, but definitely pink flowered.

'**Valfredda**' Widely distributed as 'Chocolate Chip', this smaller, more compact plant has narrow chocolate-coloured foliage. Wonderful with miniature narcissi, small golden hostas, or golden grass.

Alnus (Betulaceae)

Ostensibly not the most ornamental of trees, the primary attraction of this genus is its tremendous hardiness and tolerance of cold, wet soil; its ease of culture; and its result-ant rapidity of growth. *Alnus* will quickly and quietly form a windbreak to allow more exciting individuals to be grown within their protection. They do produce attractive catkins; males are long and more showy, while the females develop into small cones. Interestingly, most alder species have been proven to fix atmospheric nitrogen. Thus, their inclusion in impoverished woodland soils should, with time, be beneficial. Those listed here are easily and cheaply obtainable; more obscure species may be just as useable, but harder to come by.

Alnus cordata

The Italian alder develops a handsome pyramidal habit. 20m.

Alnus glutinosa

The common alder is native to Britain and Europe (where in days gone by the wood was used in the manufacture of clogs) as well as western Asia and North Africa. It has potential to grow very large (it can be coppiced to keep it in check) or not, according to the site. The cultivars are more ornamental but less utilitarian in terms of rapidly achieving protection.

> **'Aurea'** More modest in size and beautiful in late spring/early summer before the golden yellow young leaves fade to green.
>
> **'Imperialis'** Finely cut leaves provide dappled shade, with a wonderful graceful appeal; much tougher than it looks.
>
> **'Laciniata'** Stronger growing and less finely divided foliage than 'Imperialis'. A good compromise perhaps.

Alnus incana

The grey alder heralds from Europe and the Caucasus with conspicuous grey leaf undersides.

> **'Aurea'** Yellow leaves combine well with reddish yellow stems, whose colour holds through winter. Noticeable orange-red–tinted catkins.
>
> **'Laciniata'** Fetching cut-leaved foliage.

Alnus rugosa

The lenticels on the bark make this species reminiscent of many birch. This speckled alder of North America is content in moist habitats.

Alnus viridis

The green alder from central Europe is shrublike with tall, erect stems reminiscent of a hazel. Perfect for underplanting.

> **subsp.** *crispa* Larger North American counterpart has bigger, more finely toothed leaves.

Amelanchier (Rosaceae)

Amelanchier is probably my first choice for the structural planting of a small woodland bed, as it has appeal for much of the year: delightful flowers in spring, purple-black berries in summer (one common name is June berry), fantastic autumn colour, and a simple elegance when bare in winter. Perhaps most importantly, it is easy to grow. Often considered to prefer acid conditions, they prefer moisture-retentive soil, which is more important than pH. Where summers are dry, they will be susceptible to disease and have sparse foliage. Sizes quoted are the maximum, so they should not put you off; these plants should be included in every garden. Interestingly, many more named selections are available in the United States, where more of the species originate than in Britain. Unfortunately, nomenclature confusion exists among some species as well as classification of the named selections as cultivars or hybrids.

In Europe, the favoured method of propagating the cultivars is by grafting, sometimes onto *Amelanchier* seedlings, but frighteningly frequently onto *Sorbus* for greater speed and size. This is such a shame because, for me, perhaps their greatest appeal is the lovely suckering habit that provides a thicket of flowering stems. Grafting, of course, loses this and results in unsightly rootstock suckers. This issue is resolved in the United States, where these plants are often produced by tissue culture.

Amelanchier alnifolia

One of the most lime-tolerant species, this is grown in the United States for commercial fruit production, with berries of 1cm or larger in diameter. Generally forming a multi-stemmed shrub, it thrives in cold climates. Serviceberries, as they are known, mixed with buffalo meat and fat were Native American dietary staples in winter. 3–6m.

'**Honeywood**', '**Smokey**', and '**Success**' Selected for their fruit.

'**Regent**' Compact form with notable foliage and sweet fruit.

Amelanchier arborea

Considered the most treelike, as opposed to a multi-stemmed shrub, even the bark is ornamental, being suffused with red and fissured. The white flowers are held in pendulous racemes. 8m.

Amelanchier canadensis

My son has some lovely specimens in his garden which form tidy clumps of upright stems, clothed in erect racemes of white flowers, in clean contrast to the newly emerging green leaves

Amelanchier ×grandiflora

The home of most of the hybrids. Many of the newest crosses are quite disease resistant.

'**Autumn Brilliance**' Extremely durable, with long-lasting foliage. 8m.

'**Autumn Sunset**' Selected by the great plantsman Mike Dirr for its superior leaf-retention, even in drought conditions, and the spectacular pumpkin-orange autumn colours. 8m.

'**Ballerina**' A robust European selection with larger leaves and pure white flowers as well as large fruit. Thought to be a hybrid from *A. laevis*. 6–7m.

'**Princess Diana**' An excellent American selection, distinguished by lovely white flowers and good foliage, luscious berries, and outstanding red autumn colour. 8–9m.

'**Robin Hill**' A great choice for colder gardens, where the pink colouration in the buds will be retained through the open flowers. 7–9m.

'**Rubescens**' An old selection from 1920, though still worthy of cultivation. Purple-pink flower buds open to a light pink. 7–8m.

Amelanchier laevis

Allied to *A. arborea* but enhanced by the bronzy colouration of newly emerging leaves. 5–8m.

'**Snowcloud**' The *A. laevis* parentage is apparent in the upright, narrow habit. Clouds of white flowers are followed by blue-green foliage which turns lovely orange-reds in autumn. Sweet fruits. 7–8m.

Amelanchier lamarckii

An elegant species that forms a small, shrubby tree. The young leaves are decoratively flushed with bronze, coinciding with the lax racemes of palest pink-white flowers. Blue-black fruits and lovely autumn colour round off the season.

Amelanchier lamarckii

Anemone (Ranunculaceae)

This extensive genus comprises more than 100 species found across a diverse range of habitats, from moist and shady woodlands to sun-baked alpine scree. To thrive, plants must be matched with habitat; light and moisture levels are the most important factors. Many of the Mediterranean species will flower poorly in the shade of our woodland, while the high alpine species will suffer from too much moisture at the wrong time of year.

Nevertheless, many anemones are perfect for the woodland floor. They can be divided into two groups: those with underground rhizomes and tuberous types. The rhizomatous species tend to die back quickly after flowering. The rhizomes hate to be too wet once dormant, nor do they like to be too hot. They seem to thrive within the thick layer of mulch we apply annually, which gives them just enough moisture to retain their fleshiness, yet adequate drainage to prevent them damping off. *Anemone apennina* and *A. blanda* form small, nutlike corms just below the surface, naturalising by seed rather than below the ground.

The tuberous-rooted species have a slightly different growth cycle, being more akin to herbaceous perennials. They therefore need more moisture and light throughout the summer than the rhizomatous species, making them better suited to clearings and open areas; they will not thrive in heavy shade. Their seeds, being encased in woolly hairs, are easily distributed by the breeze—hence their name, meaning windflower. Many species are similar and may be more closely related than is currently understood.

Above: *Anemone apennina*

Right: *Anemone blanda* blue shades

Anemone apennina

Although native to southern Europe, care should be taken not to let the dormant rhizomes bake too much. Typically the delightful single spring flowers are blue. Such a pretty thing.

var. *albiflora* Beautiful white form with the palest blue back imaginable.

'**Petrovac**' Superb intense blue selection from southern Croatia.

Anemone blanda

Anemone blanda 'White Splendour'

A little more robust than *A. apennina*, this one comes from the mountains of the Balkans. It self-seeds readily, but it can be worth starting with some named clones to provide a good range of colours. Unnamed forms can be rather wishy-washy.

blue shades Generally a reliable selection of mid-blues.

'**Charmer**' Pale pink.

'**Ingramii**' The darkest form; violet-blue flower with a yellow centre. Found on Mount Parnassus, Greece.

'**Radar**' Spectacular selection whose intense magenta flowers contrast with their white centres.

'**White Splendour**' Huge white flowers can be up to 5cm across.

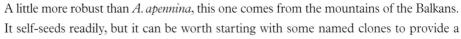

Anemone ×lipsiensis

This hybrid between *A. nemorosa* and *A. ranunculoides* is found in the wild where the parents grow together. The gorgeous plant has pale lemon-yellow flowers in early to midspring, contrasting well with rich, green, ferny foliage, touched with purple. (Previously known as both *A. ×seemannii* and *A. ×intermedia*.) Rhizomatous.

Anemone ×lipsiensis

Anemone multifida

Although tending to be short lived, this tuberous native of the Americas is easily raised from seed. Much is to be learnt about the geographical variations in this species as well as the closely allied or synonymous *A. magellanica*. The typically available form grows to 30cm tall and has up to three creamy white flowers per stalk. However, white to yellow, green, and pink forms are known in the wild.

Anemone nemorosa

This delightful Eurasian woodland plant is usually white, though even wild plants may be tinged with blue or pink, particularly on the backs of the petals. The insignificant looking twiglike rhizome starts into activity early in the winter to give flowers in mid to late spring over pretty, fernlike, deeply divided leaves. The species is perfect for naturalising over large areas, but many named forms add variety in shades of pink and blue. Extremely versatile in their use, as a carpet under an individual tree or scattered among other bulbs and similar plants, the cultivars could also be admired in a woodland rock garden. 15cm.

Left: *Anemone nemorosa*

Below: *Anemone nemorosa* 'Leeds' Variety' is more substantial in both flower and foliage than the wild *A. nemorosa*, at lower right.

> **'Allenii'** Old cultivar dating back to 1890 or earlier. Large pale blue flowers with a pinkish outside.
>
> **'Blue Bonnet'** One of the darkest blues.
>
> **'Blue Eyes'** Essentially white multi-petalled flower, developing a subtle blue eye in the centre.

'Green Fingers' An oddity; the wider than normal petals are white, but in the centre of the flower, the modified anthers and styles resemble a dense tuft of tiny frondlike leaves.

'Leeds' Variety' Larger white flowers with broader petals and less finely cut foliage.

'Robinsoniana' An old cultivar, but one of my favourites, and certainly vigorous enough to naturalise. Lilac-blue flowers over prettily purple-flushed foliage.

'Royal Blue' Large purplish blue flowers.

'Vestal' Double form with a pretty white ruff in the centre of the flower; usually one of the last to flower.

'Westwell Pink' Opens white before maturing to pink.

Above: Semi-double form of *Anemone nemorosa*

Right: *Anemone nemorosa* 'Westwell Pink'

Anemone quinquefolia

This North American native is similar to *A. nemorosa* but is considered of inferior ornamental value.

Anemone ranunculoides

Easily grown European species producing bright green feathery foliage and vivid yellow buttercup-like flowers in spring. Rhizomatous. 25cm.

'Pleniflora' Double-flowered form.

Anemone ranunculoides

subsp. *wockeana* Smaller, less vigorous form from north-central Europe, with bright yellow flowers.

Anemone rivularis

The flowers are essentially white, but the best forms have a wonderful steely blue reverse to each petal. From the Himalayas and China, it likes a damp soil, so it is best in a moist, though not too shady, area of the woodland, where other more delicate plants may struggle. It can self-seed. Tuberous. 50 cm.

Anemone sylvestris
This one definitely requires caution, with the potential to be a thug. Use it for wild areas only, because it spreads by root buds, and it needs only a very small section of root to regenerate itself. Once planted, it is very difficult to eradicate, which is a shame, because the white flowers are so delightful in early summer, and believe it or not, they look lovely in flower arrangements, with their pretty divided leaves. 30–50cm.

Anemone trifolia
Similar in principle to *A. nemorosa*, but it has heavy, non-feathery three-lobed leaves, so it proves valuable where denser groundcover is required. Rhizomatous.

Anemonella (Ranunculaceae)

As its name implies, *Anemonella* is a diminutive form of *Anemone* in all characteristics. Only one species exists in this genus.

Anemonella thalictroides
The specific name describes the foliage, implying that it resembles *Thalictrum*, with delicate fernlike leaves. Although rhizomatous like some of the anemones, *Anemonella* is slow to establish and spread; its fragile beauty can be rewarded with a special corner, where it is sheltered from harsh winds and it will not be overrun by rampaging neighbours—perhaps in the woodland rock garden. *Anemonella* resents disturbance, so if extracting outer tubers from the clump, be careful not to disturb the main mother plant. This eastern North American native produces small pinkish white flowers throughout the spring before quickly dying down.

Anemonella thalictroides

'**Alba Plena**' Double white flowers.
'**Amelia**' Clear pink single flowers.
'**Cameo**' Double pink flowers.
'**Jade Feather**' Unusual green-white flowers.
f. *rosea* 'Oscar Schoaf' Rosy pink double flowers.

Anemonopsis (Ranunculaceae)

Anemonopsis is another monotypic genus, this time heralding from Japan.

Anemonopsis macrophylla
Beautiful enough to warrant a special corner of the woodland floor, this clump-forming

herbaceous perennial has black flower stems 40–80cm tall, reaching above the fernlike foliage. The nodding flowers are quite lovely, with purplish pink petals and a distinct cup-shaped centre of white, tipped with pink.

Aquilegia (Ranunculaceae)

Although this is an extensive genus of some 70 species, few are suitable for the shady woodland. Most gardeners are familiar with the often gaudy colours of the hybrids, yet I find some of the species more appealing. It is important to choose those which live in woodland areas in the wild, as the meadow species require more sun than the woodland will allow. *Aquilegia* has several common names, columbine being widely used, but I prefer the nickname granny's bonnets, which perfectly describes the nodding flowers. These have an inner trumpet, or corolla, of petals and an outer ring which extends backward into spurs, which may be hooked or straight. Often these two sets of petals are different colours, resulting in a bicolour flower. They flower for many weeks through the summer, potentially from early summer to midautumn, and are lovely plants at an often difficult time of year for real colour in the woodland garden.

There is a fine line between a plant being invasive and merely seeding around. It usually comes down to growing conditions and how well suited they are to the plant's requirements. Those listed here are candidates for the woodland floor, but I would introduce them only into a relatively large area—although, with patience, dead flowers and therefore the seed heads can be removed to control their spread if required. If more than one species are grown together, they are likely to hybridise and will then not come true from seed.

Extremely closely related is the genus *Semiaquilegia* (literally meaning half aquilegia). A delightful species to look out for is *S. ecalcarata* from China, varying in colour

Semiaquilegia ecalcarata

from rich wine-purple to, rarely, almost white. Distinguished by its lack of spurs, it appears so dainty.

Aquilegia canadensis

This variable North American native usually has arresting flowers with a yellow corolla, red sepals, and long spurs. Expected height is 15–40cm, though it might grow taller in milder areas. Similar species are the smaller *A. elegantula* (completely red-flowered forms are known) and the taller *A. formosa*. Also closely related is *A. flavescens*, which has a pale yellow flower.

'Corbett' Uniformly yellow flowers (one wonders whether this has some *A. flavescens* in its parentage).

'Nana' Dwarf form, 15–20cm tall.

Aquilegia coerulea

The Colorado state flower has a white corolla contrasting with blue long-spurred sepals. Cultivars are scarce in Europe but plentiful in North America, though many are thought to be of hybrid origin. 20–80cm.

var. *ochroleuca* Pure white

Aquilegia viridiflora

Quite different from the preceding plants, this species from western China is at home in the woodland shade. The nodding flowers have greenish sepals with short, straight spurs and an inner corolla which varies from greenish or reddish brown to almost black. 20–50cm.

Arachniodes (Dryopteridaceae)

A member of the shield fern family, this extremely attractive, though less well-known, genus is perfect in a moisture-retentive, shady corner of the woodland floor.

Arachniodes simplicior

From Japan, the fronds can reach a height of 1.2m and are evergreen. The leaves are a rich deep green with a yellowish band along the midrib, giving the effect of subtle variegation. The rhizomes will slowly expand to form tidy clumps.

Aralia (Araliaceae)

Little is subtle about this genus, yet for the leafy verdant look through summer, you need not search further. These plants are big and bold, suitable only for large, relatively wild woodland areas. Large and leafy they may be, they are still perennials, suitable for the woodland floor; they can grow to 2m, making a major impact in the summer. Consider the scale of planting; these fellows would look silly around small and delicate trees, so ensure that enough height clearance is available to accommodate them. Bearing in mind the potentially vast surface area of the leaf, it is not surprising that a moisture-retentive soil is required; a streamside position would be ideal.

Aralia continentalis

Supposedly, this species from China and Korea is clump-forming rather than a runner, but I would still be cautious in its placing. Small white flowers in panicles adorn the 1.5–2m stems in summer, followed by black berries in autumn.

Aralia cordata

The great plant-hunter Philipp von Siebold introduced this Japanese species as long ago as the 1830s, and it is becoming increasingly popular for its architectural stature. It is rhizomatous and will spread, with a height of 1.5–2m. The greenish white flowers can last until early autumn, followed by purplish black berries.

Aralia racemosa

This North American version is also rhizomatous. In the wild, it can exceed 2m, but is often shorter in cultivation, dependent on conditions.

Arisaema (Araceae)

These are some of the strangest plants I have ever seen, yet I share my young son's interest in this genus because of its unusual character and beauty. They have no "flower" in the traditional sense. Instead, they have a spathe, which is simplest described as a tube coming out of the ground, widening to culminate in a hoodlike projection, which tends to be the most colourful part of the flower. Sometimes this hood folds down over the mouth of the tube, often ending in a spur which in some species can be long and whippy. Inside the tube is a pencil-like spadix, along which berries will form. In some species, this projects above the mouth of the tube, or it may terminate in a long spur called the spadix appendage. To children (from 8 to 80), this can look as if a little mouse is hiding in the spathe with just its tail hanging out. The whole effect is rather reminiscent of some carnivorous plants, and indeed they do attract insects—for pollination purposes rather than for breakfast.

In many species, the spathe is conspicuously vertically striped with green or deep purplish brown and white. The leaves emerge before the flowers—rarely before mid-spring, but sometimes not until early summer, June here, which is valuable because most of the classic spring woodlanders have long since finished their display by then. These can be held singly, high above the ground like a multi-lobed umbrella. They do not take up much space on the woodland floor and can easily exist among and above carpeters. The interest extends right on into the autumn, when the spathe is replaced by a spike of brightly coloured berries, resembling a primeval corncob. Naturally shade loving, they thrive among the leaf-mould of the woodland floor; indeed, the tallest plants benefit from growing among deciduous shrubs whereby their framework can support the potentially top-heavy leaves and flowers.

Sadly, not all are easy to grow. About 150 species are widely distributed across the northern hemisphere with the exception of Europe; most of the species from temperate areas are hardy, but it is probably best to start with those from North America and the Sino-Himalayan range. They dislike being too wet when dormant, so heavy soils are problematic. They need a deep root-run of friable soil which maintains moisture in summer but drains well in winter. A raised bed of adequate depth is ideal; they should be planted as much as 20cm deep. This protects the corms against extreme winter cold and slows down their emergence in spring. Many of the Japanese introductions are essentially hardy, but they become active too early, so vulnerable soft growth emerges while spring frosts are still threatening. Hardiness is such a tricky thing and gardens can have variable micro-climates, so it is often worth experimenting. However, the choicer species are best risked only if the gardener is prepared both mentally and financially for disappointment.

Those species forming good clumps can be divided in two ways: some will form tuberlets at the edge of the main tuber and others form them on the end of a stolon (an underground stem). Care needs to be taken not to damage the main tuber; if the youngsters are still attached, they are still dependent and will not survive by themselves. When mature enough to remove, the connection will be broken naturally, and these young tubers are then safe to transplant. Arisaemas will move quite happily if lifted and replanted without delay. As with so many plants with underground storage organs, they quickly dry out when lifted. This is why newly purchased plants can be so difficult to establish. Buying pot-grown plants can overcome this problem.

I have included a few of the more commonly available and amenable species. I make no apology for

Arisaema amurense

dwelling on these amazing plants in some detail. The aura of mystery surrounding their culture makes them deserving of wide appreciation, as they make such a wonderful statement of interest or even curiosity in the woodland garden. In reality, provided that they are planted in appropriate conditions, they are not as difficult to grow as their reputation might imply.

Leaf rust is a potential problem for North American enthusiasts; it occurs in the wild there, too, though it seems not to exist in Europe. Symptoms are yellowish orange spots on the underside of the leaves and spathe, causing the leaves to die back sooner than they should, thus weakening the plant. With no known cure, it is safest to burn affected plants to minimise the risk of it spreading through your collection.

Arisaema amurense

This is a rewarding species since it is undemanding in cultivation, readily forming a pleasing clump. Distributed from Siberia to China, the simple spathes are usually green with white stripes, though purple forms are known. 50cm.

Arisaema candidissimum

One of the classic and most easily grown species, this one provoked my son's interest and started our collection. Discovered originally in 1914 by the intrepid plant-hunter George Forrest, two forms exist: the original discovery was pure white, but then a rose-tinged form was found, whose beautiful pink and white–striped hood does not roll downward. Despite the order of discovery, most plants commercially available today are the pink form. The white form does not seem to have an "official" name, but when seeking it out, make sure the colour is specified. One of the smaller species, it has three lobed leaves. An unexpected bonus: its flowers are fragrant. 60cm.

Arisaema ciliatum

Another Chinese species, this one has a much taller, narrow spathe. It is variable in colour —green or purple striped with white. The leaves typically

Below: *Arisaema candidissimum*

Right: *Arisaema consanguineum*

have 12 lobes. It is unusually stoloniferous, gently spreading by underground runners, to form a goodly clump readily in favourable conditions. 90cm.

Arisaema concinnum
My first inclusion from the Sino-Himalayan zone, this is a vigorous plant with eight-lobed leaves. The generally green and white–striped spathes are relatively tall and thin, with a reasonable tail. Stoloniferous. 150cm.

Arisaema consanguineum
This is the most widespread species in Asia, and what an impressive chap it is. Each of the 13 leaf lobes terminates in a hanging thread, appearing as water running off the tips. Sometimes these statuesque leaves have a silver band along the midrib, further enhancing their beauty. At their best, arisaemas can be magnificent foliage plants. The spathes tend to have shades of both green and purple on the same flower. Its vast distribution means that it has adapted to a wide range of growing conditions. 180cm.

Arisaema elephas
This shorter grower is found from Bhutan to China. The name does not refer to the stature so much as the resemblance of the spadix appendage to an elephant's trunk. 40cm.

Arisaema fargesii
This species clumps rapidly when established. From western China, it has a broad habit; examples have been found in which the central leaflet of the trilobed leaf extends to 0.25 square metre. That is vast. They have the added attraction of turning bright yellow as they die back. The spathes are a lovely shape—an elegant, narrow tube with strongly recurved mouth margins and a deeply overhanging hood. 60cm.

Arisaema griffithii
It can be difficult to find some distinctive feature to typify the different species, because many are so similar. This Himalayan endemic is unique. Personal taste determines whether you call it spectacular or bizarre, but it will certainly be a talking point. The hood of the spathe widens dramatically above the tube, to as much as 20cm, and rolls forward to cover completely the mouth and the source of the long, winding spadix appendage. This reptilian resemblance has prompted its nickname, cobra lily. The spathe is dark purple with green stripes, and even the leaves can be dark purple as they unfurl. Just 60cm tall but 80cm wide due to the substantial leaves, each with three rounded lobes.

Arisaema jacquemontii
This lovely Himalayan species is intolerant of summer heat, so deep in the woodland is the perfect place. Of medium height, with five lobed leaves, the tall, elegant, thin green

and white spathes exhibit long tails from both spathe and the contrasting purple spadix appendage. 80cm.

Arisaema lichiangense

Although closely related to, and often growing together in the wild in Western China with *A. fargesii* and *A. candidissimum*, it has a distinctive spathe in that the hood is almost vertical, allowing full sight of both it and the gently curving spadix appendage. In colour, it shades from purple and white through to green and purple. 50cm.

Arisaema propinquum

The shorter, squatter flower tends to be held below the substantial trilobed leaves. It is widely distributed throughout the Himalayas so is tolerant of cultivation within the parameters discussed. The spathe is darker in colour than most, shading through green and dark purple, usually with little white. The hood bends over, hiding the mouth of the tube, but the long mouse-tail of the spadix appendage is clearly visible. 80cm.

Arisaema ringens

Although Japanese in origin, this species is surprisingly tolerant of colder conditions in cultivation than those it would be exposed to in the wild. A substantial plant, lacking the willowy grace of some, it will grow to 110cm by a massive 80cm due to the paired chunky, trifoliate leaves. The spathe is solid and helmet-shaped; both predominantly green and purple forms are known.

Arisaema sikokianum

Arisaema sikokianum

How frustrating that my favourite has the reputation for being short-lived. This Japanese woodlander is quite distinctive; a white clublike spadix protrudes from the pure white mouth of the tubular spathe, with an elegant green and purple hood rising behind it. Modest in stature, the leaves can be beautiful, with silver markings. 70cm.

Arisaema speciosum

Mottled markings, reminiscent of snakeskin, appear on the leaf stem of this wide-ranging Himalayan species. The leaves can be a rich purple beneath, particularly in *A. speciosum* var. *mirabile*. The spathe has a long spadix appendage. 70cm.

Arisaema tortuosum

This species is widely distributed from the Himalayas to India and China, explaining its inherent variability. This also has its disadvantages; the forms from low altitude can be markedly more tender, so it can be useful to know the provenance of the stock. If in doubt, plant it deep and hope. The leaves are quite different from the others considered here. Instead of all lobes emerging from a central point, they (usually 13) are arranged around an arc, with the lobes at the extremities being smaller; the effect is similar to a tiara. The stem and emerging leaves are beautifully marked with green and black mottling. The spathes are narrow and elegant, usually pale green and white, but with a long, often upward-tilting spadix appendage. 50cm.

Arisaema triphyllum

No collection of *Arisaema* could be complete without this North American native, known locally as Jack in the pulpit. American Indians made effective culinary use of it, earning it the nickname Indian turnip as well as diverse medicinal applications to treat rheumatism, bronchitis, and snakebite. More variability exists in this species than perhaps in any other, with all combinations of green, red, and black on both spathe and spadix; all should be happy enough in moisture-retentive shady sites, forming nice clumps due to its stoloniferous nature. 80cm.

Arisarum (Araceae)

Arisarum could be described as miniature versions of *Arisaema*, or even their European equivalent, as they come primarily from Mediterranean regions.

Arisarum proboscideum

My son was given a tiny plant years ago, and we planted it in a fairly prominent locale, where he could watch it easily. That was a mistake, since it spreads prodigiously underground. It needs to be planted where it has space to be left to its own devices. The flowers resemble those of *Arisaema*, but they are only a few centimetres long and hidden beneath the leaves. Yet they have a long brown spadix appendage which is clearly visible and looks like a mouse's tail peeking out from the foliage—hence the nickname mouse plant.

Arum (Araceae)

Widespread across Europe and North Africa, in Britain this is known affectionately as cuckoo-pint or lords and ladies. Unfortunately the brightly coloured spikes of berries (produced on a pencil-sized spike from within the inflorescence) are toxic. It is generally accepted that *Arum* does not flower well in heavy shade. Hardiness is an issue in colder climates, where prolonged periods of extreme cold or snow would spoil that lovely winter foliage, though it is incredible how it stands up again following a short period of sub-zero temperatures. The hooded flower, which resembles that of *Arisaema*, has an amazing ability to generate heat; the leaves fold around themselves to preserve warmth on a cold night and maintain their lure to pollinating insects.

Plant arums deep in the woodland for maximum shade, where you can enjoy the arrowhead-shaped leaves without worrying about the berries or snow damage. For plants so clearly comfortable in seasonally wet sites, their summer dormancy gives them great tolerance of dry shade.

Arum italicum

New research suggests that two of the subspecies are not distinct enough to warrant separation. It is proposed that *A. italicum* subsp. *italicum* should include the populations previously known as subsp. *italicum* and subsp. *neglectum*. This simplifies matters considerably.

subsp. *albispathum* Distinguished by a pure white spathe rather than the normal yellowish.

subsp. *italicum* Selections with particularly attractive leaves have been made.

subsp. *italicum* '**Chameleon**' Distinctive selection with a broad green margin surrounding a leaf centre that is largely creamy silver, heavily veined in green.

subsp. *italicum* '**Marmoratum**' (syn. 'Pictum') The most widely available form with beautiful silver marked foliage.

subsp. *italicum* '**Miss Janay Hall**' Irregular variegation is cream-coloured rather than silver.

subsp. *italicum* '**Spotted Jack**' Typical attractive silver mottling is overlaid with black spots.

Arum italicum subsp. *italicum* 'Spotted Jack'

Arum maculatum

This species generally has a plainer leaf, but more purple pigment appears through the plant, manifesting itself in maroon blotches on the spathe and sometimes the foliage.

'**Painted Lady**' Cream and pale yellow variegation.

'**Pleddel**' Notably dark maroon leaf markings.

Aruncus (Rosaceae)

Many years ago, members of this genus were nicknamed goat's beard as a reference to the shaggy white flowerheads. This genus is widespread through the shady woodlands of the northern hemisphere, all with similar characteristics though varying in size. From late spring to late summer, location determining, aruncus are magnificent in flower; what they lack in size they certainly make up for in quantity, with billowing plumes of creamy white flowers held above pretty fernlike foliage. They can be interesting alternatives to ferns, with the added benefit of spring flowers. The dead flower spikes remain long into autumn after the leaves have died down, adding welcome structure to the winter woodland. The larger-growing species combine beautifully with large-leaved hostas, providing a wonderful contrast of foliage and form as well as disguising the less interesting lower half of the aruncus. They need a moisture-retentive soil in summer to support their plentiful growth.

Aruncus is a dioecious genus, so both male and female plants are required to set seed. If a large self-seeding colony is required (potentially they will do this quite readily), both male and female plants are needed. Clonal plants will allow tighter control of the colony to be maintained. This can be several plants of a named form or a single specimen, split and replanted as it grows.

Aruncus aethusifolius
This Asiatic species makes a compact mound to 40cm in all directions. The bright yellow autumn colour is an extra bonus.
'Hillside Gem' and **'Little Gem'** Excellent but scarce selections.

Aruncus asiaticus
By contrast, expect heights approaching 1.4m for this statuesque species. The leafy stems are topped with fluffy flower spikes through summer, before developing lovely yellow autumn colour.

Aruncus dioicus
This larger-growing North American version can make nearly 2m in height. Extremely hardy, it struggles in hot, dry summers. The Native Americans derived all manner of uses from the plant, including a poultice to treat bee stings. It develops a woody rootstock at maturity, which makes propagation by division from an older plant more difficult. Male plants have creamy white flowers while those of females are nodding and a more greenish white.
'Glasnevin' Creamy white flower plumes. 1.5m.
'Kneiffii' Smaller stature and particularly fernlike foliage. 1m.
A. **'Southern White'** A hybrid between *A. aethusifolius* and *A. dioicus* with considerable tolerance of summer heat. Dense and numerous slender flower spikes.

Asarum (Aristolochiaceae)

I remember so clearly my first *Asarum*; I thought it was a cyclamen. Known colloquial-ly as wild ginger, *Asarum* is not actually related to true ginger; however, when bruised, it emits a scent reminiscent of that spicy root. Dwelling on the woodland floor, approxi-mately 100 species are found in North America and Eurasia. Their popularity has exploded almost into obsession in Japan, with vast amounts of money changing hands for the most desirable forms.

Unfortunately, hardiness is an issue. Seemingly the most beautiful forms are a little too tender to include here, but they are worthy of experimentation in a kind site. The foliage is remarkable. Most are evergreen, though top growth can be safely lost as a defence mechanism during extreme weather. The rounded to heart-shaped leaves of many are marked with exquisite patterns, which reminds me of cyclamen. They create a rich green backdrop for the delicate upright leaves of small bulbs.

Asarum species are variable, so these descriptions can only be a guide. They flower in mid to late spring, and they definitely fit into the "odd" category, being like small pitchers, often tucked away beneath the leaves. They revel in the humus-rich soil of the woodland floor, developing deep root systems which permit some tolerance of brief dry spells in summer. However, having long, stringy roots with few root hairs, they are unable to react quickly to a reduction in moisture levels, so they should not dry out. Considering the significant surface area of leaf, it becomes obvious why they need shade. Great care must be taken when transplanting *Asarum* that the exposed roots do not desiccate. For this reason they can be rather tricky to establish, but they are actually not difficult to grow if they are given the right conditions. But that could be true of any-thing and rather summarises the art of gardening.

Asarum arifolium

This species immediately seems to contradict much of what I have just explained. It comes from the southeast coast of the United States and therefore has evolved to toler-ate heat and drought. Indeed, it can rot if subjected to conditions that are overly wet. Typically the leaves are arrow-shaped with the usual profusion of colour variations. The flowers look like little brown jugs.

Asarum caudatum

Native of the western seaboard of the United States, this species needs rather more summer moisture than its cousin *A. arifolium*. The glossy, heart-shaped green leaves lack the silver markings of others, but they will be luxuriant, given plenty of moisture and shade. The relatively large flowers open in late spring to early summer and are dark purple-red with conspicuous white patches in the violet throats. Amusingly, each of their three lobes terminates in a tail, which can be as long as 5cm.

'**Album**' White flowers.

Asarum europaeum

Sadly, the generally green foliage of this species is not the most inspiring, but it is as hardy as they come, being accustomed to the winters of eastern Europe. Kidney-shaped, glossy green leaves make nice groundcover, suppressing the weeds, trapping fallen leaves, and creating a simple foil for other more colourful woodlanders.

Asarum hartwegii

I may be ambivalent about some, but I am thrilled with my developing colony of this plant. The heart-

Asarum hartwegii

shaped leaves are glossy and beautifully marked. The aromas are less like ginger and more like citrus peel. From the US West Coast, it is arguably the best of the American species, with a surprising resistance to drought.

Asarum maximum

I had intended to include only the very hardiest species, but I fell for this one at a plant sale and defy anybody to walk away from a plant in flower. The flowers are frequently described as "panda-like" (the species is from China, too), with huge violet-black blooms sporting a big white eye. Magnificent. The leaves are large and leathery and as variable as any species; some have exotic markings, others are plain. Subsequently, I realised that my expensive acquisition was a recently imported chunk of root, even more recently popped in a pot. It quickly wilted and died. However, it was so beautiful that I shall try again, though I will be more careful how I buy it and nurture it a little more carefully until it is fully re-established.

Asarum splendens

Leaves of this Chinese species resemble cyclamen, and it is arguably the easiest to grow, spreading readily to form good-sized colonies. The dark purple and white urn-shaped flowers are produced in late spring but are almost superfluous.

Asplenium (Aspleniaceae)

Found in all corners of the globe, few of these 600 species of ferns are hardy. Most are evergreen, forming tufted clumps, though some are rhizomatous and will gently spread. The frond shapes vary and in some cases are not at all fernlike. However, the hardy species will enjoy humus-rich, freely draining soil and are a valuable addition to the woodland floor, particularly for the structure and texture they bring in winter.

Asplenium ceterach

(syn. *Ceterach officinarum*) Native of much of Europe and North Africa, it is often found in dry walls and on rocks. It is perfect for crevices in the woodland rock garden, as the fronds rarely exceed 10cm wide. Sometimes called the rusty-back fern, alluding to the dense layer of rust-coloured spores on the underside of the leaf.

Asplenium ×ebenoides

This hybrid between *A. rhizophyllum* and *A. platyneuron* occurs naturally in Alabama and exhibits characteristics of both parents. The long, narrow fronds are divided in a more traditionally fernlike manner, courtesy of the *A. platyneuron* genes, but they also occasionally produce new plantlets at the end of the fronds as in *A. rhizophyllum*. Delightful at 15cm tall by 25cm wide.

Asplenium platyneuron

Variable in its habitat in eastern North America, but not difficult to grow, the sterile fronds are low, floppy, and of little consequence; but the spore-bearing, fertile fronds are impressive, rising to 50cm tall. Not of grand stature, but quite different from other smaller ferns, its unusual habit makes it a great companion plant to anything small.

Asplenium rhizophyllum

This North American fern is quite special and guaranteed to attract comment. The leaves are totally unique, being long (20cm), narrow (2cm), and arrow shaped, lying flat on the ground. It is known locally as the walking fern, since it produces a new plant at the leaf tip, where it touches the soil. It is not the easiest to grow since it enjoys constant moisture during the growing season and shelter from desiccating winds in winter. Tuck it into a moist corner of the woodland rock garden or, better still, establish it in a wild area where it can meander over rotting logs.

Asplenium scolopendrium

The archetypal species in this genus is distributed through Europe and Asia to North Africa. A bewildering array of cultivars is available; the species frequently produces bizarrely crested mutants. Commonly called the hart's tongue fern on account of its long fronds, it is tolerant of all manner of habitats and is diverse in detail.

>   **Crispum Group** Wavy fronds. Selected from this group are 'Crispum Bolton's Nobile', with large, broad fronds; 'Golden Queen', of an unusual greenish yellow colour; and 'Moly', which has distinctly ruffled edges.

>   **Cristatum Group** Crested tips.

>   **Fimbriatum Group** Heavily fringed.

>   **'Kaye's Lacerated'** Deeply but elegantly incised fronds appear shredded. They may also display crested tips.

>   **Marginatum Group** Toothed and irregular margins with ridged leaves.

'**Ramocristatum**' Fronds are branched at the tip; each branch is crested.

Ramomarginatum Group Branched fronds; each branch is toothed or irregularly margined.

'**Sagittatum**' Elongated arrowhead-shaped fronds 45cm long are created by the presence of lobes at the base. 'Sagittatocristatum' has the same frond shape, but with crested tips.

Undulatum Group More deeply undulate (wavy) fronds than the Crispum Group.

Left: *Asplenium scolopendrium* 'Moly'

Above: *Asplenium scolopendrium* Fimbriatum Group

Asplenium trichomanes

With global distribution and a hugely adaptable character, I particularly like the way this asplenium colonises shady walls. Fronds are produced in rosettes, being narrow with tiny rounded leaflets on dark, wiry stems. Not often differentiated commercially, it may be relevant to know that subsp. *quadrivalens* is usually the more robust form, preferring alkaline soil, while subsp. *trichomanes* requires acid soil. 20cm.

Cristatum Group Crested at the tips.

Incisum Group Incised leaflets.

'**Ramocristatum**' Branched leaflets with crested tips.

Astilbe (Saxifragaceae)

This gorgeous genus of truly hardy plants provides so much colour and interest in return for so little. They prefer a shady but reliably moisture-retentive area of the woodland floor; they are often grown as bog plants, perfect for areas benefiting from seepage from natural springs. They are considered to be deer-resistant.

Native to North America, but mainly found in southeast Asia, their wonderful ferny foliage gives superb contrast with bolder leaved plants such as hostas, while their upright spikes of fluffy flowers dazzle through the heady days of midsummer, with a variety of colours, from glistening whites through soft creams and delicate pinks to electrifying reds and robust purples. With differences in heights and vigours, there is an *Astilbe* to suit every colour scheme and taste.

They form rhizomatous clumps which slowly spread, so it is important to choose the appropriate sized plant for the site. Conveniently, even the tallest flower spikes stand up tidily by themselves with no need of support. (To my mind, supporting herbaceous plants in the woodland is not an option; they must fend for themselves as nature intended.) Accordingly, they can be left to overwinter, or in a more visual area, the tops can be tidied once they have died down. In a large area, massed planting of just one cultivar looks spectacular; alternatively, smaller clumps punctuating the verdant calm can be dramatic. With so many named cultivars (more than 200), I can only skim the surface here and have chosen a few of my favourites.

Astilbe ×arendsii

A superb group of hybrids between *A. chinensis*, *A. astilboides*, *A. japonica*, and *A. thunbergii* were raised initially in Germany between 1909 and 1955 by Georg Arends. They have certainly stood the test of time, though naming confusion due to translations of original German names is an issue. Technically, anglicised translations are not valid names. Other problems occur because of the involvement of four species. Current nomenclature transfers some hybrids out of this group to be assigned to the species with perhaps the most claim to parenthood, so I have tried to follow that here. These hybrids are recognised as members of the ×*arendsii* group.

Opposite: *Astilbe* 'Spinell' contrasts with a bold variegated hosta in the background.

A. 'Cattleya' Delightful lilac-pink cultivar from 1955. 90cm.

A. 'Fanal' Classic from 1933 with vivid red flowers, slightly early in the season. 60cm.

A. 'Irrlicht' Dense white panicles. 45cm.

A. 'Rosa Perle' Rose-pink flowers. 70cm.

A. 'Spinell' One of the tallest red-flowered selections with fine, narrow plumes contrasting handsomely with rich, deep red young foliage. 90cm.

Astilbe chinensis

A Chinese species with a number of subspecies showing natural variation in flower colour, size, and sun/drought tolerance. Many named cultivars have been selected for these different parameters.

var. *taquetii* 'Purpurlanze' The flower spikes are tall and thin and of a wonderful shade of pinky purple, almost magenta. The name translates as purple lance, which puts it rather well. More drought tolerant than others. 120cm.

'Visions' Dwarf selection from *A. chinensis* var. *pumila*, with lovely, dense flower spikes of a delicious raspberry-pink. Also more drought tolerant. 35cm.

Astilbe japonica

This Japanese species definitely enjoys moisture. These hybrids are derived from *A. japonica*.

- *A.* **'Bonn'** Rich, dark pink flowers are produced slightly earlier in the season than others. 45cm.
- *A.* **'Deutschland'** Another older but still worthwhile cultivar from Arends, having substantial white panicles. 50cm.
- *A.* **'Montgomery'** An exquisite selection in which deep red flowers contrast magnificently with dark red-bronze young foliage. 50cm.

Astilbe rivularis

This Himalayan species has unusual shaped foliage. The leaves are more solid and much less fernlike than others, and the plant tends to be taller, making a handsome backdrop with creamy white flowers from midsummer to early autumn. It is perhaps a better plant for the more natural woodland than cultivars and hybrids, which are almost too ornamental.

var. *myriantha* From southwest China, with more drooping white panicles.

Astilbe simplicifolia

Scarce in the wild and in cultivation, *A. simplicifolia* produces informal, shaggy white flower spikes. These selections have inherited the smaller stature of this Japanese species.

- *A.* **'Bronce Elegans'** Lovely coral-pink tones with bronze-flushed foliage. 30–45cm.
- *A.* **'Sprite'** Short dense heads of shell-pink flowers hover above finely cut, deep purple-brown foliage. 30cm.

A. 'Willie Buchanan' Late season, creamy white flowers are flushed with light pink above dense mounds of bronze foliage. 20–25cm.

Athyrium (Woodsiaceae)

As with most ferns, many of the 180 species of *Athyrium* are tropical. However, this genus includes some ethereal greys and silvers flushed with red. They require humus-rich soil which retains moisture through the summer. Most are deciduous. In cultivation, *Athyrium* is represented by few species, but many cultivars and hybrids are available.

Athyrium filix-femina

Widespread throughout the northern temperate zone and down into South America, this elegant fern known as lady fern came to the fore in Victorian times, when ferneries became a popular status symbol. With a justifiable reputation for adaptability and ease of growth, its popularity continues today. The basic species forms upright leafy clumps to nearly 1m tall with individual leaves 20cm across when thriving. The heavily crested types are less weather resistant due to their weight; however, new fronds are continuously produced throughout the growing season, so any wind damage can be removed if necessary without leaving an unsightly gap for long.

var. *angustum* 'Lady in Red' This recent introduction was selected in New England. Amazing dark red-violet stipes (stems) support light green lacy foliage.

Cristatum Group Traditional English selection with finely cut and heavily crested fronds.

'Frizelliae' Discovered in Ireland in 1857, the tatting fern is still unique. The narrow fronds are only 2cm wide and clothed on both sides by green lobes. They were thought to resemble a piece of sewing fashionable at the time.

'Minutissimum' Delightful dwarf selection. 15cm.

'Plumosum Axminster' The golden colour of the young growth makes this one distinctive. Combine with chartreuse hostas and *Euphorbia* for subtlety or dark colours for impact.

'Vernoniae' First introduced to England in 1873, it grows to 60 cm in all directions and forms a substantial yet graceful clump of deeply cut and slightly crested, feathery fronds.

'Vernoniae Cristatum' More heavily crested.

'Victoriae' Considered the ultimate fern in Victorian times with its cruciate (crossed-over) fronds. Derivatives propagated by spores exhibit this frond shape, but 'Lady Victoria' has recently been singled out as worthy of propagation by tissue culture.

Athyrium niponicum

Two colour forms of this gently creeping rhizomatous species occur in its native north-east Asia. The standard wild type is green.

> **var.** *pictum* This decorative, widely cultivated variety with shorter fronds and reddish midribs has acquired the common name Japanese painted fern. Several colourful cultivars have been selected for commercial propagation, making a subtle statement in the woodland garden. 30cm.

> **var.** *pictum* '**Burgundy Lace**' New fronds unfurl rich purple, highlighted with silver stripes along the veins and at the tips, maturing to silver-green with contrasting purple midribs. Similarly, look out for 'Pewter Lace' and 'Ursula's Red'.

> **var.** *pictum* '**Silver Falls**' The most silvery selection to date, with elegant long-arching fronds with glamorous contrasting red-purple veining.

> **var.** *pictum* '**Wildwood Twist**' A recent hybrid of *A. niponicum* × *A. otophorum*, creating a magical silvery apparition of smoky grey and green slightly twisted fronds, with the subtlest hints of gold.

Above: *Athyrium niponicum* var. *pictum*

Right: *Athyrium* 'Ghost'

Athyrium otophorum

A more statuesque Oriental species that displays an irresistible combination of pewter-coloured fronds which unfurl the same reddish purple as the midribs remain. 80cm.

> **var. okanum** A yellow-green base colour to the fronds, with red-stained veins, for a completely unique ambience.

Athyrium thelypteroides

(syn. *Deparia acrostichoides*) For a more natural effect, this eastern North American native makes an impressive clump. In optimum conditions, the wavy fronds can reach 1m in length, gracefully swaying in the breeze to reveal the silvery spore cases on their underside, which coupled with fine yellow hairs make the plant positively shimmer.

Athyrium cultivars

When grown from spores (the fern equivalent of seed), certain parental characteristics are retained by the offspring. However, to replicate the beautiful cultivars and modern hybrids exactly, vegetative reproduction is necessary. Technical advances have made commercial propagation by tissue culture viable and encouraged breeders to experiment. These hybrids between *A. niponicum* var. *pictum* and *A. filix-femina* are superb.

    A. **'Branford Beauty'** Steely grey fronds. Grows vigorously to 45cm.

    A. **'Branford Rambler'** Light green feathery fronds. Gently spreading.

    A. **'Ghost'** Combines the silvery foliage of its Asian parent with the habit of the lady fern for a ghostlike effect.

Beesia (Ranunculaceae)

Closely related to *Actaea* (but more visually akin to *Asarum*), this evergreen carpeter from the mountainous forests of China is rare but eminently growable in woodland floor conditions. It is normally represented in cultivation by the species *B. calthifolia*.

Beesia calthifolia

Apparently embossed veining enhances the glossy, leathery, heart-shaped leaves. Upright spikes of starry white flowers are produced from midspring into summer. *Beesia deltophylla* is similar.

Beesia calthifolia

Bergenia (Saxifragaceae)

Although only six species of *Bergenia* are found in eastern Asia, many more hybrids and cultivars have been derived from these, most of which have been raised in cultivation in Europe. All are evergreen and closely related to *Saxifraga*, which I find surprising when mentally comparing the tiny rosettes on my scree bed to the massive elephant ears of these leaves. Bergenias are extremely handsome; their lustrous foliage is the richest glossy green and often warmly flushed with red in winter, when they clothe many a bare patch. The spring flowers are extremely impressive, ranging in colour from white through baby pinks, to vivid magenta and bright red. Inevitably in view of the size of the leaf, they need a moisture-retentive site on the woodland floor.

Purple late-winter foliage of *Bergenia* 'Ballawley' creates a wonderful textural contrast to the spiky bluebell foliage.

Bergenia cultivars

Aesthetically, I would be reluctant to plant a species in this case, since the cultivars have been selected for colour and for quality of bloom, generally flowering more freely than the species.

'Abendglut' I rarely enthuse about double-flowered forms, but this one is spectacular, even in a none-too-subtle shade of magenta, from midspring to early summer.

'Ballawley' (syn. 'Delbees') The glossy green, crinkly edged leaves take on rich purple tones through winter. Vivid magenta flowers are produced on red stalks. Many hybrids are derived from this selection.

'Beethoven' What a fantastic contrast between the pure white flowers with dark centres and the gleaming, deep green foliage.

'Britten' This one is more to my taste—a delicate pale pink with a darker eye.

'Overture' The taller, glowing magenta flowerheads are held above the foliage, which is distinctly red in winter. The particular advantage of this cultivar is its

Bergenia 'Rosi Klose'

greater tolerance of dry shade such as we find closer to the base of trees. Imagine this one around a silver birch; that would be quite some contrast.

'Pink Dragonfly' This one is not so bulky, with narrower leaves and a more graceful appearance, turning plum-red in winter. Exquisite coral-pink flowers.

'Rosi Klose' Gorgeous apricot-pink flowers. 30cm.

Betula (Betulaceae)

I have become completely smitten by this genus, by their gorgeous winter silhouette when the differing bark colours paint a spectacular picture. There is so much more to *Betula* than the archetypal silver birch, beautiful as those glistening white stems undoubtedly are. No tree could be easier to grow, even on our heavy clay soil; their only disadvantage is their shallow root system, which by maturity can make it difficult to establish woodland carpeters at their base.

Approximately 60 species are distributed through the northern temperate regions and although all are theoretically suitable, several are particularly outstanding. Worthy of introduction into mature woodland, where their bark can be enjoyed, they are also superb to plant as a group to create an almost instant woodland to whatever scale is required. A single tree or a group of three can planted as close as possible to appear as a multi-stemmed whole. If space permits, a larger bed can be an indulgence, where the differing colours and textures of bark can contrast with one another.

Each tree bears both male and female catkins, the males longer and more showy, while the smaller females stand erect. Most forms greet the winter with a flourish of butter-yellow foliage in autumn. Juvenile bark does not peel, so the true bark colour is rarely evident on very young trees. New planting will require patience until such time as the contrast of the older peeling bark with the darker young stems can be fully appreciated.

Considering that 334 species of invertebrates feed on the birch of Scotland, we should be thankful that the majority cause no aesthetic damage. In North America, the most serious pest is the bronze birch borer, *Agrilus anxius*, prompting breeding programs to produce resistant trees. The beetle is small and slender, but the larva is devastating, feeding just under the bark. When this ring-barks a branch, the resultant loss of sap flow causes sudden wilting and potential death. Fortunately, birches are less prone to attack in shady, cool, and moist wooded areas. Caterpillars and saw-fly larvae can be a nuisance, too, sometimes feeding on the leaves until just their skeletons remain.

Betula albosinensis

This Ernest Wilson discovery (China, 1901) is my favourite species. The rich, often orange-red or pink bark peels off in scrolls to reveal a more subtly coloured layer beneath, covered in a white bloom.

'China Ruby' This lovely form was selected at Stone Lane Gardens in Devon from seed collected by the Chinese Forestry Service in Gansu, China, with opulent reddish brown outer bark which can appear almost scarlet when wet.

'**Kenneth Ashburner**' Cinnamon-coloured bark peels to reveal a pinky red underlayer which is initially covered in a white bloom, giving a silvery pink effect. Wonderful, tidy, symmetrically upright habit.

'**Ness**' Initially shorter and bushier by comparison, but the pink-flushed bark colours are exquisite.

var. *septentrionalis* '**Purdom**' Arguably the best selection of this subspecies with grey-pink bark, first collected by the redoubtable Wilson in 1908.

Betula dahurica

The dark bark of this Oriental species does not peel, so much as erupt from the trunk.

'**Stone Farm**' This selection epitomises the craggy nature of this species; almost like a giant bonsai, it gives the air of living a hard life, even when it is thriving. Full of character and an inspired contrast with the usual graceful fountains. A full two weeks earlier into leaf than the other species, this one gets spring off to a head start.

Betula ermanii

This graceful Asian species freely branches to provide a bushy effect, encouraging full appreciation of the delightful bark.

'**Grayswood Hill**' The definitive selection of this gorgeous species. Soft orange-brown bark peels to reveal a straw-coloured underlayer. I love the shaggy effect, which somehow seems more natural than the glossy perfection of the *B. utilis* selections.

Betula nigra

The river birch is particularly suited to damp ground, where it will develop shaggy, pinkish orange bark that becomes furrowed and ridged with age. Beneficial in areas to be underplanted, it develops fewer surface roots.

'**Heritage**' Superlative American selection which has become the standard for the species.

Betula pendula

The silver birch is common throughought the woods of Europe and also found in North America where it is known as the European white birch. Its tiny leaves and drooping branches bring elegance to the natural canopy, but the bark lacks the excitement of the others listed here.

'**Bungor**' Attractively divided, small, fernlike leaves, but a vigorous tree.

Betula szechuanica

A handsome Chinese species to rival *B. utilis* for bark effect.

'**Liuba White**' Selected from a Roy Lancaster collection, this vigorous form has

Betula albosinensis 'Ness'   *Betula dahurica* 'Stone Farm'

Betula utilis 'Fascination'   *Betula utilis* var. *jacquemontii* 'Doorenbos'

almost blue-green leaves and brilliant white mature bark, contrasting magnificently with rich chestnut-coloured younger stems.

Betula utilis

Although the archetypal silver birch has white stems, this extensive Himalayan species also includes forms with orange or coppery brown bark, particularly in the eastern areas of its distribution. With so many cultivars from which to choose, there is one to suit every mood.

'**Fascination**' Deep orange to mahogany bark peels to reveal an almost polished layer beneath.

var. *jacquemontii* Heralding from the western extent of the species' range, this variety has whiter bark than the variable species.

var. *jacquemontii* '**Doorenbos**' An early Dutch selection, with spectacular white bark which is is almost orange when freshly exposed.

var. *jacquemontii* '**Grayswood Ghost**' Fast becoming a classic, even in this exalted company. Glistening white, softened by a flush of cream.

var. *jacquemontii* '**Jermyns**' Vigorous, upright English selection. Long, showy catkins are a bonus.

var. *jacquemontii* '**Silver Shadow**' A classic selection with ice-white bark and deceptively large leaves.

'**Wakehurst Place Chocolate**' What a contrast this is with dark brown, almost black, bark.

Betula cultivar

'**Royal Frost**' This fabulous American hybrid (*B. populifolia* 'Whitespire' × *B.* 'Crimson Frost') brings contrast to the *Betula* glade, boasting rich purple leaves through summer. With white lenticels punctuating the very dark young bark and exceptionally fine orange-red autumn colour, there is no limit to its attractions.

Blechnum (Blechnaceae)

Most of the 200 species of *Blechnum* come from the southern hemisphere and are not hardy. They have simple fronds; wide and closely-spaced pinnae (lobes) make them appear more solid and coarse. These are not graceful, airy creatures; some can make great primeval clumps, primitive in their simplicity, while others are tiny carpeters. Fascinating diversity.

Blechnum chilense

From South America, this species will reward with the stature of a tree fern when happy, though it does not develop a trunk. Spreading by underground rhizomes, with time a large area can be colonised.

Blechnum penna-marina

This adorable little evergreen fern creeps gently, covering the ground with simple yet richly coloured young fronds. It comes in two flavours, though the subspecies distinction is not always made in commerce.

subsp. *alpinum* The smaller form from New Zealand.

'**Cristatum**' Crested fronds.

subsp. *penna-marina* From South America, this is the preferred subspecies, a little more substantial than subsp. *alpinum*. The new growth has a more orange-red colour which matures to a fresh green. With the increase in plant-hunters collecting in South America, it is likely that selections will be made for particularly good colour with different size options. 10–20cm.

'**Shishi**' A crested Japanese selection.

Blechnum spicant

Native of Europe, including Britain, the deer fern prefers moist acid soil, particularly in association with conifers. The sterile fronds look like little ladders and can be up to 50cm long, lying flat in a basal rosette, from which rise erect fertile fronds, potentially to 75cm high. Very architectural.

'**Cristatum**' 25cm long fronds terminate in a crest.

'**Rickard's Serrate**' Serrated pinnae may overlap.

Blechnum spicant

Boykinia (Saxifragaceae)

This is a small genus of eight species, whose relationship with *Saxifraga* is clearly visible in the clump-forming habit, the appearance of the basal leaves, and the way the flowers are held in clusters in summer. They enjoy shade, preferring a humus-rich, moisture-retentive area of the woodland floor. Mainly originating in North America they have representation in eastern Asia. See also *Peltoboykinia*.

Boykinia aconitifolia

Pretty white flowers adorn 60cm stems for several weeks, above kidney-shaped evergreen leaves which form a dense carpet. *Boykinia major* is similar.

Boykinia jamesii

(syn. *B. heucheriformis*) The resemblance with *Heuchera* is apparent. Five to twenty-five dusky pink, almost bell-shaped flowers are held in single-sided clusters on 20cm stems. Typical basal foliage.

Boykinia occidentalis

Previously known as *B. elata*, this species from the US Pacific Northwest differs from others in its more open, airy panicles of smaller flowers.

Boykinia rotundifolia

More rounded leaves distinguish this California native. White flower clusters.

Brunnera (Boraginaceae)

This genus has grown on me and is now an indispensable part of my woodland garden. I rarely choose to incorporate variegated plants, but I am prepared to make an exception for some of these. They are absolutely fantastic for brightening up a dark corner of the woodland floor or as accent plants to punctuate the surrounding green. I love their blue flowers, like old-fashioned forget-me-nots, held above the leaves to a height of 50cm. They have large leaves through the summer, so it is important that they do not dry out. They are wonderful in association with *Bergenia*; their pretty leaves will take over as the flowers of the *Bergenia* fade, and the glossy green of the latter make a superb foil for the variegation here. I am careful not to overdo it though; a little bit of variegation goes a long way in an otherwise natural woodland. But that is a matter of personal taste.

Brunnera macrophylla

Not quite the only species, but certainly the main player. From Siberia, its hardiness is not a concern.

Brunnera macrophylla
'Jack Frost'

'**Betty Bowring**' A more conservative selection, with discreet green leaves but pretty heads of pure white flowers in midspring to early summer.

'**Dawson's White**' White-edged leaves are pretty against the pale blue flowers produced from late winter to early summer, but it will scorch in sun or if it dries out.

'**Hadspen Cream**' Different variegation, being cream-edged. Still the same clouds of pretty blue flowers in midspring to early summer.

'**Jack Frost**' This one is predominantly silver-leaved with a green edge and prominent green veining. The sprays of blue flowers from late winter to early summer and beyond have the slightest touch of lilac.

'**Looking Glass**' Lacking the green veins of 'Jack Frost', this one is silver all over. So pretty with its blue flowers.

Buxus (Buxaceae)

Though not necessarily the first plant to spring to mind for the woodland, as it has such a strong association with parterres and formal gardens, *Buxus* is a perfect choice. Its only drawback as far as I am concerned is that it is so slow. I was amazed to discover that 30 species exist, ranging from western Europe across the Mediterranean area to Asia, Central America, and even the West Indies. They are tremendously shade tolerant, but they do not like to sit in stagnant water over winter, so their site needs to be adequately free-draining.

Buxus are easy to grow. A fungal disease, *Cylindrocladium buxicola*, was first identified in Europe and New Zealand in 1994. It starts as black spots on the leaves, and severe defoliation can follow. It is best to destroy infected plants. However, it would be a shame if this discouraged the planting of these simple, useful and architectural plants.

Buxus sempervirens

These can be incorporated into the woodland garden as nice, dense, bushy plants to provide structure in winter and protection for precious winter bulbs. Almost any of the variegated cultivars (for example, 'Elegantissima') can be used in exactly the same way if desired. If left to grow naturally rather than being clipped, they can become gnarled and leggy. If, perhaps, an unloved older plant has been kept in a pot, tucked around the corner, "out of sight and out of mind", it may have started out as a neatly clipped sphere or other shape, but inattention has rendered it a shaggy mess. These are perfect to thin out and plant as a "tree", which can then be underplanted with all manner of carpeters to enhance the architectural structure. The smallest cultivars, such as 'Myrtifolia', can even be used in a woodland rock garden to provide structure, as a change from dwarf conifers.

Cardamine (Brassicaceae)

Lady's smock, as we used to call it, *Cardamine pratensis* was one of my favourite mead-ow flowers as a child. Sadly much rarer now, it is satisfying to be able to grow some of its relations on the woodland floor, in light shade where adequate moisture is retained even through summer. There the creeping underground rhizomes will gently spread out to form a tidy little colony. Of the 130 species from the temperate zones around the world, not all are suitable for the shade of our woodland. This is a captivating genus of real treasures, a relationship to be built with time and familiarity, because these plants are not meant to be garish and vulgar—their simplicity is part of the attraction of the natural woodland garden. Plants included here flower in mid to late spring unless other-wise stated.

Cardamine bulbifera
This one is a novelty. Though a member of the cabbage family, it produces bulbils in the leaf axils up the stem, just as some lilies do. (Think brussels sprouts.) The stems grow to a heady 70cm, topped with a cluster of pretty pink flowers in midspring to early summer. Native of damp oak and beech woods from Britain east to Iran.

Cardamine concatenata
(syn. *C. laciniata*) Distinctive dark green, deeply divided foliage lasts well into summer, spreading readily to form a handsome colony. From eastern North America, the vari-able flowers may be pale purple to white. 20–30cm.

Cardamine diphylla
This white-flowered species to 35cm has leaves which are altogether heavier, with three broad lobes.

Cardamine enneaphylla
The individual white or pale yellow flowers are like bells, hanging in clusters on shorter stems, to 30cm or less. The young growth as it emerges is a rich purplish colour, green-ing with maturity. From central Europe.

Cardamine heptaphylla
Taller, western European species to 30cm or more, with larger pinnate leaves, forming clumps or small colonies from thick rhizomes. Variable in colour, it can be pink to rose-purple but is usually white.

Cardamine kitaibelii
From central to southeastern Europe, this is chunkier, with less loosely held flower heads of white to pale yellow. 20–30cm.

Cardamine macrophylla

Large leaved, as the name suggests, it has proportion-ally larger pink flowers on upright stems to 70cm.

Cardamine quinquefolia

A delightful little chap, not making much more than 20cm in height but gently creeping to form a pretty colony topped with pink flowers in spring. Allow it space to spread. By the end of January in my garden, it is already coming into growth—a real harbinger of spring.

Cardamine quinquefolia

Cardamine trifolia

Usually white, though pink is known, this is another central European endemic.

Cardamine waldsteinii

Pleasingly large flowers are white with attractive violet anthers. 30cm or more.

Cardiandra (Hydrangeaceae)

An unexpected member of the hydrangea family, this genus is herbaceous, so it is a candidate for the woodland floor, which should be moist and ideally acidic.

Cardiandra alternifolia

First documented in 1830, it remained almost unknown (it is scarce, even now) until the modern-day American plant-hunter Dan Hinkley rediscovered it in the early 1980s. In midsummer to early autumn, when fresh colour is most welcome on the woodland floor, the white or pale pink flower heads are the familiar hydrangea-like mix of sterile bracts around the centrally held fertile florets, at the top of a 70cm tall stem.

Cardiocrinum (Liliaceae)

This small genus of bulbs has a limited distribution from the Himalayas to China and Japan. In Nepal, the hollow stems are used as pipes to make music, but it is summed up best in Chinese, where *lily* means forever in love.

The flowers are similar to those of giant lilies, but the leaves are distinctively heart-shaped. They are remarkable plants, erupting out of the ground in spring to produce flowering stems as tall as 4m by midsummer. The new leaves are often richly flushed with purplish bronze. With such a prodigious growth rate, they need a rich, moisture-retentive soil to reach their potential, although they hate to be too wet when dormant over the winter. The shade of the woodland floor replicates their natural habitat, also sheltering them from the wind.

The awe-inspiring flowers are great white trumpets, reaching out from their lofty stems to as much as 35cm, having beautiful maroon markings within. Each individual flower may not last long, but their succession will give colour and fragrance for several weeks. Their life-cycle is notable. Taking up to seven years to flower from seed, the bulbs then die. Fortunately, however, they will have produced new bulbous offsets which will perpetuate the plant, themselves producing flowers after another four-year wait. This is not a plant for the instant gardener. It is usually best, where feasible, to dig up the bulbs after flowering and replant the new offsets.

Cardiocrinum cordatum

This modest Japanese species, to just 120cm, is considered more adaptable to warmer climates than its Himalayan counterpart and is unique in its ability to send up a second flower shoot in early autumn when conditions permit.

> **var.** *glehnii* Where the species has 4 to 10 flowers per stem, this variety can have up to 20. The flowers are greenish cream as opposed to white.

Cardiocrinum giganteum

The archetypal Himalayan lily was discovered in 1821 by Nathaniel Wallich, a Danish born surgeon who was instrumental in its introduction to Europe in 1852.

> **var.** *yunnanense* The Chinese equivalent is a little different in flower. Instead of the petals being effectively fused together to form a trumpet, they are more individually held, giving the flower a ragged look. It also exposes the maroon markings on the inside, making it appear darker.

Cardiocrinum giganteum

Carex (Cyperaceae)

In general, grasses need more light than is available on the woodland floor, yet certain sedges are quite tolerant of the shade, adding a vertical accent with their distinctive straplike foliage and long-lasting flower stalks. I have tried other grasses and was not satisfied with the results; too many are prone to rust, while I have had problems with the deciduous species rotting off in winter. Clearly they need to be drier in dormancy than our soil allows.

Carex oshimensis 'Evergold'
Part of my justification for including this one is that it is evergreen, or as the name reminds me, evergold, since the leaves are conspicuously striped with golden yellow. A perfect contrast with large-leaved plants at any time of year.

Caulophyllum (Berberidaceae)

Berberidaceae is a revelation, an extraordinary family with such diversity, including a surprising number of fabulous herbaceous woodland genera. Perfectly adapted to life on the woodland floor, *Caulophyllum* are tolerant even of the dense and often dry shade cast by deciduous trees. They spread very slowly by underground runners.

Caulophyllum thalictroides
Native of North America, but not a widely known plant, the young growth is richly tinged with purple as it unfurls. The entire plant is often prettily covered with a white dusting in early spring. With typical resourcefulness, the Native Americans discovered all manner of medicinal uses for the rhizomes, although it should be noted that the lustrous blue, marble-sized berries—which are perhaps their greatest asset, adding an unusual contribution to the autumn display—are poisonous. The flowers in mid to late spring are more interesting than showy, being small and starlike though held in clusters of greenish brown above the leaves, which comprise several leaflets.

   subsp. *robustum* The similar Asiatic equivalent has yellowish green flowers.

Chamaelirium (Melanthiaceae)

This family has been subdivided from Liliaceae, which tends to imply a completely false impression of the characteristics of this unusual North American wildflower. It is close to unknown in Europe, which is a shame because it is rather sweet and totally hardy, though with a preference for moisture-retentive acid soils. Choose therefore a humus-rich area of your woodland floor into which a little light will penetrate before lunch.

They will not provide bold drifts of colour, since these are little treasures to be tucked away in corners, perfect for the woodland rock garden. Used extensively for medicinal purposes by Native Americans, it is still utilised today in gynaecology.

Chamaelirium luteum
Plants will be either male or female, and the male has by far the showier flower spike, springing from a little cluster of ordinary leaves at ground level. The individual tiny flowers open white and as they mature to greenish yellow; the entire spike bends over.

Chelonopsis (Lamiaceae)

One thing I was particularly keen to achieve with our woodland areas was to extend the interest for as much of the year as I could. I adore the exuberance of spring as everything bursts into life, and I love the simplicity of summer when so many shades of green dominate the garden, but it is fun to find the odd flower at an unexpected time of year. Hence my enthusiasm for this one. Since it is active in the summer and flowers in late summer to early autumn, it inevitably needs a slightly more open but moisture-retentive position on the woodland floor.

Chelonopsis moschata
From Japan, the slender stems grow to as much as 1m tall from a woody rootstock, with leaves in pairs along its length. The flowers develop in the leaf axils near the top; it will grow well enough in heavier shade, but the flowers will be sparser and the plant leggier as it looks for the light. The tubular flowers can be 4cm or more in length and are a pretty pink, stained darker in the throat.

Chionodoxa (Hyacinthaceae)

This is a delightful genus of dwarf, purple-blue flowers from the eastern Mediterranean, where they inhabit high mountain habitats, flowering as the snow melts; hence their moniker, glory of the snow. They can tolerate woodland floor conditions under deciduous canopy solely because of this early flowering. They spring forth, dazzle us with their beauty, and disappear again before the trees develop enough leaf to shade them. However, they do need good drainage, so they are ideal planted at the base of large trees, whose water usage will keep the bulbs dry while they are dormant. In heavy or evergreen shade, the flowers will be disappointing and the foliage straggly. Take advantage of their early growth cycle and scatter them around hostas (provided the soil surface is not too wet), giving colour while the big guys continue to sleep. Confusion surrounds their nomenclature; all eight species are similar but the waters are muddied by the ease with which they hybridise.

Chionodoxa luciliae

(previously *C. gigantea*) Recognisable by the largest, upward facing flowers, though paler lavender in colour. Definitely quality over quantity.

'**Alba**' Pure white flowers. Delightful.

Chionodoxa sardensis

Smaller growing with four to twelve flowers per stem. These are deep blue with no white shading on the petals, though the white cone of stamens can appear as a white eye.

Chionodoxa siehei

The most commonly cultivated species, and rightly so, in view of its ability to seed about freely to create large colonies. The violet-blue flowers have conspicuous white centres.

Chionodoxa siehei

Chionodoxa cultivar

C. '**Pink Giant**' Uniformly pink flowers are not as large as the name implies.

Claytonia (Portulacaceae)

Mainly North American, the genus name honours John Clayton (1693–1779), an eminent early Virginia botanist. *Claytonia* enjoys moisture-retentive, humus-rich soil, where it will spread gently by small, dark cormous tubers; "fairy spuds" with their chestnut-like flavour were a favoured food among Native Americans. The flowers and leaves are also edible, being compared to lettuce or spinach; apparently they are high in vitamins A and C.

Claytonia sibirica

Claytonia sibirica

(syn. *Montia sibirica*) Distributed up the West Coast of North America into Alaska as well as Siberia, this species is extremely hardy. Its attraction is in its longer flowering time—potentially from midspring to early autumn—with equally persistent foliage. The delightful light pink flowers with deep magenta veining have five notched petals. Sometimes short-lived, so allow it to seed around.

Claytonia virginica

These delightful flowers are the epitome of spring. As the increasing sunlight warms the woodland floor through the bare twigs of the deciduous canopy, life starts to stir once again and fleshy leaves appear through the leaf litter, to be followed by misty carpets of these lovely flowers that are similar to anemones. They may be ephemeral, but therein lies the character and beauty of the spring woodland. No wonder they are referred to as spring beauty. Loose racemes of tiny, pale pink flowers, often with darker veining, are held on 30cm stems. The similar *C. caroliniana* has broader leaves. Allow for its exuberant, lax habit when positioning, perhaps around late emergers such as ferns and hostas.

Clematis (Ranunculaceae)

Clematis like to have their heads in the sun while their roots are cool and shaded. Training climbers up into the trees is a great way to make the most of every bit of woodland space. It is important to match their proportions, since too vigorous a scrambler could topple a young sapling. Pruning tends to be the first thought when considering clematis. In nature, no pruning is done, and in a woodland setting I would leave them to grow naturally.

Clematis is a vast genus of more than 200 species (though not all are climbers) not to mention the numerous named cultivars. As a result, the genus is divided into groups of closely related species to which the hybrids are assigned according to their breeding. By understanding the characteristics of the group, the requirements and qualities of any given hybrid can be ascertained. Most members of these groups should be happy in our woodland conditions, so select your individuals according to preference and availability.

Armandii Group

Evergreen, so not the hardiest species, *C. armandii* forms the backbone of this group, producing exquisite scented flowers in early spring. First introduced by E. H. Wilson from China in 1900, it was named after another renowned plant collector, French missionary Père Armand David.

C. 'Apple Blossom' Pinker in bud opening to white.

C. armandii 'Snowdrift' Pure white.

Atragene Group

These small-flowered clematis have experienced a dramatic increase in popularity. Originally introduced from China in 1910, *C. macropetala* is perhaps the major influence. Incredibly hardy and robust, though slender stemmed and delicate in structure, it will not overwhelm a smaller tree. Indeed I would consider this group to be the most suited to our woodland requirements. The bell-shaped flowers appear almost double thanks to modified stamens and are freely produced in late spring to early summer. Sporadic blooming for the rest of the summer is a desirable feature. Other related species contributing to this gene pool include *C. alpina*, *C. chiisanensis*, and *C. koreana*.

C. 'Columella' Bred by Swede Magnus Johnson, who is responsible for many of the new initiatives in breeding within this group. Four simple, rich deep pink petals are softly outlined with palest pink.

C. '**Georg**' Soft purple flowers are produced right through until early autumn.

C. '**Jan Lindmark**' Rich violet-purple.

C. '**Rosy O'Grady**' Elegant pale pink petals are veined and flushed with deep magenta-pink.

C. '**White Swan**' Graceful, pure white flowers.

Cirrhosa Group

Hardier than literature often implies, *C. cirrhosa* will be clothed with primrose-yellow bells, often stippled with purple inside, in winter. Native of scrubby woodlands of southern Europe and Asia Minor, the silky seed heads extend their attraction.

C. cirrhosa var. *purpurascens* '**Freckles**' Strongly freckled with purple.

C. cirrhosa '**Wisley Cream**' Less spotted cream-coloured flowers.

Montana Group

Introduced from the Himalayas by Lady Amherst (of pheasant fame) in 1831, initial plants of *C. montana* displayed white flowers which resembled anemones. Much excitement greeted the subsequent arrival of a pink form from China, *C. montana* var. *rubens*, which also has attractive bronze-flushed young leaves.

C. '**Broughton Star**' Wonderful velvety dusky pink, the four main petals are augmented by additional smaller ones in the centre giving a very distinctive appearance. Slightly more modest in dimensions than some.

C. '**Mayleen**' Delightfully fragrant pale pink flowers are large and nicely rounded. Purple-flushed young leaves from var. *rubens* origins.

C. montana '**Alexander**' Creamy-white sweetly scented flowers.

C. '**Pleniflora**' Think of *Magnolia stellata*, apply that to a clematis, and this Swiss selection is the result. Fully double white flowers with narrow petals.

Tangutica Group

Smothered in yellow floral lanterns from late summer, *C. tangutica* is a Chinese species which thrives on neglect. I remember one escaping from the confines of the garden, wandering over the drive and up into the woods, where it was beautiful for most of the year. When the flowers finally faded, the silky seedpods glistened through a layer of frost. Never pruned, it flourished. *Clematis orientalis* is similar.

C. '**Bill MacKenzie**' Even larger thickly textured, mustard-yellow flowers start in early summer and continue until the first frosts.

Viticella Group

From southern Europe and cultivated since the sixteenth century, *C. viticella* and its derivatives are wonderful where space can accommodate their vigour and proliferation of small but beautiful flowers in early autumn. Many of its hybrids are showier than the species because the bell-shaped flowers open wider. In large landscapes, leave them to their own devices, to roam through the treetops where they will flower on the current season's growth as it cascades from the canopy. They may not flower as densely when left unpruned, but blooms in any quantity at that time of year are a welcome sight. In more restricted areas, plants of the Viticella group can be cut to the ground in spring.

C. **'Etoile Violette'** This one has been around since 1885. The flowers are more outward-facing than many so that intense violet-purple colour can really be appreciated.

C. **'Kermesina'** Even older, still one of the most beautiful in a luxuriant shade of deep pinkish red around a subtle white throat.

C. **'Minuet'** Bicoloured flowers dance at the tips of slender stems. The four petals are broadly rimmed with magenta-purple around pale pink centres.

C. **'Paul Farges'** (syn. 'Summer Snow') Beautiful, scented white flowers with four to seven widely spaced, narrow petals and prominent stamens smother the plant in early summer. Originally bred in the Ukraine in 1962, it combines the hardiness of British native *C. vitalba* without its invasiveness, with the prettiness of *C. potaninii* var. *fargesii*, giving a greater profusion of flower. Although vigorous, the leaves are nicely spaced so the canopy never becomes heavy and overwhelming.

Clintonia (Convallariaceae)

This small genus mainly from North America was named in honour of DeWitt Clinton (1769–1828), an early naturalist and New York governor. Short rhizomatous rootstocks give rise to large, glossy basal leaves and a flower stem in late spring to midsummer, with small, funnel-shaped flowers. The flowers are pretty rather than spectacular, but the subsequent Prussian-blue berries (hence the moniker, bluebead) certainly make up for any deficiency in their floral display. Well-drained but humus-rich soil on the woodland floor suits them, with the western North American species appreciating conifer litter. The attractive berries are poisonous, though the young leaves are edible, tasting a little like cucumber.

Clintonia andrewsiana
This species is the showiest, with many tiny reddish purple flowers in umbels on 25–50cm stems.

Clintonia borealis
Reminiscent of *Erythronium tuolumnense*, with four to eight nodding, greenish yellow flowers on 15–30cm tall stems. No *Erythronium* sports blue berries like these, though. Hunters are said to have rubbed the roots on their traps, since bears were attracted to their smell.

Clintonia umbellulata

Spreading well to form a nice colony, 15–30cm tall. The white flowers held in umbels open widely—sometimes to reveal purple markings—followed by small black fruits.

Clintonia uniflora

The smallest, to 10–20cm, and least easy to please, with solitary white anemone-like six-tepalled flowers looking up at you from a pair of basal leaves. Most appealing though.

Convallaria (Convallariaceae)

Lily of the valley is an evocative plant, with so many memories of special people and places, that no garden of mine will ever be without it—and to think that some people consider it a weed. Every part of the plant is toxic, but that should not discourage the planting of some of the most archetypal woodland plants.

Convallaria majalis

Its vast natural distribution covers much of Europe, including northern England, Japan, and the North American Appalachians. Diverse of habitat, but perfectly at home on the woodland floor, it will gently spread to fill the area with a delicious fragrance when the tiny, bell-shaped flowers open in spring. Five to thirteen flowers are suspended on 20cm stems, separate from the leaves, so they make a wonderful posy for a special person or the kitchen table. Variations can be found in wild populations, with others occurring in cultivation. Inevitably, coloured leaf forms exist, but for me, variegation distracts

Convallaria majalis

from the simplicity of this special plant. This is one occasion when I prefer to stick with the species.

'**Albostriata**' Leaves striped with narrow bands of white.

'**Fortin's Giant**' Bigger is not necessarily better. The leaves are heavier, and the flowers, although marginally larger, seem to be held closer together on the stem, detracting from its grace.

'**Prolificans**' Prolific it may be, but the flowers are small and often deformed.

var. *rosea* This is a pretty variant, common in the wild in parts of central and eastern Europe. Often smaller in stature, but with delightful shell-pink flowers.

Coptis (Ranunculaceae)

These quaint little evergreens are from North America and Asia, creeping by fine shallow rhizomes; they prefer humus-rich, moisture-retentive soil in full shade. Small white flowers sparkle above the glossy green, multi-lobed foliage in mid to late spring. Keep companion planting in proportion; dwarf bulbs are perfect, including *Fritillaria* later in the spring and small feathery ferns. *Coptis* resent disturbance.

Coptis quinquefolia

The leaves of this delightful Asian species have five lobes, while the white flowers are reminiscent of *Hepatica*.

Coptis trifolia

The common name, threeleaf goldthread, describes not only the foliage but the threadlike, golden yellow rhizomes. From North America and Japan, the petals are narrower, for a more starlike appearance to the white flowers.

Cornus (Cornaceae)

There is a *Cornus* for every level of the woodland and because the genus is so diverse, I divide it into three groups according to size, main characteristics, and application.

Middle Canopy Cornus *Grown for Floral Bracts*

Small to midsized trees are perfect to underplant within a mature woodland or to become the canopy in their own right in a more modest area. Tree cornus, or flowering dogwoods, are an attractive group of small trees not as widely known and used in Europe as they deservedly are in North America; indeed, many cultivars have been selected there.

It is best to choose a grafted, named cultivar. The species would generally be grown from seed, and this naturally gives rise to variation. Such plants can take several years to flower and then prove to be indifferent; so many superlative selected forms are available, yet many gardeners are unaware of the possibilities.

By grafting, we can perpetuate a particular feature, whether flower bract size and colour, growth habit and size, or foliage variegation. *Cornus nuttallii*, particularly, is not a happy plant in damp winters, being prone to sudden death when grown from seed. By grafting it onto a tougher rootstock, we not only make it easier to grow, but we can guarantee its flowering characteristics, also ensuring that the plants flower from an early age.

The attractive parts of the flowerhead are actually bracts, which resemble petals and surround the tiny, almost green, true flowers in the centre. These bracts are usually white, but many pink cultivars are available. Bracts are actually more allied to a leaf, so their size and exact colour can be influenced by their growing conditions—particularly soil moisture levels in summer (if they are too dry, the bracts can be small and disappointing). However, interest is maintained for longer, often starting green and starlike before expanding to a more rounded shape as the true flowers open. In some cultivars, the bracts mature to pink.

Cornus florida

From the eastern seaboard of the United States, and the least well adapted to the infamous British weather, *C. florida* prefers a more continental climate. They hate to dry out but need high light and heat levels in the summer to ripen the wood. This promotes flower and bract development for the following year, but it also increases their hardiness through the winter. Thus, they are not suitable for growing in heavily shaded conditions within a woodland; the wood does not ripen and is prone to die-back over the winter. However, in appropriate conditions, they make superb small trees to create the canopy in a "garden-sized" woodland glade. They can provide lovely autumn colour for many weeks.

They flower just before they come into leaf in late spring, and the four bracts may be pink or white. My inclination is to choose more upright plants where underplanting is required. The many variegated cultivars of *C. florida* can be very pretty but difficult to place in this type of planting. Fruit are rarely produced in Britain due to the climate.

    'Cherokee Chief' Upright habit and a lovely white bloom on the twigs enhance their appeal even in the winter. Pinky red bracts have noticeable white veining. A selection from *C. florida* var. *rubra*.

    'Cherokee Princess' White-bracted equivalent.

Cornus kousa

This Asiatic species is the latest flowering of the group, at its best in early to midsummer. More naturally a woodland tree growing perfectly in shade, it is equally well-suited to planting as the middle canopy beneath established mature trees or as the canopy itself on a smaller scale. The four bracts are predominantly creamy or white, though sometimes pink. Their mature shape varies from starlike, where the bracts are narrower and more pointed, to quite rounded and almost overlapping. Fruit are freely produced on many cultivars, being red—not dissimilar to a strawberry in fact—and can be nearly as large as a golf ball. With so many good forms from which to choose, very often the precise choice is irrelevant, so long as it is a grafted, named cultivar.

'**Big Apple**' Large spreading tree with heavy textured, dark green leaves and extremely large fruit.

'**Blue Shadow**' Another fantastic robust American selection. The leaves are larger and more substantial than most, a rich blue-green in colour that turns reddish in autumn.

var. *chinensis* If it was essential to plant a species rather than a cultivar, I would choose this variant as it is slightly more vigorous and the bracts are usually larger.

var. *chinensis* '**Bodnant Form**' From the renowned National Trust garden in North Wales, with beautiful, big creamy white bracts and distinctly purple young stems.

var. *chinensis* '**China Girl**' One of the most readily available, with an upright habit and white bracts.

var. *chinensis* '**Snowflake**' The leaves, and particularly the bracts, have delightful wavy edges, making it a graceful tree.

'**Galilean**' Very upright, the bracts of this American selection are enormous, and it fruits freely. An excellent recent selection.

'**National**' This magnificent cultivar is of dense, rounded habit, and the large bracts are freely produced. They open white, maturing to pink, to give an interesting bicolour effect across the whole plant, maximising the time of interest.

'**Satomi**' Exquisite pink bracts, though the exact colour will be influenced by light levels, being creamier in heavy shade.

'**Teutonia**' Huge bracts up to 13.5cm across have been known on this cultivar, which reliably develops the best autumn colour here.

'**Tsukabanomine**' Another recent selection; its horizontal branching habit creates an effect not unlike *Viburnum plicatum*. Much more exclusive, though, and quite different from the other flowering dogwoods we grow.

Cornus nuttallii and its hybrids

The largest known *C. nuttallii* specimen in Britain is around 13m tall, but that is exceptional. The species has two distinct types of growth habit: the vigorous upright grower and the more cascading shrubby one. The latter, tending to be more typical of the hybrids with *C. florida*, can be difficult to underplant when it forms a curtain to the ground. All have particularly good red and yellow autumn colours.

This species from the US West Coast, and its derivatives, have arguably the most spectacular flower bracts of all dogwoods and certainly the earliest, in mid to late spring, sometimes even providing a second flush in early autumn. Like *C. florida*, they need persistent summer moisture and adequate light to ripen the wood and promote

Cornus kousa 'Satomi'

Cornus kousa 'Teutonia'
autumn colour

flower development and hardiness, so lighter sites are preferable. Though rarely produced in Britain, fruits are akin to those of *C. florida*, with only a few seeds held within individual fleshy red berries, then clustered together. The six bracts of *C. nuttallii* (the hybrids have just four) evolve from greenish white to cream-coloured, sometimes developing a pink flush with age. The cluster of true flowers in the centre of the bracts is larger than in other species and noticeably scented.

I also include the hybrids between *C. nuttallii* and *C. florida* because they reflect their *C. nuttallii* parentage both visually and culturally.

'Colrigo Giant' This vigorous American form, named after the Columbia River Gorge in which it was discovered, is a magnificent small tree of upright habit with enormous rounded flower heads up to 15cm across. 'Portlemouth' is the English equivalent from Devon.

C. **'Eddie's White Wonder'** This is a hybrid with *C. florida*, but I include it because its appearance is much closer to its *C. nuttallii* parentage. An American selection with a layered, arching habit which bracts prolifically.

134

Cornus nuttallii
'Portlemouth'

Cornus 'Eddie's White
Wonder'

By mid-November,
Cornus 'Pink Blush' has
already formed next
year's flower buds; these
will not be hurt by winter
frost.

'**North Star**' Upright habit with incredibly large flower bracts, frequently producing a second flush in the autumn. The bracts do not expand to overlap, creating a starlike effect.

C. '**Ormonde**' Another of the hybrid group, but a more vigorous plant with a more statuesque and tiered habit.

C. '**Pink Blush**' Also a hybrid with *C. florida*, the bracts are rose-flushed with maturity.

Dogwood anthracnose

A fungal disease, dogwood anthracnose, affecting *C. florida* and *C. nuttallii* forms, has become problematic in North America, where both native and cultivated trees are affected. Known in Britain but not serious, with good management and awareness by both gardeners and nurseryman, there is no reason for it to become so. It is caused by the pathogen *Discula destructiva*, which first manifests itself on the foliage as small, purple-rimmed spots or larger tan blotches that may enlarge to kill the entire leaf. Once the infection begins, it can spread very quickly, particularly in a humid, damp spring, resulting in the tree's death. These dogwoods are shallow rooted and vulnerable to summer drought; if under stress in this way, they will be more susceptible to disease. However, other less serious fungal infections can look very similar. Removing and destroying any infected material is a wise precaution, as is sterilising the secateurs (pruners) after pruning. Mulching the tree will help maintain moisture levels while annual fertiliser application will keep it growing strongly. *Cornus kousa* and its derivatives are resistant, along with the new Rutgers hybrids. Some fungicides may be beneficial.

Hybrids from Rutgers University

In 1964, a hybridisation program was begun by Elwin Orton at Rutgers University, New Jersey, to combine the best features of the local favourite *C. florida* with the greater disease resistance and stress tolerance of *C. kousa*. This he achieved with overwhelming success, with six hybrids eventually named as the "Stellar" Series, blooming prolifically in late spring. Naming conventions used for these hybrids include the trademarked trade name and the cultivar name in parentheses.

AURORA ('**Rutban**') Vigorous and upright; large, rounded, pure white overlapping bracts.

RUTH ELLEN ('**Rutlan**') Lower and more spreading habit, the slightly earlier bracts are narrower at the base and separate. Pure white before becoming pink flushed at maturity.

STELLAR PINK ('**Rutgan**') Not as pink as the equivalent *C. florida* selections, but the large bracts are an exquisite creamy pink. Upright habit.

Dr. Orton moved on to cross *C. kousa* and *C. nuttallii* and has achieved the new

"Jersey Star" Series. These amazing trees have cream-coloured bracts the size of *C. nuttallii* (reputedly 20cm across) but they appear just before *C. kousa*. Of course they are disease resistant, too. Brand new to the trade in 2005, it is an exciting time to be planting dogwoods.

> **VENUS** ('**XKN30-8**') Four great overlapping bracts.
>
> **STARLIGHT** ('**KN4-43**') The wide rounded bracts taper towards the base to be held a little more individually.

Cornus STELLAR PINK ('Rutgan')

Shrubby Cornus for Winter Stem Colour

These extremely hardy deciduous shrubs can be used to great effect within the woodland to provide interest and wind filtration in the winter with their vividly coloured stems. All are easy to grow in almost any soil, whether it has a tendency to wet or dry.

Young shoots have the best colour, and popular wisdom frequently decrees cutting the whole plant back to ground level in winter to generate new growth and maximise the following year's display. I prefer a more conservative approach, whereby the oldest third of the stems are cut back hard; over a three-year period, the whole plant is rejuvenated, with some new stems each year, while maintaining a more natural looking plant.

Cornus alba

Cultivated since 1741, all the many cultivars of this Eurasian shrub have brilliant red stems. If left unpruned, a height of some 3m can be achieved.

Cornus alba 'Siberian Pearls'

'Bloodgood' Arguably the best American selection for stem colour.

'Elegantissima' Classic creamy white edging to greyish green leaves.

IVORY HALO ('**Bailhalo**') Compact white variegated selection; pink-flushed.

'Kesselringii' Distinctive black stems.

'Siberian Pearls' Following an enhanced floral display, a profusion of white fruits turn blue with age.

'Sibirica' As seen to such dramatic effect at Westonbirt Arboretum in Gloucester, the standard against which all other red-stemmed *Cornus* are compared.

'Sibirica Variegata' Compact white variegated selection flushed with pink.

'Spaethii' Conspicuous yellow-margined leaves. 'Gouchaultii' is similar.

Cornus amomum

Less common, the North American silky dogwood has greyish white hairs on the leaf veins and a soft purple pubescence on the young winter stems.

'Blue Cloud' Produces clouds of blue berries in autumn; appreciated by wildlife.

Cornus sanguinea

Rather boring European hedgerow species, but its named cultivars are spectacular.

'Anny's Winter Orange' Raised in Holland in 1995, arguably the brightest colour of all dogwoods grown for winter stem effect. Coral-red shades to orange at the base.

'Midwinter Fire' Twiggier structure than the more substantial *C. alba* cultivars. Wonderful winter colour, shading from amber-orange on the older wood to scarlet at the tips.

Cornus sericea

Formerly known as *C. stolonifera*, this vigorous American species follows the same principles as *C. alba*.

'Flaviramea' Yellow stems.

'Hedgerow's Gold' Vigorous wild sport with golden variegated leaves.

'Isanti' Compact habit, bright red stem colour, and free berrying.

'Kelseyi' Very dwarf, forming a neat mound; useful for hiding leggy stems behind it.

'White Gold' Lovely golden leaf edging matures to creamy white with chartreuse stems. 'Silver and Gold' is a similar American introduction.

Left: *Cornus sericea* 'Hedgerow's Gold'

Above *Cornus sericea* 'White Gold'

Other Cornus Species

The diversity within this invaluable genus is remarkable. Sometimes the family likeness is unmistakable; tiny *C. canadensis* produces a floral display exactly like its Asiatic cousin, *C. kousa*. Yet on occasion, I wonder how taxonomists justify the classification.

Above: *Cornus canadensis* in spring

Right: *Cornus canadensis* in late autumn

Cornus mas is such a different plant with its yellow flowers; it is almost as impressive as *Hamamelis* and certainly easier to grow. Perhaps the aristocrat of the genus is *C. controversa*, particularly its variegated selection which can create a magical focal point in any woodland scheme.

Cornus alternifolia

The North American pagoda dogwood develops a layered habit, growing to 8m or taller by a potentially greater width. Flat-topped clusters of white flowers cover the horizontal branches in late spring and early summer, but the species itself is rarely cultivated, being generally represented by the exquisite variegated cultivar.

'**Argentea**' Modest in dimension, the white-margined leaves of this beautiful shrubby tree make it stand out in any situation. A particularly fine woodland feature plant.

'**Silver Giant**' Sported at our nursery. Less variegated than the classic 'Argentea', with a more glaucous central green portion, it has larger leaves so is more vigorous. A superb compromise where something a little more interesting than the species is required, but without the extreme ornamentation of 'Argentea'.

Cornus controversa 'Variegata'

Cornus canadensis

At 20cm tall, this North American woodland carpeter produces four-bracted "flowers" in midspring followed by seemingly impossibly large and heavy, succulent orange berries.

Cornus controversa

The Asian equivalent is similar in principle to *C. alternifolia* but on a larger scale.

'**Variegata**' Known as the wedding cake tree on account of the tiered habit, it benefits from woodland protection, where it will develop into an eye-catching specimen.

Cornus mas

Further exemplifying the diversity within the genus, this Eurasian species flowers on bare twigs in late winter, producing numerous clusters of yellow stamens, dazzling despite their lack of petals. Easily tough enough to create the structure of a small-scale woodland area, eventually to 5–7m, though the smaller, variegated selections prefer some shade. Named forms guarantee floral quality, while bright red edible berries are an added bonus.

'**Flava**' Yellow fruit.

'**Golden Glory**' The current standard against which all others are judged. Upright in habit and abundant in flower and fruit.

'**Jolico**' Probably the first form bred for fruit production to gain acceptance in British gardens; others are following from eastern Europe and the United States.

'**Spring Glow**' The best choice for milder gardens, where the floral performance of this cold-loving species can be disappointing.

'**Variegata**' Superb accent plant with bright, creamy white leaf margins; good flower and fruit. Great year-round interest.

Cortusa (Primulaceae)

Very closely related to *Primula*, separated only by minor botanical differences, these pretty little plants are ideal for the woodland rock garden, where their delicacy can be closely admired. Few of the eight or so species are widely available, even from specialist alpine growers.

Cortusa matthioli

The purple-violet nodding flowers are held on 20–35cm tall stems in late spring to summer. From the European Alps east to Russia and Japan, it requires moisture-retentive, humus-rich soil and shade. Various similar geographical variants exist.

'**Alba**' White flowers.

Corydalis (Papaveraceae)

This is a vast genus of some 300 species, so it is vital to choose the right one for the job; some are annuals rather than perennials, others are specialist alpines, and some frankly can be thugs. The classic concept of a weed simply being a plant in the wrong place springs to mind, because if the woodland floor is large and left to its own devices, a pretty little plant that freely seeds around and jostles with its neighbours may be ideal. Yet in a small and more controlled area of delicate treasures, it would definitely be too much of a good thing. One way of curtailing the invasion is simply to plant it somewhere where it can survive but not thrive.

Most are delightful plants if a little ephemeral. Just when you are enjoying their apparently fragile beauty, they disappear for the summer. However, that is part of the fun of woodland gardening, the way in which plants pop up here and there before dying back down again to make room for the next performer. Perfect for those of us with a short concentration span who cannot wait for the next plant to flower.

Distributed throughout the northern temperate zone, most species have lovely dissected fernlike foliage, which is very much part of their appeal. It is tempting to believe that nothing this delicate in appearance could possibly be a thug. The flowers are held in racemes, but individually they remind my children of snapdragons. Four narrow petals overlap to form a tube, with two almost hooded outer petals—the upper one pointing backwards and often becoming a spur. Thus when the sides of the tube are gently squeezed, the mouth seems to open.

There is considerable variation in their root system; some form small tubers while others are rhizomatous or even fibrous rooted. Generally the woodlanders do better in cooler areas; they appreciate a moisture-retentive soil while they are in growth, but, although they do not want to be baked when dormant, few will tolerate overly wet conditions at that stage. Few are suitable for the heaviest shade deep in the woodland, partial shade being more to their liking.

Corydalis ×*allenii*
Considered to be a hybrid between *C. bracteata* and *C. solida*, it has pink flowers with cream-coloured spurs.

Corydalis cashmeriana
From a cluster of small oval tubers spring a mass of stems and bright green ferny leaves to 10–15cm. However, the exact shade of brightest blue flowers on this lovely Himalayan species actually varies with the temperature.

Corydalis caucasica
The tuberous rootstock renews itself annually, splitting into two. From the Caucasus, the flowers are variable in colour, being pink, purple, or white with a distinct spur.

Corydalis cava

A large, corky tuber becomes hollow with age. This can be worrying, but it is not actually rotting. A native of the Balkans eastwards, the flowers are cream to yellow.

'**Albiflora**' White flowers.

Corydalis cheilanthifolia

This Chinese species behaves more like a fern, not only in view of the appearance of the foliage but also by virtue of the wonderful bronze hues which develop in autumn and are held through the winter. The yellow flowers are held in dense racemes, prolifically in early summer but sporadically throughout the season. This one seeds about for us, but in a nice way, not aggressively. The seeds lodge in crevices, as it pops up in completely inaccessible and unlikely places. Well worth trying on a large woodland rock garden; if seed is available, try sowing it in tiny gaps between rocks, even where they are at a steep angle to vertical.

Left: *Corydalis cheilanthifolia*

Above: *Corydalis flexuosa* 'Purple Leaf'

Corydalis elata

I love these blue-flowered species; this one is from China and usefully flowers later than most, into midsummer. Taller growing to 50cm.

Corydalis flexuosa

Perhaps the most popular *Corydalis* at the moment, this Chinese species comes in a range of subtly different shades of blue, flowering from midspring to midsummer and again in autumn if moisture levels are maintained through the summer. In the wild, it looks exquisite flowering among swathes of emerging shuttlecocks of *Matteuccia*.

'**Blue Panda**' Possibly my favourite, the flowers being clear blue and white.
'**China Blue**' Bright light blue.
'**Golden Panda**' The yellow leaves are unusual and can make quite an arresting sight.
'**Père David**' A richer mid-blue.
'**Purple Leaf**' This one has more purple pigment through the plant, in the leaf and also the flower.

Corydalis lutea

This European species can be invasive, which is a shame because it is pretty, with bright yellow flowers over a long period. Introduce it into wilder areas only, where its neighbours will not be overcome. It will thrive on banks and rocky places with limited soil to preclude the establishment of less-tolerant individuals. A measure of its ability to make itself at home is that it has naturalised in the British Isles.

Corydalis malkensis

Similar in principle to the better known *C. solida*, but with pure white flowers. Unlike that species, the corms of *C. malkensis* do not divide; it spreads by virtue of lots of seeds. Not aggressive enough to be a nuisance, it is gorgeous together with blue scillas. Flowering so early, it disappears by late spring to make room for later risers.

Corydalis solida subsp. *solida* 'George Baker'

Corydalis ochroleuca

Similar to *C. lutea* in behaviour, this species from the mountains of southeastern Europe has delightful creamy flowers.

Corydalis scouleri

What a contrast to the tiny alpines. This big North American species makes as much as 60cm in height and spreads rapidly by underground rhizomes; take care in its placing. The flowers are pretty pink with darker spurs.

Corydalis solida

Plant this diminutive species in the woodland rock garden and enjoy the extensive selection of named clones in an amazing range of flower colours—shades of pink, red, and purple. The flowers are almost disproportionally big by comparison to the rest of the plant. Dozens of named forms are available from specialist growers, but they will not come true from seed. Not too much shade and lightly moist soil.

Corylopsis (Hamamelidaceae)

Often dismissed as acid-loving, these stupendous deciduous shrubs require typical woodland soil: humus rich, moisture retentive in summer but adequately drained in winter. Hanging racemes of tiny cup-shaped fragrant yellow flowers dance from naked branches in early spring. A small genus, but unfortunately one within which nomenclature confusion and alterations abound. Upright when young, most mature to large, broad-headed shrubs.

Corylopsis glabrescens

Vigorous species with larger, more rounded leaves having an almost bluish tinge, even more pronounced in *C. glabrescens* var. *gotoana*. 3–4m.

Corylopsis pauciflora

The smallest *Corylopsis* with the daintiest leaves but ironically the largest flowers (primrose-coloured and cowslip scented), held in small clusters of two or three rather than the usual raceme. Rarely exceeding 2m.

Corylopsis sinensis

An elegant Chinese species, usually represented by the following variants. 4m.

> **var. *calvescens* f. *veitchiana*** Commonly referred to just by the latter name for simplicity, this is arguably the most tolerant form. Upright in habit and prolific in flower, which for me are the best scented of the genus.

> **var. *sinensis* 'Spring Purple'** Plum-purple young shoots and leaves mature to green. Although appreciating our woodland conditions, adequate light is needed to maximise the foliage colour.

Corylopsis spicata

The yellow flowers display conspicuous red stamens projecting beyond their tepals. Heart-shaped leaves. 3m.

Corylus (Corylaceae)

The humble hazel is of huge importance to the ecology of the woodland. Long cultivated in a natural setting in Britain and Europe (it was one of the first colonisers after the last ice age), it is the perfect backbone for a woodland glade in difficult conditions. Although 10 species are distributed throughout the northern hemisphere, forgive me

Left: *Corylopsis glabrescens* autumn colour

Above: *Corylopsis sinensis* var. *calvescens* f. *veitchiana*

for concentrating on *C. avellana*, which is found in Britain, across Europe, into Asia and North Africa.

Catkins wait dormant for months to swell and release their pollen as winter loosens its icy grasp on the countryside. The showy catkins, known to country folk as lamb's tails, are actually clusters of male flowers; the females are like tiny red sea urchins. Being wind-pollinated, showy flowers are not needed to attract insects.

Hazels have been farmed in Britain for around 4000 years. Traditionally the hazel was coppiced (the main trunk pruned close to the ground in winter) to produce lots of strong, tall trunks and a resultant diverse wildlife habitat. Over the years, forms of cob nuts with larger fruit have been selected, so planting these trees can definitely be of mutual benefit to both gardener and wildlife. Such is the reverence in which these trees are held; folklore has it that carrying hazel nuts defends one against illness and the forces of evil.

The species can easily be grown from seed. The cultivars can be layered, which is a slow process, or grafted. Grafting *Corylus* is unsatisfactory due to the suckering nature of the rootstock. To plant up a glade, it is simplest to acquire a single large-fruited named form, and sow the fruit from that. The resulting plants may not be quite up to the standard of the cultivar and should certainly not be named as such, but they will make excellent plants for the woodland structure.

Corylus americana

All the hazels are very similar, being little more than geographical variants. This 5–6m, particularly hardy species is from eastern North America. Hybrids between this and *C. avellana* are known but not commercially available in Britain.

Corylus avellana

Can be coppiced; if left to grow, will make a tree of 4–5m.

> **'Contorta'** The corkscrew hazel is an amusing plant with its zigzag stems; it was originally found in an English hedgerow in 1863. Rather fun for very small-scale woodlands.

> **'Webb's Prize Cob'** Selected for superior fruit, as are 'Cosford Cob' and 'Pearson's Prolific'.

Corylus colurna

This Turkish species grows enormous by comparison, at 15m or more, though it can be coppiced. It has larger nuts, too. The hybrid *C.* ×*colurnoides* (and cultivar 'Chinoka') between this and *C. avellana* have promise.

Corylus maxima

Try the selections of this for bigger nuts, differentiated as a filbert rather than a cob nut. Many commercial nuts are actually a cross between this and *C. avellana*—for example, *C. maxima* 'Kentish Cob'. 'Red Filbert' and 'White Filbert' are two commercial fruiting clones.

Crataegus (Rosaceae)

Crataegus is a huge genus—dependent on the system of classification, it includes between 200 and 1000 species. These quintessential hedgerow trees are incredibly tough, tolerating the worst the weather can throw at them, from coastal to mountain locations. A mass of flower in late spring (small individuals held in great bunches) and resplendent in berry in autumn, hawthorns provide multi-season interest, making them ideal trees to form the canopy of a new woodland glade, as they prefer a sunny site. Local availability will influence choice, which will be more extensive than I can list here, but consider the preferred flower and berry colour and, importantly, the degree of thorniness. Some can be rather vicious and are best planted away from paths. *Crataegus* means strength and refers to the immense strength of the wood itself.

Hawthorns are a fireblight host, so they should be monitored, particularly after a warm, damp spring. Their movement between countries is therefore restricted. Rust is of concern in North America, particularly in drier hotter zones, but is rarely an issue in Britain.

Crataegus coccinioides
The highly adaptable American Kansas hawthorn is tolerant of more shade than most, and of wet soils, but it can also take drought once established if protected from wind. Typical white flowers and red berries.

Crataegus laevigata
(syn. *C. oxyacantha*) A British native less well-known but similar to *C. coccinioides*.
  'Crimson Cloud' Single scarlet flowers with a white eye.
  'Paul's Scarlet' Double scarlet.

Crataegus monogyna
Ubiquitous in British hedgerows, hawthorn is nonetheless valuable with fragrant white flowers in late spring and red haws in autumn. Pink and double selections are also common. Many of the named cultivars are probably hybrids between this and *C. laevigata*.
  'Aureum' Yellow fruits.
  'Biflora' (syn. 'Praecox') Legend has it that after the crucifixion of Christ, Joseph of Arimathea came to England to establish Christianity. While at Glastonbury, he prayed for a miracle to convince the people of his divinity. He plunged his staff into the ground and it immediately burst into leaf and flower despite it being Christmas Day. Hence this form is known as the Glastonbury thorn; some flowers are generally produced in winter, with the rest at the normal time.

Crataegus persimilis **'Prunifolia'**
(syn. *C. prunifolia*) Smaller growing with glossy oval leaves. Fantastic in autumn when they colour alongside much larger red berries. The thorns are vicious.

Crataegus punctata

The dotted hawthorn is spectacular in flower and prolific in fruit.

f. *aurea* Yellow fruits.

var. *inermis* Improvement on the type due to lack of thorns.

Crataegus tanacetifolia

Delightful Asian species with small, soft, grey downy leaves and few, if any, thorns. Large yellow fruit.

Crataegus viridis 'Winter King'

This selection may be a hybrid, as it is not completely typical of the species. Raised in the United States in 1955, it is a great all-rounder. Its vase-shaped structure creates a lovely rounded habit and in autumn drips with red fruit, which are large and held for a long time. Exfoliating soft-grey bark is a winter bonus, revealing a cinnamon-coloured underlayer.

Crocus (Iridaceae)

Crocus can be divided into two groups: those flowering in spring and those flowering in autumn. The desired flowering time is therefore the first decision, dependent on the other planting with which they are to be associated. The majority are better suited to open, sunny sites with sharp drainage when dormant, making them unsuitable for the woodland. Their forte, however, is under a single specimen tree, where good light is often available, particularly in the winter and early spring when the sun's low rays can easily penetrate beneath and through the bare canopy. They need only a very shallow root run so the established root system of the tree is not in conflict with their requirements; indeed it helps to keep them dry in summer. Crocus can easily be added into a little gritty leaf-mould in the pockets created by the big buttress root systems on ancient trees.

Some species are subtle in colour and size, others will beckon you from across the garden; that choice is entirely personal. I have considered just the species here, rather than the modern hybrids which are available in such a wide range of colours. Most produce large flowers in the spring, surviving well enough where light levels are adequate, but many are sterile so will not naturalise in the same way as the true species.

Wildlife can wreak havoc with crocus. Squirrels can be such a nuisance digging up the dormant corms that it is often recommended to lay a piece of small-gauge chicken wire over them, just beneath the surface. This is all very well when establishing through grass, but less satisfactory in a woodland unless you are sufficiently organised to plant all the bulbs, and only bulbs, in an area at the same time. Bizarrely, I have an issue with blackbirds. I watch them in February as I sit writing this, delighting in taking apparently random pecks of my orange crocus as they wander past. They seem to be attracted

A haze of crocus creates a simple spring carpet under deciduous shrubs.

only to the orange forms; perhaps they think they are berries and quickly move on in disappointment.

Crocus angustifolius

In the spring, this yellow-flowered Crimean species is striped with brown on the outsides. 7cm.

Crocus flavus

This wonderful species from the Balkans has tall, rich orange-yellow flowers in spring. 12cm.

Crocus imperati

In spring (actually late winter), this Italian species sports deep lilac flowers with yellow or orange throats and a buff exterior, variably striped with purple. 12cm. *Crocus etruscus* is similar, with 'Zwanenberg' a vigorous selection.

    subsp. *imperati* **'De Jager'** Robust, earlier flowering selection.

Crocus ochroleucus

Small, elegant, creamy white flowers with orange throats are produced from midautumn to early winter. Naturalises well, but is best in a sheltered place to prevent physical damage from the winter weather.

Crocus robertianus

This uncommon autumn-blooming Greek species is surprisingly tolerant of the worst autumn weather, producing rounded deep-purple flowers with a contrasting yellow throat.

Crocus speciosus

In autumn, large lilac-purple flowers are often mistaken for *Colchicum*, but the silvery leaves are rather smaller. Distributed through the Caucasus are three botanically distinct, but aesthetically similar, subspecies as well as various named selections. The intensity of colour will vary, and some have yellow throats. 25cm.

'**Albus**' White flowers.

Crocus tommasinianus

From southeastern Europe, this spring flowerer is one of the best for naturalising, increasing freely by seed and offsets. Smaller flowers are lilac-purple, with a white throat or cream exterior. 13cm.

'**Eric Smith**' Pure white with a suggestion of tiny purple specks on the outside.

var. *roseus* Rose-pink inside and a sophisticated creamy pink exterior.

'**Ruby Giant**' and '**Whitewell Purple**' Excellent large deep purple forms.

'**Taplow Ruby**' Reddish purple.

Crocus versicolor

From a relatively small area of southern Europe, the 12cm tall flowers in spring are white or pale lilac, sometimes with purple feathering striping the outside for a more subtle display.

'**Picturatus**' Particularly well-marked petals.

Cyclamen (Primulaceae)

At Christmas time, the shops are full of perfect pots of these exquisite gems, but these are tender, destined for the windowsill. Fortunately, a pleasing number of species are able to withstand the rigours of the garden. Surprisingly, most of these Mediterranean plants actually prefer a shady position. Not suited to the moist and shady depths of our woodland floor, they are perfect at its edges or in smaller scale woodland beds and at the foot of mature trees.

Although the flowers, with swept-back, twisted petals, are all variations on a theme of pink and white, huge interest can be gained from their leaves alone, and at different times of year. The toughest without a doubt is *C. hederifolium*, which needs the thinnest layer of gritty substrate so it can be introduced into the harshest of sites, simply by mixing some seeds or baby corms into a bucket of soil and sprinkling the mixture over the surface. It will naturalise, even in the pockets created by buttress roots at the foot of great trees, perhaps in combination with small ferns and crocus for year-round interest. Others should be planted more deeply to maximise their hardiness, while some enjoy a slightly more moisture-retentive soil; whichever you choose, they are mesmeric little plants.

Cyclamen hederifolium corms can grow into plate-sized discs, while *C. coum* is much smaller, like a smooth pebble. Many subtle variations in leaf and flower colour have been given cultivar names, but detailed differences will be impossible to replicate without isolation, since seed is the only method of propagation. If the separate named forms are planted in discrete groups, perhaps around particular trees, they will breed remarkably true. Any inconsistencies can always be rogued out as they become apparent.

Take care when acquiring new plants. Many wild populations have been decimated by unscrupulous harvesting, so ensure that they are cultivated, not wild-collected corms. Few tolerate drying out while out of the ground and require planting as freshly lifted as possible; they can be obtained from specialist growers in pots in active growth. Once established, most species will set seed freely to colonise the area. The seedpods look like marbles; although their stems are like coiled springs, they do seem to drop much of their seed on top of the existing corm, which is not ideal from a distribution point of view. However, insects will spread them. Alternatively, collect and scatter the ripening seedpods; most will germinate readily but take several years to flower.

Cyclamen coum

This variable species is a true classic, flowering in late winter. The leaves are rather rounded or kidney-shaped and sometimes completely green. Some forms have beautiful symmetrical markings, while others are almost completely silver. Flowers are normally deep magenta-pink but paler variants are common. Pure white is highly prized. This species likes to be planted deep (at least 3cm).

Left: *Cyclamen coum* thrives beneath the canopy of a fissured pine.

Above *Cyclamen coum* Pewter Group 'Blush' and 'Maurice Dryden' intermingle.

subsp. *coum* f. *pallidum* 'Album' White flowers with a conspicuous pink nose over green leaves. Usually referred to as *C. coum* 'Album'.

Pewter Group General name referring to those with pewter-coloured foliage, often edged in green. Flowers may be any colour from pale pink to rich magenta, including bicoloured forms. Seldom used, the botanically correct name is *C. coum* subsp. *coum* f. *coum* Pewter Group. 'Maurice Dryden' has typical Pewter Group foliage but delightful white flowers with magenta noses. Some seedlings from this will be pale pink and are named 'Blush'.

Above: *Cyclamen hederifolium*

Right: *Cyclamen purpurascens* Lake Garda form

Cyclamen hederifolium

The most vigorous species potentially forms great colonies of exquisitely marked leaves. Although they seldom hybridise, this one is best kept to itself to prevent it swamping smaller species.

f. *albiflorum* White flowers.

Silver-leaved Group Lacking any green markings at all, these iridescent leaves will make an eye-catching carpet below and among all manner of other gentle woodlanders. Selected forms have either pink or white flowers.

Cyclamen purpurascens

Where soil moisture levels are adequate, this cyclamen will remain evergreen, flowering from the start of summer until the first autumn frosts. Fragrant, too, they are true gems, but not as easily established as the other species; they are certainly not likely to produce great drifts of pink. Plant them deep (up to 20cm) in leafy soil enriched with pine needles, perhaps among rocks where they will remain cool and moist. Most have fairly plain green foliage, but strains from specific areas have silver-marked leaves.

Cyclamen repandum

This Mediterranean species sensibly waits for the warmer spring weather before showing its sweetly scented flowers, relatively narrow and often with twisted petals, usually bright pink and rarely white. The large leaves have deeply scalloped edges and, in some forms, amazing silvery patterns. Considered slightly less hardy than other cyclamens listed, deeper planting provides additional protection.

Cyclamen repandum

Cyrtomium (Dryopteridaceae)

Known as holly ferns in recognition of their thick, glossy, leaflike fronds, their boldness is a far cry from the softness of the traditional ethereal fern but adds a tropical touch to the woodland floor. They are tolerant of heavy shade and even drought, though the crowns benefit from the protection of a thick mulch in cold areas where they will become deciduous.

Cyrtomium falcatum
Asian, with typically shiny, arching holly-like fronds, to as much as 90cm long by 25cm wide.

    '**Rochfordianum**' Considered the best form; vigorous, with coarsely toothed pinnae.

Cyrtomium fortunei
We can learn much from nature. I can think of few better combinations than *C. fortunei* growing among *Disporum flavum* in its native Asia. This species is similar to *C. falcatum*, though the stems and midribs are stained with purple, with the bonus of increased hardiness.

Cyrtomium macrophyllum
These ferns are so shiny as to almost appear metallic. Position them where the sun's rays penetrate the canopy for just a short while early in the day, and enjoy their radiant beauty. Fewer, broader pinnae and a more spreading habit.

Cystopteris (Woodsiaceae)

By fern standards, the bladder ferns are a small genus, with just 18 species. Potentially small enough for the woodland rock garden or tucked into smaller corners of the woodland floor, they thrive in humus-rich, moisture-retentive soil. All are deciduous and have triangular shaped fronds that are lacy, with toothed pinnae.

Cystopteris bulbifera
Widespread in North America, little green bulblets form on the underside of the fronds, dropping off to grow into graceful new ferns, hence the name bulblet fern. It also spreads by virtue of its creeping rootstock. Copy Mother Nature and plant them with *Aquilegia*; they work together. 30cm.

Cystopteris dickieana

Only one colony of this fern is thought to exist in Scotland; otherwise, it is found in arctic Europe and Asia. It has a tufted habit, with short multi-branched rhizomes and heavy fronds. 10cm.

Cystopteris fragilis

The fragile fern is widely distributed through the temperate regions of the northern hemisphere and suitably adaptable as a result; it will tolerate most conditions, including thin soil over rock and full sun. How versatile it is, yet elegant. Clump forming. 20cm.

Cystopteris montana

From northern Europe and Canada. Rhizomatous, so it is colony forming. 20cm.

Daphne (Thymelaeaceae)

Guaranteed to produce gasps of wonder or grimaces of despair, daphnes will always inspire comment with their exquisite scent and beautiful flowers. The secret to growing daphnes is to maintain a constant moisture level—not too wet in winter, not too dry in summer—so it is important not to plant them too near to the base of big trees. However, they are very deep rooting, so provided they can manage to establish, they will send their roots down to find moisture.

Those listed here are evergreen, unless described otherwise, making rounded bushes to 1m (with the exception of the larger *D. bholua*). As well as being superb flowering shrubs in their own right, they provide valuable low protection to smaller treasures. Their fragrance is unrivalled; most are moth-pollinated so they are often at their best on a warm evening.

Daphnes have a habit of "moulting". As the sap starts to rise in spring (after the early species have finished flowering), the old leaves turn yellow, hang, and drop as the new growth starts to emerge. The worst offender is *D. bholua* 'Jacqueline Postill'. Since one parent is deciduous, it can look decidedly scruffy for a week or two, but this is nothing to worry about.

Daphnes are prone to virus spread by aphids, though the evergreens are generally less susceptible. It shows as yellow veining and streaking through the leaves but should not be confused with chlorosis caused by hunger or a nutrient imbalance. It cannot be treated and infected plants should be destroyed.

Daphne bholua 'Alba'

Once used as a purgative by itinerant "quacks", daphnes are highly toxic in all their parts. Their sap can also cause skin irritation.

Daphne bholua var. *glacialis* 'Gurkha'

Daphne acutiloba

An evergreen Chinese shrub of upright, bushy habit. Typical heads of white flowers are produced in mid-spring. Plants grown from seed vary.

> **'Fragrant Cloud'** Collected in China in the early 1990s under collection number CD&R626, this is a superior selection with large, fragrant blooms.

Daphne bholua

One of the finest winter-flowering shrubs, this Himalayan species can start blooming by midwinter (Christmas here) and still be a delight in midspring. Amazing. Their scent is exquisite; imagine it drifting through the glade as winter sun filters through the trees. They reach 2m in height in 10 years, but they can exceed that in woodland conditions to their liking.

Daphne bholua 'Jacqueline Postill'

> **'Alba'** The most compact form; almost pure white flowers with just the faintest touch of pale pink. Lovely glossy dark green leaves.
>
> **var.** *glacialis* **'Gurkha'** Uniquely deciduous and upright, this form was collected by Major Tom Spring-Smyth in 1962 on the Milke Banjyang Ridge, Nepal.
>
> **'Jacqueline Postill'** Spectacular selection with large clusters of deep magenta-purple flower buds opening paler.

Daphne jezoensis

Daphne odora 'Aureamarginata'

Daphne laureola subsp. *philippi* provides a
valuable winter element.

Daphne tangutica

Daphne jezoensis

This daphne is like no other. For a start, it is summer deciduous, meaning that it loses
its leaves in spring and starts into growth in autumn with fresh new foliage, at a time
when so much else is looking tatty. The flowers are its main attraction, though; brilliant
yellow trumpets are held in globular clusters in midwinter to early spring. Deliciously
citrus-scented, they are exquisite. Native to Russia's Kamtschatica peninsula, one of the
harshest corners of the globe, pure hardiness is not an issue. However, the very difference in the climate found in most gardens can make this a challenging plant to keep.

Daphne laureola

Useful rather than spectacular, yellowish green flowers clothe the upright stems of this British native in early spring.

subsp. *philippi* Endemic to the Pyrénées, this dwarf form has deep, rich green leaves and a low bushy habit with none of the legginess typical of the species.

Daphne odora

The archetypal daphne with the most sweetly scented flowers imaginable in early spring, opening white from dark purple buds.

'Aureamarginata' The most common form with narrow gold margins to the leaves. Unusually, this variegated selection is hardier than the basic species, with a fragrance just as good. The level of variegation is variable and a number of more richly margined clones are in cultivation, like our own 'Double Cream'.

'Sakiwaka' Pure white.

Daphne pontica

One of the most resilient daphnes, with larger leaves and quite uniquely shaped, spidery yellow flowers in early to midspring. Black berries. The red-berried *D. albowiana* is similar.

Daphne tangutica

Perhaps the easiest of all daphnes and arguably the most rewarding, flowering from midspring and then sequentially until the frosts. Deep purple buds open to white flowers. Inevitably, if the shade is too heavy, flowering will diminish.

Darmera (Saxifragaceae)

A magnificent foliage plant from the American Northwest, where it is found along stream banks in evergreen forests. Despite this, it needs some sun, perhaps in the morning. Its requirement for moisture is undisputed; having huge leaves reminiscent of rhubarb or *Gunnera*, it is easy to see why.

Darmera peltata

Sometimes known incorrectly as *Peltiphyllum peltatum*. The leaves can reach 1m tall by 60cm across, developing from a creeping rhizome. The pinky white flowers are most unexpected, emerging from the ground in midspring before the leaves. They can be vulnerable to frost, but for me the leaves are the reason for growing this plant. They add such an exotic feel to a moist or even boggy area of the woodland floor, particularly as they are tinged with reddish purple as they unfold.

'Nana' For smaller scale plantings, this dwarf form is about half the size in all dimensions. Still an impressive leafy plant.

Deinanthe (Hydrangeaceae)

This Oriental herbaceous perennial has gained popularity in Western gardens only recently. Although in the hydrangea family, *Deinanthe* flowers look nothing like the classic hydrangea; instead, they are held in clusters of downward-facing, small anemone-like blooms in late summer. The large leaves, however, are reminiscent of hydrangea, and are vulnerable to damage from drying wind. Classic woodland conditions are perfect: a shady, sheltered site with plenty of moisture through the summer to support all that lush growth. In summer, they make a wonderful backdrop to lilies, for instance, that can look a little lost by themselves.

Deinanthe bifida
From late spring to late summer, the white flowers with yellow stamens are nicely displayed above rich green foliage on leafy shoots rising to 60cm.

Deinanthe caerulea
Flowers can be up to 4cm across and of an unusual waxy blue to bluish violet with blue stamens, held similarly to those of *D. bifida*. 45cm.

Dicentra (Papaveraceae)

Sometimes a single bad experience can easily cloud your feelings for a whole genus. So it is for me with *Dicentra*; one plant has run amok across my woodland floor, trampling all before it. Perhaps I exaggerate, but clearly there was inadequate room for it at that position, even though it was so pretty.

The individual flowers have two enlarged spurs, sometimes likened to breeches. Before opening, these are often heart-shaped, giving rise to the common name bleeding heart. They are held above the leaves in arching racemes and range in colour from white through pink to almost red. Classic woodland floor conditions suit them admirably; they appreciate the shade, do not care to dry out, but dislike being too wet when dormant. Most need only a shallow run for their rhizomatous root system, so they will exist in little more than a thick mulch. The beguiling fernlike foliage shades from a bright light green to my favourite almost blue-grey. They flower in spring to early summer and quickly disappear as temperatures rise. *Dicentra* can be toxic if ingested.

Dicentra canadensis
From northeastern America, this lovely and manageable little species has grey-green leaves and fragrant white flowers. 30cm.

Dicentra cucullaria

Larger than *D. canadensis*, it has a similar distribution plus an isolated population in the US Northwest. The flowers are generally white, but pink is known.

Dicentra eximia

From eastern North America, this forms pretty mounds of fine-textured blue-green foliage. The typical pink flowers are produced in abundance in spring, potentially continuing through the summer if the soil remains adequately moist. Known locally as staggerweed, in reference to the effect its ingestion can have on cattle. A delightful plant in the wild, though it can become invasive in artificially enhanced garden conditions. 45cm.

'Snowdrift' A less boisterous, white-flowered selection.

Dicentra formosa

Similar to *D. eximia*, this species from the North American Pacific coast is showier but coarser, being more floriferous, with larger pink flowers and heavier foliage.

'Alba' White flowers.

subsp. *oregona* Glaucous foliage and creamy flowers.

Dicentra spectabilis 'Alba'

Dicentra spectabilis

For me, this is the archetypal dicentra that evokes memories of my childhood garden. From Korea and north China, this larger, distinctive species makes a substantial clump but does not run. The pink flowers are large, too. 60cm.

'Alba' I love the simple contrast of the pure white flowers and green leaves.

Dicentra 'Bacchanal'

Dicentra cultivars

Dicentra eximia and *D. formosa* hybridise freely, and it was with one of these offspring that I had my disagreement. The mat of rhizomes becomes so dense that nothing else can survive within it. Thus, when they have died down, there is nothing to take over from it. In truth, if the soil were moister, these species and their derivatives would have the potential to stay in growth all summer. The cultivars are generally showier garden plants than the species, though all will seed about. They need adequate space or robust neighbours who will not be easily overcome. Nevertheless it is worth finding the right spot, because they are very pretty.

'Adrian Bloom' Delightful foliage is more divided and not quite so vigorous. Reddish pink flowers.

'Bacchanal' Rich, velvety maroon flowers hover over feathery foliage.

'King of Hearts' A more recent hybrid, arguably regarded as the best yet. Certainly more compact, the substantial flowers are an intense shade of pinky red above lovely blue-green leaves. It will flower potentially from midspring to late autumn if moisture levels are adequate; drought will stop the show prematurely.

'Pearl Drops' Vigorous grower but so pretty; pink-flushed white flowers over silver-grey foliage.

'Stuart Boothman' Smaller, with very narrow leaflets and deep pink flowers.

Digitalis (Scrophulariacea)

The ubiquitous foxglove, a classic British wildflower, is one of more than 20 species of annuals and perennials distributed across Europe and Asia. Its popular name derives from the fingerless-glove appearance of the individual flowers. In late spring to early summer, tall spires of funnel-shaped flowers, often beautifully speckled within, rise from leafy basal rosettes—a clear invitation to any passing bee. Naturally biennial, they freely seed around to maintain a natural-looking colony; they are perennial if the old flower stems are removed. Foxgloves are easily grown across the woodland floor and may be tolerant of drought, but they are happiest where soil is moisture-retentive. Other species may be woodlanders in their native habitat, seeking respite from their much hotter and drier climates in the woodland shade. Although beautiful and desirable, they need more sunlight than northern woodland gardens can provide, to maintain hardiness and avoid fungal problems.

All parts of the plants are highly poisonous. The cardiotonic drug digitalin is extracted from the leaves, though a synthetic form has been developed.

Digitalis grandiflora

Essentially a European native, though naturalised in other locations as diverse as North America and Kashmir. Pale yellow flowers may sometimes have interior brown veining.

'**Temple Bells**' Large flowers.

Digitalis ×mertonensis

Even in 1925, botanists were experimenting. At London's John Innes Horticultural Institution, colchicine treatment resulted in this tetraploid hybrid between *D. grandiflora* and *D. purpurea*. Large, showy flowers are an interesting mix of pinkish buff, salmon, or reddish pink colours above evergreen leaves.

Digitalis purpurea

Another European native, it usually occurs in shades of vivid pinkish purple, but its white forms are particularly beautiful in the shady woodland setting. Many named forms are seed selections rather than genuine cultivars, so they will breed true when grown in isolation. In mixed colonies, the results will be more unpredictable, though potentially spectacular. If left entirely to their own devices, the purple of the species will dominate the gene pool. 150–180cm.

Excelsior Group Good mix of colours from white, to yellow, pink, and darker rose. Sturdy plants of varying heights.

'**Pam's Choice**' Selected form of *D. purpurea* f. *albiflora*; white with maroon throats.

'**Primrose Carousel**' Delightful shorter selection with 75cm spikes of large yellow flowers with conspicuously claret-speckled throats.

Left: The white form of *Digitalis purpurea* adds a vertical accent through lush summer foliage, here *Acer palmatum* var. *dissectum*.

Above: *Digitalis purpurea* f. *albiflora*

Diphylleia (Berberidaceae)

Life in the woodland is always full of surprises, and nowhere is this more apparent than in Berberidaceae. How varied they are, yet it seems increasingly that *Berberis* itself is the odd one out. *Diphylleia* is represented in Asia and North America by herbaceous perennials for the woodland floor, developing great leafy umbrellas, though with pointed lobes, held in pairs when the shoot is mature enough to flower. As should be expected of such luxuriant growth, moisture-retentive leafy soil is required, while shade is essential. The effect is similar to that of *Podophyllum*, though *Diphylleia* has the advantage of holding the flowers above the leaves where they can be appreciated. These are held in clusters in late spring to early summer, to be followed in autumn by waxy blue grapelike fruits. They provide contrast with graceful ferns and other more delicately structured plants, but make sure each has the right amount of space. At the time of planting or when plants are dormant, it is all too easy to put things too close together, because it is hard to believe just how much room these large-leaved plants will occupy. Surround them with spring bulbs to fill the space while the larger plants are dormant.

Diphylleia cymosa
Indigenous to northeastern America, it was used medicinally by Native Americans. Nowadays, a stimulating prospect is the development of an anti-cancer drug based on a component in this plant. The leaves can reach 1m in height and up to 40 cm across. Up to 10 white flowers are held clustered together above them.

Diphylleia grayi
This Japanese equivalent is perfect for smaller scale woodlands, just two-thirds the size in all its parts, with slightly less strongly lobed leaves.

Disporopsis (Convallariaceae)

All the genera in this family are classic woodland floor plants. The graceful arching stems with bell-shaped flowers hanging from the leaf axils in late spring to early summer look wonderful in combination with our bigger leaved, more luxuriant occupants. The advantage of this particular Asian genus is that it is evergreen. Unfortunately, by definition this makes it more vulnerable in the winter, but woodland conditions will provide significant protection anyway. Even if foliage becomes a little tatty as winter takes its toll, the old shoots can be cut down before new growth starts in spring and the plant will be none the worse for it.

Disporopsis fuscopicta
Much naming confusion surrounds this genus, complicated by the introduction of

newly discovered species. This one is distinguished by its creeping rhizome, resembling a string of beads. Tremendously glossy leaves at their best look almost artificial, and it produces the largest individual flowers in the genus.

Disporopsis pernyi

(syn. *D. arisanensis*) This most widely available species, from the Yunnan province of China, is perhaps also the most floriferous, with gorgeous, white (occasionally marked with purple), scented bells and then violet-blue berries. Purple-spotted, erect, dark green stems zigzag at the top. 40cm.

Disporum (Convallariaceae)

These have earned the common name fairy bells with good reason. Interest in and appreciation of this genus is gathering momentum with the introduction of new species from North America and especially Asia. I think they are delightful and perfect in the woodland garden, where they love the shade; they do better with constant moisture, so they are best not planted too close to the base of a large tree. In that situation, they will die down much sooner in the summer, and the red berries of autumn which complete their season will be missed. The dainty flowers hang like bells from the leaf axils in late spring and early summer and are typical of plants in this family, though variation in shape, size, and, particularly excitingly, colour exists in this large genus.

Disporum bodinieri

This Chinese species reaches a whopping 2m, so locating it requires some forethought. Fortunately it is not invasive; in fact, it seems to balance its elevated stature against a lesser number of stems. The stems are multi-branched, with creamy flowers hanging in clusters; the gold stamens extend below the flared mouth. Large blue-black fruit follow in autumn.

Disporum cantoniense

Widespread through Asia, this species purportedly reaches 2m in the wild; in cultivation, growing conditions will dictate the height, which could be between 60cm and 150cm. An attractive plant, flower colours vary from white to pink, to sundry shades of red and even purple. Forms are available with a collection number, identifying the expedition and the people who collected it, so it is possible therefore to reference the colour. The flowers themselves are held closer to the stem and are quite chunky, the sides of the bell being almost parallel rather than flaring.

> **'Aureovariegata'** A subtly variegated form from Japan, with green-yellow leaves within green margins.

Disporum flavens

This species is almost more like a *Uvularia* with intense yellow flowers suspended beneath pleated, bright green leaves. 100cm.

Disporum lanuginosum

Hanging from branched stems, the petals of the yellow flower bells are pointed at the base rather like a tattered skirt. Orange-red berries. 60cm.

Disporum maculatum

This North America species has spotted flowers. 60cm.

Disporum megalanthum

An extremely sought-after evergreen Chinese species with relatively large, flared white flowers, followed by blue-black berries. 30cm.

Disporum megalanthum

Disporum sessile

This robust Japanese species forms colonies fairly rapidly from underground rhizomes. It would not be wise to plant it among delicate treasures. The creamy white flowers are greener at the mouth, while golden yellow autumn colour is a bonus if summer moisture is adequate to support the plant for long enough. 45cm.

> **'Variegatum'** It is strange that the variegated form of this species is actually more common than the species itself; indeed it is probably the most widely available disporum, certainly in Britain. Green and white–striped leaves are cheerfully pleasing in a shady woodland situation.

Disporum smilacinum

This smaller Japanese species has more starlike flowers, usually held singly rather than in clusters. The leaves are broader, too, so the colony becomes dense as it slowly expands. The Japanese have found many variegated sports of both this species and *D. sessile*.

> **'Aureovariegatum'** The original and most widely available selection with narrow, irregular white variegation, mostly along the margins. Newer clones are difficult to obtain, indeed few have made it to Britain yet, but they include all manner of white and yellow variegation options. Some are attractive, others are downright bizarre.

Disporum smithii

Found along the western North American coastal ranges, where its native forest habitat is threatened by clearance, this species has perhaps the largest flowers in the genus. The creamy flowers hang in groups of two to four on red-spotted, branched stems, followed by orange-red berries. 60cm.

Disporum uniflorum

I am captivated by this species from China and Korea, again with branched stems. The large flowers dangle as much as 6cm below the leaf axils, causing the stem to arch, displaying the flowers in all their magnificence. Not widely available, but worth searching out. 1m.

Dodecatheon (Primulaceae)

Dodecatheons can be so tiny that they are easy to lose on the woodland floor, though a drift of one of the larger species would be a wonderful sight. They are certainly worthy of a corner on the woodland rock garden in any event. Not all are for shady sites, but those which are suitable thrive in humus-rich, cool, and moist soil. Native mainly to North America, their growth cycle is early in the year, so they can be planted in the lee of deciduous shrubs where the light will penetrate in spring, avoiding the deepest and driest shade. Known commonly as shooting stars due to their flower shape, swept back petals reveal prominent stamens atop a stem springing from a rosette of leaves that reminds me of primrose.

Dodecatheon dentatum

From moist woodlands of western North America, the flowers are mainly white, revealing a cone of deep reddish purple stamens. 40cm.

Dodecatheon hendersonii

Found along the West Coast of the United States, the flowers are more variable in this species; they may be magenta, lavender, or even white, on 45cm tall stems. As many as

Above: *Dodecatheon hendersonii*

Right: *Dodecatheon meadia* f. *album*

17 flowers may appear on a single stem. *Dodecatheon jeffreyi* is extremely similar in all respects.

Dodecatheon meadia

Unbelievably, species with 125 flowers to a head have been found. Although colour is variable in the wild, cultivated plants are usually magenta-pink.

    f. *album* White flowers.

Dodecatheon pulchellum

Aesthetically, little difference exists among many of these species. I have selected some which are more robust and suited to normal cultivation in shady sites, and it may well be that the right one to start with is the first one acquired. This species is reasonably obtainable. Typically pink, white forms are known.

    subsp. *pulchellum* 'Red Wings' Selected form with richer colouring.

    'Sooke Variety' Sturdy grower from Canada's Vancouver Island with a mid-pink flower.

Dracunculus (Araceae)

Dracunculus is another weird and wonderful favourite of my son. In fact, this one is even better (so far as he is concerned at least) because it smells—actually, it stinks of rotten meat. Some plants have exquisite flowers to attract pollinators; this one uses the foul smell to catch the attention of local flies. Although I would not want it downwind of my patio, it is a tremendous foliage plant for a moisture-retentive spot on the woodland floor. Not as hardy as most plants listed, but a thick mulch in autumn will act as an insulator. I dislike using hardiness zones because pure temperature is only part of the story, but this is certainly fine with no protection to zone 7.

Dracunculus vulgaris

Reminiscent of *Arisaema* in many ways, the jug-shaped flowers in early to midsummer are actually rather magnificent, greenish on the outside but a rich burgundy colour inside. The leaves are like a segmented umbrella, the whole thing reaching almost 1m tall. They are rather amusing in small clumps for accent.

Dryopteris (Dryopteridaceae)

These classic wood ferns are of tremendous value in a woodland garden, with 150 species distributed around the world. Forming dense clumps from thick, often scaly rhizomes, they will thrive with little attention on the woodland floor.

Dryopteris affinis

With handsome, shuttlecock-shaped rosettes of fronds, the stalks are clad in orange scales, giving rise to the common name golden shield fern. The foliage is held well through the winter before literally disintegrating in spring—self-pruning plants save so much time. Many forms are available of this Eurasian fern. 60cm.

Left: *Dryopteris affinis* subsp. *borreri*

Above: *Dryopteris affinis* 'Crispa Barnes'

subsp. *borreri* Forms handsome colonies of dark green fronds.

'Crispa Barnes' Crimped golden-green new fronds develop into a substantial yet tidy colony of crowns.

'Cristata' Sometimes known as 'The King', this selection has graceful drooping fronds with crested pinnae.

'Pinderi' Elegant upright form with narrow, tapering fronds.

Dryopteris bissetiana

Known as the beaded fern due to the unique beaded effect of the triangular fronds, it is evergreen. Since new growth does not start until early to midsummer, it is perfect to take over from spring treasures. 45cm.

Dryopteris carthusiana

Distributed through the northern temperate zone, it often grows in swamps. Although it will tolerate a range of conditions, it clearly thrives with ample moisture, where it can become invasive. Drier conditions will contain its exuberance. Sometimes known as the fancy fern, aptly referring to the finely divided fronds, which potentially grow to 1m long; it is a favourite among flower arrangers.

Dryopteris championii

Evergreen fronds of this Oriental fern remain upright through the winter, giving much needed structure to the woodland floor. Remarkably weather resistant, at their best, fronds are dark and glossy. As with so many in this genus, they will tolerate dry soils to good effect but will spread more rapidly, producing much lusher growth in moister sites. 1m.

Dryopteris crassirhizoma

From Asia, solitary vase-shaped crowns are normally produced rather than clumps. Thick textured, almost tropical in appearance and semi-evergreen, the fronds remain green in winter but lie flat on the ground, making a wonderful insulating natural mulch for potentially more tender neighbours—perfect for arisaemas perhaps, which have the strength to push up through the decaying fronds, but delicate early spring risers could be smothered by their warm embrace. 1m.

Dryopteris cristata

This rare British native is not as crested as the name implies.

Dryopteris cycadina

It is amazing how much textural variation as well as colour is seen among ferns which are essentially green. Another exotic-looking Chinese species with semi-evergreen, heavily textured, dark green foliage, this one is notable for the black hairs on the back of the stipe (stem).

Dryopteris dilatata

A large fern with vast wild distribution, through North America, Eurasia (including Britain), and even South Africa, from which it has evolved to be exceedingly adaptable to differing conditions. Semi-evergreen according to climate, it is large at nearly 1m tall, with a number of smaller growing variants. Various of the names included here describe physical characteristics, and other forms exist, combining these features and names (for example, 'Lepidota Crispa Cristata', finely divided, crisped, and crested).

'Crispa Whiteside' Smaller growing, paler green in colour and evenly crisped. 35cm.

'Grandiceps' Heavily crested.

'Lepidota Cristata' Finely divided crested fronds give a lacy appearance.

'Recurvata' Fronds become almost tubular as the pinnae recurve.

Dryopteris erythrosora

This Oriental fern is one of my favourites, since new copper-red fronds emerge in early summer to create a colourful mix with mature green fronds. 95cm.

'Brilliance' Selected form with even richer colour.

var. *prolifica* Dwarf form with cinnamon-red new growth, but, amusingly, new plantlets are produced along the edge of the lacy, slightly crinkled fronds. 30cm.

var. *purpurascens* Sometimes classified as a species in its own right (*D. purpurella*), this one is majestic. As colourful as the species, but twice the size.

Dryopteris filix-mas 'Crispa Cristata'

Dryopteris filix-mas

The easily grown male fern is widely distributed through the northern temperate zone. Usually deciduous unless the climate is mild, in optimum conditions, it can make a whopping 150cm tall. Fortunately, many of the variants are significantly more compact.

'Barnesii' Elegant tall form with narrow leaflets.

'Crispa' Crisped fronds with densely overlapping leaflets. 50cm. 'Crispa Cristata' is crisped and crested.

Cristata Group The most crested forms have been given cultivar names. 'Cristata Martindale' has small crests on leaflets which curve towards the tip of the frond. 60cm.

'Grandiceps Wills' Found in the wild in 1870, displaying tassled terminal crests and leaflets. 70cm.

'Linearis' Slender crisped, finely divided leaflets. 'Linearis Polydactyla' has additional branching with forked and crested pinnae, the result being both complex and airy.

Dryopteris filix-mas
'Linearis'

'Parsley' An American selection with crinkled and crested fronds. 50 cm.

Dryopteris goldiana

In this American species, the fiddleheads are brown, developing into 120cm long, dark green fronds. This majestic evergreen fern loves moisture but tolerates drought. That really sums up this wonderful genus.

Dryopteris marginalis

This is considered a weed in its native United States, only because it is so tough and adaptable. The tidy, evergreen, vase-shaped clumps are 60cm wide by 45cm tall.

Dryopteris sieboldii

With so many ferns, the differences are subtle or by virtue of assorted crests and crinkles. This one from Japan and Korea is unique. Usually deciduous unless particularly protected, the leaflets are thick, leathery, and almost straplike; more akin to *Cyrtomium* than *Dryopteris*.

Dryopteris tokyoensis

Of similar distribution, this little-known gem forms clumps of upright fronds. The fern's neatness makes it easy to plant other woodlanders around and under it without fear of their being suffocated. 60cm.

Dryopteris uniformis

An elegant, amenable Oriental evergreen with yellowish green new fronds which recurve outwards.

'Cristata' Crested variant. 60cm.

Dryopteris wallichiana

This elegant, vase-shaped fern has yellow-green new fronds that contrast well with the black, hairy midrib and stems. Widespread natural distribution as apparently diverse as the Orient, South America, Africa, Madagascar, and even Hawaii. It needs humus-rich soil which remains moist in summer. 100cm.

Epimedium (Berberidaceae)

Native of two discrete zones, Asia and the Mediterranean, epimediums have been grown ornamentally in Western gardens since the nineteenth century. Inevitably, the newer introductions are considered the most desirable and indeed many are exquisite; the evergreens benefit from shelter from cold winter winds, so woodland protection is perfect. The older, traditional selections are extremely resilient with robust leaves and durable rhizomes, so many will survive in dry shade; though, of course, they will do better in a more hospitable area of the woodland floor. Sometimes planting in difficult conditions can be a method of damping the exuberance of a vigorous spreader and it is often a shame to waste perfect conditions on a more tolerant species. Something choicer always awaits that special location.

Some epimediums are deciduous, others are evergreen; some form tidy clumps only slowly, while others spread at varying rates by shallow, creeping underground runners. These will cover the ground with their magnificent foliage, suppressing the weeds and providing a backdrop to other more ephemeral plants. Some of my favourites have wonderfully shaped leaves which are dramatic as they unfurl, being tinted and mottled in shades of copper and burgundy. The deciduous species often have smaller, apparently more delicate new leaves and display vibrant autumn colours before they die back for their winter rest. If circumstances allow, old growth can be removed in spring to make the emerging leaves and flowers more visible, but this is not practical on substantial areas of woodland planting and can make a natural area look too manicured. Cutting back also takes away the plant's natural protection against late frost.

My preference is for species in which the flowers are held above the leaves, where they are more easily admired; they are usually held in racemes containing a variable number of flowers from just a few to more than 100. These flowers consist, in simple terms, of three layers: an inner cup of petals, four inner sepals, and four outer sepals. Think of them as layers 1, 2, and 3, where 1 is the innermost layer, 2 is the inner sepal layer, and 3 is the outer sepals. It is the varying level of development of these layers which gives the flowers their characteristic but differing shapes, while the layers need not all be the same colour. Sometimes a layer is so underdeveloped as to almost cease to exist (layer 3 often falls soon after opening); in others, two layers have fused together to appear as a multicoloured whole. Layer 2 is of varying size. Layer 1 forms the major part of the flower and can comprise four simple petals, or petals can extend at the top into spurs of varying length protruding beneath layer 2; this inverted crownlike shape has given rise to one common name, bishop's hat. In the centre is a cluster of stamens; sometimes it is invisible within a cup-shaped layer 1, at the other extreme the inner layer of petals is effectively absent, with a flower resembling a shooting star, with long exserted stamens protruding beyond the petals.

All epimediums are beautiful; space necessitates that I make these descriptions somewhat clinical in an endeavour to simplify the complicated flower structure and to convey their differences. Botanically dodgy but descriptively revealing, I will adopt my layer analogy to describe the flowers.

Vine weevils are fond of epimediums; the adult beetle can notch the leaves while the larvae can strip away the feeder roots. However, it is not generally terminal in garden situations on established clumps where the roots regenerate faster than they are being eaten. It is worth checking newly acquired plants to make sure you are not planting any of the wretched pests with them.

Epimedium campanulatum

Lots of pure primrose-yellow flowers are held like bells above the leaves. The inner layer 1 forms the bell while layer 2 is tiny and spurless. It will creep, but very slowly. Long, tapering leaflets are prettily mottled with red as they unfurl. *Epimedium platypetalum* and *E. ecalcaratum* are similar.

Epimedium davidii

First described in western Sichuan by the French missionary Père David in 1869, it was not until 1985, when Chinese regulations were relaxed, that botanist Martyn Rix returned to the same location and introduced it to cultivation. It is clump-forming, so slow to increase. The gorgeous flowers are the most intense golden yellow imaginable. Layer 2 is small and distinctly red flushed. Layer 1 forms a deep cup but is modified into downward pointing spurs. The leaves are relatively small and quite spiny, but beautifully flushed red when young. *Epimedium fangii* is similar but with straight petal spurs and a more creeping rhizome. In the same group, the more delicate *E. flavum* is distinguished by yellow inner sepals (layer 2).

Above: *Epimedium davidii*

Right: *Epimedium epsteinii*

Epimedium diphyllum

This was the first Japanese species to reach Europe in the 1830s, having a very distinctive flower. Layer 1 petals are "normal", in as much as they have no spurs and do not overlap. Layer 2 is barely different, so the overall effect is of a pretty, dangling, somewhat shaggy white flower. The young arrowhead-shaped leaflets are slightly folded inwards down their edges and a rich brown in colour. These mature to green with an almost silvery tone through the major veins. Deciduous.

Epimedium epsteinii

First described as recently as 1994, this large (to 3cm across) bicoloured flower is impressive. Layer 1 petals are chocolate-purple, creating a bell-like centre before extending into four long spurs. Above these, layer 2 has large, broad, and almost pure white sepals—hence the dramatic contrast. Emerging from a gently creeping rhizome, the pointed, spiny green leaves are prettily flushed with copper in spring.

Epimedium fargesii

A dainty species, the flowers on tall stems to 50cm remind me of *Dodecatheon*; the central cluster of long stamens, then the tiny purple layer 1, and the long, narrow, white layer 2 sepals are all strongly reflexed. Capping it all until fully open is the violet-tinged layer 3. *Epimedium dolichostemon* is similar, differing by shorter, straight layers 1 and 2—the whole effect therefore is less swept-back.

'Pink Constellation' Darker flowers due to layer 2 being pink.

Epimedium grandiflorum

This was the first long-spurred species to be cultivated in European gardens in the early nineteenth century and was to remain the only one until a century and a half later. Knowing the interest surrounding the current rash of introductions, it is easy to imagine the excitement this must have created in 1830. The extensive distribution of this species explains the diversity of flower colour now known. Deciduous, the new leaves are small and soft on emergence from the clump-forming rootstock in spring. In many selections, the almost lime-green leaf is conspicuously margined with red, fading to mid-green with maturity before taking on orange and red tints in autumn. The bell-like layer 1 tapers to long, arching spurs. Layer 2 is fairly narrow and flattened over these spurs. Layer 3 falls as the flower opens, but the sepals' red flush contrasts beautifully with the bud in the white-flowered cultivars.

Epimedium grandiflorum 'Saturn'

'Lilafee' Low-growing selection with rich purple-flushed foliage and purple flowers.

'Nanum' The tiniest of the epimediums we grow, it does not spread by underground rhizomes. White flowers contrast prettily with the red-rimmed new leaves.

'Saturn' and 'Sirius' Larger equivalents of 'Nanum' with white and palest pink flowers, respectively.

f. *violaceum* Intense reddish pink flower colour. A number of named forms have been selected from the variable wild populations in many shades of pink, but I enjoy the reddish tinge to this one. In some, the spurs of layer 1 are white at the tips and suffused with white at the centre.

'Yellow Princess' Delightful selection with pale primrose-yellow flowers.

Epimedium latisepalum

The effect of the huge flowers, up to eight per raceme, each of which can be up to 5cm across, is white, but layer 1 (which extends into substantial spurs) is speckled and flushed with green and cream. Layer 2 has pure white and broad sepals, reflexing slightly to display the spurs below. Not to be outdone, the almost blue-green foliage is handsome, too, being leathery in substance and conspicuously glaucous beneath. Spreads slowly but is very impressive.

Epimedium leptorrhizum

It is easy to be swept along on the tide of new introductions and forget the species which are long established in cultivation. This one was first collected in 1898. The huge flowers always seem too big for its modest stature, but it is a pretty thing, forming a dense carpet of heavily textured leaves close to the ground. Yellow stamens hang below the pale pinky white spurs of layer 1, topped by the pretty pink, long spurs of layer 2. *Epimedium brachyrrhizum* is a gorgeous larger, more vigorous, recently discovered (1997) clump-forming equivalent, with darker flowers and beautifully copper-flushed young foliage.

Epimedium membranaceum

Starting in midspring, it can still be blooming in late summer. Amazing. As many as 35 vivid, golden yellow flowers can be held per raceme above bright green, strongly ever-green leaves which are superbly marked with chocolate-purple when young. There is no real bell-like centre to these flowers; layer 1 tapers from a swollen base into long, horn-like spurs which can almost meet beneath the flower. Layer 2 sepals are also long and narrow over the spurs, flushed with reddish purple. *Epimedium rhizomatosum* is similar but with longer, running rhizomes and a shorter, denser flower spike with fewer individual flowers. Its leaves have more spines.

Epimedium ogisui

Unique in such a vast genus, this one is guaranteed to grab your attention in spring when the large, pure white flowers (physically similar to *E. latisepalum*) stand out against the richest bronze-purple young leaves. These eventually mature to green. The whole plant is of shorter stature and spreads slowly to form a dense carpet.

Epimedium pauciflorum

A dear little chap whose appearance belies a modest description. Very low growing to 15cm or so, the foliage produced in profusion from creeping rhizomes is reminiscent of miniature holly leaves. The comparatively small flowers are a delicate silver-pink. The bell-like element of layer 1 flares slightly at the mouth, while extending also into arching spurs beneath an elegant layer 2.

Epimedium brachyrrhizum

Epimedium ogisui

Epimedium perralderianum

Similar and closely related to *E. pinnatum* subsp. *colchicum*, these two species grew together en masse at what was to become the Royal Horticultural Society's Garden at Wisley. Seedlings were noticed and grown on to become the hybrid *E. ×perralchicum*, of which two cultivars are recognised: 'Frohnleiten' and 'Wisley'. They are extremely similar and have the vigour and resilience to overcome much drier conditions.

Epimedium pinnatum subsp. colchicum

This subspecies is the more commonly available and refers to geographical and minor botanical variation rather than anything aesthetically distinct. This could be considered an ordinary species, yet its durability and tolerance make it growable in a wide range of conditions. The evergreen leaves are tough and leathery, while the flowers are a penetrating yellow. They are held among the leaves, but the outward-facing flowers are open

Above: *Epimedium pubescens*

Right: *Epimedium myrianthum*

and their colour is such that they are easily visible. Layer 1 are yellow in the centre with short, squat brown spurs in stark contrast to the rounded sepals of layer 2. Roy Lancaster has made available one of his accessions under the collection number L321, which maintain red layer 3 sepals as further contrast. 'Black Sea' develops rich black tinges to the winter foliage; superb against white flowers such as snowdrops.

Epimedium pubescens

Somehow I would have expected this to be one of the new flush of introductions, so I was quite surprised to discover that it was first described in 1877. Up to 30 tiny flowers float in their racemes above gorgeous reddish brown young leaves. The long central stamens are surrounded by a curiously abrupt and blunt, orange brown layer 1. The airy feel of the flowers is given by the pure white layer 2, with long and thin sepals, extending far beyond layer 1. The conspicuous purple sepals of layer 3 encase the flower bud, being displaced as layer 2 extends to horizontal. Gently creeping.

Epimedium myrianthum, *E. stellulatum*, and its cultivar 'Wudang Star' are other variations on this theme which are worthy of a place. Closely related *E. sagittatum* also benefits from richly coloured arrowhead-shaped young growth.

Epimedium pubigerum

We should not choose only the gaudiest flowers; bigger is not always best. This Eurasian species was introduced in 1881. It is so pretty, the lightness of the flower spike so natural in the woodland calm. The underside of the more rounded, paler green leaflets are quite hairy. The yellow petals of layer 1 are tiny, with the broader layer 2 hanging down almost around them in a slightly open cup shape. Layer 2 is essentially white but daintily flushed with deep red from the base.

Epimedium sempervirens

This is the evergreen equivalent of *E. grandiflorum* from the opposite (western) side of Japan; it is similar florally, with both whites and pinks known.

Epimedium ×versicolor

Perhaps not the most exciting epimedium, it has a supreme ability to survive in harsher, more exposed conditions. The result of a cross between *E. grandiflorum* and *E. pinnatum* subsp. *colchicum*, several named cultivars exist. Autumn colour is spectacular on this hybrid and is retained long into the winter, by virtue of one deciduous parent and the other evergreen. They almost never lose their leaves, but they do get tatty by spring, so it can be worth tidying them up prior to flowering.

    '**Sulphureum**' Dumpy but clearly evident yellow bells from layer 1 extend into shortish spurs below a broader cream-coloured layer 2.

Epimedium wushanense

Epimedium ×warleyense

Ellen Ann Willmott was a great English gardener active at the start of the twentieth century. A hybrid between *E. alpinum* and *E. pinnatum* subsp. *colchicum* arose at Great Warley and was named thus after her Essex garden. Wonderful open, orange flowers derived from the broad, rounded layer 2 dominating the tiny, short-spurred yellow layer 1.

Epimedium wushanense

Arguably the most remarkable species, its long, arrow-shaped leaflets can be as much as 13cm long and are outstanding in spring with vivid reddish purple mottling. As many as 100 flowers can be held on tall racemes extending 1m into the air. Everything is impressive about this plant, including the large yellow flowers (up to 4cm across). Spreading by underground rhizomes, this species is worthy of space for its foliage alone.

    '**Caramel**' Layer 1 has no cup as such, becoming long,

almost horizontal spurs, giving the appearance that the caramel-coloured flowers are hovering in the air. The small layer 2 sepals are pale green suffused with pale red.

Epimedium ×youngianum

The cross between *E. diphyllum* and *E. grandiflorum* is very much intermediate between its parents. All are clump-forming and deciduous, with vibrant autumn colours. The inner layer 1 has the same shagginess as *E. diphyllum* but with a hint of a spur, while layer 2 sepals are a little flatter and broader.

'**Merlin**' Perhaps the deepest colours, all sepals and petals are rich purple-pink, shading to white and pink at the base.

'**Niveum**' Pure white contrasts beautifully against reddish brown young leaves.

'**Yenomoto**' Palest pinky white.

Above: *Epimedium ×youngianum* 'Merlin'

Right: *Epimedium ×youngianum* 'Niveum'

Eranthis (Ranunculaceae)

Just a handful of species of these tuberous rhizomes is distributed from western Europe to Japan, flowering best following low temperatures. What a wonderful splash of colour winter aconites bring, with their cheerful bright yellow flowers, like buttercups, held on short stems above prettily divided foliage, perhaps pushing up through a late sprinkling of snow. They thrive in humus-rich, free-draining soil, protected from the rigours of the winter and excess summer moisture by a dense canopy. Plant them in drifts across the woodland floor, where they can be succeeded by other treasures as spring comes to life or at the base of a mature tree. Wherever planted, they are natural companions to the pure white of snowdrops and the leafy shelter of small evergreen ferns.

The rhizomes do not like to desiccate when dormant and can be difficult to re-establish if allowed to dry out at the time of lifting. For this reason they are often sold in the green in the same way as snowdrops. Winter aconites are extremely toxic. I once read that in Cheshire, a lady died in 1822, having muddled her plants and used their roots to make a horseradish sauce.

Eranthis cilicica

From Turkey east to Afghanistan, this species is sometimes classified as a form of *E. hyemalis*. More finely divided foliage and larger flowers.

Eranthis hyemalis

The classic winter aconite is native to southern Europe, though it has naturalised across much of the continent.

'**Flore Plena**' Double flowers.

'**Orange Glow**' Richer, deeper coloured.

Eranthis pinnatifida

This Japanese species is distinctive because the flowers are white. Although perfectly hardy, they flower so early, still very much in winter, that the protection of small evergreens will minimise their battering.

Eranthis ×tubergenii

This is the general classification for the sterile hybrids between *E. cilicica* and *E. hyemalis*.

'**Guinea Gold**' The original Dutch selection has large, golden-yellow flowers over deeply divided bronze-flushed foliage.

Erythronium (Liliaceae)

Variously known as trout lily, reflecting the marbled patterns on the leaves, and dog's tooth violet, which aptly describes the shape of the bulbous rhizome of *E. dens-canis*, despite it being unrelated to violets. Although also found in Europe and Asia, many of the best species for naturalising originate from North America, where the genus is widespread. Flowering-size plants have two leaves, with a slim flower stem growing up between them, while less mature plants sport a single leaf. The hanging bells have six petals, strongly reflexing on warm spring days to reveal a contrastingly coloured throat or long stamens, in shades of white, cream, and yellow to pink.

They have a reputation for being difficult to grow; I remember, as a teenager, killing my first erythronium, a "souvenir" from Knightshayes, with kindness. Although some are snowmelt plants requiring specialist conditions, many are perfectly amenable to cultivation in well-drained, humus-rich soil on the woodland floor. All are beautiful, most are worth the effort, but those included here are the easiest to grow and the fastest to naturalise. Try the other species in special spots on the woodland rock garden; they are too captivating to ignore.

The bulbs have no protective tunic and are vulnerable to changes in humidity. They need to be planted deeper than one would expect; shallow planting can result in desiccation in a dry summer or simply prolific multiplication at the expense of flower. Thus dormant bulbs out of the ground for any length of time and allowed to dry out will be hard to resuscitate. Indeed initial establishment is often the greatest hurdle to overcome; unless obtained fresh from a specialist grower, it is often best to buy them potted, in active growth.

Erythronium californicum

Mottled brown leaves contrast with typical white flowers, three or more per stem. These have a greenish yellow centre, usually highlighted with yellow, orange or brown markings. Although an excellent plant for humus-rich soil in moist woodlands, it can be slow to colonise.

'White Beauty' In contrast, this selection, made by respected nurseryman Carl Purdy from his wild collections at the turn of the twentieth century, clumps up pleasingly rapidly. The creamy white flowers are conspicuously marked internally with reddish brown zig-zags.

Erythronium dens-canis

This European species is tolerant of slightly moister conditions than its American cousins. Lower growing, the smaller bulbs produce offsets freely, clumping up at an enviable rate. Pink flowers are held above often beautifully mottled leaves, though whites and purples abound among the many named selections.

'Old Aberdeen' My favourite cultivar with the most dramatically mottled leaves and deep violet-purple reflexing petals.

'Pink Perfection' Paler pink, broader petals held flatter, with an almost white throat.

'Purple King' Large pinkish purple flowers are stained red in the centres.

'Snowflake' Strongly reflexing white petals with a chartreuse base and a faint ring of red.

'White Splendour' The petals of this white are held flatter.

Above left: *Erythronium dens-canis* 'Old Aberdeen'

Above: This *Erythronium revolutum* hybrid is delightfully surrounded by dainty *Narcissus cyclamineus.*

Left: *Erythronium revolutum* 'Knightshayes Pink'

Erythronium oregonum

Although visually similar to *E. californicum*, this neighbouring species is often easier to naturalise as its more varied native habitat results in a greater tolerance of growing conditions. It increases nicely and self-seeds where happy.

> **subsp.** *leucandrum* Distinguished by the colour of the anthers – white as opposed to yellow in the species.

Erythronium revolutum

Arguably the best and loveliest erythronium for naturalising, it liberally self-seeds. Pink flowered, with lots of tonal variation in both flower and foliage.

> **'Knightshayes Pink'** This selection from the colonies at Knightshayes Court, Devon, reliably produces large, dark pink flowers.

Erythronium cultivars

Erythroniums are extremely promiscuous, hybridising readily with other species from the same continent. As a result, cultivar parentage is often uncertain, though many involve *E. californicum*, *E. revolutum*, and *E. tuolumnense*. Tissue culture techniques render these selections more widely available than seed-grown species. The hybrids are self-sterile, meaning that although they will cross enthusiastically with other forms, seed will not be produced within an isolated planting of a single clone.

'Citronella' This sturdy hybrid inherits the stature of yellow, shy-flowering *E. tuolumnense*, producing up to 10 magnificent creamy yellow flower spikes with great mottled leaves. 35cm. 'Kondo' and 'Pagoda' are similar.

Above: *Erythronium* 'Citronella'

Right: *Erythronium tuolumnense*

Euonymus (Celastraceae)

This large and diverse genus is widely distributed globally. Easily cultivated, *Euonymus* species fall into two categories: the well-known multicoloured evergreens and the more discreet deciduous species. The latter are of interest for the woodland. The largest can be grown as small trees tough enough to provide the upper canopy for small-scale new planting, while any can fit into the larger woodland landscape as middle canopy or even smaller. The early summer flowers are rather inconspicuous, but they give rise to spectacular seedpods which open to reveal a brightly coloured seed suspended within. Coupled with dazzling autumn colour, they perform an exuberant show before winter sets in. These plants are underrated and underplanted.

The eggs of the broad bean black fly (*Aphis fabae*) overwinter on *E. europaeus* and *E. hamiltonianus*. Other species are not troubled in Britian. Euonymus scale is of considerable irritation in the United States.

Euonymus alatus

Corky wings distinguish the stems of this large Asian shrub. I find it rather lanky and

*Euonymus alatus
'Compactus' autumn
colour*

prefer the more compact forms, all exhibiting some of the best fluorescent pinky red autumn colours.

'Compactus' Compact rather than dwarf, this extremely slow grower can eventually gain deceptive height. Corky wings are almost absent.

'Rudy Haag' Dwarf American selection to 1.5m.

'Timber Creek' This superb 1995 selection reaches about 3m in 15 years. The most prolific fruiting form.

Euonymus americanus

Upright thicket forming to 2m, the fruits are distinctive. Imagine a marble-sized, rich red, sweet chestnut case and you are nearly there. It opens to reveal the usual scarlet-orange seeds. Common names abound; my favourite is hearts-a-busting.

Euonymus bungeanus

This large shrub or small tree has a much greater elegance than some of the other, more chunky species.

'Dart's Pride' Subtle toning through the many shades of autumn. The creamy pink fruit are smaller than some but perfectly in proportion to the leaves and character.

*Euonymus bungeanus
'Dart's Pride' autumn
colour*

Euonymus cornutus

A smaller and more visually delicate Chinese species with narrow leaves and yellow autumn colour.

Euonymus cornutus var. *quinquecornutus*

Euonymus europaeus 'Red Cascade' autumn colour and fruit

var. *quinquecornutus* The fruits are remarkable, with five or six hornlike projections giving them the appearance of jesters' hats.

Euonymus europaeus

The Eurasian spindleberry is widespread through British hedgerows. Scarlet capsules open to reveal orange seeds. Assorted clones have been selected to maximise the autumn display of both fruit and leaf colour.

    'Red Cascade' Phenomenal plant with purplish red stems, unsurpassed red autumn colour, and masses of fruit.

Euonymus grandiflorus

Sino-Himalayan, my favourite species appears more like a camellia in summer, with large, thick, glossy leaves. The flowers are large, too, giving way to red seeds within

Euonymus grandiflorus 'Red Wine' shimmers under a hard frost.

Euonymus hamiltonianus 'Rising Sun'

Euonymus hamiltonianus 'Popcorn'

Euonymus hamiltonianus 'Winter Glory'

straw-coloured seedpods. The burgundy-red autumn colour starts later and lasts long into winter. Magnificent.

'Red Wine' Compact, shrubby form with narrow leaves.

Euonymus hamiltonianus

Vigorous species with large, often slightly rolled leaves. Usually yellow autumn colour can be brief, though fruiting is often spectacular.

'Indian Summer' The best for autumn colour, but turning late in the season so in full glory from midautumn until early winter. Dark pink fruit.

'Popcorn' White fruit capsules.

'**Rainbow**' Yellow variegated leaves.

'**Rising Sun**' In my garden, the most spectacular in fruit. Vivid red capsules contrast with green leaves.

subsp. *sieboldianus* '**Coral Charm**' Young stems are a pretty coral-pink in winter. Yellow autumn colour and pink fruit.

'**Snow**' White variegation.

'**Winter Glory**' One of a number selected for prolific pink fruits.

Euonymus oxyphyllus
'Waasland'

Euonymus latifolius

Upright European species which turns the brightest orange early in the autumn, with large scarlet fruits. *Euonymus planipes* is similar.

Euonymus oxyphyllus

An excellent Asiatic species developing rich, purple-flushed, red autumn colour following substantial red seedpods. The bright orange seeds contrast with their purple interiors.

'**Waasland**' Selected at the Belgian arboretum of the same name for the quality and reliability of its fruiting.

Euonymus tingens

Wonderful evergreen species reminiscent of its deciduous cousins, or even an osmanthus, except for the distinctive pink fruits. So effective against the glossy foliage.

Euphorbia (Euphorbiaceae)

With some 1600 species of *Euphorbia*, perhaps fortunately, most are found in sunny places, rendering them unsuitable for our requirements. Inevitably in such a large, widely distributed genus, some are adaptable to our shaded woodland floor, though most of these will benefit from only a lightly shaded position to prevent them becoming too leggy. They typically form evergreen clumps of tufted, leafy stems in the first year, before sending up a flowering stem in their second. Many send out underground rhizomes to become large patches. Their flowers are rather peculiar, being composed of horned glands rather than typical petals; essentially the ornamental parts are bracts behind the true flowers, which is why they are able to last for so long. Euphorbias display an amazing diversity of colour, with every shade of green, orange, and even blue.

The milky sap is notoriously caustic, particularly in sunlight. Exercise extreme care when working with them.

Euphorbia amygdaloides

This British native's habitat extends through Europe to North Africa and the Caucasus. Its long, narrow leaves clothe the deep purple upright stems and are often flushed with purple. The contrasting bracts are a pale green and commence in early spring before the trees come into leaf. With adequate light and moisture, flowering can continue until late summer. 80cm.

'**Golden Glory**' The bracts of this cultivar are as luminous as the best forms of *E. polychroma*, highlighted as they are against the darker leaves of a robust and stocky plant. Happy in shade and mildew-resistant.

var. *robbiae* Previously classified as a species in its own right, it remains a classic plant for dry shade. Low growing, with broader, darker green leaves, it spreads by underground runners. It grows well in difficult dry shade. Very heavy shade will suppress its flowering, but for me that is no bad thing as it looks tidier without, providing a lovely backdrop to taller spring bulbs pushing up through the leafy rosettes.

Euphorbia polychroma

(Previously *E. epithymoides*) My favourite woodland species is found in the scrubby woods of southeastern Europe. The mid-green leafy stems are topped by heads of acid-yellow bracts in mid to late spring. This makes a vivid combination with blue spring bulbs, *Brunnera*, *Omphalodes*, *Scilla*, and even the faithful *Myosotis*, lighting up the woodland floor. 40cm.

'**Candy**' Tremendous new introduction with rich reddish purple stems and foliage; what a combination against those almost yellow bracts. It needs some sun to show off its colouring, so it is best in an area of high canopy or a distinct clearing. 'Sonnengold' is similar.

Euphorbia polychroma and Scilla bithynica look spectacular together, combining acid-greens and blues.

'**Lacy**' The leaves are broadly margined in creamy white, so it benefits from the woodland shade. However, the intensity of colour has been lost from the bracts, leaving them essentially cream-coloured, which for me diminishes the effect. There is no arguing its ability to brighten a dull corner. Sometimes erroneously referred to as 'Variegata'. 'First Blush' is a new introduction, adding a pink flush through foliage and bracts.

'**Major**' Widely available selection that is slightly larger in all its parts. This may or may not be an advantage, according to where it is to be planted.

'**Midas**' Selected for the exceptional quality of the chartreuse bracts.

Euphorbia cultivars

E. amygdaloides var. *robbiae* is no longer the archetypal plant for difficult dry shade; these new cultivars will be harder to come by, but will surpass it in all respects.

'**Blue Lagoon**' A brand new hybrid between *E. amygdaloides* var. *robbiae* and *E.* 'Jade Dragon' with exceptional potential. Neat mounds of almost blue foliage are touched with red on the new growth, giving way to waves of acid-yellow bracts which last for months, before fading to a light burnt orange. Best of all is its tolerance of dry shade and its gently creeping nature.

'**Orange Grove**' This recent selection (*E. amygdaloides* 'Golden Glory' × *E. amygdaloides* var. *robbiae*) captures the best of all worlds. Brilliant chartreuse bracts fade to citrus-orange after emerging from the clean, red-tinted new foliage.

Fagus (Fagaceae)

Beech trees make a wonderful upper canopy, but creating a new woodland of them would definitely be planting for posterity. Perhaps a selection can be included within a new framework planting of *Betula*, *Corylus*, and *Crataegus*, for example, accepting that those others will achieve more instant gratification, to be sacrificed as the beech become established. This way the canopy will develop quickly enough to allow planting within it. This small genus of just 10 species from the northern temperate zones, includes innumerable permutations of the European beech.

Fagus grandifolia
Strangely, no selections have been made of this American equivalent of the European *F. sylvatica*, despite its vast populations.

Fagus sylvatica
This species thrives in all soils except those which waterlog. The smaller, slower, more fussy cultivars can be chosen as accent plants beneath established high canopy, and the more robust ones can become the canopy in their own right, though not in small gardens. Purple-leaved forms will need adequate light to maximise their colour, while the yellows may scorch in full sun. It seems that each habit and foliage style is now available in whichever colour is required.

'**Ansorgei**' Gorgeous, almost like a purple form of the *Acer palmatum* Linearilobum Group, with very narrow leaves. Dates back to 1891.

'**Dawyck**' Planting fastigiate trees in woodland is as personal a decision as including variegation. This original green clone was found in the wild in Scotland in 1864. Bred from it in Holland are purple and gold versions.

var. *heterophylla* '**Aspleniifolia**' The classic cut-leaved beech from 1804 becomes a magnificent tree with time. 'Rohanii' is the purple-leaved equivalent, while 'Rohan Gold' is surprisingly vigorous despite its colour.

'**Pendula**' A green weeping selection, with 'Purpurea Pendula' and 'Aurea Pendula' providing the other colour forms. 'Black Swan' and 'Purple Fountain' are narrower, more recent purple clones.

'**Purpurea**' The ubiquitous copper beech. 'Riversii' and 'Spaethiana' hold their darker colour well through summer.

'**Roseomarginata**' Pretty rose-pink border to purple leaves. 'Tricolour' is similar but with a little more cream colour.

'**Zlatia**' Selected from a native stand of *F. moesiaca* in Serbia in 1890. It may therefore belong to that species or it may be a hybrid with *F. sylvatica*. It is a beautiful though fearfully slow tree. The new leaves are a lovely yellow, fading to green through summer but rarely scorching even in full sun on our heavy clay.

Fothergilla (Hamamelidaceae)

It is amusing that nomenclature can become confused even in a genus of just two species. These gorgeous shrubs from the American Southeast dislike chalky soils but are surprisingly tolerant if the structure is right: humus-rich, moisture-retentive in summer, and well-drained in winter. Their fascinating white bottlebrush-like staminoid flowers sit erect in midspring, just before the leaves unfold. Their greatest claim to fame, however, is their spectacular autumn foliage, which can be muted in too shady a site. Woodland planting gives them valuable protection from chilling spring winds and sharp frosts as well as the full intensity of the summer sun. Many selections have been made in North America; sadly few are available in Europe.

Fothergilla gardenii

This small species gently suckers to make a thicket of wiry stems. 1m.

'**Blue Mist**' Widely available in Europe, but a little more demanding in its requirements. Astonishing blue leaves through summer change to purples and oranges in autumn.

Fothergilla major

In its native habitat, it can reach as much as 4m tall; I would expect half that in cultivation in the UK. Basically bigger in all its parts, including flower and leaf, they are a sight to behold in autumn.

Fothergilla 'Mount Airy'

Monticola Group Previously classified specifically, it is now placed in *F. major* as the differences were not sufficiently clear cut, though it is generally smaller.

Fothergilla cultivar

'**Mount Airy**' Selected by Mike Dirr, who rates its vigour and tolerance most highly. Dark blue-green summer foliage develops wonderful autumn colour.

Franklinia alatamaha

Franklinia (Theaceae)

Franklinia is a difficult but exquisite monotypic genus.

Franklinia alatamaha

It is amazing to realise that all trees in cultivation today are derived from John Bartram's original collection in the state of Georgia in 1765. None have been found in the wild since 1791. This species prefers acid soil, though, as so often, the structure is more important than the pH. The large, single white flowers with prominent yellow stamens are produced in late summer when the vibrant, dark green leaves start to develop rich shades of orange and mahogany-red.

Fritillaria (Liliaceae)

This iconic bulbous genus of more than 100 species may not be the most obvious choice for woodland planting, but they are so delightful that space should be found for just a couple. Many exciting new species are appearing from China, with the relaxation of that country's access restrictions, and it may transpire that some of these are suitable for European and North American woodlands, but for now I will stick with the tried and tested. Though they do not have the strength to push up through thick carpets of vegetation, nor to compete with vigorous neighbours, some are perfectly happy in less heavily shaded but well-drained areas of the woodland floor or rock garden. One secret seems to be to plant deep. This protects the bulbs from fluctuations in soil moisture and temperature and promotes flowering rather than just multiplication.

The bulbs are vulnerable, consisting of just one or several thick, fleshy scales from which emerges a single unbranched stem, with the leaves distributed along its length, in whorls or alternate. Immature bulbs produce a single large leaf. They lack a protective tunic so quickly shrivel if allowed to dry out. While in the ground, these are kept at an almost constant temperature and protected from physical damage which could result in a secondary fungal infection. Once lifted, they are at risk from all these outside influences, so they should be planted as soon and therefore as fresh as possible. It is crucial to start with plump and healthy bulbs. It is also important to be certain of the source of these bulbs, to ensure that they have come from cultivated stocks or have been saved from development sites rather than wild collected.

Fritillaries will appeal to those who appreciate subtlety; there is nothing ostentatious about their flowers. Instead they possess a gentle charm. Most are bell-shaped and many are quiet earthy shades of green and purplish brown, harmonising perfectly with the woodland tranquillity.

Most *Fritillaria* species are easily grown from seed, but their rice grain–sized bulblets provide a more rapid alternative in those species where they are produced. Others will bulk up when happy, with the twin-scaled bulbs dividing in half every few years.

Fritillaria acmopetala

This tall, slender species has green outer and purplish inner petals, lending a striped appearance to the bell-shaped flowers, which reflex at the mouth. 45cm.

Fritillaria affinis

Growing under trees up the west coast of North America, this species prefers slightly moister habitats in the spring while the canopy keeps them cool and dry in summer. Enormously variable, they are generally taller growing in woodland conditions, with up to four whorls of leaves. The flowers, substantial bells with clearly separate petals, are also variable; most are chequered with purple patterns to a capricious degree over a chartreuse base. The disc-shaped bulbs are covered with tiny bulblets. 90cm.

> **var. *tristulis*** From open coastal cliffs, this lower growing adaptation is better able to withstand more exposed sites.

Fritillaria camschatcensis

This species is a law unto itself, thriving with underlying moisture, rather than the drainage we rather expect, and flowering later in the spring. The neat bell-shaped flowers may be so dark as to be almost black. Tiny bulblets surround the bulbs, but the plant may also spread by stolons. 75cm.

Fritillaria meleagris

The European native snakeshead fritillary with broad-shouldered, heavily-chequered purple flowers is surprisingly adaptable to soil conditions and superb among poor grass beneath sparse canopy. They follow on well from snowdrops and winter aconites, but I love their simplicity set against dwarf evergreen ferns. 30cm.

Fritillaria meleagris

> **var. *alba*** Beautiful pure white form.

Fritillaria pallidiflora

This species is more robust in appearance; its glaucous stems carry up to five flowers. These conspicuous square-shouldered bells are primrose-yellow. They are happy in moister conditions, requiring a lesser midsummer rest. 65cm.

Fritillaria pontica

The subtle green flowers are highlighted with pinkish brown at their mouths. Good drainage during dormancy is preferable. 45cm.

Fritillaria pyrenaica

This wonderful plant is robust and adaptable to cultivation. The neat, dark purple-brown flowers are noticeably yellow inside, particularly at the flaring mouth. We traveled to the Pyrénées early one summer with the sole purpose of finding the elusive golden form. Unfortunately, we encountered unseasonable weather, being greeted by a significant depth of snow in our campsite. Botanising through knee-deep snow was frustrating though slightly mitigated by the breathtaking scenery. 30cm.

Fritillaria thunbergii

Opposite: *Galanthus elwesii* var. *monostictus* Hiemalis Group emerges through a carpet of fallen leaves in November.

This Asiatic species is widely cultivated for medicinal use even today, but it is equally valuable on a purely aesthetic basis. Slender stems are clothed with tendril-like leaves, which help support them among shrubs, topped with pretty white flowers, delicately veined with green. They should not be kept too dry. 80cm. *Fritillaria verticillata* is similar.

Fritillaria uva-vulpis

Small brownish bells atop tall, thin stems may not make this the prettiest, but it is one of the toughest, clumping up rapidly.

Galanthus (Amaryllidaceae)

Snowdrops have been revered for centuries. Few plants inspire the extremes of passion that the humble snowdrop can generate, and although I would not consider myself as besotted as some, few sights are more welcoming than the first snowdrops of spring, indicating that winter is turning the corner and lighter days will soon follow. One of my favourite combinations to drive away the winter blues is hellebores and snowdrops.

Widely distributed through Europe to Iran, from where *G. plicatus* was introduced in the 1850s by soldiers returning from the Crimean War, snowdrops became fashionable and Victorian plant-hunters went in search of new varieties. This quest continues today. However, they are such simple plants that little scope exists for significant variation; each bulb produces two narrow, tongue-shaped leaves and a stem with a single, hanging bell-shaped flower. These consist of six tepals; the outer three are usually pure white and lightly spreading, while the inner three are much smaller, usually with green markings.

These bulbs love to colonise the base of a hedgerow, appreciating the winter light when active and dryness when dormant. They will be equally at home around the base of a mature tree or creating an early snowy carpet through the woodland floor before

later spring performers emerge. Conventional wisdom dictates that they dislike being mulched. It is probably more accurate to say that too much fertiliser will result in lots of leafy growth at the expense of flowers.

For the woodland floor, it seems to me preferable to choose robust species at modest cost which will seed around, freely naturalising, rather than paying out vast sums for obscure named forms which are only very subtly unique. With little differences between them, it is almost inevitable that nomenclature will be confused.

Overcrowding can result in snowdrops loosing their vigour and flowering becoming sparse. They will benefit from being dug up, the clump divided and replanted. Traditionally sold "in the green", they are best not lifted until the foliage fades. It is a misconception that they dislike disturbance when dormant. This has evolved from the time when snowdrops were dug from the wild, which needed to be carried out when they were active simply because that was when they could be located. They dislike drying out, so at whatever time they are moved, they need replanting as quickly as possible. It is a shame to disturb them when in full growth, as roots will be damaged and energy wasted. New acquisitions should come from cultivated stock, not the wild. Many species are now rare in their native habitats due to greedy collection.

Galanthus elwesii

From the Balkans, this satisfying species has glaucous leaves, one characteristically folded inside the other, and large typical flowers, the inner tepals being well marked. Look out also for 'Fenstead End' and 'Mrs MacNamara'.

'Comet' Fine vigorous selection with tidy "drop-shaped" flowers, often with green tips, selected at the RHS Garden, Wisley.

Galanthus nivalis are dazzling en masse.

'Maidwell L' Large flowers have completely green inner segments. Early flowering.

var. *monostictus* Hiemalis Group This classification is loosely applied to any *G. elwesii* that flowers prior to midwinter, before the leaves are visible. The inner petals are marked with a narrow green inverted V. 'Barnes' is arguably the earliest cultivar of all from this group.

Galanthus nivalis

A traditional icon of winter hope, this snowdrop has naturalised in Britain but is not a native as is popularly assumed.

Though many named snowdrops have a huge desirability aura with their endless subtle variations, including doubles and those with yellow markings, for me it is hard to beat the simplicity of this delightful single. We buy a box of 500 bulbs "as lifted" every spring, establishing them along our deliberately neglected hedgerows among the primroses and bluebells. Few sights are more rewarding or more beautiful.

Galanthus plicatus

This distinctive eastern European species is identifiable by its leaf edges being folded back in the leaf sheath. The outer tepals open out wide, while the inner three are conspicuously marked with a green upside down U shape.

'Three Ships' Reliably flowering here around Christmas, this superb selection has almost horizontally held large, rounded outer tepals over the strongly marked inner three. Found in an abandoned garden in Suffolk.

'Warham' Although named in Norfolk, this excellent form with large flowers and broad leaves is thought to be one of the original Crimean collections.

'Wendy's Gold' The yellow marked forms have always attracted attention; although often weaker growing, this is perhaps the best of them. The white tepals hang from bright yellow ovaries while the inner markings are also yellow.

Galanthus reginae-olgae

A complex species from the Adriatic region; importantly they flower much earlier than traditional snowdrops. Some forms commence as early as October in Britain.

Galanthus rizehensis

From the Black Sea region, this is one of my favourite species, with elegant, deep green, glossy leaves and simple flowers as *G. nivalis*. Preferring a more humus-rich soil than many, so best sited further away from demanding tree roots.

Galanthus cultivars

Hybrid snowdrops will not breed true from seed, so will not naturalise in the same manner as the species. I have included some of the best of the many selections available today.

'Atkinsii' This English form (thought to be a hybrid between *G. nivalis* and *G. plicatus*) dates back to the late nineteenth century and remains one of the best. The substantial pear-shaped flowers with well-defined green markings on the inner tepals appear in midwinter. It colonises well, being clearly visible at a distance on account of its larger, robust stature and silver-centred, glaucous leaves.

Galanthus 'John Gray'

'John Gray' Huge rounded flowers, with a pale green X on the inner segments, are held on arching stems. Early flowering.

'Kingston Double' A double-flowered derivative of *G. elwesii*, with a ruff of inner tepals.

'Magnet' Despite the plethora of new selections, some of the oldest remain the best;

this one from 1888. The early, large flowers sway in the breeze, held away from the stem by a long slender pedicel.

'**S. Arnott**' One of the most popular snowdrops, first seen in public in London in 1951, its statuesque flowers hold their outer petals outwards, to reveal inner ones neatly marked with an inverted V.

Gentiana (Gentianaceae)

The name gentian immediately conjures up images of beautiful, intense blue flowers adorning the mountains of my favourite holiday destination. However, these alpines are not at all suited to our shady woodland floor. *Gentiana* is a surprisingly large genus with around 300 species of annuals and perennials from across the temperate areas of Australasia as well as the northern hemisphere. Putting aside the true alpines, most are meadow plants rather than true woodlanders, so choose a more open position where the canopy is high or sparse. Too much shade will result in straggly growth and lack of flowers.

Gentiana asclepiadea

One of my favourites, this European native flowers profusely in late summer when so much else is looking tired. Known as the willow gentian, owing to its tall, arching stems, which are clothed in pairs of leaves, the flowers are clustered in the leaf axils of the upper third of these. Typically shaped, long and tubular with a flared mouth, the flower colour varies from white through pink, to a slightly lilac shade of the traditional gentian blue (with or without a white throat). Named forms abound to reflect this variation. 100cm.

var. *alba* Gorgeous, pure white flowers.

'**Knightshayes**' From the Turkish form, having a white throat to the blue flower.

'**Pink Swallow**' Pretty pink flowers.

Geranium (Geraniaceae)

The wild cranesbill should not be confused with the colourful patio plants more correctly belonging to the genus *Pelargonium*. This misconception predates 1789, when the two groups were finally separated; to this day, annual pelargoniums are commonly, but incorrectly, also referred to as geraniums. Although about 300 species of *Geranium* exist worldwide, only a small percentage are suitable for the shade of the woodland garden. Planting sun-loving geraniums in shade will result in straggly, untidy plants producing few flowers. Most are typically herbaceous in habit, dormant in winter, and active in summer, requiring an adequately moisture-retentive soil.

Given these conditions, suitable plants will colonise an area and provide a bright

Perennial geraniums are hard to beat in a dense groundcover, even beneath sycamores.

Geranium erianthum 'Neptune'

display of flowers through much of the summer. Some are vigorous to the point of invasive, spreading by means of seed flung far and wide from exploding seed capsules and by underground rhizomes; as always, care should be taken to match the vigour of the plant to the size of the planting area. In tidier quarters, they can benefit from a haircut partway through the season. This can rejuvenate the plant and give a further flush of flower. In wilder areas, nature can take its course. Others can be added in lighter, more open areas, but the plants presented here are the most shade-tolerant.

Geranium aristatum

Hairy geranium from the Balkans, related to the *G. phaeum* group, with nodding reflexed flowers of pale lilac-pink.

Geranium collinum

Resistant to drought so it is particularly good under trees. Colourful spring foliage and clear lavender-pink flowers almost glow in the centre.

Geranium erianthum

Although a meadow plant in its native subalpine habitat, this extremely hardy species is ideally adapted to life on the woodland floor, its "spring-loaded" seed capsules ensuring that it will spread. Flowering commences in late spring, often the first of the blue geraniums, and continues until autumn, when the foliage takes over the display.

'Calm Sea' Pale blue flowers, enhanced by darker veins.

'Neptune' Larger, rich, violet-blue flowers and more spreading habit.

Geranium gracile

From the Caucasus, this one has distinctive crinkled leaves and funnel-shaped pink flowers with a small central white eye. The deeply notched petals have short purple veins. Pale forms are occasionally found. It enjoys cool, humus-rich, moisture-retentive conditions.

Geranium macrorrhizum

From the mountains of southern Europe, this species forms dense mats from fleshy underground rootstocks and thick rhizomes. The usually evergreen leaves are aromatic, being used in the past as a source of oil of geranium, and give surprisingly good autumn colour. Easily grown and tolerant of most conditions, they can seed around rather enthusiastically. The flat flowers in shades of pink and white with prominent stamens are held almost vertically.

'Album' Palest pink to white petals with pink stamens.

'Bevan's Variety' Bold deep magenta and carmine flowers. 'Czakor' is similar.

'Ingwersen's Variety' Pale pink 1929 collection from Montenegro.

'Lohfelden' Very pale pink flowers with dark pink veining.

'Snow Sprite' Pure white flowers.

'Spessart' Dark pink flowers.

'White-Ness' Albino form lacking any red pigmentation; pure white flowers over bright apple green leaves.

Geranium maculatum

This native of eastern North America has deeply lobed leaves and saucer-shaped, up-facing flowers of lilac-pink to brighter pink. Easy to grow on humus-rich, reasonably moisture-retentive soil.

f. *albiflorum* Pure white flowers with golden stamens.

'Beth Chatto' Soft lilac-pink flowers.

'Shameface' Pale pink flowers with a white eye.

Geranium ×monacense

Two highly shade-tolerant species *G. phaeum* and *G. reflexum* combine to produce these hybrids.

var. *anglicum* Lilac-coloured flowers are inherited from *G. phaeum* var. *lividum*.

var. *monacense* The typical form with purplish red flowers, noticeably paler in the centre.

var. *monacense* '**Muldoon**' Handsome dark flowers over mahogany-coloured mottled foliage.

Geranium nodosum

Distributed from the Pyrénées to Serbia, bluish or purplish flowers sit above larger three- or five-lobed glossy evergreen leaves from early summer until late autumn. Tolerant even of dry shade.

'**Svelte Lilac**' Pale lilac with darker veining.

'**Swish Purple**' Although dark lilac-purple, the flowers on reddish wiry stems have a luminosity which illuminates a dark corner.

'**Whiteleaf**' Rich lilac-purple flowers delicately edged in white.

Geranium oreganum

This North American species with showy pink-purple flowers is becoming increasingly rare as destruction of its habitat continues.

Geranium phaeum

This lovely species is widespread through the subalpine woods of Europe and naturalised elsewhere. Large clumps form from thick rhizomes. The distinctive seven- to nine-lobed leaves are often conspicuously spotted with reddish purple, the same colour as the dramatic flowers, which can be almost black. One of the earliest geraniums to flower, it is gorgeous with white spring bulbs or later with variegated hostas.

Geranium phaeum
'Mourning Widow'

'**Calligrapher**' Large lilac flowers with dark edging and patterning above heavily dark blotched leaves.

'**Lily Lovell**' An English garden selection with currently the largest flowers in the species; royal-purple highlighted with a white centre.

var. *lividum* '**Joan Baker**' Pale lavender flowers are typical of var. *lividum*, in this case with a darker centre.

'**Margaret Wilson**' Lilac-purple flowers with white centres over distinctive cream-coloured marbled foliage.

'**Mourning Widow**' Arguably the darkest flowered form, sometimes known simply as a black-flowered selection.

var. *phaeum* The richly mottled foliage is the main feature of this group.

var. *phaeum* '**Langthorns Blue**' Light violet-blue flowers with paler centres above well marked foliage.

var. *phaeum* '**Samobor**' Maroon blotched leaves and maroon flowers.

'**Rose Madder**' Deep pink-red flowers above light green leaves.

'**Stillingfleet Ghost**' White flowers, unmarked foliage.

'**Variegatum**' Even more interesting foliage, adding cream to the green and red of the species, complements handsome maroon flowers with a white eye.

Geranium platypetalum

Handsome species from the Caucasus. Rich purplish blue flowers with darker veining are held over substantial hairy leaves.

Geranium procurrens

A low-spreading species from the Himalayas; pretty magenta-pink flowers with black veining and eye are produced in late summer until frosts. Enjoying moisture-retentive soil, it makes a perfect groundcover through which to grow lilies. However, it can become rampant.

Geranium reflexum

Similar to *G. phaeum* but with narrower, reflexed petals.

Geranium sanguineum

The bloody cranesbill is native from Britain to the Caucasus, where it can scramble through other plants. Easily grown in most conditions, it is tolerant of drought though not the deepest of shade, excellent at the foot of a mature tree where light will be good. The foliage is finely cut and the magenta flowers are produced over a long period.

'**Album**' White flowers.

'**Ankum's Pride**' Superb Dutch selection with large pink flowers enhanced by rich reddish pink veining.

'**Max Frei**' From Germany, this tight, compact plant forms neat round hummocks of deep magenta flowers with a white eye.

var. *striatum* Palest pink flowers highlighted with dark veining over darker green foliage. Beautiful.

'**Vision**' Vigorous with deep green leaves and bright red-purple flowers.

Geranium sylvaticum

The wood cranesbill is widespread through Europe; its tufted rootstock and deep roots prefer soil that is moisture-retentive but well-drained. Flowering prolifically in early summer, colours are varied in the wild. Foliage is again deeply dissected and lobed.

'**Album**' Larger pure white flowers.

'**Amy Doncaster**' The bluest of the *G. sylvaticum* cultivars, highlighted with a white eye. Gorgeous and bold when combined with acid-green *Euphorbia polychroma* or subtle among ferns and *Polygonatum*.

'**Birch Lilac**' Mid-violet flowers. Relatively late into leaf, but flowering over a longer period.

'**Mayflower**' Large, rich violet-blue flowers have a pale eye.

f. *roseum* 'Baker's Pink' Beautiful large, pink, cup-shaped flowers on taller erect stems.

Geranium thunbergii

Lovely species with marbled leaves, distinctively blotched with brown-purple markings. Small flowers may be white to reddish purple. Extremely tolerant of dry shade.

'**Jester's Jacket**' A seed strain; the leaves are even more mottled than usual. It leafs up very early in the season, blooming all summer long. Flowers are conspicuously veined, pale pink in summer turning darker as temperatures cool in autumn.

We planted *Geranium tuberosum* and were delighted when lovely cow parsley joined in.

Geranium tuberosum

Tuberous form with a growth pattern similar to spring bulbs, it is extremely tolerant of summer drought when dormant and superb for underplanting. The earliest geranium to flower (lilac-purple with dark veins) with glaucous feathery foliage which dies away quickly before reappearing in the autumn to remain over winter.

'**Leonidas**' Lovely form with brighter, pinker flowers.

Geranium versicolor

Pretty netted flowers, like a dragonfly's wing, have lacy wine-coloured veining over white petals all summer long. Evergreen in mild climates, the foliage is attractive, with each lobe further incised. Native of southern Europe.

Geranium viscosissimum

From western North America with flat, dark-veined, purplish pink flowers with a white centre.

Geranium 'Ann Folkard'

var. *incisum* (syn. *G. nervosum*) A lime-scented variety with aromatic, slightly toothed roundish leaves. Large purplish pink flowers.

Geranium cultivar

'Ann Folkard' A distinctive, eye-catching plant raised in Lincolnshire in 1963. Bright chartreuse leaves contrast rather shockingly with magenta-purple flowers, highlighted with an almost black eye. A late starter in spring, so bulbs have time to flower around it first.

Glaucidium palmatum var. leucanthum

Glaucidium (Glaucidiaceae)

Now monotypic within its own family (previously classified under *Paeonia* or Ranunculaceae), this lovely Japanese plant enjoys cool, preferably acid, and humus-rich, moisture-retentive pockets of the woodland floor.

Glaucidium palmatum

Large palmate leaves, up to 20cm across, are like umbrellas with pointed lobes, rising from thick rhizomes. The lavender-pink flowers resemble poppies, with a conspicuous boss of golden stamens, nicely held in full view above the leaves in early summer. 30cm.

var. *leucanthum* White flowers.

Gymnocarpium (Woodsiaceae)

Just six species of colony-forming rhizomatous ferns are too vigorous for the woodland rock garden, but they are perfect for gently creeping across the woodland floor.

Gymnocarpium dryopteris

Widely distributed through the northern temperate zone as well as mountains south of that, the oak fern has broad, triangular, triple-headed fronds. Bright yellow-green when young, they rise on slender stems from blackish rhizomes. 35cm.

'**Plumosum**' Lovely form with more substantial fronds caused by the pinnae almost overlapping.

Gymnocarpium oyamense

Distinctive Asian species whose triangular fronds are held at right angles to the stem but lack the three-headed appearance of the others. Instead, the leaflets are broader with the lowest pair pointing slightly downwards towards the creeping rhizome. Distinctive colour, too, being a bright, light but almost blue-green.

Gymnocarpium robertiana

Found almost exclusively on limestone, and widespread through North America as well as Europe and the Caucasus. The central lobe of the three is clearly dominant.

Hacquetia epipactis

Hacquetia (Apiaceae)

This monotypic genus from central Europe is related to cow parsley, though it could hardly be more different in appearance.

Hacquetia epipactis

This clump-forming species is tolerant of most soil types, though it spreads faster in lighter, moister soils, typically to 40cm across, but only 15cm tall and herbaceous in habit. The leaves have five discrete lobes, and each of those is also toothed. The yellow true flowers are tiny and densely packed into a boss, behind which lies usually six lobed green-yellow bracts. It is almost difficult to tell where the leaves end and the bracts begin. First opening in late winter at little more than ground level, successive shoots become taller as the weather warms up. I love it combined with dwarf blue bulbs such as *Scilla* and even *Galanthus*. The acid-green combination makes a wonderful contrast with the stark purity of the little bulbs.

'**Thor**' Both leaves and bracts are broadly margined with creamy white.

Halesia (Styracaceae)

This tiny genus of beautiful small trees is mainly found in the southeastern United States. In late spring they are show-stoppers, known as the silver-bell or snowdrop tree, thanks to the fantastic display of white bell-shaped flowers dangling from all the branches. Naturally found as middle canopy trees, they could be chanced as structural planting where conditions are good and summers not too hot. Summer moisture is essential, though adequate winter drainage is also a requisite.

Halesia monticola var. *vestita* 'Rosea'

Halesia carolina

(syn. *H. tetraptera*) Widespread through the Appalachians, they grow potentially to 10m or more, though often smaller in cultivation. Interesting four-winged fruit follow the spectacular flowers.

'**Rosea**' Pink-flushed flowers. Several clones exist, of differing beauty, confused by the fact that environmental conditions can influence the precise colour.

'**UConn Wedding Bells**' Even more floriferous.

Halesia diptera

Differs from *H. carolina* in being slightly smaller and bushier, flowering two weeks later, with two-winged fruit.

var. *magniflora* The best form, being larger and more prolific in flower.

Halesia monticola

Some authorities, particularly in the United States, include this one under *H. carolina*. It is similar but generally larger in all its parts.

var. *vestita* The biggest of the big as it were; generally the most available form in Britain.

var. *vestita* '**Rosea**' Pink-flushed flowers with the same issues as *H. carolina* mean that identification is confused. However, some clones are definitely better than others.

Hamamelis (Hamamelidaceae)

The witch hazels are a small genus of inimitable shrubs. Few sights and scents are as evocative as these superlative shrubs, flowering their hearts out, their bare branches adorned with exquisitely fragrant spidery flowers in the depths of winter, shrugging off even the worst the weather can throw at them. Selection has given us an extended range of colours and flowering period, from early winter through to early spring. Lovely autumn colour, generally golden yellow, hints at the glory soon to unfold.

I would always buy a grafted plant of a named cultivar. Unfortunately, even some supposed cultivars have been propagated from seed, and therefore inferior plants do occur in the trade.

Hamamelis ×*intermedia*

Uncertain origin and parentage have placed most cultivars in this group. Hybrid vigour gives some of these the potential to reach 5m or more, though only after many years.

'**Angelly**' Recent bright yellow Dutch selection blooms in late winter to early spring. Vigorous, upright vase shape.

'**Arnold Promise**' Selected at the Arnold Arboretum of Harvard University. Clear yellow flowers bloom late winter to midspring, dependent on seasonal factors. Bushier, freely branching habit.

'**Diane**' The best red, but a bronzy red, from Kalmthout Arboretum in Belgium. Blooms in late winter.

'**Jelena**' Also from Kalmthout; large flowers are reddish at the base, orange in the middle, and yellow tipped, appearing coppery orange. 'Aurora' is a similarly coloured recent selection with thinner petals.

Hamamelis ×*intermedia* 'Angelly'

'**Moonlight**' Sweet perfume is reminiscent of its *H. mollis* parentage. Pale creamy flowers.

'**Pallida**' (previously *H. mollis* 'Pallida') Perhaps the best known and still one of the most desirable. Sulphur-yellow flowers with a glorious scent.

Hamamelis mollis

The great Ernest Wilson is often honoured with the introduction of this species from China in the early 1900s, though in fact it was first collected in 1879 by Charles Maries, a British plant-hunter employed by London nursery firm James Veitch & Sons. Sweetly scented golden yellow flowers in late winter typify the attraction of the genus.

'**Coombe Wood**' The sole plant of that original Maries collection to survive to maturity was named thus; today it is still a worthy cultivar. Spreading habit.

'**Goldcrest**' A basal claret stain suffuses the large, rich golden flowers, later than other forms.

Hamamelis vernalis

This North American species cannot compete with *H. mollis* for flower power, but it does produce spectacular autumn colours when conditions suit. Indeed they colour more reliably in colder climes. The commencement of flowering (individually smaller, but often prolific) varies with the season and location, from midwinter to early spring.

'**Autumn Embers**' American selection for red-purple autumn colours.

'**Red Imp**' Hillier selection; basal claret-red pales to copper at the tips.

'**Sandra**' A Hillier introduction (1962). Cadmium-yellow flowers. Plum-purple suffusion as young leaves unfold, maturing to green with purple undersides before bursting into flaming autumn colours of orange, scarlet, and red.

Hedera (Araliaceae)

It is with slight trepidation that I include this contentious genus. One of my favourite aspects of our natural woodland and hedgerow bases is the carpet of ivy clothing the ground with rich, glossy, green leaves, suppressing the weed seedlings and providing a wonderful backdrop against which snowdrops shimmer. We always leave some *Hedera* to ascend the trees; the dense mass of evergreen foliage provides nesting opportunities for countless wildlife, while the flowers are always covered by insects in late summer. Yet care has to be taken; too much ivy can be too heavy for small or brittle trees, causing them to crash to the ground in a gale. Therefore I include it somewhat conditionally. All parts of the plant are toxic.

Hedera helix

Our British native ivy grows so freely here that I find it difficult to believe that some people might have to buy this plant. Indeed I would only introduce ivy as a last resort in a really difficult site, there are many more interesting plants to enjoy on the woodland floor. Nevertheless, if it is already present, it is not imperative to remove it from a more natural area. Instead, it can itself be enhanced with the incorporation of other equally tough plants, as well as providing a wonderful rich green background for bulbs—whether the purity of snowdrops or rich yellow narcissus. Of course it does become rather a task if you need to clear it later, but even then it is not that difficult to do; *H. helix* spreads across the surface, rooting in as it goes rather than by devious hidden underground runners. Countless options of variegated forms are available, but I have reservations as to their aptness in the woodland. They are tolerant of that gardener's enigma, dry shade, and would certainly brighten up a dark corner, even beneath conifers if care is taken with establishment. There is a fine line between useful groundcover and invasive plant and, in parts of North America, English ivy has crossed that line and and its introduction should be avoided.

Helleborus (Ranunculaceae)

Hellebores seem to be one of the most fashionable plants of our time, and with good reason. One of my favourite plants, they erupt from the soil in my garden around Christmas-time and flower defiantly through the depths of winter. Modern hybridisation has resulted in a mouth-watering range of colours.

Although 15 species exist, few are widely cultivated. Those that originate in Mediterranean regions are less ideal in our woodland, but they are well placed under the light canopy of a single tree, where they are not shaded until later in the season. For many years, the popular garden hellebore was described as *H. orientalis*, but recently it has been proposed that generations of breeding has contaminated the gene pool of modern garden plants, so they are now classified as *H. ×hybridus*; it is usually this group which most interests us for the woodland floor.

To help them find constant moisture, hellebores have a deep root system, which dislikes disturbance. They are easily grown, but black spotting on the leaves or stalks should be taken as a warning. Originally thought to be a fungal infection, it has been shown to be a virus, so spraying with a fungicide will not cure it. The only solution is to destroy an infected plant as soon as possible. Do not shred or compost it back onto the garden, as this will spread the problem. It is thought that aphids spread the disease, so controlling them is a valuable exercise but not often practical in a woodland situation. Widespread chemical use is not desirable. Cutting back old leaves in midwinter helps prevent the development of this and does seem to result in a healthier plant all round.

Helleborus argutifolius
Hailing from Mediterranean islands, thus requiring dryer conditions and more sun, this species is more suited to life beneath a single tree than in the true woodland. Robust and handsomely evergreen, with almost prickly leaves, the pale green, cup-shaped flowers are held in large clusters. Potentially comparably large to 90cm.
>   'Pacific Frost' and 'Silver Lace' Variegated selections from either side of the Atlantic require more shade in summer. This makes them ideally suited to planting beneath the canopy of a tree or large shrub. Shorter than the species at only 60cm.

Helleborus foetidus
This is an uninspiring name for an attractive woodlander, with deeply divided leaves and huge heads of pendant green flowers from midwinter to early summer. The tough

plant is tolerant of surprisingly dry positions, and it usually dies after seeding; the resultant roving population is rather nice but the flowerheads can be removed after flowering if this is to be avoided. Not sweetly scented, but the odour is faint and only noticeable from close-by.

> **'Wester Flisk'** My favourite of the seed strains was originally spotted growing alongside the River Tay in Scotland. Deep purple-red stems and leaf stalks are set against greyish green leaves.

Helleborus ×hybridus

Even these adaptable hellebores need some light during the summer, so planting under a high canopy is ideal. Winter wet is definitely to be avoided for all species, even for the true woodlanders; adequate drainage is essential to prevent the crowns rotting. Although frequently inhabiting limestone areas, all have high tolerance of both acid and alkaline soils. They are, however, greedy plants, so lots of organic matter should be dug in to sustain their deep root system prior to planting, and a generous mulch in late summer is extremely valuable. This is an unusual time to apply mulch, but it fits in with their life cycle, because at that stage they are forming flower buds for the following year. It is generally recommended that the old foliage be removed prior to flowers blooming. This reduces the risk of disease infecting the new season's growth and allows the flowers to be fully appreciated in all their glory. I tend to do this for my "best" colours in more cultivated areas, but clearly it is impractical in extensive plantings. I rather like the green carpet through which the flowers emerge.

Traditionally, *Helleborus orientalis* gave us the choice of pink or white flowers; then its subspecies *guttatus* offered the additional benefit of purple speckling. It became normal to breed and select out the darkest purples, with black being the ultimate reward. At the other end of the spectrum, yellow was highly sought after and pure green the target of some. These colours have been refined with clean, even shades of bright yellow, smoky purple, and every shade in between—even apricot. No longer content with these single colours, having conquered bicolours (where dark rims overlay the dominant colour) and picotees (beautifully mottled with purple), breeders have turned their attention to "anemone-centres".

To explain this, I first need to discuss the structure of the flower, which is more complex than it looks. The large colourful bits are not actually petals; they are sepals, whose role is to protect the true flower within, and by being colourful, they attract pollinators. The true petals occur around the prominent bunch of stamens in the centre. These no longer resemble petals, since they have mutated into horn-shaped nectaries containing a sweet substance which is the target for insects, who pollinate the flower as they help themselves. These nectaries are inconspicuous in the old-fashioned ordinary flowers, but they have been the focus of breeders who have selected forms with very dark nectaries and most recently deep gold. In anemone-centred flowers, the nectaries have become enlarged, appearing as a ruffle of petals around the stamens. These can be of a darker colour than the sepals, which is beautiful and considered very desirable. The

A double-flowered selection of *Helleborus* ×*hybridus*   *Helleborus* ×*hybridus* Ashwood Garden hybrids

Helleborus ×*hybridus* Ashwood Garden hybrids   *Helleborus* ×*hybridus* Ashwood Garden hybrids

next stage sees the nectaries revert to petals, thus creating a "double" flower. Although highly sought after by gardeners, these shaggy, heavy flowers are not to my taste.

Classy hellebores are expensive, since much effort has gone into their breeding and several years pass before they flower and can be sold. They naturalise readily, and although the progeny will not be identical to their parents, if the original plants are of high quality, the gene pool will be such that nearly all the offspring will be beautiful. When starting with indifferent plants, it will take many generations of breeding, if ever, to achieve that special something. Look out for the Ashwood Garden hybrids or plants derived from them; although many breeders are painstakingly breeding and selecting hellebores, these are some of the best.

Helleborus niger

The famed Christmas rose is rarely as easy to establish as the ubiquitous *H.* ×*hybridus*. It needs a humus-rich soil in a sheltered location, with moisture-retentive but free-

Helleborus niger 'White Magic'

draining soil—perhaps in the lee of an evergreen shrub in a more open part of the woodland. The nice thing about this squatter species is that the flowers face outward and are therefore more visible. Opening glistening white, they often mature to dusky pink. 20cm.

'Potter's Wheel' and 'White Magic' Selected forms for greater vigour and better flowers.

Helleborus thibetanus

For purists who want to grow species hellebores rather than the modern hybrids, this gorgeous little plant has glaucous foliage and hanging flowers of the palest pink, all with an almost silvery sheen. Requiring a much moister site than the others listed, the foliage dies down much earlier, usually by the end of July in my garden. This is a treasure to be cherished rather than planted for massed effect. 50cm.

Helleborus torquatus

Another beauty, more delicate in appearance and smaller growing, has deeply divided foliage. The flowers vary from outward-facing to nodding and almost cup-shaped, and in colour from green through pink to purple, often with a greyish bloom. These more delicate species should not be confused with the big showy flowers to which we have become accustomed. 40cm.

Heloniopsis (Melanthiaceae)

This small genus of little-known spring-flowering plants for moist, leafy soils hails from Asia.

Heloniopsis orientalis

Clump-forming, with a rosette of narrow leaves above which the flowers are held. These are individually somewhat starry, but are clustered together prettily on 10–20cm stems in late spring/early summer. They vary in colour from white to purplish pink. Although evergreen, the leaves often turn purple in winter or become deciduous in severe conditions. By virtue of its small size, it may be better in the woodland rock garden

Hepatica (Ranunculaceae)

To say that hepaticas are in the buttercup family makes them sound ordinary, but then so are hellebores and there is certainly nothing ordinary about them. This genus has captivated me; nothing eclipses their simple beauty in spring. In Japan, particularly, they have achieved almost cult status in recent years, with astronomical sums of money changing hands for the most desirable (or sometimes weirdest) forms.

Despite complex classification, 12 species are currently known, distributed across the northern temperate zone from Europe (regretfully not Britain) across Asia to North America. The flowers emerge during mild spells through spring and are similar to many *Anemone* species, the difference being botanical. Hepaticas have three small bracts below the flowers. Blue is the normal colour of most species, though whites and pinks are common. Reds and yellows are known, but these can be prohibitively expensive. Further variation is found in flower structure, with doubles and semi-doubles in a riotous combination of these basic colours. Some are quite extraordinary, but I prefer the simplicity of the single flowers. Since such close relationships exist among the species, hybridisation is inevitable, increasing the colour range of these beauties even more. I have not included the Chinese and Korean species here because they are much less widely available and of as yet uncertain hardiness.

Hepatica americana ×
H. acutiloba.

Hepaticas favour leaf-litter in the wild, which offers them excellent drainage without drying out completely. This makes them ideal for the woodland floor no matter how small the woodland may be; they will happily live beneath a single shrub. Provided adequate moisture can be retained during summer, they are perfect candidates to occupy pockets in buttress roots or old hedges, filled with well-rotted leaf-mould. Their tiny stature and exquisite perfection also make them worthy of a highly visible corner on the woodland rock garden. More vigorous species, such as *H. transsilvanica* and *H. ×media*, will eventually carpet a surprisingly large area with often intricately marked foliage.

Hepatica acutiloba

In North America, this gorgeous extensively distributed native is sometimes known as liverwort, which sounds strange to my ears as the word is used in British nurseries to describe a pernicious algae which we work extremely hard to eradicate from our stock. The sharp-lobed, bright green leaves are almost evergreen. The flowers are held on sturdy upright stems, between early spring and early summer. Normally white, pale pinks, and blues are known. 20cm.

Hepatica acutiloba

Hepatica americana

I prefer the foliage of this alternative American species. Evergreen and kidney shaped with rounded lobes, it can often be beautifully marbled. Smaller than *H. acutiloba*, the flowers are soft pastel shades of lavender blue, shell pink, and white. 15cm.

Hepatica japonica

Today a whopping 550 named cultivars in the full range of colours are found in Japan, most of which have been collected from the wild since the 1970s, even though the species has been known there for more than 400 years. Japanese enthusiasts grow and show their hepaticas in deep pots, but many should also flourish in suitable conditions in our woodlands, because this species is closely related to the easily grown *H. nobilis*; indeed some authorities consider *H. japonica* to be merely a subspecies of *H. nobilis*. The Japanese cultivars are creeping into the European market, but it will be a long time before they are widely and cheaply available.

Hepatica japonica   *Hepatica nobilis*

Another *Hepatica nobilis*   *Hepatica nobilis* Picos Strain

Hepatica ×media

This sturdier hybrid group derived from *H. transsilvanica* grows well with a minimum of fuss and bother, including flourishing in sandy soils which dry out badly in summer. An abundance of mid-blue flowers are held over evergreen foliage, with the new leaves developing as the flowers fade. They are sterile, so propagation by division is necessary. 15cm.

'Ballardii' Large blue flowers.

'Harvington Beauty' Large powder-blue flowers.

Hepatica nobilis

Widespread through the woodlands of central Europe north almost to the Arctic Circle, there is tremendous scope for variation. Flowers vary from white through pinks and blues to deep indigo. The foliage is often beautifully marbled. 15cm.

Picos Strain Selected in the Picos de Europa mountains of northern Spain for their conspicuously mottled foliage and delightful flowers, lilac-purple in bud, opening

Hepatica transsilvanica
'De Buis'

to almost white, but with the colour staining the edges of the petals.

var. *pyrenaica* The population endemic to the Pyrénées has been given varietal status. This is a particularly well-marbled form with delightful apple-blossom–pink flowers.

Hepatica transsilvanica

Found under large trees such as beech, oak, and even sycamore that take up considerable moisture, this species is clearly tolerant of significantly drier summer conditions. This is helped by the fact that it is more robust and vigorous in its growth, though it still reaches only 15cm in height. With a tiny wild distribution by comparison to the surrounding *H. nobilis*, an amazing number of selected named forms of this species exist; this is possible because it spreads by creeping rhizomes so can be propagated vegetatively to replicate its characteristics. This enhanced ability to spread makes it perhaps the best suited to naturalising over a larger area.

'**Ada Scott**' Dark blue.

'**Alba**' Pure white.

'**De Buis**' Lovely lilac-blue rounded petals and exceptionally free-flowering.

'**Eisvogel**' Distinctive white selection having a pale blue flash on the reverse of each petal.

'**Elison Spence**' This anemone-centred semi-double was previously known as 'Flore-Plena'. Opening a strong rich blue with a tight central boss, it gradually fades and loosens.

'**Lilacina**' Not truly a cultivar name; it is a group of pink-flowered forms usually grown from seed.

'**Loddon Blue**' Pretty pale blue flowers.

Heptacodium (Caprifoliaceae)

A monotypic genus, the species was named *H. miconioides* in 1907; it was not until a joint Sino-American expedition to China in 1980 that Western gardeners became aware of this fantastic plant. In the meanwhile, specimens examined in 1952 were classified differently as *H. jasminoides*. They are now concluded to be one and the same, so the earlier name takes precedence.

Heptacodium miconioides

The starry white flowers commencing in late summer are individually small, but incredibly prolific. A great terminal head is produced, carrying many whorls of blooms, each made up of six flowers with a seventh in the centre (hence the Chinese name seven-son flower from Zhejiang). Insects love *Heptacodium*; it is a welcome late nectar source here to all manner of creatures, including red admiral butterflies topping up before the winter. But that is not all; as the flowers fade, they are subtended by rich burgundy-red bracts, giving a further display as the leaves take on appealing autumn colours. It is still of interest in winter, with attractive peeling pale-brown bark. Potentially a large shrub or small tree, this superlative plant seems able to thrive in seemingly any soil, in any position. A firm favourite. 3–4m.

Left: In mid-September, *Heptacodium miconioides* blooms prolifically.

Above: By October, the burgundy-red bracts provide autumn colour.

Heuchera (Saxifragaceae)

It is funny how plants go in waves of fashion, and on the back of the groundswell of popularity come a flurry of new cultivars. So it is with *Heuchera*. Most of the 55 species originate from North America, so unsurprisingly it is American nurserymen who are at the forefront of *Heuchera* breeding and introduction. They are tremendous plants; most have wonderful leaves in myriad shades of purple and green, superbly marked with silver, which are retained throughout the year. They are also endowed with pretty flower spikes—sturdy, erect stems clothed in lots of tiny flared bells in summer.

Partial shade is perfect; this is not a genus to bring radiance to the very shadiest areas, where they would become straggly with little flower. However, they hold their colour well in shade and make excellent groundcover if planted in blocks (they do not really spread other than by seed). They also associate well with all manner of other woodland perennials and bulbs, their lovely colours adding an extra dimension to the woodland floor without risk of them taking over. The pewter and purple foliage combinations can tone beautifully with the smaller glaucous-leaved hostas with their mauve flowers.

Early breeding programs concentrated on improving their flowering potential (most make excellent cut flowers), but recently emphasis has shifted to their foliage. When such a delightfully colourful array of cultivars awaits, it is difficult to justify choosing the species, which are in any case difficult to obtain, unless wild provenance is needed.

Sadly, the species are endangered in many of their native habitats by the lumber industry and development. It is vital that species in their purest forms do not die out, so a balance has to be found. I have included a few of the best species, but the cultivars are undoubtedly superior garden plants.

Older crowns can push themselves out of the ground, making it easy to remove sections, often with root hairs just starting to develop. Unfortunately, they act like a magnet to vine weevils. Periodically, I find a plant apparently wilting and reach down to feel the leaves; the whole plant comes away in my hand, completely chewed through at ground level. It can often be salvaged by promptly dividing the crown into sections, removing much of the foliage to reduce the stress, and placing the sections in an appropriate environment for root regeneration.

Heuchera americana

This important species, the only one from the eastern part of North America, has had significant influence on the recent hybrids, often contributing the popular silver markings, the metallic sheen, and a line of colour along the leaf edge.

Heuchera bracteata

For me, the simplicity of this one stands out against the almost predictability of the modern cultivars. From the Rocky Mountains, this small grower is ideally suited to the woodland rock garden, where the uncomplicated green leaves complement the proportionally small greenish white flower spikes. 15cm.

Heuchera sanguinea

From Arizona and Mexico, mats of dark green leaves display the attractive, rich coral-coloured flowers. Named cultivars of this species, which has been known in Britain for more than 150 years, have been superseded by newer hybrids.

Heuchera cultivars

There are too many cultivars to list all of them, and many are extremely similar, so I have chosen some of my favourites.

> **'Caramel'** Considered an improvement on *H.* 'Amber Waves', this colour break is remarkable if not to everyone's taste. It adds a splash of colour and makes a fun accent plant. Rich orange-brown young foliage matures to a slightly more muted shade. White flowers. 25cm.
>
> **'Chocolate Ruffles'** Much larger leaves are distinctly ruffled along the edges to show off their rich burgundy-coloured undersides. Small white flowers on spikes to 65cm occur in succession from late spring to late autumn.
>
> **'Coral Bouquet'** A lovely, pleasantly compact plant, arguably more natural in appearance with subdued green leaves. There is nothing shy about the lovely pink flowers, though. 45cm.
>
> **'Ebony and Ivory'** Spikes of ivory flowers over ebony-coloured foliage.

Above left: *Heuchera* 'Caramel'

Above: *Heuchera* 'Chocolate Ruffles'

Left: *Heuchera* 'Ebony and Ivory'

'**Mint Frost**' Most new heucheras seem to concentrate on the purple foliage options, but this pretty one is largely silver with prominent green veining.

'**Petite Pearl Fairy**' Cultivars in the "petite" range grow only to 20cm. This one flowers particularly well with dense spikes of rich pink flowers over deep red-purple leaves. Great for smaller scale plantings.

'**Silver Scrolls**' Pewter, silver, and purple combine in the lovely foliage but are topped by substantial creamy flower spikes extending the height from 35cm to 75cm.

'**Stormy Seas**' Gorgeous foliage, essentially pewter coloured with darker veins, purple suffused when young and rich purple below. White flowers are irrelevant. 50cm.

×*Heucherella* (Saxifragaceae)

Lovely intergeneric hybrids between *Heuchera* and *Tiarella*, these have identical cultural requirements. Breeding continues at a tremendous rate, so new cultivars are constantly arriving to tempt us. These hybrids are sterile, so they consequently flower for longer through the summer, usually from midspring to early summer and beyond. I almost prefer their slightly more subdued tones and prettily shaped leaves. Here are just a few to ponder.

×*Heucherella* cultivars

'**Kimono**' The foliage, shaped almost like that of a maple, is deeply lobed, silver-green, with deep purple veins. Pale pink, almost white flowers. 55cm.

'**Quicksilver**' Although almost purple, the silvery sheen takes the intensity out of the leaves. Particularly large bell-like flowers open pink before fading to white. 45cm.

'**Silver Streak**' A low grower to just 25cm, the foliage is subtly shaded through green and pewter, flushed with purple when young. The white flowers have that same purple flush.

'**Stoplight**' This would indeed stop you in your tracks as you wandered through the calm, green woodland. The leaves are a vibrant yellow with blood-red veining. The white flowers are quite superfluous. 25cm.

'**Viking Ship**' Differentiated from the previous cultivars by its prolific crop of coral-pink flowers held as late as midautumn over green, maple-shaped leaves. Lovely. 40cm.

Hosta (Hostaceae)

A huge genus with a history to match, these plants were known for more than a century in their native Japan and China before being named *Hosta* in 1812, some 28 years after their introduction to Europe. Nowadays they have become archetypal plants for shade gardening, but their popularity is easily understood by considering their diversity. Compare the tiny ones, with leaves the size of a matchbox or less, to the monsters of the genus which can easily rub shoulders with the shrubs, whose leaves are like elephant's ears. Then think about the range of colours: blues, greens, yellows, and white, with variegation in every possible combination. Yet the greens are almost adequate by themselves, for no two shades ever seem quite the same. But hostas are not completely dedicated to foliage; many have lovely flowers by the end of summer, in shades of lilac or white. Sometimes it is worth removing these to concentrate on the beauty of the foliage, but others are enticingly fragrant.

Contrast can be gained by using their varying habits and leaf sizes, by associating

Bold, blue-leaved *Hosta* contrasts superbly with airy white *Astilbe* for a cool, reflective combination.

them with plants with pinnate leaves, such as *Arisaema* or graceful ferns. Green is a colour of peace, tranquillity, and relaxation; too much variegation is not to my taste. It is easy to lose sight of the species in the light of the plethora of modern cultivars. This is inevitable; when there is room for just a few members of a genus, it is important to choose those which will best achieve the desired effect. Fortunately, botanic gardens are dedicated to the preservation of our species.

Hostas are herbaceous and erupt from a thick rootstock each spring. The woodland shade protects their potentially huge leaves; clearly, the bigger they are the more vulnerable they will be to windy or dry conditions, and the more water they will require in summer, so they need to be sited or selected accordingly. They benefit from the incorporation of lots of organic matter into the soil prior to planting and thorough mulching in winter.

Ferns and hostas make gorgeous companions.

Hostas are notorious for their attractiveness to molluscs and their infamous ability to decimate a plant overnight, though thicker textured leaves are less vulnerable. Everyone has their own slug control method, and some are more effective than others. Unfortunately, the moist and shady environment of our woodland floor is the perfect habitat for these creatures, so they perhaps have to be tolerated; the Japanese accept the holes as part of the game. At least there will be plenty of food for the thrushes.

Hosta lancifolia

This species forms a dense mound of arching, narrow, dark green glossy leaves, with deep purple flowers. Small to medium.

Hosta minor

Small yellowish green leaves are shiny on the reverse. Dark flowers. Dwarf.

Hosta sieboldiana **var.** *elegans*

The patriarch of blue hostas has thick, round, puckered blue leaves. White flowers have a lavender blush and sit just above the foliage. Huge.

Hosta venusta

Tiny, light green, heart-shaped leaves and lavender flowers. Dwarf.

Opposite: *Hosta* 'Lemon Lime'

Hosta cultivars

Almost 4000 cultivars are registered, a mere 500 of which are considered garden-worthy. Here is a sampling of colours and sizes.

'**Blue Moon**' Small, heart-shaped blue leaves are substantial and pest-resistant. Prolific white flowers. Dwarf.

'**Candy Hearts**' Heart-shaped, rich green leaves. Pale lavender-blue flowers. Small to medium.

'**Devon Green**' Justifiably the most popular green hosta in Europe. Shiny, dark green leaves are held almost horizontally. Beautiful habit. Medium.

'**Floradora**' Neat heart-shaped green leaves. Very floriferous. Small.

'**Fragrant Bouquet**' Bright apple-green, slightly wavy leaves with a creamy white edge. Large, white, exquisitely scented flowers. Vigorous. Medium.

'**Golden Scepter**' Heart-shaped golden leaves. Purple flowers. Small to medium.

'**Gold Standard**' Emerges green but almost immediately turns to bright limey gold with a narrow green border. Lavender flowers. Medium to large.

'**Green Fountain**' Red-spotted leaf stalks; long, arching, wavy, pointed green leaves. Pale mauve flowers. Medium to large.

'**Hadspen Blue**' Classic cultivar, still one of the best. Powdery steel-blue rounded leaves last well into the season. Medium.

'**Halcyon**' Bright powder-blue leaves of very heavy substance. Again the colour is held well. Smoky-lilac flowers. Medium.

'**Invincible**' Thick, glossy green foliage is verdant. Very fragrant, light lavender flowers. Small to medium.

'**Jade Cascade**' Long, tapering, and cascading green leaves. Very elegant. Large.

'**June**' Blue edges around creamy centre gradually changes to dark chartreuse. Light violet flowers. Medium.

'**Lemon Lime**' Clumps of vivid chartreuse, wavy leaves fade to light green,

Above: *Hosta* 'Patriot'

Right: *Hosta* 'Royal Standard'

Few plants can compete with bluebells for colour intensity, but it may be wise to consign them to wilder areas or as companions to vigorous, large-leaved summer perennials, since they develop a dense mat of foliage, bulbs, and roots.

contrasting subtly with the bright gold of the new foliage. Lavender flowers. Small but clumps up well.

'Love Pat' Intensely blue foliage, round, very cupped, and corrugated. White flowers. Large.

'Paradise Puppet' Distinctive, smooth, glossy, long green leaves. Purple flowers. Small.

'Patriot' Broad white margins contrast with dark green leaf centres. Medium.

'Piedmont Gold' Arguably the best gold hosta; commences lime-green, quickly turning to gold with slightly twisted leaves. Lavender flowers. Large.

'Royal Standard' Bold and vigorous with dark green leaves. Fragrant white flowers. Tolerates sun and lasts until the frost. Medium to large.

'Shining Tot' Elongated heart-shaped, thick, glossy, dark green leaves. Lavender-blue flowers. Dwarf.

Hyacinthoides (Hyacinthaceae)

There can be few more evocative images of the archetypal English woodland than swathes of nodding bluebells, as May sunshine filters through the fresh new leaves above. Their classification has changed several times, masquerading as *Scilla* or *Endymion*, but the beauty and popularity of these bulbs remain undiminished. They enjoy damp, shady areas of the woodland floor, often colonising the base of hedgerows.

Hyacinthoides non-scripta

Nearly half the global population is found in Britain, but the English bluebell is declining due to habitat loss and competition from the Spanish bluebell. They are such pretty flowers, violet-blue bells on graceful arching stems, that no woodland should be without them, although they will spread when happy. It is difficult for me to consider them invasive, but it would be possible in a small space.

Hydrangea (Hydrangeaceae)

Hydrangeas must be one of the most well-known shrubs, so popular in suburban gardens. The larger leaved varieties are actually woodland plants, thriving in moisture-retentive, humus-rich soil. Leafing late in the spring, their early sparseness can be camouflaged by the myriad ephemeral spring bulbs and flowers which will appreciate the protection their framework provides, yet they will be done and dusted by the time the hydrangeas take their turn on centre stage, flowering unreservedly from midsummer even into autumn.

The flattened or dome-shaped flowerheads consist of two types of flower. Sterile bracts around the outside of the head give colour and substance, while the insignificant fertile flowers in the centre give a graceful air to the lacecap types. For me, these sit much more comfortably in the woodland surroundings than the huge, almost artificial sun-loving hortensia hydrangeas which have massive heads of sterile florets.

Twenty-three species grace Asia and the Americas, though not all are appropriate for the woodland. However, the range of hybrids and cultivars available today still makes for a bewildering array. Blue flowers have a beguiling attraction, perhaps because so few are truly blue. Hydrangeas include some of the best, but frustratingly the blue colouration develops only when they grow in acid soil. The plants themselves will do well enough with higher pH, but the colours will be more towards pink. Chemicals can be added to the soil to improve the situation, but it is a temporary respite and not a long-term solution.

Hydrangeas flower on young wood, so any pruning should be carried out immediately after flowering. Winter pruning of early summer-flowering forms will be at the expense of flower that season. If the flower heads and their stalks are harvested as they fade, they may be hung upside down to dry and used in floral decoration to great effect. In the case of the earlier summer-flowering *H. arborescens*, this dead-heading often results in a second flush of flower.

Hydrangea arborescens
Small and bushy, not treelike as the name implies, in cold winters it can even be cut down almost like a herbaceous perennial. From the woods of eastern North America, it tolerates the heaviest shade.

'Annabelle' The standard by which the species is represented. This hardy Illinois selection has flowerheads the size of a football, up to 30cm across, weighing the slender branches almost to the ground. Arguably too blousy for a natural woodland, it is undoubtedly impressive.

subsp. *discolor* 'Sterilis' Distinguished by flatter topped flowerheads and silvery backed leaves. Rather more subtle and half the height.

Hydrangea aspera
'Macrophylla'

Hydrangea aspera

Magnificent Sino-Himalayan species with distinctive velvety leaves. Large lilac-blue flattened heads of fertile flowers are fringed by lilac-pink or white sterile florets.

Kawakamii Group Crûg Farm has introduced a number of selections from Taiwan. My favourite has large heads of purple, with just a few almost-white florets punctuating the circumference.

'Macrophylla' Spreading habit supports superlative flowerheads of deep bluish purple, ringed with contrastingly paler florets.

'Rocklon' More gracefully proportioned, lilac-mauve fertile flowers are interspersed with similarly coloured florets.

subsp. *sargentiana* This Chinese introduction is a sumptuous plant with thickly felted shoots and huge leaves, rendering it appreciative of our woodland protection. Large blue flowerheads are surrounded by white florets.

Villosa Group Perhaps the most common incarnation, with a more restrained habit and smaller leaves, it is similar to 'Rocklon'; this Chinese selection has been in cultivation for nearly 100 years.

Hydrangea macrophylla

The true species has all but disappeared under the weight of hundreds of cultivars assigned to it. I include just a selection of lacecaps. The proportions of fertile central flowers to outer sterile bracts varies, while soil pH will determine the exact colour.

'Kardinal' Insignificant cream-coloured fertile flowers are dominated by magenta-pink florets with a creamy eye.

'Lanarth White' Elegant well-proportioned pure white head.

'Möwe' (syn. 'Geoffrey Chadbund') Warm rose-pink.

'**Nachtigall**' From Switzerland, potentially the richest blue lacecap, starting with white centres and deepening with maturity.

'**Rotdrossel**' Bright purplish pink florets are held in a symmetrical ring around a tight circle of bluish fertile flowers.

'**Tokyo Delight**' Mounded heads with an outer ring of large white florets. Inner fertile flowers may be pinkish or bluish.

'**Veitchii**' Classic selection from 1880 with very large domed heads of fertile flowers, which mature from pink to blue, surrounded by almost white florets, subtly lilac-flushed.

Hydrangea serrata

Previously sunk into *H. macrophylla*, this hardier species (known as mountain hydrangea) is perfect for colder gardens with some wonderful new selections being made in its native Japan. Smaller in stature at 1m, with typical flowerhead structure, these are my favourites, being softer in flower and foliage than *H. macrophylla*. Their young growth is often flushed with purple and then turns a rich reddish purple in autumn. As a result of their close relationship, many designated cultivars of both species may well be hybrids.

'**Beni-gaku**' Delightful ever-changing flower colour. Central fertile flowers emerge dark purple, fading to light blue while the surrounding florets open white, progressively darkening to pink with deep red edges.

'**Kiyosumi**' Deep red-flushed foliage complements unique flowers. The outer sterile bracts are white, each dramatically edged with reddish pink.

'**Komachi**' Released in the West as 'Pretty Maiden', the outer sterile florets are a pretty pale pink, but tightly double, appearing almost like rosebuds. 'Miyama-yae-murasaki' (anglicised to 'Purple Tiers') is the same principle but with darker flowers.

'**Miranda**' Lovely mid-pink flowerheads over richly coloured foliage.

'**Shirofuji**' The double white bracts of this recent Japanese cultivar are loosely held; so despite a comparative lack of fertile flowers, its appearance is graceful and lacks the overindulgence of so many double flowers.

Hydrophyllum (Hydrophyllaceae)

Endemic to North America, this genus comprises eight species, though few are widely cultivated. Classic rhizomatous woodlanders, they require constant moisture and shade, though they do not tolerate waterlogged soil.

Hydrophyllum canadense

The long-stalked, five to seven–lobed leaves rise to as much as 70cm tall. The greeny white flowers may be small but they are delightful, individually bell-shaped but with stamens much longer than the petals, held in clusters above the leaves from early to late summer.

Hydrophyllum virginianum

Similar to *H. canadense*, the young shoots and leaves are actually edible. The flowers may be white or even dark violet.

Hylomecon (Papaveraceae)

Aptly described as the forest poppy, this small Asian genus lights up the shady woodland floor with a plethora of cheerful, yellow poppy-shaped flowers; they thrive where the soil is moisture-retentive and humus-rich.

Hylomecon hylomecoides

This rare Korean species clumps up more slowly but is smothered with clusters of lovely yellow flowers for most of the summer.

Hylomecon japonica

Spreading by short, shallow rhizomes (but rarely as aggressively as some would suggest), single cup-shaped golden flowers are freely produced from mid-spring to early summer.

Hylomecon hylomecoides

Ilex (Aquifoliaceae)

For those who consider holly a red-berried Christmas accessory, it may come as a surprise to learn that about 400 species are found globally. I love the mythology and history surrounding plants; legend endows holly with enormous powers of good over evil, with red berries warding off evil spirits. *I. aquifolium*, a native of Britain, is enormously tolerant of the notoriously difficult dry shady areas of the woodland, even at the foot of established trees where it creates valuable winter protection. Thirty-nine species of holly are native to or naturalised in North America. Most are evergreen although their tolerance of shade varies and is influenced by climate. Location will determine availability and suitability of the numerous cultivars and hybrids.

Most hollies are slow growing, and either male or female, so one of each is required to produce those desirable opulent berries. However, a single male can pollinate a number of females.

Ilex aquifolium

So many cultivars with plain green or variegated foliage exist. All are suitable; it just comes down to personal taste.

'Bacciflava' Yellow fruits.

'Ferox' The hedgehog holly, with extra spines down the backs of the leaves as well as the margins. Small bushy growth. Considered to be the oldest surviving cultivated holly type, dating back to the early seventeenth century. Male. Selected forms have cream margins ('Ferox Argentea') or gold centres ('Ferox Aurea').

Ilex aquifolium 'Ferox Aurea'

'Golden Milkboy' and **'Golden Milkmaid'** Male and female forms respectively with larger green leaves splashed with gold in the centres.

'Golden Queen' Confusingly male. Broad yellow margins, with inner dark green, pale green, and grey shading.

'Handsworth New Silver' Purple stems contrast well with creamy margins. Female.

'J. C. van Tol' My favourite holly; dark glossy green, almost spineless leaves and upright habit. Reliable and prolific berry production. Self-fertile. Silver and gold–margined derivatives are also available.

'Myrtifolia' Small green leaves with variable spikiness and purple stems. Pretty gold-margined and gold-splashed forms also exist. Male.

Ilex vomitoria

Yaupon holly is widespread through southeastern North America, colonising varied habitats from dry, sandy areas to swamps and maritime forests, even where exposed to salt-laden winds. Adaptable, but not terribly hardy, it is worth trying in southern

England, though named forms are almost unavailable in Britain. Small, oval leaves that are evergreen and shallowly toothed clothe dense, shrubby clumps of smooth limbs. Abundant flowers are produced in spring. Subsequent bright red berries last as long through winter as birds will allow. Yaupon holly is also compatible with *I. opaca* for pollination purposes. Variable and easily grown from seed, many cultivars have been selected. 6-7m.

Ilex vomitoria is emetic (causes vomiting—hence the name). An infusion from the young leaves containing caffeine, known as "black drink", was used by native Americans as a ceremonial intoxicant to cleanse body and soul of impurities, and for medicinal purposes.

'**Nana**' Various smaller growers have been selected. Expect 2m high by 3m wide. Enhanced by purple young shoots, 'Schillings' is even more compact. Male.

'**Pendula**' A rather general name for plants with weeping habit. There is suggestion that it should be a form rather than a cultivar since their seedlings are usually pendulous too. Male and female versions exist.

'**Saratoga Yellow**' Vigorous, yellow-fruited selection from 1951. Similarly coloured alternatives include 'Dodd's Yellow' and 'Katherine'.

Ipheion 'Alberto Castillo'

Ipheion (Alliaceae)

Although about 25 species of this genus are found in South America, only one is commonly cultivated. A faint garlicky aroma alludes to their classification in the allium family. It naturalises beautifully from offset bulbs and by self-seeding, colonising an area fairly rapidly. It is best in more informal positions where the shade is not too dense, being tolerant of seasonal dryness beneath specimen trees, where it can be left to its own devices in a thin layer of additional soil. Although it forms dense clumps, it is not to the exclusion of all else; other bulbs can spring up through it for a pretty mix of colours. In my garden, it shares a corner with *Scilla*, *Muscari*, and *Narcissus*.

Ipheion uniflorum

Small, fleshy rooted bulbs spring into life in the autumn to produce leafy, grasslike patches. By late winter, or even earlier in mild years, they will be smothered by pretty six-petalled, pale violet starlike flowers, continuing often until midspring.

'Charlotte Bishop' Rosy pink.

'Froyle Mill' Dark violet.

'Wisley Blue' Light blue.

Ipheion cultivars

'Alberto Castillo' Of uncertain hybrid origin, its large white flowers and glaucous leaves make this a distinct improvement on the basic white-flowered selection of *I. uniflorum*.

'Rolf Fiedler' From Uruguay, blue-green leaves set off cobalt-blue flowers, though it produces fewer blooms per stem than *I. uniflorum*.

Iris (Iridaceae)

Naming a genus for the Greek goddess of the rainbow certainly sums up the diversity of colours through the 300 or so species, and that is discounting modern breeding programs. However, few are suitable for our woodland conditions. A number of these prefer shallow planting in drier sites, since the rhizomes are prone to rot when dormant. Other iris by contrast enjoy significantly moister sites, so they are perfect contenders for the more open glade.

To describe the flowers succinctly, a little understanding of their structure is useful. In simple terms, they consist of six tepals (petals); the outer three, known as the falls, arch outwards and hang down. Between these, the other three, the standards, are usually narrower and often erect, though they may arch in some species.

Iris are easily split with a spade through the clump after flowering to create extra plants to distribute to envious friends or to speed up the development of a new area.

Iris *Species for Shallow Planting in Drier Sites*

These species are perfect choices beneath a specimen tree, where the sun will slant beneath the canopy in spring, with the tree roots keeping them dry and hungry in summer. They would be equally happy along the sunny side of a mature hedgerow. Some are so tiny that they need to be safely perched on the woodland rock garden, benefiting from the rain shadow of a rock.

Iris douglasiana

North America has a rich heritage of flora; this is yet another plant endemic to the west coast. Large flowers, blooming late spring to early summer, are variable in colour within the purple spectrum, but often with darker veining and a yellow zone on the falls. 30–40cm.

Iris gracilipes

Scarce in Britain, it is perfectly hardy and well suited to a place on the woodland rock garden, with grasslike leaves. The flowers are proportionally small, usually lilac-blue; the falls have a white, purple-veined patch and a yellow-tipped crest. The standards are spreading, forming an apparently flatter flower. 10–15cm.

Iris innominata

This plant is lovely in all its forms. Hybrids are common, even in the wild, and this species is a major influence in the group broadly known as the Pacific Coast or Californian hybrids, which first opened my eyes to the possibilities of growing iris beneath trees. Until then, I had always associated the genus with extremes: alpines, water plants, or the sun-loving bearded iris. However, this group is superb beneath a specimen tree, where some sun can penetrate beneath the canopy. They revel in dry summer conditions, with a profusion of blooms in midspring to early summer. The range of colours is endless, from the familiar blues and lilac-purples through to white and yellow, with some peachy tints in between. Named forms are available, while it is also common to buy them "to colour". 15–25cm.

Iris Californian hybrids are available in many colours.

Iris japonica

Despite its reputation for slight tenderness, this surprisingly tolerant plant will grow almost anywhere, in the lee of a wall or under a big tree (even under sycamores), quickly establishing healthy clumps of evergreen foliage. The rather flat but frilly spring flower has a base colour of pale lilac, beautifully highlighted with purple and a gold splash on the falls. The shallow rhizomes are easily divided. 30cm.

'**Aphrodite**' White flowers are stained with lavender and highlighted by an orange crest. Green and white–striped leaves.

'**Eco Easter**' Floriferous American selection with lavender-blue flowers.

'**Ledger**' Typical colour but reputedly the hardiest selection.

Iris longipetala

Sturdy species with as many as eight flowers to a stem. These are almost white, with prominent lilac-purple veining, particularly on the falls, along with a yellow flash. Wonderful in a well-drained spot beneath light canopy. 30–40cm.

Iris missouriensis

Variable, but generally more elegant than close relative *I. longipetala*. The glaucous leaves are narrower, but the flowers are similar in late spring to early summer.

Iris purdyi

Needing a well-drained position, with a particular liking for sandy soils, its unbranched flower stems reach 35cm tall in late spring to early summer, with the plant forming a loose clump. Flower colour varies from creamy yellow to pale blue, often with noticeable veining. The rather narrow standards and falls are elegant.

Iris ruthenica

Just 15cm tall in bloom, though the leaves can extend to 30cm, the surprisingly scented blue-lavender flowers in early to midsummer are stained violet with white falls. Worthy of a special site on the woodland rock garden, where the scent can be appreciated. Needs free drainage.

Iris suaveolens

This one enjoys shade and dryness beneath a specimen tree, with two main forms, yellow or purple, but bicolours are also known. Very squat and low at just 8–15cm, the large flowers can take up half this height.

Iris tenax

Another Pacific Coast species of influence in those hybrids. The species varies from deep blue-purple through pale lavender, cream, and white to the less common buff-yellow and creamy pinks. Rare in the wild, yet popular in cultivation.

Iris tenuissima

This Californian iris is surprisingly rare in cultivation. Again variable, the early summer flowers are cream with purple or brown veining. 15–30cm.

Iris *Species for the Woodland Floor*

Many of these generally larger growing species tolerate much moister sites, though some prefer the higher light levels of a woodland glade.

Iris chrysographes

One of my favourites in this group, though it does not perform to its best in too much shade. It does, however, enjoy the rich, moist soil often found in a woodland glade, producing the most gorgeous velvety purple, almost black flowers. Look out for vegetatively propagated named clones such as 'Black Knight' and 'Black Velvet' for richest colour. 45cm.

Iris foetidissima

Frost-covered *Osmanthus delavayi* contrasts dramatically with *Iris foetidissima* berries.

Britain's native iris grows wild here. Its evergreen swordlike leaves punctuate our hedgerows, though the flowers themselves are a rather wishy-washy lavender colour and not very impressive, despite their stature. However, it really comes into its own over the winter with red-orange seeds held in open pods. They are long-lasting; although visually attractive to birds, they are not actually edible for them. Scarce variants have yellow or even white seeds. 90cm.

Iris germanica

This eastern Mediterranean species may itself be a hybrid. Certainly it is quite happy in the dry shade of deciduous trees, flowering in early to late spring, several heads to a stem. The pretty lavender-purple flowers have a white splash on the falls and are scented.

Iris graminea

This very hardy European species extends as far east as Poland. Flowering in late spring to early summer, the flowers are said to smell of plums, and that certainly describes their luxuriant base colour, with the falls richly marked with yellow. Leafy soil in partial shade. 40cm.

Iris lazica

Closely related to *I. unguicularis*, popular in the UK for its winter flowers, this Turkish species comes from a moister area than its Mediterranean cousin, though it still appreciates the shade. Flowering from late winter to midspring, when temperature permits, the flowers are deep purplish blue with darker spotting on the falls and a pale yellow stripe. Very hardy, though the evergreen leaves can be cut back by severe cold below −10°C. 30cm.

Iris sibirica

Another classic species, enjoying much the same conditions as *I. chrysographes*—moist, but not too heavily shaded. The habit and flower size is comparable, too, but not the colour. Essentially blue in all its shades, a huge number of named forms increase the colour spectrum with yellows, whites, and purples. Allow plenty of space for both these species as they rapidly bulk up to form large clumps with almost evergreen foliage.

Iris variegata

Unusually, this name refers to the flowers, not the foliage. More shade-tolerant than most, although too much shade will reduce flower production. A parent of many of our modern bearded iris, the flowers in late spring/early summer are remarkable, with bright yellow standards, while the falls are almost striped, being banded with red or black on white. 40cm.

Iris verna

The flowers extend 4–6cm tall, with the leaves reaching dizzy heights at 15cm, making it better suited to life on the woodland rock garden. Bright blue flowers in spring to early summer boast an orange stripe to their falls.

Isopyrum (Ranunculaceae)

A genus of about 30 species, few are readily available or seen in cultivation. Ranunculaceae is often considered the buttercup family, but I prefer to associate it with the delightful anemones. This genus is aesthetically closer to *Anemonella*, usually with basal leaves and further leaves on the branched flowering stems. Rooting in a similar manner through slender rhizomes often including tiny tubers, they form clumps and small colonies. Some species can cover larger areas of the woodland floor almost to the point of invasive given favourable conditions; others are tiny and desirable enough to warrant special treatment on the woodland rock garden. I can think of many worse things than an invasion by these delightful little spring flowerers, who all too soon die down for their summer rest.

The little tubers that form along the rhizomes remind me of celandines; this does make them surprisingly difficult to remove, because it takes only one of these little grains left behind to allow a new plant to generate itself. Others may be even more desirable, but those listed here are more obtainable.

Isopyrum biternatum
From eastern North America, this colony-forming species is of medium vigour, the root system including both rhizomes and tubers. Several white flowers up to 2cm across are held above the basal bright green leaves. 30cm.

Isopyrum nipponicum
More compact in habit, with numerous, although individually smaller, flowers. Usually pale greenish yellow to white, purple tinting is known. This Japanese species requires a moist position. 25cm.

Isopyrum thalictroides
The most vigorous listed here spreads by slender rhizomes and is the most adaptable as a result of its wider distribution, from central Europe to the Himalayas. This also explains the variability in flower size, so it can be worth selecting out particularly good forms; white in colour. 15cm.

Itea (Escalloniaceae)

The relevant members of this fascinating and varied small genus are still little known in Britain; indeed no cultivars, even in its native North America, were known before 1982. Now it has established itself as an invaluable small shrub for a moisture-retentive, humus-rich corner of the woodland. Some light filtering through the canopy will maximise the gorgeous autumn colours.

Itea virginica

Delightful thicket-forming, suckering shrub varying from 1m to 2m tall. Upright racemes of small but sweetly scented white flowers appear in late spring to early summer. Burgundy-red autumn colours last long into winter. In mild locations, leaves may be held all year, reverting to green as the sap rises in the spring.

'Henry's Garnet' The first named cultivar, selected for outstanding autumn colour.

'Long Spire' Taller, vigorous habit with amazing flower spikes potentially 20cm long.

'Merlot' My favourite; more compact and red wine–coloured in autumn.

'Sarah Eve' Pinky white flowers.

Jeffersonia (Berberidaceae)

Yet another member of this diverse family; I am fond of these and treat them to a prime spot on the woodland floor or indeed the woodland rock garden, where they can be easily appreciated. Characterised by a deeply divided single leaf that appears to be two separate ones, these little clump-formers love a humus-rich, moisture-retentive soil and are deceptively tough. Although flowering in mid to late spring, their foliage is retained for much longer than many other more ephemeral woodlanders, being joined in autumn by strange seedpods, which can be likened to a smoker's pipe.

Jeffersonia diphylla

The delightful single white anemone-like flowers of this North American species are held above the glaucous leaves in clear view.

Jeffersonia dubia

The Asian equivalent is not so sturdy in habit, but pretty, with lavender-blue flowers. The leaves are less deeply divided, more kidney-shaped than *J. diphylla* and often richly flushed with purple on emergence.

var. *alba* Beautiful, naturally occurring white-flowered variant.

Jeffersonia dubia var. alba

Kirengeshoma (Hydrangeaceae)

This summer woodlander retains its foliage into the autumn, long after the lovely yellow flowers have faded. They consequently enjoy a moisture-retentive site, though with adequate drainage. Spreading by virtue of their rhizomatous rootstock to form a lovely colony, these essential plants give a gorgeous splash of colour in midsummer, a difficult time in woodlands relying too heavily on spring bulbs for their glory.

Kirengeshoma palmata

The nodding, rich yellow bells are so perfect it is almost as though they were made from wax, hanging in clusters in early summer from arching stems. A native of Japan, their leaves are rather maple-shaped. 1.5m.

> **Koreana Group** Sometimes given the status of a distinct species, or just deemed a geographical variant. In reality, the differences are minor; this Korean form often has more erect stems to 2m tall and the paler yellow flowers are a little more flared. The petals may be slightly narrower, too.

Lamium (Lamiaceae)

As a small child, I saw wild lamiums in the woods and was convinced that they were the fearsome stinging nettle. Indeed the leaves are sufficiently similar, both in terms of shape and their toothed margins, that they are often known as deadnettles. Forty species of annuals and perennials are distributed from Europe to Asia and North Africa. They layer themselves, rooting where the stems touch the soil, and some can definitely be invasive, so care should be taken to match the scale of the plant to the desired location. The flowers are held in the upper leaf axils and look like snapdragons; pretty rather than spectacular, there are many colours from which to choose. Some have variegated foliage, which can brighten a dull and difficult corner, thriving in the shady woodland environs. These are easy plants to grow, certainly not requiring prime sites. They enjoy considerable moisture but will grow with adequate vigour even in very dry shade. They can be delightful jostling for position among other plants of equal vigour in a wild part of the garden but are inappropriate among tiny treasures.

Lamium galeobdolon subsp. montanum 'Florentinum' emerges through a dense carpet of Isopyrum thalictroides.

Lamium album

White flowers produced from midspring to late summer. 60cm.

> **'Friday'** A somewhat random epithet for a variegated form.
>
> **'Goldflake'** New shoots are golden in colour.
>
> **'Pale Peril'** Similar. Pale refers to the foliage colour, and you can probably guess the Peril part.

Lamium galeobdolon

This is the classic yellow-flowered deadnettle of my childhood and is not itself generally cultivated. However, a number of named forms, many of which are variegated, can be effective in suitably large and informal areas, though it can be invasive, so be cautious in its selection.

> **'Hermann's Pride'** Arguably the best of the many variegated selections, being robust, with beautifully silver-marked leaves. I love it combined with blue flowers, such as bluebells and forget-me-nots, or lovely *Omphalodes*.

> **subsp.** *montanum* **'Florentinum'** Often known simply as *L.* 'Variegatum'. I am in two minds about this one: certainly, if it is planted in too manicured or restricted an area it will quickly be considered invasive, yet in larger areas of more natural woodland it can be useful to plant some easy groundcover. This is pretty, particularly the young growth which matures to a simpler green and silver variegation. The yellow flowers are typical of the genus.

Lamium garganicum

My favourite species, I love the darker markings in the throats of the pale pink flowers. A number of subtly different geographical variants come from the mountains of southern Europe, preferring drier conditions than those enjoyed by lower level brethren.

Lamium maculatum

Also European (though not Britain), from Scandinavia east to Iran, both pink- and white-flowered forms are found.

Lamium orvala

> **'Beacon Silver'** Almost entirely silver leaves are highlighted by a narrow green margin. Pale pink to lilac flowers are of secondary importance. Wonderful beneath blue hostas.

> **'Roseum'** (syn. 'Shell Pink') Pale pink flowers tone nicely with the leaves, which have a white central splash. A frequently found wild combination, various named forms have similar appearance, such as 'Chequers'.

> **'White Nancy'** Leaves have silvery overtones and the flowers are pure white. 'Pink Nancy' and 'Red Nancy' have appropriately coloured flowers.

Lamium orvala

A brilliant species because it clumps rather than spreads. Large purple flowers are held in typical whorled spikes. 60cm.

> **'Album'** White flowers.

> **'Silva'** Silver-marked leaves.

Lathraea clandestina

Lathraea (Scrophulariaceae)

This European native is a true oddity, a remarkable plant, and a fascinating conversation piece.

Lathraea clandestina

The purple toothwort is actually a parasitic plant, living on the roots of trees, preferring *Salix*, *Alnus*, and *Populus*. The amazing purple flowers, appearing in spring, are the only part visible above ground. The British equivalent, *L. squamaria*, prefers *Corylus* and *Ilex*.

Lathyrus (Papilionaceae)

Most of the familiar sweet peas require more sun than the woodland is likely to provide. These clump-forming species prefer the more open areas of a partially shaded woodland glade.

Lathyrus aureus

Established clumps can be divided in early spring. Plants spread by seed, but I do not find them persistent enough to be a problem. In the garden, I cut it back to ground level in the autumn and let the shoots start afresh in the spring. In a woodland, old stems can be left on most plants; they disintegrate eventually, adding their contribution to the ecosystem.

Lathyrus aureus

Distinctive and unusual amber-yellow flowers lend this plant a striking subtlety. 45cm.

Lathyrus vernus

This pretty, widely distributed European species blooms from midspring to early summer. The flowers are typical of the pea family, and a number of different coloured, though unimaginatively named, forms are in cultivation, making small clumps to 40cm tall. From var. *albus* (white) and 'Alboroseus' (pink and white) through f. *roseus* (pink) to 'Cyaneus' and 'Caeruleus' (bluish purple). These named forms are not "true" cultivars; they are colour strains, which breed true from seed.

Leucojum (Amaryllidaceae)

These delightful European bulbs, fittingly known as snowflakes, are reminiscent of large snowdrops, their pendant bell-like flowers differing in having six tepals of equal length. Not true woodland plants, they are nonetheless large enough to survive on the woodland floor and happy in dappled shade; some authorities state that shade is vital to avoid them being ravished by the narcissus fly. Since the smaller growers were transferred back to *Acis*, only two species are now classified under *Leucojum*, with characteristic green tips to their white flowers.

Leucojum aestivum

Found from Europe to northwestern Asia, it appreciates a moist site, often being found near rivers and even in waterlogged conditions. The inflated seedpod is filled with air to allow it to float and be dispersed by water. Up to eight flowers, prettily edged with green, may be held on a single stem in mid to late spring. 60cm.

'**Gravetye Giant**' Larger flowers.

Leucojum vernum

From central Europe, similar to *L. aestivum* but with larger green-tipped flowers on shorter stems. 35cm.

var. *carpathicum* Yellow-tipped flowers.

Leucojum aestivum
'Gravetye Giant'

Lilium (Liliaceae)

Lilies are evocative flowers, familiar even to the most dedicated nongardener. They flower and grow in the summer, so a certain amount of light must penetrate through or below the canopy to sustain them, ensuring enough food reserves are stored to give flower in subsequent years, although the bulb itself likes to remain cool. Dappled shade in fertile, leafy, humus-rich but well-drained soil is perfect for a number of species. They are happiest in more open clearings or at the woodland edge, where they can rise up above bushy smaller plants such as ferns, hostas, daphnes, and *Ruscus*. These give structure and hide the sometimes tatty lower stems of the lilies. They grow from a loose, scaly bulb which lacks a protective covering. The flowers are borne on erect leafy stems and may be trumpet-shaped or pendant Turk's-caps with reflexed petals.

Although beautiful, lilies do have their share of difficulties, virus being the most troublesome. This manifests itself in distorted, yellow-streaked foliage, weakening and eventually killing the plant. It is highly contagious, so affected plants should be destroyed. Control of aphids which transmit the virus is also important. Lilies grow best in cooler climates where these are less prevalent. The bright red lily beetle is another nuisance.

Lilies are best produced from seed. Most will germinate readily, but in two ways. In epigeal germination, a grasslike leaf is produced and the seedling grows away in the usual manner. In hypogeal germination, a rooted tiny bulb forms, but leaves are not produced until the following season. Cultivars need to be vegetatively propagated, but offset bulblets are often readily produced, sometimes in the leaf axils, too. Care should be taken not to propagate vegetatively from virused plants, though the disease cannot be transmitted through the seed.

Lilium duchartrei

This unique Chinese species was discovered by Père David in 1869 and loves a moist but not wet humus-rich soil where it will gradually spread by stolons. The stem may grow to 45–150cm tall, topped with exquisite, large Turk's-cap flowers, marble-white with conspicuous purple spots.

Lilium mackliniae

Not the toughest, but certainly one of the most beautiful species, at the time of its introduction from Burma in 1949, it was classified as *Nomocharis*. This is an understandable mistake when considering the open, bell-shaped flowers which are creamy white and delightfully flushed with pink. Up to eight flowers can be held on stems 30–70cm tall. One of my absolute favourites.

Lilium martagon

The name is derived from a Turkish word for a type of turban; hence the Turk's-cap lily. Probably the best woodland species, being found in such conditions through continental Europe. Usually up to 13 flowers clothe the leafy stems, but 50 has been recorded in cultivation. As a result of their vast natural distribution, the flower colour of these geographical variants is variable, from pure white through pale pink and darker, often heavily speckled. 120–180cm.

This amenable species has been utilised in hybridisation programmes, including orange-red *L. hansonii* to create *L. ×dalhansonii* and *L. ×marhan*. The second generation gives a wide range of colours, including the American Paisley hybrids and the British Backhouse hybrids. Enjoy these as a group or seek the individually named cultivars.

> **var.** *albiflorum* White flowers spotted with carmine-pink.
>
> **var.** *album* Unspeckled pure white flowers. An effective yet simple contrast with green and leafy companions.
>
> **var.** *cattaniae* (syn. var. *dalmaticum*) Statuesque form with large heads of amazing deep wine-coloured flowers.

Lilium pyrenaicum

Extending east from the Pyrénées to the Caucasus, the wide distribution renders this a varied and adaptable lily. Known since 1590, it has naturalised in hedgerows, reminding us that it appreciates some light. Many narrow, horizontally held, often silver leaves clothe the stems. The flowers are typically shaped and usually yellow with subtle black spotting.

Lilium martagon var. album

It is a complex species, having a number of similar and previously separately classified species brought into it. Scottish lily breeder Chris North utilised *L. pyrenaicum* as the seed parent in many of his superb crosses. 30–120cm.

> **subsp.** *carniolicum* **var.** *albanicum* Lower growing Balkan form; the amber-yellow flowers are marked with cinnabar-red.
>
> **subsp.** *pyrenaicum* **var.** *rubrum* Pretty Spanish form with brown-spotted, orange-red flowers.

Liquidambar (Hamamelidaceae)

Sweetgum, like maples, have deeply lobed leaves and spectacular autumn colour. Eventually large, they make wonderful accent plants in new woodland structural planting among *Crataegus* and *Betula*. They are tough enough to start out with them, but they have the potential to become long-term trees to take over the mantle of upper canopy as the interim planting starts to fade.

Liquidambar acalycina

Large three-lobed leaves are rich reddish purple when young, maturing to green, with fiery purples and oranges in autumn, for a long season of colour.

> **'Burgundy Flush'** The typical colouration is particularly vivid in this selection.

Above: *Liquidambar acalycina* 'Burgundy Flush' autumn foliage

Above right: *Liquidambar styraciflua* 'Golden Treasure' autumn foliage

Right: *Liquidambar styraciflua* 'Stared' autumn foliage

Liquidambar orientalis

Superb species, smaller in all its parts. Neat little leaves and tidy habit, still with tremendous autumn colours.

Liquidambar styraciflua

This most common species from North America resembles a maple with five to seven-lobed leaves and is extremely tolerant of wet soils. Seed-grown plants will vary in their autumn display and may disappoint; this is a shame when so many tried and tested named selections are available. Corky bark is a further attraction. Many variegated options exist.

'**Burgundy**' Deepest burgundy-purple autumn colour.

'**Festival**' Tidy habit but exciting displays of kaleidoscopic autumn colours, from yellows through peachy pinks to orange and red.

'**Golden Treasure**' Preferring the shelter of the middle canopy due to its variegation and much smaller stature, the leaves are margined with golden yellow. The progressive onset of autumn colour is a sight to behold.

'**Parasol**' Similar in colour to 'Festival', but broader in habit, the branches gently droop at the tips.

'**Rotundiloba**' The leaves have conspicuously rounded (as opposed to pointed) lobes and develop deep burgundy colour late in the season. Apparently no seed is set, which is considered an advantage in the United States—climatic differences dictate that seed-set is a rare occurrence on any *Liquidambar* in Britain.

'**Stared**' Wonderful selection with deeply divided, starlike leaves progressing through the colours of autumn to culminate in a rich red.

'**Worplesdon**' An English selection. Excellent autumn colour and tidy upright habit with nicely shaped leaves.

Liriope (Convallariaceae)

These useful evergreen plants are able to carpet even the most difficult areas of the woodland floor. However, there is a fine line between an easy-to-grow plant making a dense and extensive colony and it becoming an invasive thug. Usually it comes down to growing conditions. Problems can often occur in garden situations where higher fertiliser levels may exist. Woodland conditions can be allowed to be harsher; indeed, *Liriope* will be perfectly content at the foot of larger trees where less nutrients and moisture are available.

They are tremendous plants. Their upright, narrow, straplike leaves give structure all year, long after the ephemeral spring flowers have disappeared, while contrasting so well with many other shapes and textures of foliage.

The five species are of Asian origin, though recent times have seen a surge in the development of named cultivars, including those with variegated foliage. All are indispensable in the shade of the woodland garden, where they flower in that most difficult of seasons, bridging the gap between summer exuberance and the fiery displays of autumn, with dense spikes of colourful flowers protruding from their leafy midst. Clusters of berries reliably follow, thus extending their interest. In extreme winters or environments, they can relinquish their foliage, but this is rarely to their detriment. They form clumps to 40cm high from tuberous roots and spread accordingly.

Reversion can be an issue with the variegated cultivars, but in established colonies it is not always possible to tell whether the green sections are new seedlings (these variants do not breed true) or whether they are reversions from the variegated clump. The combination can actually be rather effective, enhancing the attraction of the variegated leaves, though care has to be taken that these green sections do not take over, since they are inevitably more vigorous than their variegated counterparts.

Liriope exiliflora

This most vigorous spreader may need to be exiled to the compost heap if not carefully located.

'**Ariaka-janshige**' This Japanese cultivar (incorrectly transcribed as Silvery Sunproof) is altogether gentler, with creamy white striped leaves beneath pretty pale violet flowers held more loosely than the other species. Black berries.

Liriope muscari

Liriope muscari

The most commonly found species in all its many incarnations, it is clump-forming with less inclination to run, hence its wider application.

'Big Blue' Hardly imaginative, but aptly descriptive. The flowers are a violet-blue rather than a true-blue.

'Christmas Tree' Less common form; the name alludes to the shape of the pale lilac flower spike which is wider at the base, narrowing to the top.

'Gold-banded' Superior selection from 'Variegata', in which the leaves have dark green margins of variable width surrounding a bright yellow centre. Purple flowers contrast magnificently.

'Monroe White' White flowers against a dark green leafy background is a favourite combination.

'Royal Purple' Clean purple flowers.

'Silver Ribbon' and **'Silvery Midget'** White variegation contrasts nicely with the purple flowers.

'Webster Wideleaf' Vigorous selection for where a leafy plant is needed; at 2cm wide, they are the most substantial in the genus. Purple flowers.

Liriope spicata

From China and Taiwan, as the others, this is the only species not also represented in Japan. Lower growing but spreading rapidly with mauve flowers held more loosely. 30cm.

'Alba' White flowers.

'Gin-ryu' Anglicised to Silver Dragon, the leaves are vividly striped with silver. Pale purple flower spikes reach only 25cm, followed by pale green berries. The correct name is the first name under which it was described, regardless of language. Although tempting to render the name more accessible to Western tongues, to do so is bad practice. (Translating names causes confusion and, more fundamentally, is rude.)

Lonicera (Caprifoliaceae)

Incredibly, the climbing honeysuckle's native range is from the Arctic Circle to the Malayan Archipelago and Mexico. Although many honeysuckles are shrubby, they prefer sunnier sites, so I shall concentrate on the climbers which are surprisingly happy in shade, even if some do flower better once their heads find the sun. They look tremendous scrambling through trees and hedges, just as nature intended, where their elongated trumpet-shaped flowers fill the air with delicious perfume in summer, often to be followed by orange or red berries in autumn. Easy to establish at the foot of modest trees or a little further away from greedy, mature root systems, they are a perfect way to enliven tall, bare trunks in mature woodland.

The flowers are held in pairs, or in terminal six-flowered whorls. Individually, long thin trumpets flaring into two "lips" reveal long stamens.

Lonicera ×*americana*
(*L. caprifolium* × *L. etrusca*) Spectacular vigorous hybrid. Eventually deep yellow, the flowers open white and mature through primrose, tinged purple on the outside.
> **'Pam's Pink'** New introduction; combination of blue-green foliage and pink flower buds opening to white.

Lonicera caprifolium
Upper pairs of leaves are perfoliate (that is, the stem appears to grow through the centre of an extra large leaf). Creamy white flowers are tinged pink. Native to Europe (not Britain, though it has naturalised here) east to Asia Minor.
> **'Anna Fletcher'** Creamy white flowers mature to pale yellow with no trace of pink. Midspring to midsummer.
> **'Inga'** Delightful recent selection with almost beige flowers and orange berries.

Lonicera ×*heckrottii*
(*L.* ×*americana* × *L. sempervirens*) Early hybrid predating 1895. Yellow flowers are richly flushed with purple.
> **'American Beauty'** Amazing form. Purple buds open to reveal brilliant orange trumpets with yellow centres from early summer to early autumn. Orange-purple berries.

Lonicera henryi

Vigorous and evergreen. The smaller but intensely coloured flowers open yellow, stained red at the base. Introduced from western China by Wilson in 1908.

'**Copper Beauty**' Floriferous and early, flowering in late spring/early summer. Large glossy leaves are deep bronze when young.

Lonicera periclymenum

Widespread through European hedgerows, its range extends south to Morocco. The flowerheads are an exuberant mix of purple and cream, typically produced from early summer to early autumn. The alluring scent increases in the evening as they strive to attract their hawk-moth pollinators.

'**Belgica**' Classic early form flowering initially in late spring/early summer and often again in late summer. 'Serotina' is similar but flowers later.

'**Cream Cloud**' Creamy green buds open to primrose flowers. Late spring to early autumn.

'**Graham Thomas**' The lovely, long-lasting, primrose-yellow flowers are tinted copper with maturity.

'**Heaven Scent**' Purple in bud, opening white, maturing to yellow. Late spring to late summer.

'**Red Gables**' Elegant form. Reddish purple in bud, the flowers flare to almost vertical as they open to reveal pale pink insides.

'**Sweet Sue**' Found by Roy Lancaster on a Swedish beach and named after his wife, it produces a long succession of very fragrant, large pale yellow flowers.

Lonicera ×tellmanniana

(*L. sempervirens* × *L. tragophylla*) This Hungarian hybrid is fantastic in even heavy shade. Large flowers open coppery yellow from reddish buds.

'**Joan Sayer**' Recent more floriferous form.

Lonicera tragophylla

Another treasure from western China. Huge bright yellow flowers in early to midsummer. Like its progeny *L. ×tellmanniana*, best in heavy shade.

Lunaria (Brassicaceae)

Known familiarly as honesty, I vividly remember the biennial version from childhood. My mother is a great flower arranger, and we picked the spent heads to use in the winter. A papery layer can be peeled from each side of the flat, round seedpod to reveal a sparkling disc, giving rise to another common name, money plant.

Lunaria rediviva

This perennial species inhabits subalpine woods of much of Europe, though nowhere is it widespread. It produces surprisingly fragrant pale pink flowers in clusters above soft, heart-shaped leaves from late spring to midsummer. Delightful summer colour in larger woodland landscapes. 140cm.

Luzula (Juncaceae)

Luzula is often touted as a great foliage plant for moist, shaded areas, and though it is without the bonus of colourful flowers as found in *Liriope*, the grasslike foliage is uncannily similar. This genus could be the solution where the ground is moist to the point of boggy and a dense carpet of foliage is needed to suppress the weeds and provide a sensation of luxuriance. Out of the 80 or so known species, only a handful are relevant here, forming tufted cushions.

Luzula nivea

Tiny white hairs edge the leaves, almost appearing as a silvery margin.

Luzula sylvatica

The most commonly grown species, forming gently creeping leafy tussocks. Of the various selections of this central European species, many are courtesy of the Munich Botanic Garden. 25cm.

> **'Aurea'** Broad leaves colour according to light levels, developing rich golden tones in good light in summer, and greenish yellow in heavy shade or winter.

> **'Marginata'** Green leaves neatly margined with creamy yellow, rather pleasantly complementing the humble brownish drooping flower spikes.

> **'Taggart's Cream'** New leaves emerge so pale as to be almost white, maturing to cream and finally dark green; new growth is in sharp contrast to the darkness of the older leaves.

> **'Tauernpass'** Low, flat rosettes of rich green leaves maintain their verdure throughout even the harshest winter weather.

Luzula cultivar

> **'Ruby Stiletto'** Supremely hardy selection from the mountains of British Columbia. The compact mounds of narrower leaves are tinted with red through winter and early spring. What a wonderful foil for the first snowdrops of the season.

Magnolia (Magnoliaceae)

No one who has experienced the gardens of Cornwall in the spring will need convincing of the necessity of including magnolias in every woodland garden. Indeed, few sights are more inspiring than a magnolia in all its glory. Yet I prefer to intersperse them through the woodland, as accent trees among the simple greenery and those with other season interest, rather than to be bowled over by a mass of colour as they all flower together. Such is the beauty of gardening, that there should be no single solution.

Magnolias are perfectly at home in a woodland setting.

The Asiatic species may be the aristocrats of the genus, but they grow to a vast size and take many years to flower. Modern breeding programs and selection around the world have brought together an endless range of hybrids to suit every aesthetic taste; these are grafted to flower from a very young age for almost instant gratification. Excitement surrounds the quest for a pure yellow flower, but their advantage is their later flowering, often not until late spring. Not only does this extend their season, but they escape the worst of the damaging late-spring frosts. Magnolias are more tolerant of soil pH than is widely appreciated, the soil structure being more important since they have a large leaf and hate to dry out in summer. However, on high pH soils, choose cultivars derived from the following species: *M. acuminata*, *M. kobus*, *M. ×loebneri*, and *M. wilsonii*. I have included a personal selection of more durable cultivars.

Magnolia ×*kewensis* 'Wada's Memory'
(*M. kobus* × *M. salicifolia*) Eventually a large but well-branched tree with slightly floppy, narrow-tepalled, pure white, fragrant flowers. What the flowers lack in size, they make

up for in quantity. Sometimes these smaller flowered clones can be more at ease with nature. Young leaves are flushed bronze-red.

Magnolia ×loebneri

(*M. kobus* × *M. stellata*) Magnolia hybridisation is not a recent innovation; Max Loebner was experimenting with this cross in Germany before the First World War. Although happy in light shade, they do well in full sun; their extreme frost hardiness and soil tolerance makes them ideal candidates for structural planting in a small woodland. The flowers' narrow petals reflect their parentage.

> **'Ballerina'** Compact small tree. Up to 30 tepals per flower, fragrant, white, flushed pink at the base.
>
> **'Donna'** Upright, densely branched shrubby tree. Twelve to thirteen broader pure white tepals.
>
> **'Leonard Messel'** Classic selection from 1955, less vigorous, with pale to rich pink flowers. Twelve tepals.
>
> **'Merrill'** From Harvard's Arnold Arboretum, the most vigorous clone, forming a broad-spreading tree to 9m or more. Pure white flowers with 15 tepals.

Magnolia sargentiana var. robusta

Discovered by Wilson in China in 1910, this was named for the then director of the Arnold Arboretum, Charles Sprague Sargent, whose unselfish foresight and generosity allowed this magnificent plant to become established in Western gardens. Being much more exposure-tolerant than its species, this is one of my favourite magnolias for the upper canopy, where, given time and appropriate conditions, it can reach majestic proportions. Potentially smothered in exquisite rose-purple blooms, shading to pale pink at the tips, the flowers were originally described as "open parachutes of coloured paper". The few named clones are hard to find but its influence is enjoyed in many modern hybrids.

> **'Blood Moon'** The darkest coloured selection.

Magnolia sprengeri

Another Wilson collection from China, this time on behalf of an English nursery. Existing in the wild as two distinct forms, having either pink or white flowers, it is a wonderful choice for the upper canopy. Various seedlings have been named while modern hybrids have benefited from its genetic influence.

> **'Diva'** One of the original Wilson seedlings, it eventually flowered at Caerhays Castle, Cornwall, in rich, crimson-pink. 15m.
>
> **var. *elongata*** This smaller form is more elegant in appearance. Resembling miniature water lilies, the creamy white flowers are flushed with rose-pink. 9m.
>
> **'Eric Savill'** Seed from the original 'Diva' flowered in the Savill Garden, England, after 17 years. Deep wine-red flowers fade to pink inside. More modest stature.

Above: *Magnolia*
×wieseneri

Above right: *Magnolia*
'Athene'

Right: *Magnolia*
'Butterflies'

Magnolia stellata

Shrubby in habit with narrow straplike tepals, many cultivars are available in shades of pink and white. Generally flowering best in a sunnier site, so it is suitable within an open, high-canopy woodland where its elegance can be exquisite.

Magnolia ×wieseneri

(syn. *M. watsonii*) (*M. obovata* × *M. sieboldii*) Becoming a small tree, often multi-stemmed, the imposing upward-facing flowers open in early to midsummer. Rounded white buds open to richly fragrant, creamy white flowers with prominent rose-crimson stamens.

Magnolia wilsonii

A charming member of the summer-flowering group, this Chinese native has tiny flowers by comparison with *M. ×wieseneri*. One of the best woodland magnolias, there can be no prettier sight than these nodding, red-stamened white blooms dangling from the almost black limbs of a bushy small tree. Another Wilson introduction, *M. sieboldii* is similar but exceptionally winter-cold hardy.

Magnolia cultivars

'Apollo' (*M. campbellii* subsp. *mollicomata* 'Lanarth' × *M. liliiflora* 'Nigra') Rich pink-purple buds open to reveal flowers with paler insides. Narrower petals open fully, almost reflexing, to flaunt the prominent boss of red stamens.

'Athene' (*M.* 'Mark Jury' × *M.* ×*soulangeana* 'Lennei Alba') Enormous fragrant flowers of cup and saucer structure may be 30cm across. Pink shading darker to the base outside, paler inside. Later spring flowering.

'Butterflies' (*M. acuminata* 'Fertile Myrtle' × *M. denudata*) A more recent American yellow hybrid, the flower is smaller than the traditional spring-flowering selections, but such a pretty colour.

'Columbus' (*M. denudata* × *M.* ×*veitchii* 'Peter Veitch') Although bred at the United States National Arboretum, it was selected by the late John Bond, then keeper of the gardens at Windsor. He named it to mark the 500th anniversary of Columbus's voyage, with oblique reference to the magnolia's cross-Atlantic journey. It freely produces large, cup-shaped white flowers, with the potential to become a large tree.

'Elizabeth' (*M. acuminata* × *M. denudata*) A lovely cultivar from the Brooklyn Botanic Garden. The cross was made in 1956 in an early attempt to produce a truly yellow magnolia, but it was not selected until 1977. The creamy yellow flowers with red stamens are produced later in the spring and are extremely weather resistant.

'Gold Star' (*M. acuminata* var. *subcordata* 'Miss Honeybee' × *M. stellata* 'Rubra') The unique flowers are primrose-yellow while their form is reminiscent of *M. stellata*, being 10cm across but consisting of 13 to 15 relatively narrow tepals. Growing larger than its parent, but retaining its free-branching tendency, 'Gold Star' grows vigorously when young. The larger than usual leaves are attractively bronze flushed when young and slightly furry. The most resilient of all magnolia we grow, it is one of my favourites.

'Lois' (*M. acuminata* × *M. denudata*) Recent selection considered to be the finest yellow yet. The primrose-yellow colour is held through four to six weeks of floral wonder.

'Margaret Helen' (*M. liliiflora* 'Nigra' × *M. campbellii* subsp. *mollicomata*) Rich rosy red bowl-shaped blooms are leant an air of elegance by narrower petals.

'Milky Way' (*M.* 'Mark Jury' × *M.* ×*soulangeana* 'Alba') Fragrant, icy white flowers in midspring are shaded rose-pink toward the base and pure white inside. An erect, neatly rounded tree.

'Star Wars' (*M. liliiflora* × *M. campbellii*) The outside of the flower is pink, but somehow a different pink to the others—more apricot-pink than purple, and creamy white within. The large but elegant flowers are more star-shaped than most and last for up to a month. Free-branching to make a broad headed, small tree.

'Susan' In the 1950s, a breeding program was undertaken at the US National Arboretum involving *M. stellata* and *M. liliiflora* clones, from which a number of cultivars were selected, to become known as the "eight little girls". These have larger flowers than *M. stellata* and flower later, thus avoiding the worst of the frosts. Their growth habit is shrubby, intermediate between their parents, making all members of this group (known as the Kosar-de Vos hybrids) perfect middle-canopy plants. 'Susan' has dark reddish purple flowers that open from slender, upright buds.

Mahonia aquifolium 'Green Ripple'

Mahonia (Berberidaceae)

Some 70 species are distributed from the Himalayas into Asia and the Americas. All are evergreen; some are sun-lovers, but the shade-dwellers are useful as well as being pleasant to look at. Easily established in seemingly hopeless areas, even infamous dry shade, they add valuable structure and low-down winter protection. Most produce showy, dense racemes of tiny yellow flowers in winter or early spring, cheerful against lustrous, glossy pinnate leaves. Native Americans were resourceful with their indigenous plants; the roots and stems contain the drug berberine, while the characteristic yellow roots were used as a dye. Apparently the berries make a delicious jelly, unless the bears get there first. Fortunately this is not a problem here in Somerset!

Mahonia aquifolium

The state flower of Oregon, hence the moniker Oregon grape, which recognises the blue-black berries. Glossy leaves may turn red with winter cold. The many named forms are all superb, small evergreens, perfect in woodland conditions, growing to about 1m and gradually broadening to make a dense thicket.

'Apollo' Vigorous but low-spreading. 'Smaragd' is similar.

'Atropurpurea' Particularly fine reddish winter colour.

'Green Ripple' Unusual wavy-edged, glossy green leaves turn purple in winter.

'Orange Flame' Fiery orange new growth contrasts with wine-red or deep green mature leaves.

Mahonia nervosa

Other species akin to *M. aquifolium* are found elsewhere in North America. This one is distributed through the western coastal mountain ranges, with coarsely serrated leaflets.

Mahonia nervosa

Mahonia pinnata

Confined to California and Oregon, its leaves are dull green above, glaucous grey beneath, reddish purple in winter. A little more upright.

Mahonia repens

Stoloniferous and lower growing, its dull blue-green leaves turn rich purple in winter.

Mahonia ×wagneri

This cross between *M. aquifolium* and *M. pinnata* includes these cultivars:

Frost-dusted *Mahonia ×wagneri* 'Hastings Elegant'

- **'Hastings Elegant'** Upright selection with sharply lobed, very shiny leaves.
- **'Moseri'** Bronze and orange young leaves develop from pretty apricot-coloured new growth, turning to apple-green and finally dark green.
- **'Pinnacle'** Previously attributed to *M. pinnata*, with vigorous upright habit and bronze young foliage.
- **'Sunset'** Spectacular colour through autumn into winter.

Maianthemum (Convallariaceae)

This unassuming genus includes those species previously known as *Smilacina* and still commonly referred to as such. However, it is burgeoning with recent introductions from China, giving us plenty more choice of leafy stems to add verdancy to our woodland floor. Thriving in the humus-rich, moisture-retentive shade, upright stems emerge from underground rhizomes in early spring, clothed with simple, alternate leaves and topped with starry or bell-like flowers between midspring and midsummer. Many species complete the display with a crop of bright red berries while developing radiant yellow autumn colours seldom rivalled by herbaceous species. I have included none of the latest South American introductions until more understanding of their hardiness is gained, though they are distinctive and attractive, with pendulous racemes of flowers.

Maianthemum dilatatum

Maianthemum dilatatum

(syn. *M. kamtschaticum*) Its range extends from the west coast of North America, to Russia and Japan. Do not waste prime conditions on it, or the dense, low foliage will become rampant; it is tolerant of even the darkest, driest sites, covering them through summer with short stems supporting two to three almost heart-shaped leaves. This green carpet is sprinkled with spikes of white flowers, but rarely until early summer, followed by red berries. Despite the fact that their leaves remain through summer, they will grow in areas more normally associated with summer-dormant spring woodlanders, being tolerant of the dry shade at the base of a tree, where they will continue to give cover long after their more spectacular spring companions have gone. Herein lies their strength.

Maianthemum formosanum

(previously *Smilacina formosana*) Clouds of scented white flowers hang above substantial, ribbed, deep green leaves on mahogany-red arching stems. Red fruits follow, in this luxuriant Taiwanese species. 100cm.

Maianthemum fuscum

(previously *Smilacina fusca*) Most members of Convallariaceae are white, so it is nice to vary the flower colour. Drooping racemes of relatively large purple flowers are followed by red fruits. 30cm.

Maianthemum japonicum

(previously *Smilacina japonica*) Native of Japan, but also Siberia, with glossy, dark green leaves. The individual white flowers are rather like bells and are densely clustered at the ends of 45–60cm tall stems. Bright red pea-sized berries follow. Known in Japan but yet to reach the West in quantity are various interesting sports; white margins and yellow fruit have been reported.

Maianthemum oleraceum

(previously *Smilacina oleracea*) Native of the Himalayas and China, I love the contrast of white flowers dangling like bells from the tips of rich ruby-red arching stems, followed by red berries. Deep green, glossy leaves are deeply veined. Its extra height adds to the drama. 150cm.

Maianthemum purpureum

(previously *Smilacina purpurea*) From China, purple pigmentation conspicuously stains the outer areas of the wide flowers and margins the otherwise dark green leaves. 70cm.

Maianthemum racemosum

(previously *Smilacina racemosa*) The most widely available species and rightly so, this North American native produces lots of small creamy white flowers held in feathery clusters at the ends of the stems. Lustrous red berries follow. 30–90cm.

Maianthemum racemosum

Maianthemum tatsienense

(previously *Smilacina tatsiensis*) This recently introduced Chinese species is completely different, having panicles of dainty yellow star-shaped blooms and orange berries. 40–90cm.

Matteuccia (Woodsiaceae)

This small genus is from North America and Eurasia.

Matteuccia struthiopteris

The most commonly cultivated species of fern is largely archetypal of the genus, although not the only member. It is nicknamed the ostrich fern, alluding to the plume-like fronds, yet in Britain it is known as the shuttlecock fern due to the clump's hollow shape, occurring because the sterile fronds form a symmetrical ring, in the centre of which fertile fronds arise in mid to late summer. These can make magnificent specimens, enjoying very moist or even boggy soil, where they may spread by stout rhizomes. In drier conditions, they will be more modest in stature. Until recently, the North American version of this was classified separately as *M. pennsylvanica*. Although wild plants should never be eaten, I was fascinated to discover that in New England and adjacent Canada, the still coiled young fiddleheads (sterile fronds) are collected in early spring and considered a delicacy, being canned commercially. 150cm.

Meconopsis (Papaveraceae)

The definitive blue poppy must be one of the most desirable garden plants; I admire it every time I visit gardens that accommodate it with acidic soil conditions, even though it will not grow in my soil. Unfortunately, those gorgeous blue-flowered species, such as

M. betonicifolia, *M. grandis*, and their hybrids, are singularly intransient in their soil requirements, rarely thriving in soils of higher pH no matter how well prepared. This group prefers a sandy, peaty soil that stays moist in summer.

Meconopsis cambrica

There is more to *Meconopsis* than blue poppies. This European native (including Britain) is a delightful plant, thriving in shady woodland conditions even on dry soil. The bright yellow flowers are held in early to late summer above prettily divided foliage. These bring the sunshine into the woodland through the heady days of summer. 60cm.

Seed is produced in vast abundance in pepper-pot like capsules, best sown direct, letting nature do the work. This long-lived perennial produces a branching taproot, so once established it cannot be transplanted, nor does it allow for division.

Yellow *Meconopsis cambrica* and orange *M. cambrica* var. *aurantiaca*

var. *aurantiaca* Orange-flowered form.

'Flore Pleno' Unusual double-flowered form, which also comes true from seed in both yellow and orange.

'Frances Perry' Arguably the darkest flowered selection, being reddish orange.

Meehania (Lamiaceae)

Closely related to *Lamium*, this one should be used with equal care, or it will colonise to the point of invasion. The long stoloniferous shoots wander along at ground level, rooting as they go and sending up stems from each node, each terminating in a pretty flowering spike. The purplish flowers in midspring to early summer are typical of the deadnettle family, with particularly attractive markings in the throat, while the virtually evergreen leaves are reminiscent of the ubiquitous stinging nettle.

Meehania cordata

This American species is a good compromise—creeping and spreading, but not too boldly. Flowering shoots reach 20cm tall, topped with dense clusters of pretty pinkish purple flowers.

Meehania fargesii

Difficult to obtain, this Chinese species rarely produces troublesome stolons; nor does *M. montis-koyae* from Japan. Flowers are more than 4cm long. A very pretty plant for a moist area of the woodland floor. 40cm.

Meehania urticifolia

The most widely available species needs careful siting, since it definitely can become rampant, though the attractive blue flowers are the largest in the genus. Widespread in moist Asian woodlands, there can be no disputing its quality as groundcover. Drier soil will diminish its enthusiasm to some degree. It can become deciduous in cold winters.

Melittis (Lamiaceae)

A pretty monotypic member of this useful family, spreading through Europe, east to Russia and Turkey.

Melittis melissophyllum

This clump-former (not a runner like its cousins) is variable across its wide distribution, so it is tolerant of a broad range of conditions. Its habit will be determined by the levels of moisture, nutrient, and shade. Thus, in full sun on poor, dry soil it will stay small and compact, while at the other extreme in shade, on moist and rich soil, it will grow more expansively to 40cm or even 70cm. The snapdragon-like flowers in late spring to early summer may be white, pink, purple, or a combination thereof according to its origin; plants from western Europe are usually pink to purple, while subsp. *carpatica* and subsp. *albida* from further east have larger leaves and white flowers, often with a purplish lip. A delightful plant for those difficult drier, shadier positions, colourfully following on from the spring bulbs.

Mertensia (Boraginaceae)

I find blue flowers in the woodland so restful in combination with the luxuriant green foliage (though it can be fun to punctuate the scene with a little bright yellow). There are actually around 50 perennial species of *Mertensia* with a varied distribution from Europe to eastern Asia, as well as the Americas. Most have basal clusters of leaves from which rise stems supporting hanging racemes of blue bell-like flowers in late spring to early summer. Many are pinkish while still in bud.

The standard few are widely available, but recent years have seen a number of seed collections of less common species being made, particularly in the Himalayas and Rocky Mountains. Not all are suitable for woodland purposes, but some are sure to establish themselves as essential plants as we gain experience of their requirements. Although most species will tolerate at least some shade, they will become leggy with sparse flowering if it is too dense. A few are actually native of sandy shores, so clearly these are not at all adapted to woodland culture. Nomenclature confusion exists in this genus; several species are known under two names and opinion differs as to which is now considered to be correct.

Mertensia ciliata

From the American Northwest, this species flowers later than many, in late spring to late summer. The root system is rhizomatous, but not invasive, forming small, tidy clumps of pleated leaves with pretty lilac flowers. 60cm. *Mertensia primuloides* from the Rocky Mountains is similar.

var. *stomatechoides* From coniferous forests, it is tolerant of heavier shade.

Mertensia echioides

As yet not widely grown, this undemanding yet rewarding Himalayan species has dense clusters of intense, deep blue flowers. It prefers rich soil that drains adequately in winter. Perhaps even worthy of a spot on the woodland rock garden. 20cm. Similar in stature and requirements is *M. moltkioides*, whose flowers are even prettier, having a delightful white or yellow eye.

Mertensia virginica

Mertensia sibirica

(syn. *M. pterocarpa*) This excellent choice should be much easier to obtain than others. Satisfyingly, it remains in growth for much longer through the summer, forming dense clumps. 40cm.

Mertensia virginica

(syn. *M. pulmonarioides*) A classic North American wildflower, whose only disadvantage is that it dies down so quickly after flowering in the spring. Position carefully to minimise the impact of a suddenly empty space; plant it adjacent to a late emerger, preferably one that needs a lot of space later in summer. Hostas are an obvious choice; with their huge leaves, they can need much more space by the height of the season than their winter absence deserves. Surrounding them with these pretty blue flowers in spring is the ideal solution to both problems.

'**Alba**' White flowers.

Milium (Poaceae)

Grasses have become almost a fashion accessory in recent years, particularly coupled with the trend towards prairie-style and drought-tolerant planting. Few are suitable for the shade of our woodland floor, but this European native is ideal.

Milium effusum

The tufted rootstock produces an elegant clump of broad leaves, each to 1cm wide and arching like ribbons as much as 120cm long.

'**Aureum**' (syn. 'Bowles' Golden Grass') The species itself is undistinguished, but this smaller cultivar adds a striking colour accent through the underplanting without being garish. Loose clusters of tiny yellow flowers are formed in midsummer but are incidental to the display. It can be short-lived, so it is useful that it comes true from self-sown seed. That also means it is unlikely to outlive its welcome.

'**Yaffle**' Recently selected, robust variegated form; the leaves are like soft green ribbons with a narrow golden stripe down their midrib. 1m.

Mitchella (Rubiaceae)

From North America or Japan, just two species of this genus exist. The evergreen, woody plants completely cover the ground, in much the same way that ivy can. Little room is left for plants other than bulbs to penetrate the mat of crisscrossing stems, though it will rarely bother to strangle another woody plant, nor does it climb. A perfect groundcover, therefore, where the changing seasons are not required to be marked by the arrival and departure of woodland perennials. It prefers acid soil, though tolerance of higher pH is shown if the soil is rich and moisture-retentive. The flowers are of great botanical interest, since they occur in pairs, the ovaries of each being united. The detail of each flower differs slightly to assure cross-pollination, reliably producing large red berries—one from each pair of flowers. These are much loved by the birds, but where they permit, they will remain on the plant for a whole season, creating a wonderful display along with the following year's flowers. It also makes a most attractive decoration at Christmas-time.

Mitchella repens

The classic American species. A white-berried form (f. *leucocarpa*) is known but scarce.

Mitchella undulata

The Japanese equivalent is arguably more ornamental, since it has larger leaves and fruit. The flowers are more pinkish in colour.

Mukdenia (Saxifragaceae)

This Asian endemic enjoys a cooler climate and will struggle with hot summers. Shade will help reduce the effect of warmer temperatures, but too much will mean fewer flowers. Its leaves are attractively shaped like those of maples. They require ample water in summer.

Mukdenia rossii

Mukdenia acanthifolia

The scarcer of the two species in cultivation, though first described back in 1941, this one hails from Korea. Both species are extremely similar, differing only in the precise leaf shape; this has more shallowly lobed leaves.

Mukdenia rossii

Rhizomatous and clump-forming in much the same way as *Heuchera* and others, with pretty white (occasionally pale pink) flowers held in clusters on 45cm tall stems in late spring to early summer. The deeply lobed, attractive leaves resemble maple leaves and account for its former name, *Aceriphyllum rossii*. The generic name now in use, *Mukdenia*, is derived from Mukden, the ancestral capital of the Manchu Dynasty and the old capital of Manchuria.

'**Crimson Fans**' A new introduction with leaves that almost rival those of *Heuchera* for colour—and they certainly exceed them for size. They emerge bronze-green and age to mid-green splashed with bright red as the summer progresses. The show gets even better into autumn as the green areas change to gold. The white bell-shaped flowers are held in their branched panicles above the beautiful foliage from late winter to midspring.

Muscari (Hyacinthaceae)

The ubiquitous grape hyacinth offers so much more than is often appreciated. With some 60 bulbous species from which to choose, they are distributed in the wild from the Mediterranean basin east into Asia. The flowers form in a conical pyramid on a short stem emerging from a tuft of basal leaves. Individually they are grape shaped, tiny urns with constricted mouths, with the top ones usually sterile and of a different colour. The basic colour is generally blue, from the palest to a deep violet. Many will thrive in open, sunny sites but they will do well in all but the deepest shade. Though some dislike baking in summer, others are resilient enough to tolerate the drier sites at the base of the mature tree. I love the traditional colour combination of blue and yellow, so these work well with primroses and *Narcissus*, but many are tough enough to stand their ground among larger but late developers. Colonise difficult areas around hostas or among the yet-to-show patch of *Convallaria* and *Polygonatum*. The darker forms look wonderful against the silvery variegation of *Pulmonaria* or *Brunnera*, toning with the latter's pale blue flowers. Imagine a rich blue carpet beneath a white magnolia.

Muscari armeniacum

The leaves of this easy but variable species will be fully developed by midwinter. This is advantageous in the context of a year-round green presence, but it does leave them vulnerable to the ravages of winter weather, though any damage will be superficial rather than of long-term significance. In its best forms, this is a gorgeous species. Accepting that the named forms will not breed true, if they are to be naturalised and allowed to seed around, it could be said not to matter (provided subsequent seedlings are not distributed under the cultivar name). The superior genes of the named clone will be reflected in the seedlings, enhancing the colony as a whole. 30cm.

Muscari armeniacum

    '**Christmas Pearl**' Commencing flowering in mid-February in my garden, some three weeks earlier than typical *M. armeniacum*, this cultivar creates an early splash of violet-blue to plant with snowdrops and *Eranthis*. 'Blue Pearl' is similar.

    '**Saffier**' This selection is sterile, so the flowers never open out to produce seeds. This enhances the grape analogy and limits its rate of spread while lasting in full flower for significantly longer—potentially into late spring.

Muscari armeniacum
'Valerie Finnis'

'Valerie Finnis' Masses of delightful pale violet-blue flowers (darkening slightly toward the base of the spike) disguise the slightly tatty senescent foliage.

Muscari aucheri

This dear little Turkish species may be better suited to the woodland rock garden or alongside meandering paths. Much less foliage than many *Muscari*; only two or three grey-green leaves emerge in spring shortly before the inflorescence. Rounded flowers are dark blue at the base of the squat spike, paling to almost white at the top. 10cm.

Muscari azureum

What an amazing colour this one is, sky-blue as the name suggests. Also Turkish, it enjoys the cooler, moister climes of our woodland floor. The 15cm spikes carry numerous tiny flowers, which are more flared at the mouth.

'Album' Beautiful white form.

Muscari latifolium

This larger species, from the Balkans east to Iran, is one of the best for naturalising, boasting a tidy habit with broader upright foliage. The lower flowers are a very deep violet-blue, contrastingly topped with much paler sterile flowers. 15cm.

Muscari macrocarpum

I am unable to resist including this gem from the Aegean and Turkey for the woodland rock garden.

Muscari latifolium

Thick perennial roots delve deeply down to find moisture. The lower flowers are bright yellow, opening from purple buds, creating an unlikely bicoloured effect initially. A member of the musk hyacinth group, it unexpectedly emits a delicious fruity fragrance. Look out for the selection 'Golden Fragrance'.

Muscari neglectum

For many of us, this is the archetypal grape hyacinth, which spreads by offsets to colonise potentially vast areas. I have childhood memories of a particularly uncompromising patch of garden bursting with these; among them exquisitely fragrant, pure white lily of the valley (*Convallaria majalis*) would emerge in sharp contrast. The foliage can be untidy but is almost evergreen, while the flowers are a deep blue. Certainly better than bare soil in a difficult site, but the other species are definitely more refined.

Muscari cultivar

'**Jenny Robinson**' (syn. 'Baby's Breath') A sublime collection from Cyprus by the British collection holder. The uniformly soft powder-blue flowers are reminiscent of *M. armeniacum* 'Valerie Finnis' but the grey-green leaves of 'Jenny Robinson' maintain their appearance better.

Myosotis (Boraginaceae)

The captivating blue flowers of the forget-me-not are part of my earliest gardening memories. It is easy to dismiss such plants as being too common and boring and to spend vast amounts of money and time struggling with exotics which prove to dislike the soil or the climate. Perhaps we should enjoy the simpler things in life and make the most of the plants which are so undemanding. After all, there is little aesthetic difference between the humble forget-me-not and the more fashionable *Omphalodes* or *Brunnera*.

Myosotis form mats or rosettes of leaves from which emerge the flower stems, to delight us with their traditional cluster of usually brilliant blue flowers from late spring to early autumn. Many of the 75 or so species come from the lightly wooded areas of New Zealand and they are unsuitable for climates with wet winters.

Myosotis alpestris

This variable European endemic grows to 20cm tall. It complicates matters when many extremely similar species exist with their geographical variants.

Myosotis rehsteineri

This one could be homed on the woodland rock garden since it should not exceed 10cm in height, extending potentially to 30cm across. It does need moist soil, though, and it will reward with proportionally larger blue flowers over a longer season.

Myosotis scorpioides

Sometimes called the water forget-me-not, this species thrives in wet places, though its distribution is vast—from northern Europe, south to the Crimea and east to India. It has naturalised in eastern North America as well as California and also Japan. Provided adequate moisture is available, it will revel in the dappled shade of a woodland clearing, where it will be long-lived, flowering on stems as tall as 1m, though normally nearer 30cm. Usually the expected lovely blue, several clones have been named. The creeping stems will root in at the nodes if the ground is moist enough.

> MAYTIME ('**Blaqua**') Attractive leaves broadly margined with cream set off the bright blue flowers. Much slower growing.
>
> '**Mermaid**' Robust selection with brilliant blue flowers.
>
> '**Pinkie**' Pretty pink flowers.
>
> '**Snowflakes**' Clear white flowers with a yellow eye. 'Alba' is similar.

Myosotis sylvatica

A true woodlander, occurring in most of Europe as well as the Himalayas and Japan, though often shorter lived than *M. scorpioides*. It self-seeds to offer replacement plants. Each individual flower can be almost 1cm across, while the flowering stem reaches 45cm in height. Usually blue, pink and white forms are known.

Nandina (Berberidaceae)

Certainly the most diverse and arguably the most valuable family for woodland planting, this representative is an Oriental monotypic genus, introduced to the West at the beginning of the nineteenth century.

Nandina domestica

Known as sacred bamboo, their often tall, unbranched stems are covered in an attractive white bloom and topped with compound leaves. These may be purple-flushed in spring, becoming green in summer before giving fantastic autumn colour provided light levels are adequate. They will grow extremely well in shade, even dry shade once established, though they will colour better in moister, fertile areas of the woodland floor under high canopy. In heavy shade, they can become leggy at the base, but they provide great height and structure, so the bareness can be disguised with lower evergreens—*Mahonia* or *Sarcococca* perhaps. Regular pruning helps regenerate new growth low down. Large terminal panicles of white flowers are produced in early summer and sometimes again in autumn, followed by spectacular bunches of usually red (occasionally white) berries, much loved by birds. Fruiting can be enhanced by planting two clones to aid pollination. Although limited choice is available in the UK, in the United States and Japan, recent selections have increased the range to more than 50 dwarf and variegated forms.

Sufficiently adaptable to have naturalised in parts of Florida, they look beautiful and at home in the natural woodland environment. Native flora is at risk in Florida, but it is unlikely to have the same effect in Britain due to the different climate.

'**Firepower**' Dense, compact habit with fiery bright red winter colour. 'Wood's Dwarf' is similar.

'**Harbor Dwarf**' Spreads by underground rhizomes to form colonies of graceful leafy stems. 1m.

PLUM PASSION ('**Monum**') Plum-purple new growth and pink-flushed flowers.

'**Richmond**' Vigorous selection with bright red winter colour.

Narcissus (Amaryllidaceae)

There can be few closer associations with spring than cheerful yellow daffodils, flowering their hearts out in almost every garden. Regularly offered as a "naturalising mix", but to my mind, so often these are just inappropriate random selections of modern cultivars, excessive in their height, vulgar in their shape and colour combinations. For me the answer is clear. The best *Narcissus* to naturalise through our woodland floor are those that would occur there naturally, along with their close allies.

Nandina domestica
'Richmond'

With many of the 56 species emanating from Spain, their distribution extends through Europe into Asia and North Africa. Their familiar flowers have a distinct corona (trumpet), which may be minimal (small and cuplike) or longer, backed by six tepals, usually held vertically. Sometimes the flowers are held singly; in other species as many as 20 appear per stem and up to four stems per bulb. Their natural habitats are diverse, but many appreciate surprisingly moist conditions while active.

Narcissus bulbs are made up of layer upon layer, as an onion. This protects the vital core even if the outer layers desiccate, allowing them to survive surprisingly dry conditions during dormancy. This is not difficult to achieve when positioned among tree roots, but avoid too heavily shaded an area since adequate light is required to enable energy to be stored for subsequent flowering. High canopy is ideal, as are woodland margins and clearings, hedgerow bases, and the foot of mature trees. The bulbs can rot if too wet over winter. Plant the bulbs deep in rich soil; in impoverished conditions, application of appropriate fertiliser after flowering will help replenish their vital starch reserves.

Planting combinations are limited only by the gardener's imagination, but it is important that the leaves are left to die down naturally to maximise their food conversion. It can be useful therefore to distribute them among later emergers who will disguise their demise.

Virus and nematodes afflict *Narcissus*, both manifesting themselves in yellow streaked foliage. Neither is treatable; it is better to destroy infected plants immediately to reduce the risk of infecting adjacent colonies.

Narcissus bulbocodium

Distinctive in its preference for a moisture-retentive site, this miniature and its derivatives will reward with almost evergreen foliage and abundant bright yellow hoop-petticoat–shaped trumpets in early spring.

Narcissus cyclamineus

This adorable little Spanish and Portuguese species is worryingly rare in the wild but naturalises beautifully in sparse grass beneath trees, though it does prefer moisture-retentive acid soil. Solitary bright yellow flowers in early spring are characterised by their long trumpets and petals which are so swept back as to be almost parallel with the corona. 10–15cm.

Narcissus cyclamineus

Narcissus obvallaris

With so many cultivars available, it is easy to lose sight of how nature intended daffodils to look. Classification and identification issues have dogged the history of this species, found in south Wales and other (though possibly introduced) isolated British locations. Known locally as the Tenby daffodil and adopted as the Welsh symbol of Saint David's Day, it is an excellent plant for a woodland. This classic daffodil has shallowly fringed golden yellow flowers. 20cm.

Narcissus pallidiflorus

A classic daffodil in shape but distinct in colour, being creamy yellow, paler than *N. pseudonarcissus*. Varying with altitude in its native Pyrénées, it may flower in midwinter in cultivation.

Narcissus pseudonarcissus

Having naturalised in so many places (including opposite corners of the United States), the exact extent of this species' natural distribution, though essentially European, is uncertain. Likely even to predate its first reference of 1570, the nodding flowers are widespread throughout the British Isles, with creamy yellow tepals and golden yellow trumpets. Nomenclature confusion abounds among its derivatives, many of which are too sun-loving to warrant inclusion here. 35cm.

> **'Lobularis'** Known as the Lent lily in recognition of its flowering time.

Narcissus pseudonarcissus 'Lobularis'

Narcissus triandrus

This gorgeous dwarf species is distributed from Spain into Portugal. Up to six nodding flowers appear per stem with reflexed petals (shorter than those of *N. cyclamineus*) and a cup-shaped corona. Their delicate beauty is best suited to the woodland rock garden or small-scale woodland plantings. In cultivation it is normally represented by the pale yellow *N. triandrus* subsp. *triandrus*.

Narcissus cultivars

More than 12,000 named hybrids of *Narcissus* are divided into divisions according to their origins and characteristics. These clump up nicely but will not come true from seed. I have included a very personal selection, influenced by cultural considerations.

Division 1

Trumpet daffodils, one flower to a stem with a corona as long as, or longer than, the tepals, provide classic daffodil appearance in early spring.

> **'Little Beauty'** Essentially a miniature version, white tepals contrasting with lemon trumpets. 10cm.
>
> **'Little Gem'** Pale gold, uniformly coloured flowers. 15cm.
>
> **'W. P. Milner'** Lovely creamy white flowers to 25cm.

Division 5

Derivatives of *N. triandrus* display similar characteristics but have a sturdier constitution, each stem bearing up to three flowers.

> **'Ice Wings'** Slightly taller with more rounded tepals and longer, less flared corona.
>
> **'Liberty Bells'** Delightful lemon-yellow flowers with darker cups.
>
> **'Petrel'** Excellent American selection, generally easier to cultivate than the similar well-known 'Hawera'. Pure white flowers in midspring. 20cm.
>
> **'Thalia'** White flowers with large tepals and small coronas. 30cm.

Division 6

Derived from *N. cyclamineus*, these cultivars share a more modest version of their distinctive swept-back flower shape, but often with greater vigour and soil adaptability, in a range of colour combinations.

'**February Gold**' Earlier flowering with golden yellow tepals and slightly darker trumpet. 30cm.

'**Jack Snipe**' Long, cream-coloured tepals contrast with a bright yellow cup in early spring. 25cm.

'**Jenny**' One of my favourites, the lemon-yellow trumpet fades to the same milky white as the tepals. Later flowering. 35cm.

'**Jetfire**' Classic selection from America, with vibrant colours and robust nature. The bright orange trumpet leaps out from golden tepals. 25cm.

'**Lemon Silk**' Wonderful colour, though slower to clump up. Exquisite, pale lemon–coloured nodding flowers in early spring. 35cm.

'**Mite**' Stronger version of the species with rich golden yellow flowers. 25cm.

Narcissus 'Mite'

'**Peeping Tom**' The same golden yellow swept-back tepals, but the trumpet is also flared. Taller and earlier flowering, from late winter. 40cm.

'**Trena**' Recent addition to the group with slender lemon-yellow trumpet and white tepals. Long-lasting flowers. 30cm.

Division 12

These daffodils do not fall into any other division.

'**Jumblie**' Two or three flowers adorn each stem, with golden yellow tepals and deeper trumpets. 20cm.

'Tête-à-tête' One of the best for naturalising, it flowers prolifically over a long period from late winter to early spring. The lightly reflexed golden tepals and neat trumpets are held on stout, 15cm stems.

Nomocharis (Liliaceae)

A native of Tibet, China, and Burma, this exquisite genus has a flower intermediate between a lily and a fritillaria. Like lilies, active and flowering in summer, they require adequate light and moisture at that time. However, they also appreciate a cool, humid environment, so the woodland floor can be ideal, where the soil is humus-rich but well-drained and the shade cooling rather than oppressive. These are too pretty to lose among larger ostentatious neighbours, deserving of that most special of positions, perhaps with small soft ferns at their feet to disguise their stems. Scaly bulbs and erect leafy stems are reminiscent of lilies, while the saucer-shaped flowers are more open. They are not the easiest to please, though an understanding of their requirements will help; I find this genus utterly captivating.

Nomocharis aperta

Nomocharis aperta
From western China, with up to six rose-pink flowers with black centres and a scattering of often ring-shaped crimson spots. 60cm.

Nomocharis ×finlayorum
A group of hybrids involving *N. mairei* and *N. pardanthina* which occurred spontaneously in Scotland. Intermediate between their parents, but most importantly boasting hybrid vigour, they are more easily cultivated than the species.

Nomocharis pardanthina
This charming Himalayan species is basically white; the three inner tepals are heavily spotted with pink and noticeably fringed. Variable, with less spotted or even pure white forms. Up to eight outward-facing flowers per 100cm stem can individually be an amazing 9cm or more across. *Nomocharis mairei* from western China is very similar.

Nomocharis saluenensis
Up to five gorgeous nodding flowers are rose-purple with a purple-spotted centre. Widespread through the genus's distribution. 60–90cm.

Omphalodes (Boraginaceae)

My first awareness of this genus came when visiting a local garden with my young son. He fell in love with it and insisted we should have one. Of course, I was unable to refuse, so we duly came home with our new treasure and found a shaded site for it, where it has thrived ever since. Subsequently, we discovered the existence of a number of named forms and our delight in them has never waned. Although just one species, *O. cappadocica*, dominates cultivation in the UK, the genus includes nearly thirty, some of which are annuals. The perennials form tufted clumps of simple leaves topped by clusters of blue flowers reminiscent of forget-me-nots. They could not be easier to grow in shaded conditions, though they do not like to bake in summer. These woodlanders combine beautifully with many other plants, depending on the atmosphere to be created. It can be quiet or moody with glaucous or silver foliage as found in many *Pulmonaria*, or it can be vibrant when juxtaposed among the acid-yellow of *Euphorbia polychroma* and *Narcissus*. Blue can tell one story among subtle pastel pinks or quite another against the clarity of white flowers and variegated foliage.

Above: *Omphalodes cappadocica* 'Cherry Ingram'

Right: *Omphalodes cappadocica* 'Starry Eyes'

Omphalodes cappadocica

This species is endemic to a relatively small area of northeastern Turkey and the Republic of Georgia. Clouds of dainty blue flowers drift over simple clumps of evergreen leaves in early to late spring. Delightful in itself, several clones have been named.

'**Alba**' White flowers.

'**Cherry Ingram**' Arguably the best blue selection with large, vibrant flowers.

'**Lilac Mist**' Lilac-pink flowers are pretty, but I prefer the true blue.

'**Parisian Skies**' More recent selection, perhaps set to supersede 'Cherry Ingram'.

'**Starry Eyes**' Almost bicolour, the blue flowers are noticeably edged with lilac, becoming white.

Omphalodes nitida

This taller European species, from Portugal and Spain, needs a moist site. The habit may be laxer, but the summer flowers are just as blue, marked with yellow in the folds between the lobes.

Omphalodes verna

From the central European mountains, this species will spread faster than *O. cappadocica* or *O. nitida*, by virtue of its short stolons. Vivid blue flowers are borne in spring.

    'Alba' White flowers.

    'Elfenauge' German selection with pale blue, airy flowers.

Onoclea (Woodsiaceae)

A small genus largely represented by one extremely popular fern.

Onoclea sensibilis

Early settlers observed that it was very sensitive to frost, being knocked to the ground by the first frosts of autumn, so the common name sensitive fern was born. Despite the implication of the name, it is actually extremely hardy, just deciduous. From North America and Asia, and naturalised in western Europe, this distinctive fern loves moist soils but is adaptable. The somewhat shaggy, arching sterile fronds are coarse and leathery, with broader light green leaflets. Fertile fronds by contrast are half the height and produced in late summer, with hard, beadlike brown secondary leaflets, remaining through the winter to distribute their spores the following spring. With shallow, creeping rhizomes, pretty colonies will develop but are rarely aggressive. 60cm.

Ophiopogon (Convallariaceae)

Much prized for carpeting the woodland floor, this genus includes some architectural plants which can add an extra dimension. I refer of course to the infamous black mondo grass, *O. planiscapus* 'Nigrescens', which can be used to good effect in so many different ways. These are not actually grasses, as can be seen from the family name; they are allied to *Convallaria* (the flowers are similar in structure though usually smaller) and are particularly closely akin to *Liriope*, differing mainly in their fruit colour (black in *Liriope*, blue in *Ophiopogon*). Confined to Asia, most are evergreen so offer dramatic effect even in winter. With up to 50 species, few are well represented in cultivation in the West. All, however, are at home even in very dry shade and will succeed at the foot of large evergreens.

Ophiopogon bodinieri

Above the clumps of grassy green foliage are held nodding clusters of white flowers, strongly tipped with purple. Collected in China by Chris Brickell, the collection number B&L12505 has more consistently purple flowers.

Ophiopogon japonicus

Very popular in Japan, though also found in China and Korea, this species forms colonies, spreading by slender rhizomes. They are well behaved in difficult conditions but overly vigorous in too ideal a position. The arching, 20–30cm long, green leaves are fairly undistinguished, as are the typical white flowers, but some quite amazing (bizarre even) variegated selections are available.

'Kigimafukiduma' The surprisingly erect green and white–striped foliage sparkles to the point of appearing silver. Most effective and a wonderful accent plant. Variegation should be used sparingly, but this colouring can work with anything. Plants listed as 'Silver Mist' should carry this name instead (though I can almost sympathise with Anglicising this name).

'Kyoto' Standing just 7cm tall, this cultivar almost takes dwarf to extremes, but it spreads to form a carpet. That opens up all sorts of possibilities, allowing even a small shrub to be underplanted. It would be fun to combine it with dwarf bulbs, particularly those too small to mix with the usual range of woodland carpeters— tiny *Crocus* perhaps or the smallest of the miniature *Narcissus*. Definitely a possibility for the woodland rock garden or anywhere that needs tiny planting, even under an *Acer* in a large pot. There are other extremely dwarf cultivars, too.

'Variegatus' Green leaves are narrowly margined with yellow.

Ophiopogon planiscapus

Another Japanese native, the species itself is seldom cultivated.

'Nigrescens' This black-leaved incarnation has become legendary, complemented with delicate pink-flushed flowers. Although very tolerant of dry conditions, the full intensity of colour is revealed only with adequate light, making it perfectly suited to growing at the base of a big tree, where light will penetrate from the sides. If you like strong contrasts, consider yellow flowers or foliage against the black leaves, or use it as a subtle background.

Ornithogalum (Hyacinthaceae)

It is little wonder that the botanists divided up the massive Liliaceae into more manageable chunks; 120 or so species are in this genus alone, from Europe, Asia, and Africa, though it is surprising how few are in cultivation. One or more basal leaves is produced by each bulb, followed by a leafless stem topped by usually white, rather starlike flowers.

Many *Ornithogalum* will naturalise readily, but they usually prefer more open meadow conditions. The species listed here are happy on the shaded woodland floor. They will tolerate dry conditions when dormant so are ideally adapted to planting under specimen trees where the light will be good.

Ornithogalum nutans

The most suitable species for these shady conditions is native to the Balkans but naturalised in many parts of Europe. Green buds open into white, outward-facing flowers. 25–45cm.

Ornithogalum pyrenaicum

Although the name gives away its Pyrénéan origins, this species is also distributed through Europe into England, to the point that at one stage it was known locally as Bath asparagus, owing to the production of an abundance of edible young flowering stems near that city. These rise to 30–60cm tall, topped by up to 50 white flowers, flushed yellow. They can benefit from being planted among other foliage to disguise their fading midsummer leaves.

Ornithogalum umbellatum

From southern Europe across to the eastern Mediterranean, this species forms dense clumps, thanks to its proliferation of bulblets. It will easily colonise an area with its pretty white flowers—up to 20 per 30cm stem, individually up to 4cm across.

Osmanthus (Oleaceae)

Fifteen evergreen species represent this genus, found in North America, Asia, and the Pacific Islands. The hardy forms listed here are extremely easy to grow almost anywhere, thriving in the woodland conditions where they will give valuable winter protection as well as being spectacular and fragrant in flower themselves. Their flowers may be individually small, but en masse they create a breathtaking display.

Osmanthus armatus

Statuesque, with oblong leaves to 18cm long, flowering in autumn. Another Wilson introduction from China in 1902.

Osmanthus ×burkwoodii

(*O. delavayi* × *O. decorus*) Previously classified as *Osmarea* ×*burkwoodii*, it is now back in its rightful place. Crossing two excellent species is a good recipe for a successful plant, and this is a tough customer, growing tidily to 3m, with dark green leaves and masses of fragrant white flowers in early to midspring.

Osmanthus decorus

Large, leathery leaves lack the spininess typical of this genus. Masses of tiny white spring flowers give rise to a splendid crop of purplish black berries. From the south-eastern coast of the Black Sea.

'**Angustifolius**' Narrower leaves.

Osmanthus delavayi

The white spring flowers are gorgeous, resembling jasmine. Although capable of reaching 3m, this species from the Chinese Yunnan province is much slower growing, with tiny, scallop-edged, deep green leaves. Though tolerant of driest shade, this will reduce its vigour. The Himalayan *O. suavis* is closely related but has much longer leaves (8cm) and a more upright habit.

'**Latifolius**' Bigger in all its parts, so the better choice where more instant gratification is required.

Osmunda asiatica

Osmanthus heterophyllus

It is an unexpected treat in midautumn to enjoy the sweet scent of this Japanese introduction dating back to 1856. The holly-like leaves are often at their spiniest while young.

'**Aureomarginatus**' Leaves margined deep yellow.

'**Gulftide**' Compact, upright form with very glossy foliage, paler green when young.

'**Ogon**' Effective but painfully slow accent plant. Bright golden young growth matures to green, upright habit.

'**Sasaba**' Amazing pointed, angular, spiny leaves defy description and are most unpleasant to weed around.

'**Variegatus**' Conspicuous creamy margins make this cultivar lighten a dark and shady corner.

Osmunda (Osmundaceae)

Osmunda are found on every continent save Australasia. In moist or even boggy soils, they will reward with some of the most statuesque, though deciduous, clumps. They will tolerate drier conditions but will not perform to their full potential. The species was named for the Saxon god, Osmunder the Waterman, who legend has it hid his family from danger in a clump of these ferns. Fibre found near the frond bases is used in the potting of orchids.

Osmunda asiatica

This scarce but very elegant species has a tidy, upright habit.

Osmunda cinnamomea

Distinctive fertile fronds are shorter but become a rich cinnamon-brown, held vertically in the centre of the clump of tall, vase-shaped sterile fronds which are twice divided and stately, developing unexpectedly pretty yellow and bronze autumn colours. North America is just part of its wild distribution, but it is an important plant in the ecology of the continent. 150cm.

Osmunda claytoniana

Distributed through North America and eastern Europe across to Asia, it is strangely nicknamed the interrupted fern on account of the brown fertile leaflets which are much smaller, to "interrupt" the green sterile leaflets on some fronds. Among the earliest ferns to emerge in spring from the thickly matted, stout, creeping rootstock, it forms a stately clump. 1m.

Osmunda regalis

The royal fern is the species most associated with the genus. Spring fiddleheads are not as brown and woolly as in *O. cinnamomea* or *O. claytoniana*, but they develop into a sight to behold. In rich, wet ground *O. regalis* can easily reach 2m tall as well as colonising an area 3m across, but in the drier conditions more normally found on the woodland floor, half that size is more realistic. Sometimes also called the flowering fern, alluding to the tassel-like clusters of spores at the tips of the fronds, which are broad with well-spaced pinnae (each leaflet rather reminiscent of a wisteria leaf). Yellow-brown autumn colour is an unexpected bonus.

Osmunda regalis

   'Cristata' Smaller growing with crested leaflets.
   'Purpurascens' New fronds are tinted reddish purple in spring.
   var. *spectabilis* Considered to be the North American incarnation of this species, not growing quite as tall as the European and Asian type form, *O. regalis* var. *regalis*.
   'Undulata' Crisped margins.

Ourisia (Scrophulariaceae)

Ourisia is an elusive genus; many are just a bit too demanding to grow in normal conditions. Originating in South America, New Zealand, and Tasmania, far too many need alpine house or other specialist treatment, although those listed here are said to prefer cooler climates. They are extremely happy with woodland shade and require a rich, moist soil containing abundant humus. The woodland rock garden is just the place to try them, where their unique beauty can be admired close up and their position prepared with extra attention to detail.

Ourisia coccinea

Ourisia coccinea

This exquisite little plant should thrive in the conditions just described. Long, funnel-shaped flowers in summer flare at the mouth and are the most amazing shade of scarlet, held in clusters on stems above a mat of evergreen, toothed, deep green leaves. This species may spread too widely; but what a wonderful concept. 25cm.

Ourisia macrocarpa

With flowering spikes to 70cm tall, this is one of the largest in the genus. A native of New Zealand, it seems perfectly tolerant of garden culture, though it needs more space on the woodland floor. The white flowers occur in whorls of up to nine up the stem, but individually they are of a similar trumpet shape. *Ourisia macrophylla* is similar, though usually a little shorter. Reputedly disappointing after a few years; dividing and replanting into enriched soil seems to solve the problem, as they simply exhaust the nutrients available to them before fading.

Ourisia cultivars

'**Loch Ewe**' This hybrid between *O. coccinea* and *O. macrophylla* is from the National Trust for Scotland garden at Inverewe. The structure of the plant is basically the same as others in the genus, but it has salmon-pink flowers.

'**Snowflake**' Much smaller, this white-flowered hybrid between *O. macrocarpa* and *O. caespitosa* reaches just 10cm when it flowers in late spring.

Oxalis (Oxalidaceae)

I have spent sufficient time over the years carefully extracting every vestige of root of some *Oxalis* from assorted beds and pots that I hold a deep and abiding fear for them as cultivated plants. However, *Oxalis* can make a wonderful groundcover, swathed in brightly coloured flowers. Clearly, it is important to choose the right species and hybrids. Considering that more than 500 species exist in this one genus, that is not an easy task. Widely distributed around the world, thus becoming adapted to all manner of environments, some are annuals and a few are even woody. North American and European gardeners can rule out most of the southern hemisphere plants as being too tender for our purposes. Most have trilobed leaves which endearingly fold up in the evening, opening as the sun comes up.

Frustratingly, the majority of the well-behaved *Oxalis* are alpines, sun-lovers whose limits are controlled by the severity of their environment more than by genetics. The problem is that woodland *Oxalis* are by nature opportunists that will take every opportunity to colonise an area. They prefer a humus-rich soil, but provided with that, they often become invasive, spreading both by seed and slender rhizomes just beneath soil level. One way of controlling their spread is to make them work hard, to plant them in conditions less to their liking. In summary, therefore, a shade-loving *Oxalis* is best introduced only to an area of the woodland where it can run amok, avoiding smaller spaces already bulging with treasures.

Here are some to avoid. *Oxalis corniculata* is a pernicious weed in all its forms, including the purple-leaved *O. corniculata* var. *atropurpurea*. It has naturalised itself so effectively in so many places that its origin is uncertain. The same warning applies to *O. europaea*, yellow *O. stricta*, *O. pes-caprae*, and also *O. exilis* from Australasia, though at first the latter looks small and pretty. Add the Mexican *O. latifolia* to the unwanted list, too; it has also naturalised through much of western Europe.

Oxalis acetosella

Widespread in Europe, from Iceland to the Mediterranean and Japan, as well as North America, it is superbly adapted to woodland conditions, so plant it only where it can run riot without regret. Pretty white flowers are veined with lilac and are produced in abundance from midspring to early summer, and sometimes even in early autumn. *Oxalis montana* is the almost identical American equivalent.

   var. *rosea* Pink flowers (lilac and purple forms are also recorded).

Oxalis magellanica

This mat-forming species from South America has foliage prettily flushed or margined with purple and glaucous below while the flowers are white, being displayed from late spring until autumn. Pretty but invasive in moist, humus-rich soil. *Oxalis lactea* from Australasia is extremely similar or synonymous—perhaps a geographical variant.

   'Nelson' (syn. 'Flore Pleno') Occurring naturally on the Falkland Islands, with double flowers.

Oxalis oregana

Probably the most garden-worthy species, it comes from the redwood forests of the North American Pacific coast. The foliage is attractively shaded with grey above and glaucous below. The relatively large solitary flowers from midspring to early autumn are often bright magenta-pink with a white eye, though whites and purple veining are known. Another similar and closely allied species is *O. trillifolia*.

   f. *smalliana* Deep rose-purple flowers.

Oxalis triangularis

Quite distinct foliage in this one: each of the three lobes is acutely triangular, joined at the centre on a point. Reddish purple or green leaved forms are known. White flowers are produced intermittently from late spring until autumn.

Oxalis violacea

Distributed across North America, the larger leaves of this bulbous species are often sufficiently purple beneath to make you want to turn them over, while the flowers are held in umbels rather than individually. They may be purple, violet, or white, with a yellow eye.

Pachyphragma (Brassicaceae)

When so many spring woodlanders are ephemeral, it is a relief to find something which will stay around for a while. Native of western Asia though naturalised in Britain, this monotypic genus is related to the humble cabbage, but there is nothing humble about its contribution to the woodland floor, where it will tolerate most positions, including dry shade.

Pachyphragma
macrophyllum

Pachyphragma macrophyllum

Clouds of white flowers carpet the ground in early spring, just as the snowdrops melt away. Almost evergreen, the large, rounded leaves emerge from persistent basal rosettes as their flowers fade, to suppress the weeds until the following winter, long after the autumn carnival above has had its day. Imagine the possibilities of these simple flowers jostling for position with purple hellebores, blue *Omphalodes*, pink *Cardamine*, or even beneath yellow *Corylopsis*.

Pachysandra (Buxaceae)

Ever since its introduction from Japan in 1843, *Pachysandra terminalis* has been specified in landscape design as the answer to every dry and shady corner. This widespread use, and indeed often abuse, in dreadful soil and ill-maintained schemes has given this plant a reputation that is difficult to shed. In a woodland, planted with other like-minded plants, it is a different thing altogether. All are evergreen and exceptionally capable of surviving, or even thriving, in dry shade.

Pachysandra axillaris

The least common of the genus is quite unlike the familiar groundcover forms, in that it is distinctly taller growing, almost to the point of shrubby. White spring flowers are held in long panicles.

Pachysandra procumbens

I like this gently creeping North American native, with its richly mottled leaves ascending to 30cm or so; they remain folded as they emerge, rendering the upright spikes of petal-less white flowers clearly visible between and under them. This species is much less dominant than its Japanese neighbour, *P. terminalis*, and will cohabit with other plants.

Pachysandra axillaris

Pachysandra terminalis

The more common Japanese species spreads by stolons to form a matted carpet of intertwining stems, often to the exclusion of all else. This is probably a plant best confined to a difficult area where you do not wish to grow anything else with it or through it. The male flowers are held in terminal clusters above the leaves, while the female flowers are hidden below. Large white berries are produced by wild plants but rarely, if ever, in cultivation.

    'Variegata' Slightly less vigorous, glaucous leaves are variably margined in creamy white.

Paris (Trilliaceae)

Paris is not necessarily a genus to grab your attention instantly, since at first glance it is of little consequence. However, it is one of those occasions when the more you look, the more you see. And the more you see, the more fascinating *Paris* becomes.

In 1994 just five species were known. By 2004, eighteen were listed in the *RHS Plant Finder*, plus assorted varieties and collection numbers. Many of these newly described species come from China, which has once again become the mecca for planthunters with the lifting of many access restrictions. Nomenclature has changed, too; Asian botanists often refer to them by their Himalayan name (*Daiswa*) or the Japanese equivalent (*Kinugasa*), though *Paris* is generally accepted as the correct name.

Native to the woodlands of Europe and eastern Asia, these delicate little plants are perfectly adapted to their shady, moist environment, thriving in deep, humus-rich soil that is moisture-retentive yet adequately free-drained during their dormancy. Their growth cycle coincides with other spring woodlanders, so they can make the most of early-season sunshine filtering through the bare framework of the deciduous trees before retreating below ground during the heat and dryness of summer.

Arguably, these are plants for the enthusiast, not because they are difficult, but because they simply will not appeal to those gardeners who need to be rewarded by lots of brightly coloured flowers. Erect stems emerge from the ground and develop a whorl of four or more leaves at the top. Just above these sits the flower, in the same manner as in a trillium. It has four to six narrow sepals and the same number of even narrower petals, all of them usually in shades of green. Then, finally, in the centre are four to ten stamens, sometimes having long filaments, which are retained even after the seed capsule has formed. The subtleties differentiating these plants are difficult to convey in a necessarily short description.

Naming conflicts still occur, which is not helped by the variability of many of the Asian species owing to their extensive distribution.

Paris delavayi

One of the few non-green species of *Paris*, the flowers are shades of purple and brown, usually with five sepals. This makes them much more conspicuous above the whorl of green leaves. 20–50cm.

Paris japonica

In some ways, this is the least weird species, being the one with the nearest to a "normal" flower. 80cm.

Above: *Paris japonica*

Right: *Paris lancifolia*

Paris lancifolia

An amazing species, its tall stem is bare below the terminal flower and whorl of leaves, so it should be planted through lower leafy but not dominant plants. 80cm.

Paris luquanensis

Only recently separated from *P. violacea*, it is distinguished by its broader, more overlapping leaves. These have a purplish underside, but more importantly they are beautifully mottled with silver on the upper surface.

Paris marmorata

Not easy to obtain, this dwarf plant is well worth a prime site on the woodland rock garden. Beautiful mottled leaves have an almost blue base colour and are narrower and do not overlap, to give a more starlike effect. The blue colouring extends into the flower bracts, but they are so small that they merely contribute to the overall picture.

Paris polyphylla

Widely available, extensive native distribution from China through the Himalayas into India as well as Thailand and Taiwan results in geographical variants of differing hardiness and heat tolerance. Often the origin of the plant is unknown, so it can be advantageous to buy from a specialist, while plants with collection numbers are of known provenance. Usually having whorls of six leaves and essentially green bracts, the whole effect is more substantial and leafy than many. The long filaments are yellow, an attractive bonus. Brilliant red berries are reliably produced in autumn, completing the effect. An excellent species with which to start a collection, it is one of the group previously classified under *Daisca*.

Paris quadrifolia

Widespread through Eurasia, the green and yellow spidery flower appears above four broad leaves, the outline of which is positively square. 15–40cm.

Left: *Paris polyphylla*

Above: *Paris quadrifolia*

Parrotia (Hamamelidaceae)

With just one species, *Parrotia* is an underrated tree, cultivated since 1840 but endemic only to a small area adjoining the Caspian Sea. It was named after its discoverer, F. W. Parrot, a German naturalist and explorer who found it, reputedly, while looking for

Noah's Ark. Such an easy and rewarding tree to grow, though slow, it is an excellent choice for structural planting as the roots are not demanding. Tolerant of dry conditions once established, it will suffer in standing water in winter. The wood is close-grained, hard, and strong, hence its common name Persian ironwood.

Parrotia persica autumn foliage

Parrotia persica in flower

Parrotia persica

New leaves are light green with a burgundy edge, maturing to green. It flowers, too, with tight clusters of pleasing red stamens in midwinter. Angular branch structure is softened by exfoliating grey and tan bark to give interest even when dormant. The habit of individuals varies considerably, though most are more upright when young, becoming widespreading at maturity. There is little variation other than habit; sometimes it is possible to obtain plants derived from famous magnificent specimens.

'**Burgundy**' We selected this form, noting its prominent burgundy-margined young growth but also its autumn colours, which include more purple than usually seen within the species.

'**Lamplighter**' Less vigorous, shade-requiring novelty, with vividly creamy white variegated leaves.

'**Vanessa**' Distinctly upright columnar form.

Parrotiopsis (Hamamelidaceae)

This monotypic Himalayan genus, related to *Parrotia* and *Hamamelis*, was introduced as long ago as 1879 but never became common in cultivation. Happy in the woodland shade, it appreciates moisture-retentive but free-draining, humus-rich soil.

Parrotiopsis jacquemontiana
This fascinating plant makes a large, upright shrub, which never looks quite at home in this illustrious family. The leaves are more rounded, but the flowers stand it apart. They are simplest described as reminiscent of *Cornus florida*. White bracts surround a cluster of yellow staminoid true flowers to give a most unusual effect in mid to late spring. Yellow autumn colour.

Patrinia (Valerianaceae)

Fifteen species are distributed from Europe through the Himalayas to eastern Asia, but few are available in cultivation. Easily grown in humus-rich, moisture-retentive soil, the Japanese species included here will thrive in a lightly shaded area of our woodland floor, to form clumps and small colonies.

Patrinia gibbosa
This species has yellow flowers all summer and rounded, prettily divided foliage.

Patrinia triloba
Usually represented in cultivation by *P. triloba* var. *palmata*, it is clump-forming at first but will subsequently spread by stolons to form a colony just 15cm tall. The foliage is prettily lobed, shaped rather like a maple leaf, often taking on delightful red hues in autumn. The yellow flowers are freely produced in late summer, giving a welcome splash of colour at a florally challenged time of year.

Peltoboykinia (Saxifragaceae)

A small Japanese genus, recently separated from *Boykinia*, differs in its peltate (shield-like) lower leaves. These magnificent foliage plants have large leaves, like umbrellas, and are suited only to the moister, fertile areas of the woodland floor, where they will contribute superbly with their luxuriant, leafy exuberance, gently spreading by underground rhizomes. I have barely spared a thought for the flowers as they are of little significance, being clusters of yellowish bells on upright stems in late summer. The foliage can be exploited to highlight the flowers of adjacent plantings—perhaps the airy spires of *Astilbe* and *Aruncus* or the leafy fountains of a variegated grass. These potentially large plants should be sited accordingly.

Peltoboykinia tellimoides
The leaves may be up to 30cm across and are slightly lobed from a heart-shaped outline.

Peltoboykinia watanabei

Peltoboykinia watanabei
This is the more impressive of the two species, with deeply divided leaves reminiscent of a giant *Tiarella*.

Persicaria (Polygonaceae)

Such a fine line can be drawn between a plant which thrives and naturalises and one which simply becomes a thug. This genus can easily fall into the latter category—Japanese knotweed being the ultimate example, though perhaps that is a little extreme. Nonetheless, they will need space. Even those forms which do not spread rampantly can arch over, with the sheer exuberance of their growth easily suffocating more delicate neighbours in the process; this is particularly the case if the soil dries out in the summer. Where it remains moist, the plant stays more tidily upright, an advantage since they are less likely to spread by rooting in where the nodes of sagging stems touch the soil.

Many provide lovely mid to late summer colour, drifting through large-scale woodland plantings where it will not matter if they run riot, rubbing shoulders with other plants of equal vigour, intergrowing to make a coherent whole. If the soil is not excessively wet, spring bulbs can carpet the ground before persicarias start growing vigorously in later spring. The light shade of high canopy is perfect, while they will tolerate a wide range of soil conditions—the secret of their success. Many persicarias were classified under *Polygonum* until recently, so nomenclature can be confused. The flowers are held in upright or arching spikes arising from the leaf axils on the upper part of the stems. Many are deer-resistant.

Persicaria amplexicaulis

From Afghanistan and China, one of the most variable species develops large clumps of arching stems. Many named forms have been selected to represent the different colour options. 1.5m.

>   **'Alba'** White flowers.
>
>   **'Firetail'** Rich, deep red flowers.
>
>   **'Inverleith'** Extremely useful, significantly smaller form, rarely exceeding 50cm in height. Crimson flowers.
>
>   **'Rosea'** Soft pink flowers.

Persicaria amplexicaulis
'Inverleith'

Persicaria campanulata

This pretty plant is intolerant of summer dryness; it is definitely one for the wetter areas where it will reach 1m or more in height, with spikes of white or pale salmon bell-like flowers.

>   **'Rosenrot'** Pink flowers.
>
>   **'Southcombe White'** White flowers.

Persicaria microcephala

Represented in cultivation by various hybrids, the most notable of which until recently was 'Red Dragon'. However, the hybridisers have continued to play and have developed some improvements. They are wonderful foliage plants but give of their best with adequate light, so they cannot be buried too deeply into the woodland.

'**Chocolate Dragon**' More compact and free-branching, forming a low mound of richly marked leaves; purple when young, maturing to a tasty chocolate brown with silvery olive markings. As light levels reduce with the approach of autumn, they fade to green with a dark basal blotch.

'**Red Dragon**' The original selection boasts rich burgundy-purple leaves which are marked with lance-shaped mint-green and silver chevrons. Superfluous pale, almost white, flowers are a pretty contrast.

'**Silver Dragon**' Silvered leaves are stained with reddish edges and topped with white flowers late in summer.

Persicaria polymorpha

Arguably the most showy species in bloom, with great plumes of white flowers above rather pleasant leaves which have a deep red midrib. Clump-forming; not a runner. 1m.

Phlox (Polemoniaceae)

These classic perennials need not be confined to the border; indeed most of the 70 or so species grow in woods in their native North American habitat. Those that specifically require full sun are the garden hybrids bred from *P. paniculata*. Interestingly enough, even that species is a woodlander in the wild, so this is an occasion when it is better to seek out the wild forms rather than the ostensibly improved cultivars.

Some are small enough to deserve a place on the woodland rock garden, but they can be difficult to obtain (from specialist alpine growers only) and in many cases are fussy, preferring acid soil and disliking winter wet. Their larger brethren will enjoy a humus-rich, moisture-retentive area of the woodland floor under high canopy, where the shade is not too intense. Some are prostrate, others erect; all have opposite pairs of simple bright green leaves while the flowers are held in terminal panicles. Individually, these consist of a slender tubular base, flaring at the mouth into five broad, widespreading petal lobes. Colours vary from white through all the pinks to lavender-purples, often with a contrasting eye, generally in full glory from late spring into early summer. The taller cultivated forms need support in the border; but the wonderful part of planting with nature, as one does in the woodland almost unintentionally, is that other nearby plants hold up the stems or hide the sparser nether regions. In the border, one looks for big, bold flowers and lots of them; yet the woodland looks so much more natural with less consistency; lighter, more open flowerheads; and a more informal approach as plants jostle for position.

Phlox adsurgens

This midsized species from Oregon prefers acid soil, forming mats to 40cm across, with the flowering shoots reaching 30cm tall. Flower colour is variable in the wild, within the spectrum of the genus, with a darker basal stripe to each petal lobe and a paler eye. Several wild selections have been named.

'**Alba**' Excellent white form.

'**Wagon Wheel**' Long, narrow salmon-pink petals. Very distinctive.

Phlox carolina

From southeastern North America, the erect flowering stems normally grow to at least 40cm, but 100cm is attainable in rich, moist soil. Usually pink to purple (occasionally white) flowers, held in clusters of 30 to 60, are quite a sight. The stems are attractively stained with ebony-red.

'**Magnificence**' Reliably taller growing and pretty carmine-pink.

'**Miss Lingard**' Small, white-flowered form. 45cm.

Phlox divaricata

Widespread through eastern North America, their prostrate, almost evergreen shoots root at the nodes to form loose mats from which erect flowering stems rise 20–40cm. Typically light violet-blue flowers in clusters of between nine and twenty-four are often pleasingly fragrant. Some selections of the woodland phlox have distinctly notched petals which adds an extra dimension. They will gently seed around, but a number of eminently suitable named forms as well as closely related hybrids exist.

'**Blue Dreams**' Dan Hinkley, formerly of Heronswood Nursery, enthuses about this Piet Oudolf selection and that pedigree is enough recommendation for me. Fragrant lilac-blue flowers are produced in profusion from early spring. 25cm.

'**Blue Perfume**' Similarly coloured and marginally taller, reputedly the most highly scented of this delightful species; flowers attract some of the first butterflies of spring. 'White Perfume' is a white-flowered equivalent.

'**Dirigo Icc**' Large lilac-coloured flowers.

'**Eco Texas Purple**' Unique light purple flowers are highlighted with deep magenta eyes. Vigorous and durable.

'**Fuller's White**' Fragrant, pure white flowers with pretty yellow stamens.

subsp. *laphamii* '**Chattahoochee**' Collected in northern Florida, rooting creeping stems are rarely produced, which can be a mixed blessing depending on whether or not there is room for it to spread. Produced through a long season, at 3cm across, the pale pink flowers with a darker red eye are huge. The longer tubes and petals are characteristic of the subspecies.

Phlox latifolia

(syn. *P. ovata*) Concentrated in the Appalachians, the mountain phlox sends up short flowering stems from almost evergreen creeping shoots. Usually bright pink flowers.

Phlox maculata

Widespread through east-central North America, this moisture-loving species produces tall, erect stems from a shallow rootstock. A number of cultivars have been named, covering the range of colours.

'**Alpha**' Lilac-pink flowers with darker centres. 80cm.

'**Delta**' Pure white with pink eyes. 100cm.

'**Omega**' White flowers with a violet eye. 80cm.

'**Reine du Jour**' Similar to 'Omega' but smaller. 45cm.

'**Rosalinde**' A delightful shade of purple-pink but not widely available.

'**Schneelawine**' (syn. 'Avalanche') Tall-growing, white form. 100cm.

Phlox paniculata

Similar in many respects to *P. maculata*, this species was used extensively in breeding, having been introduced to Europe in 1730. The many resultant garden cultivars have their place, but not in the woodland garden. The species itself, however, is perfectly suited and is a lovely plant with airy, graceful flowerheads in shades of pink and purple or occasionally white.

Phlox stolonifera

Spreads by creeping, nonflowering shoots, which end in a rosette of leaves from which flowering stems emerge. The flowers, to 3cm across, are often sweetly scented but not notched. Found through the Appalachian Mountains, several selections have been named. 25cm.

'**Ariane**' The preferred white form.

'**Blue Ridge**' This, like other Ridge selections from Virginia, are self-explanatory as to their colours.

'**Sherwood Purple**' Vigorous floriferous purple selection.

Podophyllum (Berberidaceae)

These magnificent plants for the woodland floor have large leaves, which can be beautifully marked and mottled; like snowflakes and *Cyclamen*, no two are ever quite the same. *Podophyllum peltatum*, the sole North American species, is the most robust, while those from Asia are slightly less hardy, developing a colony more slowly. They are too big for the woodland rock garden, but they deserve a visual position. Spreading by a rhizomatous rootstock, they appreciate a typical humus-rich woodland soil.

The structure of the leaf is quite something—best described as umbrella-like, with a stalk appearing to emerge from its centre. In reality, the leaf has two to three lobes which wrap around to make a more or less solid leaf, taking on rather geometric shapes to appear almost square or hexagonal at times. Leaves are held about 30cm above the ground, so they may be underplanted. Dwarf *Ophiopogon* selections could provide an effective contrast, but I like the simple and traditional woodland effect of a carpet of brown leaves.

An element of naming dissent exists within this genus; there is talk that the Himalayan species should form a new genus, *Sinopodophyllum*, while the other Asian species would be listed under *Dysosma*. Since this would leave just the American *P. peltatum* under *Podophyllum*, I find it a little puzzling.

These plants affect people in different ways. Some will shake their heads at the impossibility of it all and walk on, while others like myself will be captivated by them, unable to resist purchasing yet another plant because its markings are just a little bit more pronounced than the previous equally lovingly acquired example.

Podophyllum aurantiocaule

The most recently introduced species hails from eastern India and western China. Mature plants will produce up to three large leaves, with bronze zoning over a green base, all covered with golden bristles, such that the stem appears golden. The flowers are reminiscent of *Dodecatheon* in the way the petals are reflexed back and held in clusters of one to eight among the foliage, usually white or cream-coloured but occasionally tinged pink. Bright red fruits are freely produced. This species seems less tolerant of wet conditions while dormant than the others.

Podophyllum delavayi

(syn. *P. veitchii*) From China, juvenile leaves are spectacularly marked with shades of bronze, black and white and overlain with a rich red that is maintained well into the season. The attractively lobed foliage is sufficiently ornamental to compensate for the fact that they hide their deep red flowers beneath their leaves.

Podophyllum difforme

Starting into growth early in the season, the leaves are angular with a paler central zone and variable purple markings. The nodding red bell-shaped flowers hang beneath the leaves in clusters of three to nine in mid to late spring. This Chinese species spreads from rhizomes. New stems are initially clothed in whitish hairs.

Podophyllum difforme

Podophyllum hexandrum

(syn. *P. emodi*) From the Himalayas and Afghanistan to west-central China, this species has gorgeous, deeply lobed, almost glaucous foliage, the variable mottling particularly pronounced on young leaves. These can reach 40cm in height and up to 25 cm in diameter. Lovely solitary flowers are held above the leaves in midspring to early summer, where they can be appreciated against the foliage. They can be up to 4cm across and are white or pale pink with prominent yellow anthers, followed by large, red, fleshy berries. Widely distributed, this species is variable, so plants of known provenance with collection numbers can be distinct. For example, a certain strain of seed collected in Bhutan reliably produces plants with smaller fruits.

Podophyllum hexandrum 'Chinense'

'Chinense' This geographical variant normally has deeper pink flowers and more deeply divided lobes.

'Majus' Supposedly larger in all its parts.

Podophyllum mairei

Podophyllum mairei

This gorgeous Chinese species has rounded but toothed leaves which are usually beautifully marked. Pear-shaped, deep purple flowers hang from the junction of these leaf pairs.

Podophyllum peltatum

The American species is quite a plant. As with so much of their indigenous flora, Native Americans discovered both medicinal and culinary uses for them. All parts of these plants are poisonous, with the exception of the ripe fruit which were eaten raw, in preserves, or in refreshing summer drinks. They are equally popular with the local wildlife. Apparently no less than 16 compounds have been identified within this plant, including one now utilised in chemotherapy. Although great news, previous overzealous and detrimental collection of wild populations is troublesome. Fortunately, this species is easy to grow and spreads rapidly, so colonies can develop with consummate ease.

If space is at a premium, *P. peltatum* should be avoided, as it can crowd out smaller, more delicate plants. However, it associates well with other larger woodlanders, particularly large ferns and *Polygonatum* with its contrasting foliage textures and shapes. Podophyllum's tall leaf stems, to perhaps 60cm, support large leaves deeply divided into three to nine lobes, which are themselves cleft (shallowly divided) into two. This enhances their appearance, making them seem less heavy and dense. It also facilitates the view down through them to the flowers which are held individually just beneath their protective canopy. Normally white with pretty yellow stamens, pink forms are known. These are followed by the fruit, giving rise to most of the plant's common names: mayapple and raccoon berry being just two examples. The former is not necessarily accurate, however, since it depends on location. Here it flowers in April and sets fruit in June.

f. *deamii* Pink-tinged flowers.

Podophyllum pleianthum

Held pristinely until the frosts, the foliage is wonderful, but these lack the mottling so remarkable in the other species. Instead, centred on the leaf stem, the leaf wraps around to form a circular whole which is then shallowly divided evenly into five to nine lobes, each of which is pointed. These rich green leaves are in marked contrast to almost white stems, punctuated at their same level by bunches of deep maroon flowers, which have a less than pleasant smell to attract their insect pollinators.

Podophyllum pleianthum

Podophyllum versipelle

Easiest described as the Chinese version of *P. pleianthum*, with minor botanical differences, but the most relevant distinctions are that this species has a non-creeping rhizome and much less evenly lobed but more deeply divided leaves. This is perhaps the most summer drought-resistant species since with time the rhizomes will pull themselves deep into the ground.

Podophyllum cultivars

'Kaleidoscope' Of undeclared hybrid origin, to me the amazing foliage visually resembles that of *P. difforme*—umbrella-like and almost hexagonal in shape but with little lobing. The base colour is a bright lime-green central star extending to the points of the leaf and defined by rich burgundy mottling. Outside of this star are liberal splashes of darker green and bronze. Even more incredibly, it produces as many as 20 burgundy-red flowers in a cluster, each being as much as 5cm long.

'Spotty Dotty' What a corny name for such a beautiful plant. The leaves of this hybrid are essentially hexagonal but deeply divided. They are broadly margined with a rich array of chocolate-brown markings, the colour of which extends down the flower stalks and also into the huge flowers which hang beneath the leaves. Inevitably, the colour diminishes as the foliage matures. Sometimes the new fresh leaves of *Podophyllum* can be damaged by late frost, but this one has been selected as being particularly tolerant of such.

Polemonium (Polemoniaceae)

This interesting genus of about 30 species is from varying habitats across the Americas, Asia, and Europe. We are concerned here with the larger species, many of which come from woodland habitats; the smaller alpine types require the much sharper drainage associated with scree conditions.

Polemonium form an almost evergreen basal cluster of pinnate leaves, which are rather frondlike, from which emerge leafy stems topped with clusters of pretty flowers, simplest described as flared trumpets. Blue is the most common colour, but pink-, white-, and even yellow-flowered species are available. They are commonly known as Jacob's ladder; supposedly the arrangement of the leaflets along the leaf stalk resemble a ladder, as the one in biblical Jacob's dream.

Some of the named forms are actually seed strains which will come true from seed. This is confusing when I have placed such importance on propagating named forms only by vegetative means. Their names have been assigned for marketing purposes rather than in the interests of botanical accuracy.

Polemonium caeruleum

This species and its derivatives can self-seed prodigiously to become a nuisance, which is a shame because they are attractive. Perhaps it may be possible to find an area where they can fight it out for floor space among other equally successful plants. In this native of Europe and the west coast of North America, blue is the dominant flower colour. With such a wide distribution, various subspecies as well as a number of named selections are available, most flowering from early summer to midsummer.

'**Bambino Blue**' Height 30cm or more with a 30cm spread and lavender-blue flowers.

BRISE D'ANJOU ('Blanjou') Elegant creamy yellow variegated foliage and violet-blue flowers. 60cm.

subsp. *caeruleum* f. *album* Sparkling white flowers. Often but incorrectly called *P. caeruleum* 'Album'. 60cm.

'**Snow and Sapphires**' Similar to, but an improvement on, BRISE D'ANJOU in terms of robustness of habit and both quantity and quality of flower.

Polemonium pauciflorum

This unique species has pretty yellow flowers with long tubes, richly flushed with pinky red. Coming from southeastern Arizona and Mexico, it is perfectly hardy but does appreciate good drainage coupled with adequate moisture. Self-seeding, though with the reputation for being short-lived, this ongoing replacement ensures continuation of the colony without it ever becoming a problem. Avoid too heavily shaded a planting spot for this species. 45cm.

>subsp. *pauciflorum* Pretty silver-leaved form, usually known more informatively as *P. pauciflorum* Silver Leaf form.

Polemonium pulcherrimum

From northwestern North America, often found growing under spruce, it will tolerate extremely dry soil. However, this can be at the cost of flower, so a compromise needs to be found. On the other hand, dry shade under conifers is probably the most difficult site to fill, and a lovely leafy carpet, albeit of flowerless *Polemonium*, could be better than nothing. The flowers are beautiful, being blue with a white or yellow eye. Generally a shorter, neater species, the exact height depends on the provenance of the clone, with high altitude forms being less than 20cm, while lower altitude collections can reach nearer 50cm.

Polemonium reptans

From eastern North America with a low spreading habit to just 30cm, it is classified as blue, though I think it is more lilac than true blue. It also has a pretty greeny yellow eye.

>'Blue Pearl' Lovely selection with blue flowers.

>'Pink Dawn' Less widely available but the pinky mauve flowers are effective above bronze-flushed foliage.

>'Stairway to Heaven' This recent introduction is regarded as significantly better than the former star, BRISE D'ANJOU. The New England selection is considered to be more vigorous, with pretty leaves broadly margined with creamy white. I love the combination with the blue flowers in midspring.

>'Virginia White' Recent selection with pure white flowers.

Polygonatum (Convallariaceae)

I love this genus, and all members of it are perfectly suited to the shady woodland floor. Most of the 55 or so species come from Asia, with North American and European representation. They are ridiculously easy to grow, yet so rewarding given typical woodland conditions. Tolerant of heavy shade and a wide range of soil types, they do not care to waterlog when dormant. Clearly, the better the soil structure and the richer it is, the better they will perform and the taller they will grow. If conditions become tough in mid to late summer, they will respond by going dormant sooner.

They have creeping rhizomes from which spring unbranched stems, arching gracefully under the weight of the flowers from late spring to midsummer. Usually white or greeny white, these are narrowly tubular and hang individually or in clusters from the upper leaf axils. Many species are rather similar and rarely spectacular in flower, but that is not why I grow them. They possess an elegance and charm that works so well with so many other woodland plants, rising through and above their leafy carpets. The list of possible planting combinations is endless. The collector in me wants to include them all, though realistically some have more obvious aesthetic floral appeal than others so I restrict myself to distinctive species. Some variegated cultivars can also be effective, particularly when coupled with foliage plants such as ferns or others with insignificant flowers.

The generic name is derived from the Greek and equates to many knees; this refers to the many nodes and joints along the rhizomatous rootstock. Not quite so clear is why the common name became Solomon's seal, but it is first recorded as such in 1534. Lots of new and variegated selections have been introduced from Asia in recent years, and taxonomic changes have occurred among bewilderingly similar plants, resulting in extensive nomenclature confusion.

Late in the summer, sawfly larva can feast on the leaves until little remains save a rather unsightly skeleton. In the garden where they are more visual, I take this as a hint that it is time to cut them back, but it does no harm to leave them to nature.

Polygonatum biflorum

The greenish flushed bell-like flowers of this North American native dangle from the leaf axils of arching stems, usually in pairs, followed by blue berries. Arching stems. 100cm. Showier *P. commutatum*, with more flowers on taller stems, has a slightly more southerly distribution. There is debate as to whether it is a distinct species or part of *P. biflorum*. 180cm.

Polygonatum cirrhifolium

I include this Sino-Himalayan species not for its flowers (typical but small) but for its foliage. The leaves are long and narrow but most unusually held in whorls of six. With stem height varying from 30 to 90cm, this is an elegant plant.

Polygonatum cryptanthum

A most unusual Japanese species, the name means hidden flower. This is not to imply that they are so tucked away beneath the leaves as to be invisible. Instead, each flower wears a hat of three large pale green bracts which actually serve to make the flower appear larger. Quite unique and relatively short. 40cm.

Polygonatum curvistylum

This lovely arching species comes from western China, with narrow leaves and flowers of a wonderful shade of pinky purple. The fineness of the foliage ensures that the flowers can be fully appreciated and adds to its elegance. 80cm.

Polygonatum falcatum

This Japanese species is rarely grown since it has relatively wide leaves concealing the tiny flowers. However, variegated forms can be valuable for their foliage alone, though the colour differential can be lost in too shady a position.

'**Silver Stripe**' Bold leaves have a stripe down their centres, appearing gold or silver, dependent on their age. The white flowers are small but pretty. Slow to bulk up and rather short, it should be carefully positioned for accent.

Polygonatum graminifolium

Collected in Nepal, this tiny plant is definitely one for the woodland rock garden. The flowers beneath grasslike leaves are a delightful shade of lilac-pink with long tubes flaring daintily at the mouth. Pink berries follow. The flowers are scented, so it does repay the effort to plant it where it can be given the appreciation it deserves. 15cm.

Polygonatum hookeri

Another species for the woodland rock garden, it is so low that the flowers are held among the leaves at little more than ground level. Appealingly, they are a dainty shade of pale lilac-pink. Although short in stature, this is a deceptively easy plant which is distributed through the eastern Himalayas and western China.

Polygonatum ×hybridum

A vigorous hybrid between *P. multiflorum* and *P. odoratum*.

'**Betburg**' Named for the site from which it was collected in the Black Forest, this is definitely a plant to look out for. Considerably more substantial and distinguished by its colour, its new stems and leaves are richly stained with chocolate-brown over a glaucous base. The flowers are typical, hanging in clusters of up to five, before giving way to fleshy purple berries. 60–75cm.

'**Striatum**' (previously *P. odoratum* 'Grace Barker') Much in the style of the modern Japanese selections, although known for many years, this colourful cultivar has conspicuously creamy white–striped leaves.

Polygonatum inflatum

Deep green ribbed leaves highlight the suspended white flowers which are tipped green in this amusing species from Japan and Korea. Their distinctive feature is a curious bulge part way down the tube—like our cat when he has just eaten a rabbit.

Polygonatum multiflorum

A vigorous plant to 45cm or more in rich soil, with correspondingly broad leaves and pretty bell-shaped flowers held in clusters of two to four, in their typical colour scheme of white tipped with green. Widespread through Europe and Asia, it is variable as a result. The true species is actually rather scarce; many of those labelled such are in fact *P. ×hybridum*.

Polygonatum odoratum

The archetypal Solomon's seal is tolerant of a wide range of conditions thanks to its vast natural distribution through Europe, including the British Isles, and Asia. Distinction of

Polygonatum ×*hybridum* grows so fast in the spring that one can almost watch it emerge from the ground, like a snake from a basket.

Polygonatum ×*hybridum* 'Striatum'

Polygonatum ×*hybridum* 'Betburg'

Polygonatum odoratum var. *maximowiczii*

various resultant subspecies is rarely made in commercial stocks and if required is best sought from seed collections of known provenance. The stems, which are triangular in cross section, are clothed with thickly textured, pleated green leaves with the familiar green tipped, white flowers hanging from the leaf axils. Best of all, they are deliciously fragrant and make wonderful cut flowers where a few stems can be spared from the clump. 30–85cm.

'Flore Pleno' I am not a great enthusiast for double flowers, usually preferring the simplicity of the natural single, yet this one is worth planting. Fully double, creating a wider, larger flower, the effect is delightful. Less vigorous than the species, it forms a tight clump. 45cm.

var. *maximowiczii* In a genus of such similarity, this rare form has noticeably rounder leaves. Its classification is under debate; it may prove to be a separate species.

var. *pluriflorum* 'Variegatum' (syn. *P. falcatum* 'Variegatum') Wide green leaves have the narrowest white margin, widening at the tip, contrasting well with purple-tinged stems; still the flowers are tiny. Probably the most common clone in cultivation.

'**Silver Wings**' Quite different from anything else in this genus, the leaves are twisted and held upright from the stems to display their silvery backs, like surreal birds perched above the creamy bells hanging below. Smaller growing to 40cm.

Polygonatum oppositifolium

This species from China and Nepal holds its leaves in opposite pairs; most unusual in this genus.

Polygonatum roseum

One of the pink-flowered minority, the pretty flowers are unusually held in pairs, with up to three pairs hanging from a single leaf axil. The leafy stems are graceful, reaching only 50cm or a little more in height. From western Siberia to China.

Polygonatum stewartianum

This species heralds from eastern Europe and Asia, with leafy stems reminiscent of a lily. The leaves are much narrower than in the most familiar *Polygonatum*, and many more of them are held more closely together on the stem. Pale, dusky pink flowers are like hanging urns, the tube fatter than many and constricting slightly before flaring at the mouth. 90cm.

Polygonatum verticillatum

Whorled leaves distinguish this variable plant which is widely distributed from Europe to the Himalayas. As so often with large natural populations spread over vast areas, tremendous differences exist among clones. Willowy forms taller than a metre are known in the Himalayas, while those from Siberia barely exceed 40cm. Collection numbers will indicate their potential stature, but the soil will also influence this. The typical green-and-white flowers are tightly clustered and often speckled with red, to be followed by conspicuous red berries.

Polygonatum verticillatum 'Rubrum'

'**Rubrum**' Opinion is mixed as to whether this should be given varietal or cultivar status. Whatever the case, it is a pretty plant with red staining to the stems and petioles which continues into the flowers, to give them a pink flush.

Polypodium (Polypodiaceae)

This rhizomatous genus of about 75 species of globally distributed terrestrial and epiphytic ferns enjoys humus-rich but well-drained soil. Most species are summer deciduous (though they can stay evergreen if soil is moist enough), fading away in late spring with new growth starting in early autumn. It is heartening in autumn to see new life starting at the same time that so much else is dying back, and they are uplifting in the depths of winter. Nomenclature confusion abounds in this genus.

Polypodium cambricum

(syn. *P. australe*) Native of much of Europe, including Britain, this lovely and elegant fern has almost triangular fronds, with the lowest pinnae bent inwards. 35cm.

'Cristatum' Crested pinnae are all nearly the same length, resulting in a long, thin frond. 30cm.

'Grandiceps Fox' More heavily crested and a much broader frond.

'Richard Kayse' First discovered by Richard Kayse in the Cambrian Mountains of Wales in 1668. Many collections were taken over the years, but the now protected wild population still survives. The pinnae are incised and broad, almost overlapping. A lovely form. 45cm.

Polypodium glycyrrhiza

The variable appearance of this western North American fern is almost of secondary importance. Known affectionately as the liquorice fern because its rhizomes contain a compound 3000 times sweeter than sucrose, Native Americans used them as a sweetener and to ease throat infections. Not to be recommended at home! Often epiphytic in the wild, they favour *Acer macrophyllum* trunks and stumps. However, they are equally at ease on moss-encrusted rocks and roadside banks. If no decaying timber languishes in the woodland, try them in a humid, moisture-retentive spot on the woodland floor. 60cm.

'Longicaudatum' The almost pinnate fronds have long, drawn-out tips.

Polypodium interjectum

Closely related to *P. vulgare*, but more robust in habit, this European species (including the British Isles) has lance-shaped fronds widest just below the middle. Unlike most of the other species, this one dislikes humidity, being happier in cooler conditions. 15–30cm.

Polypodium vulgare

Small fern widespread through North America and Eurasia with creeping matted rhizomes, colonising banks and hedgerows or trees where humidity is high enough. Usually evergreen, young leaves do not start to be produced until late summer. The fronds consist of 51 pinnae, with those in the lower two-thirds being the same length. Old herbalists had all manner of uses for all parts of *P. vulgare*, but modern research has identified a carcinogenic compound within it. 25cm.

'Bifidomultifidum' Long, narrow, spear-shaped frond with crested lower pinnae and a large crest at the tip.

'Trichomanoides Backhouse' Amazing mixture of plain and lacy fronds which are divided three or even four times.

Above left: *Polypodium vulgare*

Above: *Polypodium vulgare*
'Bifidomultifidum'

Polystichum acrostichoides newly
emerging fronds are often referred
to as fiddleheads.

Polystichum (Dryopteridaceae)

Some of the best evergreen ferns for humus-rich areas of the woodland floor are included among the 135 species distributed globally. Most are amenable to cultivation, forming relatively dense, mounded clumps of frothy foliage. They continue to look so good through the winter that they can be combined with other seasonal plants, such as *Daphne bholua* and hellebores, to dazzling effect. The European species are often referred to as shield ferns because they have a distinctive cover over the spori.

Traditional wisdom recommended cutting off all the fronds in late winter as new growth begins. However, common sense and recent research suggests that it is better to remove only dead and damaged fronds, to tidy the clump coming out of winter.

Polystichum acrostichoides

Known as the Christmas fern, this strongly evergreen, eastern North American native looks particularly good in winter, making it excellent for cutting for seasonal decoration. The fiddleheads in spring are silvery, eventually developing into a fountain of leathery, lance-shaped fronds. Fertile fronds are taller and more upright, narrowing at the tip. Rhizomatous but nonspreading, well-drained soil is required to avoid crown rot in wet winters. 60cm.

Polystichum aculeatum

The European hard shield fern has a distinct bristle on the tip of each leaflet. In the wild, these rather solitary growers favour harsher sites on rocky outcrops, steep banks, and hedgerows, tolerating dry conditions admirably. The dense, leathery, and glossy fronds have an erect, arching habit, forming clumps to 90cm.

Polystichum braunii

Widely distributed through North America and Eurasia, fronds gently arch to form tidy clumps. Dark green fronds are widest in the middle, narrowing to both tip and base, and are covered in scales on their undersides. 30–40cm.

Polystichum makinoi

From India east to the Philippines, this lovely fern has a glossy, almost metallic sheen to the fronds. The leaflets are held evenly and horizontally, so tidily as to look as if they have been clipped to shape. 60cm.

Polystichum munitum

The name means armed with teeth, referring to the regimented rows of toothy leaflets which make up each frond. These are tall and thin, tapering to a point at both ends and often seductively curved. Beautiful even in the depths of winter, combine them with almost anything, including lower, more bushy ferns. 120cm. The indigenous people of its native North America were creative with uses for their local plants. Apparently this fern was the focus of a game in which children competed to see who could pull off the most leaflets while holding their breath and saying "pala" with each leaflet.

Polystichum polyblepharum

Common names will never replace the precision of the Latin for me, but their derivation can be both enlightening and amusing. This name means many eyelashes, which perhaps starts to conjure an image of its appearance. Elegant green, symmetrical, lance shaped fronds with long, thin leaflets, each of which is made up of neat lobes, all narrowing to the tips, are arranged in 75cm tall shuttlecocks. Golden bristles cover them in spring. Their elegance makes them fine companions for flowers, whether in the woodland or in a bouquet. From Japan and particularly Korea.

Polystichum setiferum

The European soft shield fern is an essential plant for every woodland, but it does occur in a bewildering number of variations. The species itself is evergreen, having a soft texture and lacy appearance, being easily grown in almost any soils, including those impoverished and dry. None are more effective in dry shady sites, but they deserve better than to be hidden away in dark corners. The fronds can reach 100cm tall while the stems bear tiny bulbils. All are beautiful and equally easy, but here are just a few to whet the appetite.

Congestum Group Ferns derived from this group have densely congested and overlapping pinnae.

Cristatum Group Crested fronds.

'Cruciatum Kaye' Long, narrow fronds are overlapping.

Divisilobum Group Finely divided fronds. 'Dahlem' is unusually tall and erect, with lance-shaped fronds. 100cm. 'Herrenhausen' has frothy mounds of bright green, thrice-divided fronds, arching and twisting as they grow, to swirl around the middle of the clump. 65cm. The lacy foliage is shown off by rounder leaved neighbours such as *Hosta* or *Brunnera*. For ultimate spatial efficiency, underplant with *Asarum*.

'Grandiceps' Large terminal crest.

Plumosodivisilobum Group Four times divided leaves. *Polystichum setiferum* 'Baldwinii' is considered the best of this group.

'Plumosomultilobum' Found in 1878, this small, mossy textured fern has light green multi-lobed fronds. 40cm.

'Pulcherrimum Bevis' Graceful but sterile English cultivar, discovered in Devon in 1876, needs

Above: *Polystichum setiferum* 'Plumosomultilobum'.

Left: *Polystichum setiferum* 'Pulcherrimum Bevis'

Polystichum setiferum
Rotundatum Group

to be propagated by division. Narrow pinnae curve toward the frond's tip.

> **Rotundatum Group** Each pinnae is rounded rather than pointed.
>
> **'Wollaston'** Long, lacy exceptionally graceful fronds.

Polystichum tsussimense

This delightful Oriental dwarf fern lights up shady positions since its distinctive holly-like tips are covered in silvery white scales. Black stems and semi-evergreen. 30cm.

Polystichum xiphophyllum

Native of China and India, this is one of the scarcer species in this valuable genus. The stiffly upright fronds appear almost artificial. 45cm.

Primula (Primulaceae)

Primroses, *P. vulgaris*, flowering beneath the hedgerows around my home are one of the surest signs of the approach of spring; indeed flowering seems to commence earlier every year. I vividly remember as a child the annual Sunday School ritual of collecting primroses to make into posies to give to our mothers on Mother's Day, a few weeks before Easter. Of course I am ashamed to admit it now and would never dream of letting my children pick wildflowers of any sort, but back in those days such things were done without a second thought. Today many cultivated forms of *Primula* offer a range of gaudy colours; all are very pretty in their pots but rarely manage to survive to flower again the following year. For me, the beauty of Mother Nature cannot be improved upon in this case. Our woodlands, hedgerows, and even dry stone walls are full of these delightful signs of spring as I write. However, once they have finished flowering, their foliage soon disappears unless the soil retains ample moisture. They are rather fun planted around the base of great hostas as well as associating in a much more traditional way with bluebells and narcissi.

A huge genus with nearly 400 species, many are alpines, but plenty enjoy shady conditions. Disliking hot summers and preferring cooler areas, the shade of the woodland floor will help, but most of this group also need summer moisture, so are often found along watercourses and in boggy areas. Most of those occurring naturally in moist meadows will adapt to the woodland, provided that the shade is not too oppressive and soil is adequately damp. This renders them less ideal for planting at the base of large trees, even in the woodland, where they will dry out in summer; however, *P. vulgaris* is very happy in such a site.

All have a basal rosette of leaves from which the flowers emerge in early spring or later through the summer. *Primula vulgaris* holds its flowers individually on long stems almost among the leaves, while other species may produce an umbel in which a number of flowers are clustered on top of a stout stem. Coupled with a surprisingly rich range of colours, the variety is remarkable. Many *Primula* species have what is known as farina; the flowers are covered with a white dusting, like flour, which gives them a sultriness.

The subspecies and varieties will come true from seed if grown in reasonably discrete populations. Many plants offered with cultivar names will be seed-strain, not divisions, because the latter is not a cost-effective method of commercial production, although tissue culture is utilised. Some of the named candelabra hybrids are sterile and must be divided anyway, as will any specific colour breaks in order to replicate their characteristics completely.

Primula alpicola

The dense, globular heads of the drumstick group are not my favourite primula; I prefer these laxer clusters with funnel-shaped flowers that hang in a rather one-sided umbel on 60cm stems (though 90cm has been recorded). Dusted with farina, flowers also offer a delightful fragrance. The different colours have been subdivided into varieties, all preferring moist soil. *Primula alpicola* var. *alpicola* is yellow (the variety meant when none is specified), var. *alba* is white, and var. *violacea* is dusky purple, often with a white eye.

Primula elatior

A British native, whose locale extends into Finland and Russia, to Iran and Spain. Known locally as oxslip (its close relation, cowslip, is a meadow plant preferring sunnier sites), it has two to ten primrose-yellow flowers held in umbels on stems to 15cm tall. It is particularly satisfactory planted along the base of a hedgerow.

Primula florindae

Primula florindae

This Chinese species is one of the largest, with flower stalks that can rise to 120cm. They thrive when situated close to running water, where their great leaves can be satiated. They bloom in early to late summer, when up to 80 gently drooping, trumpet-shaped flowers appear in the umbel. Similar in principle to *P. alpicola* only larger, the basic colour is pale yellow (primrose-coloured) but some dusky reds can be found, all dusted with farina. If all colours are planted together, most seedlings will be yellow, since that colour is dominant.

Primula bulleyana

Primula japonica

Native to Japan and Taiwan, this is an easy member of the candelabra group whose flowers are arranged in layers or whorls around the stem. Typically this species has six whorls on 50cm tall stems and prefers a very moist site. The flowers in early to midsummer are usually purplish red.

A number of species in the candelabra group come from different parts of the world, with essentially the same characteristics, differing mainly in flower colour. A great many hybrids exist between them. These include *P. aurantiaca*, *P. bulleyana*, and *P. chungensis* from China, in shades of orange. *Primula prolifera* is bright yellow. *Primula pulverulenta* is red with a darker eye. Derived from the latter are the pink Bartley hybrids.

'Miller's Crimson' Reddish pink.

'Postford White' White with a yellow eye.

Primula sieboldii

A delightful Japanese species with pretty, ruffled foliage and distinctive flowers in which the petals are narrower at the base, not overlapping, to give a multi-bladed effect like a propeller. The basic species is pale pink, but they have been avidly collected in Japan, resulting in numerous named cultivars in shades of pink, purple, and my favourite white.

Primula vulgaris

Although one of my favourite native plants, this primrose is not confined to the British Isles but extends into eastern Europe and even the Atlas Mountains of North Africa. All the different coloured subspecies will seed around in a delightfully natural way. Of all the *Primula* listed, *P. vulgaris* is the most drought-tolerant, growing naturally beneath trees.

subsp. *balearica* White, from Mallorca.

subsp. *sibthorpii* Pale pink, from eastern Europe.

Prunus (Rosaceae)

Prunus are not suitable trees to use as structural planting for a new woodland, which is rather a shame as their spring flowers are so beautiful. Unfortunately, they have very aggressive, shallow root systems; the competition for moisture as they develop make it exceptionally difficult for most plants to thrive beneath them. My next suggestion, however, may be controversial: laurel.

Highly toxic if ingested, laurel leaves contain amygdalin, a compound of prussic acid (HCN) and glucose, which is also found in bitter almond kernels. (They release that distinctive smell when cut or crushed.)

Prunus laurocerasus

This is known in the United States as English laurel but it is in fact a native of eastern Europe and Asia Minor that was introduced to Britain from Turkey in 1576. It can be a real thug where it has been established for centuries. Nonetheless, it does a fine job of providing a backdrop and, more importantly, it generates winter shelter rapidly and in difficult conditions, even on horrible soil. Sometimes it is useful or even necessary to achieve this evergreen protection quickly, and laurel is hard to beat. Many other evergreens may be more sophisticated, but none are so adaptable and rapid. Perhaps there is scope for compromise by planting a mix and then removing the laurel before it becomes a problem and just as its more desirable companions start to achieve the desired effect. In its favour is the fact that it does bloom; upright spikes of white flowers are produced in midspring, followed by blue-black fruit that resembles cherries (hence the common name, cherry laurel). More refined alternatives to the common species are available. Heights are anticipated after 10 years.

'**Herbergii**' Extremely hardy; dense and compact upright habit. 2m.

'**Miky**' Superb smaller form; dense with narrow leaves. Masses of flowers. 1m.

'**Mount Vernon**' Very low form. 50cm.

'**Otto Luyken**' A classic. Low, compact habit; very dark, glossy foliage; and extremely free flowering. 1m.

'**Reynvaanii**' Vigorous but compact and dense, forming a tidy conical shape. 2m.

'**Schipkaensis**' One of the hardiest selections with a narrower habit. 2.5m.

'**Van Nes**' Wonderful lustrous foliage. 1.5m.

'**Zabeliana**' Low-growing, with long, arching branches clothed in narrow leaves. Flowers prolifically. 1m.

Pulmonaria (Boraginaceae)

This genus has seen a virtual explosion in popularity in recent years. With only 14 or so species, a considerable number of named cultivars are available, many of which seem similar to one another. Perfectly adapted to life on the woodland floor, and spreading by rhizomes to form leafy colonies, their funnel-shaped flowers are held in clusters in spring, starting in late winter, before the leaves have properly developed. Their foliage can be as attractive as their flowers, since many have vivid spotting and mottling, lasting through summer for as long as adequate moisture remains. Although theoretically tolerant of very dry shade, they will perform much better in a slightly moister position, so they are best not planted at the base of a tree.

These plants are often given too dry a site. Then the foliage succumbs to mildew soon after flowering and they look dreadful. Robust plants are frequently relegated to the difficult sites in the perception that they are tough enough to cope. That may be the case, but they will perform significantly better in nicer conditions. Other genera will do well in dry shade, so there is no need to compromise these lovely plants.

They create some wonderful effects on the woodland floor. I particularly like the silver-leaved cultivars and their combination with ferns. The species hybridise freely so many of the modern cultivars are of unknown parentage. Sometimes I prefer the naturalness of species, but in the case of *Pulmonaria* I would choose named cultivars that have been selected for quality of both flower and foliage. Colours range from white through all shades of pink to purple with a number described as blue. However, many of the blues are nearer to purple in my opinion; they rarely compare with the clarity of *Omphalodes* and *Myosotis*. With so many available, I can include only a selection of my favourites to cover the range of colour combinations.

Pulmonaria longifolia

Native of much of Europe including southern England, *P. longifolia* contributes the long, narrow, spotted leaves evident in many cultivars.

'**Ankum**' Well-known cultivar with intense blue flowers over lovely silvered foliage.

'**Bertram Anderson**' Purplish pink flowers.

'**Coral Spring**' Such a pretty pinky orange colour, though the mouth of the trumpet-shaped flower is curiously split.

Pulmonaria rubra

Red flowers contrast effectively with plain green leaves.

'**Redstart**' My preference, for bigger, richer red flowers.

Pulmonaria saccharata

A variable species, with red-violet, violet, or white flowers displayed over attractively white-spotted green leaves.

'**Leopard**' Silver blotched, pale green foliage contrasts prettily with soft red flowers.

Pulmonaria cultivars

'**Berries and Cream**' Recent hybrid between two beauties (*P.* 'Excalibur' and *P. rubra* 'Redstart'), creating a fabulous contrast of raspberry-pink flowers against silver foliage. Mildew resistant.

'**Blue Ensign**' A gorgeous colour; the standard against which all new blue-flowered *Pulmonaria* are measured. Large deep blue flowers are displayed against rich green leaves.

'**Diana Clare**' Large flowers open deep pink with a longitudinal purple stripe, maturing to rich violet-purple. Silver leaves are initially narrowly margined with green.

'**Lewis Palmer**' Vigorous cultivar with long, narrow deep green leaves, spotted and blotched greenish white. Rich violet-blue flowers.

'**Majesté**' Pink and violet flowers; then superb silver leaves.

Pulmonaria saccharata 'Leopard'   Pulmonaria 'Blue Ensign'

Pulmonaria 'Diana Clare'   Pulmonaria OPAL ('Ocupol')

OPAL ('Ocupol') Opalescent flowers are almost white with a lilac flush. The green leaves are flecked with silver.

'Roy Davidson' Derived from *P. longifolia*, with even more conspicuously marked leaves and pale blue flowers.

'Sissinghurst White' A particularly neat and tidy white-flowered selection.

Puschkinia (Hyacinthaceae)

This Middle Eastern monotypic genus is similar to *Scilla*. Although snowmelt plants in the wild, they are remarkably easy to grow, enjoying rather dry conditions when dormant. They are quite at home among tree roots, though deep shade is not to their liking; beneath a mature deciduous tree is perfect.

Puschkinia scilloides

Two or three leaves emerge from the bulb along with a flowering spike topped with up to 10 bell-shaped flowers in early to midspring. These are usually ice-blue with darker stripes, though beautiful pure white forms are available; even green flowers are known in the wild. 10cm.

Quercus (Fagaceae)

I may inexorably associate the oak with the English countryside, but only two species are actually British natives (*Q. petraea* and *Q. robur*). By contrast, North America is home to over 200 species and natural hybrids. Remarkable. Others are distributed across the northern hemisphere. Valued for their timber, many traditional woodlands contain great numbers of these majestic trees which can live to a ripe old age. They are superb in the upper canopy because their roots go deep which means that, despite their immense size, they are not taking water from the upper soil levels and can therefore be underplanted. All have distinctive, interesting shapes, and some develop fantastic autumn colour, but many of the species are similar. One thing is certain, however: planting an oak is a labour of love for generations to come, because these venerable trees are slow. Perhaps compromise is called for, mixing them with quicker maturing trees such as *Betula*, *Cratageus*, and *Corylus*, which can be sacrificed in the future as the oaks develop. Alternatively, authenticity can be exchanged for more rapid effect by selecting a faster growing species.

With 600 species, it is impossible to do them justice here. Suffice it to say that these are aristocratic trees to be planted for the pleasure of our grandchildren where space allows. The temptation may be to choose the species familiar to the locality, but it can be worthwhile to look further afield. The American red oaks (including *Q. coccinea*, *Q. palustris*, *Q. rubra*, *Q. velutina*, and their derivatives) are some of the most statuesque trees imaginable, thriving on moisture-retentive soil where they are pleasingly rapid in their growth while their scarlet autumn colours, dramatised by often large leaves, are breathtaking. The slower British native, *Q. robur*, however, is tolerant of even unimproved heavy clay. Selections of all these species and more are available, with subtly different foliage colours, variegation, or variation in shape, size, and habit. Circumstances and taste will dictate the choice. Whichever are selected, such patience and foresight will be rewarded in the years to come with magnificent trees able to dominate the woodland environment, yet so protective and tolerant of the beauty thriving at their feet.

Due to their deep root system, oaks do not like to be transplanted when too large. This is definitely one instance when small is beautiful; youngsters will get off to a more rapid start. *Phytophthora ramorum* (sudden oak death) can affect *Quercus*. Buy your plants from an inspected source and look out for sudden die-back.

Ramonda (Gesneriaceae)

A little gem to try in a shady crevice on the woodland rock garden, *Ramonda* appreciates moisture-retentive soil though is surprisingly tolerant of dry conditions. The flowers are a little like those of *Primula*, peering outwards from multiple flower stems which emerge from small rosettes of thickly textured, evergreen leaves from late spring to early summer. Only three species come from isolated areas in the Pyrénées, northeastern Spain, and the Balkans. 8–12cm.

Ramonda myconi

I first saw these beautiful little plants growing at the edge of a scenic footpath in the Pyrénées. That colony was deep violet in colour, but some bloom in white (var. *alba*) and pink ('Rosea'). This is the more robust species, adaptable to woodland cultivation; others are safer in an alpine house.

Ranunculus (Ranunculaceae)

Perhaps as many as 400 globally distributed species are available, including the ubiquitous buttercup. Fortunately, not all are as all-conquering; indeed many are high alpines needing very careful culture, while some delightful woodlanders will colonise areas of the woodland floor in the same way as the closely related and visually similar anemones. These enjoy similar conditions, too, waking early while the trees are still bare before going dormant as the soil starts to dry. Most naturalise perfectly beneath the trees while others have a later growth cycle and prefer moister sites. Many are yellow, like traditional buttercups, but whites and oranges can also be found.

Ranunculus aconitifolius

Native of moisture-retentive spots in the mountains across central Europe, basal clumps of three to five-lobed leaves are formed with the flowering stems reaching 60cm. The 2cm wide white flowers are produced all summer.

    'Flore Pleno' Popular double-flowered form whose tight pom-pom flowers have graced our gardens for more than 400 years.

Ranunculus ficaria

I am always skeptical of pretty flowered versions of what would otherwise be deemed a weed. This creature is the infamous celandine. I happen to like celandines, but given moist and fertile soil, they will spread and be extremely difficult to control. However, I am happy to have the species weaving its way through the ivy at the base of the hedgerows. So the answer could be to make them suffer; after all, they are about as tough as it comes, so there is no need to waste prime sites on them.

I have them in the very summer-dry shade among shallow-rooted *Betula*. They grow in clumps, with the roots terminating in little tubers. This is why they are so difficult to remove manually; even if the main clump can be extracted, it is almost inevitable that some of these tubers will have been left to grow into more plants. Commencing into growth so early in the season, the foliage often accompanies the snowdrops, shortly to be followed by intense yellow flowers. Their display is but brief, however, for by midsummer there is no trace of them left above the ground. This makes them perfect for applications as varied as the foot of even the most mature deciduous tree or surrounding giant hostas.

Recent years have seen a flurry of new cultivars reaching our gardens, with every imaginable combination of markings on the heart-shaped leaves and flower colour, in shades from white through cream to yellow, of course, then golds, oranges, and even bronze. *Plant Finder* lists nearly 100 variants, but I include here a few of my favourites. They will colonise, but neither so rapidly nor so densely rooted as to smother everyone else in their passage. These could easily become an obsession in the same way that *Hepatica* has become in Japan, yet they are much more affordable.

var. *aurantiacus* (syn. *R. ficaria* 'Cupreus') Wonderful golden orange, narrow pointed, star-shaped petals with a darker, slightly tufted centre.

'Brazen Hussy' One of the most popular and widely available, with vivid yellow flowers over the richest chocolate-purple foliage imaginable. A great combination with later snowdrops, dwarf narcissi, or even the white form of *Fritillaria meleagris*.

'Collarette' Quite different, the centre of the flower is tightly double, surrounded by squat, noticeably rounded petals, all in bright yellow—exactly how a young child might paint the sun.

'Double Mud' Despite its name, the flower is distinctive, reminding me of a tiny waterlily. The wide, double creamy white flowers are quite flat, sitting on green leaves.

'Limelight' Lots of lemon-yellow petals overlap to form a substantial flower around a central ruff of the same colour. Reminiscent of a miniature chrysanthemum.

'Orange Sorbet' One of a number of selections made at the Royal Horticultural Society gardens. Soft orange single flowers.

'Salmon's White' Pretty mottled leaves. Large flowers, creamy white backed with silver.

'Tortoiseshell' The markings on the leaves are almost as good as a cyclamen's, with rich chocolate staining around the edges and central veins to show off single yellow flowers.

Below: *Ranunculus ficaria* 'Salmon's White'

Right: *Ranunculus ficaria* 'Tortoiseshell'

Ranzania (Berberidaceae)

Almost 35 percent of Japan's 5600 native species of flora is endemic (that is, found nowhere else in the world). Amazing. *Ranzania* is represented by a single species and is rare even in Japan, where it is found only in the high mountains from central to northern Honshu.

Ranzania japonica

This gem is definitely special enough for the woodland rock garden, where it will enjoy fertile, humus-rich soil in light shade. Its close relationship to *Jeffersonia* is evident in the heart-shaped, green leaves and even in the gorgeous, relatively large, cup-shaped lilac flowers. It grows from a creeping rhizome in the same way as many species of *Epimedium* (to which it is also related), so with patience will form small colonies. New growth and flowers emerge early in the spring and can be vulnerable to late frosts. 40cm.

Reineckea (Convallariaceae)

Sometimes with an uncommon genus, it can be easiest to compare it to a better known plant. Therefore, for *Reineckea*, think *Liriope*.

Reineckea carnea

Native of the Himalayas, China, and Japan, it is tolerant of even heavy shade, though this can reduce its flowering potential. It would still provide an excellent leafy groundcover, evergreen in mildish climates. The flowers are held on spikes to 20cm and are usually white or pale pink and faintly fragrant.

   'Variegata' Cream-striped leaves.

Rodgersia (Saxifragaceae)

Allied to *Astilbe*, these Asian plants need a deep, rich soil that most importantly is extremely moisture-retentive in summer. Woodlands can provide such diverse habitats, but these are definitely not suitable for dry shade under trees; they thrive in conditions wet to the point of boggy. Here their majestic leaves will add a tropical dimension to an area, even though they are absolutely bone hardy. The feathery clouds of flowers sailing above the 1m tall leaves in mid to late summer are almost incidental to their aesthetics.

   The dramatic leaves can act like sails in windy conditions, and the stems snap with ease, so shelter is valuable. It is vital to provide middle-canopy planting, to give protection to more vulnerable plants such as this. Deciduous shrubs are adequate to shelter rodgersias since they will be dormant in winter.

These will spread, not to the point of invasiveness, but certainly enough that care needs to be taken when siting them to prevent more delicate neighbours being trampled by their chunky rhizomes or overshadowed by their leafy canopy. Their moisture requirement generally makes them unsuitable planting companions to spring bulbs which could colour the early spring (though *Leucojum* would be worth a try), but they do work well with large-leaved hostas for seriously leafy summer impact. Their autumn appeal should not be underestimated either, for they develop bonfire shades to rival even maples.

Nomenclature discrepancies seem to abound in this genus, with translations of original German names adding to the confusion. Many named cultivars and hybrids exist in addition to half a dozen species. I discuss a few of my favourites only, since their moisture requirements and sizes render them of limited application in many woodlands.

Rodgersia henrici

The leaves are held like deeply lobed umbrellas. Flowers are usually red, though white forms are known.

Rodgersia pinnata

Perhaps the most common species, *R. pinnata* is a native of western China. The pinnate leaves are deep green, though often richly flushed with red when young. Naturally pink, various flower colours are available. These are easily obtainable, but look out for salmon-coloured forms too.

'**Alba**' Dense spikes of white.

'**Superba**' Bright pink.

Rodgersia podophylla

Undoubtedly my favourite species; I love the deeply lobed leaves which turn fiery shades of crimson in autumn.

Rodgersia podophylla
'Braunlaub'

'**Braunlaub**' The bronze-brown colour of the amazing leaves is held well into summer before becoming deep green as the cream-flushed red flowers are produced
in early summer. Selected by German plantsman Ernst Pagels.

'**Rotlaub**' An equally dramatic equivalent with deep red–flushed leaves.

Rodgersia cultivars

'**Irish Bronze**' Foliage is most effective, emerging green before developing tints of
bronze as spring progresses, to become completely bronze by the time the contrasting white flowers are produced.

'**Parasol**' The red-tinted leaves of this one are deeply divided, adding to their attraction. White flowers.

Rosa (Rosaceae)

Roses might not be top of the list as woodland plants, but there is one I would not want
to be without.

Rosa canina

The dog rose is a rambler and a familiar sight in English hedgerows, scrambling
through trees to a height of 4–5m. Native of much of Europe and western Asia, it was
introduced to North America in the seventeenth century and has naturalised there. The
scented flowers appear as a curtain of pinky white in early summer to be followed by
bright red egg-shaped hips (fruit). It may be that this rose suffers from black spot and
mildew like any other, but high up in the tree the flowers can be appreciated without
having to deal with the foliar problems.

Roscoea (Zingiberaceae)

These completely hardy members of the ginger family are visually more like baby
orchids but are not as difficult to grow as they may appear. Seventeen species are distributed through the Himalayas and western China. Forming clumps from fleshy or
tuberous roots, they appreciate that popular soil condition—moisture-retentive but
well-drained and humus-rich. Although appropriate for woodland floor conditions,
they give better flower colour with some sunshine, so the densest shade should be
avoided. Not emerging until late spring or even early summer, they undergo a long dormancy period, when they dislike being too wet. Most species are variable and increasingly selections are being made to exploit these opportunities.

Roscoea auriculata

This Himalayan species fills that midsummer slot which is often a difficult time in the woodland garden. The sequential, large, violet-purple flowers with their distinctive pure white throats are marvellous all summer. 50cm.

Roscoea cautleyoides

Probably the most commercially available species, and suitably easy to grow, its tapering leaves clasp the erect stems topped by up to three gorgeous, pale yellow orchidlike flowers with characteristically large, single upper and two smaller lower petals. There is great variation in flowering time between different selections, from midspring to late summer, while purple and white forms are also known. 40cm.

'Jeffrey Thomas' Selected form with large flowers.

'Kew Beauty' Wonderful almost white flowers. Said to be a hybrid with *R. humeana.*

Roscoea purpurea

Roscoea humeana

Although generally flowering in late spring, the leaves are rarely developed enough to be too apparent at that stage, which can be rather dramatic, particularly since several flowers may open together. Usually purple, white or even yellow forms are known. 35cm.

Roscoea purpurea

The latest to flower, and variable in its wild Himalayan habitat, it shows potential for selections to be named. Usually to 50cm, stems as tall as 90cm are known in cultivation. Flowers may be completely purple, or purple and white bicolour. Scarce red forms also exist.

Roscoea scillifolia

This smaller species, arguably more elegant and undisputedly pretty, has pale pink to deep violet flowers. The earliest will bloom in midsummer, potentially continuing into the autumn. Self-seeds freely so perfect for naturalising. 10–45cm.

Roscoea cultivars

'Beesiana' This has become a group rather than one specific cultivar, representing many incidences of the cross between *R. cautleyoides* and *R. auriculata.* They will be variable, though some growers vegetatively propagate selected forms. The large, pale creamy yellow flowers are vividly marked with deep reddish purple.

'Monique' A superb Dutch selection from *R.* 'Beesiana', pure white with a speckling of purple.

Rubus (Rosaceae)

Sometimes it is difficult to see beyond the obvious; with 250 globally distributed species, there is more to *Rubus* than brambles and berries. Many of the best for floral effect are at their most floriferous in sunny sites; care should be taken as even the most ornamental can become invasive, though jolly useful to colonise areas too poor and difficult for much else to survive.

Rubus cockburnianus

The flowers of this Chinese species may be insignificant, but great thickets of tall, arching, thorny stems are produced; these are essentially purple, but mature stems are overlaid with a white bloom to give a ghostly appearance that is particularly noticeable in winter. The greyish white leaf undersides add to the silvery effect of the plant. Superb in winter where space allows.

Rubus thibetanus 'Silver Fern' is similar to *R. cockburnianus* in principle but rather more dainty with ferny foliage. *Rubus leucodermis* also has white-dusted stems. It could be argued that if the aggressive nature of this group was to be permitted, one might as well benefit from the delicious fruit of the latter.

'Goldenvale' A slightly less rampant selection with pretty golden leaves.

Ghostly white stems of *Rubus cockburnianus* with *Scilla bithynica* beneath

Rubus parviflorus

Considered invasive in its native North American habitat (one man's weed is another man's treasure), this thicket-forming thimbleberrry does produce scrumptious fruit in the same way as a raspberry. Best in part shade, it will lose vigour in heavy shade, which could be beneficial. Great autumn colours.

'Sunshine Spreader' Prostrate form with golden foliage.

Rubus rolfei

Populations previously known as *R. calycinoides* and *R. pentalobus* have been brought together under *R. rolfei*. A superb groundcover for tough locations, this Asiatic species will form dense mats of lobed, rich green leaves, softly felted beneath, rooting as it goes. White flowers are almost invisible, hidden beneath the leaves, followed by orange berries. As temperatures drop in winter, the leaves become richly flushed with purple.

'**Emerald Carpet**' More compact form.

'**Golden Quilt**' Bright yellow young growth all season gives a bicolour effect against the mature green foliage.

Rubus spectabilis

The salmonberry from western North America has lovely magenta-rose flowers followed by orange-yellow berries, performing well even beneath trees.

'**Olympic Double**' Pretty double form.

Rubus tricolor

A more effective groundcover would be hard to find, but the carpet becomes too dense and extensive to allow even bulbs to come up through it. Although attractive, perhaps a last resort.

Ruscus (Ruscaceae)

A most unusual plant, although ostensibly woody, *Ruscus* is related to the likes of *Convallaria majalis*, spreading slowly by fleshy rhizomes. The apparent leaves are actually modified, flattened stems, which is why the flowers and subsequent berries appear stuck to the middle of the leaf. Male and female flowers are produced on separate plants unless a hermaphrodite is obtained. The latter is advantageous in that just one plant is required to produce berries, though they do look superb en masse. The berries are like small, bright red cherries, ripening in autumn and remaining until flowering time the following spring.

Ruscus aculeatus

Primarily from southern Europe, so-called butcher's broom is also found in southern England.

'**Wheeler's Variety**' This elusive hermaphrodite form is more compact, producing marble-sized red berries in winter in great abundance.

Ruscus hypoglossum

This species is less common in England. Attractive for its larger, softer leaves, it is the most extensively grown florist's crop in Israel.

Frost-coated *Ruscus aculeatus* 'Wheeler's Variety' in fruit

Sanguinaria (Papaveraceae)

Yet another surprise from the poppy family, this little chap is a true early spring delight. The name derives from the Latin *sanguinarius*, meaning blood, and refers to the redness of the root, with the common name bloodroot.

The roots quickly deteriorate out of the ground, so divisions should be replanted promptly. All parts of the plant are highly toxic, but this did not discourage the Native Americans, who utilised it for all manner of medicinal cures as well as to produce dyes for war paint, textiles, and baskets. It is considered to have medicinal applications even today, and harvesting of the rhizomes from the wild has threatened populations in some areas. Do ensure that potential new acquisitions are raised in cultivation.

Sanguinaria canadensis f. *multiplex* 'Plena'

Sanguinaria canadensis

Widely distributed across eastern North America, each branch of the spreading rhizome bears a single leaf supporting a dazzling white flower that resembles a waterlily. As the flowers fade, the leaves expand to reach as much as 15cm across. Each flower may be fleeting, but the succession ensures an alluring display for several weeks in early spring.

> f. *multiplex* Double flowers are sterile so last for longer; the single flowers of the species drop their petals immediately after fertilisation.
>
> f. *multiplex* 'Plena' This one is semi-double, which seems naming-wise to be the wrong way round. It is a prettier plant with more petals but without the heaviness of the fully double.
>
> 'Peter Harrison' Desirable, scarce selection with pink-backed flowers.

Sarcococca (Buxaceae)

This genus of small evergreen shrubs from Asia is known as Christmas box, alluding to both its flowering time and growth habit. No garden or woodland should be without it. These winter flowerers are perfect to scatter through the woodland in even heavy shade, where they will not only brighten the winter display with their pretty flowers and exquisite perfume, but provide low-down protection to emerging treasures. Generally white, the small flowers are held in the leaf axils in mid to late winter; lacking true petals, they consist of little more than a bunch of stamens. Although not individually spectacular, the flowers are produced in such profusion for such a long period that the effect is supreme. Their preference is for humus-rich, moisture-retentive soil, but they are surprisingly tolerant of drought once established.

Above: *Sarcococca confusa*

Right: Frost-glazed *Sarcococca hookeriana*

Sarcococca confusa

This dense, compact shrub has white flowers that contrast with dark green leaves, followed by black berries. 1m.

Sarcococca hookeriana

More upright stems spread by rhizomes to form a thicket. Longer leaves by comparison with *S. confusa*. Creamy white flowers. 1m.

> **var. *digyna*** This variant is more common in Britain than the species, featuring distinctive purple stems and pink-flushed flowers.
> **var. *humilis*** Particularly hardy dwarf shrub suckers to form dense clumps. 60cm.

Sarcococca orientalis

Discovered in China by Roy Lancaster as recently as 1980, this stout, small, but vigorous shrub has larger leaves. Flowering before the others in early winter, it neatly extends the season of interest. 1m.

Sarcococca ruscifolia

Similar to *S. confusa* but with red berries and slightly larger leaves. 1m.

> **'Dragon Gate'** Also collected in Yunnan by Lancaster in 1980, tiny by comparison, with small, mid-green leaves and an amazing amount of flowers for its size. Wonderful on the woodland rock garden perhaps. 50cm.

Sarcococca ruscifolia
'Dragon Gate'

Saruma (Aristolochiaceae)

This extremely hardy monotypic genus was introduced from China in the early 1900s. Its affinity to another genus in the same family was recognised and reflected in naming it as an anagram of *Asarum*.

Saruma henryi

The leaves may be heart-shaped, but they are almost furry and produced alternately on stems to 45–60cm rather than in a basal cluster like most *Asarum* species. The flowers are much more showy, too, being yellow flattened cups with three distinct petal-lobes and a deeper, orange centre. Forming a lovely clump, it is definitely worthy of a place on the woodland floor.

Saruma henryi

Saxifraga (Saxifragaceae)

With nearly 500 species, there is definitely more to this genus than the traditional little mossy alpines. As is often the case in such large genera, they are divided into sections according to their characteristics, two of which are of relevance to us, though a number of species in the alpine sections could be considered for the woodland rock garden. A surprising percentage of them appreciate some shade rather than the dry baking we traditionally subject them to on our exposed garden rockeries. Section 11 includes the so-called London pride species, which I remember with little enthusiasm from my childhood. Section 5 is a different matter. The flowers usually have two petals longer than the others, which lends a winglike feel to them, so that en masse they appear to float above the foliage, which is often valuable in its own right. Those described here are clump-forming perennials, often spreading by long, threadlike stolons, terminating in rosettes of palmate basal leaves. This group is ideally suited to humus-rich areas of our woodland floor, being highly decorative for much of the year.

Although clearly attributable to certain species, most modern selections are classified by cultivar names alone. To understand their characteristics and requirements, I have listed the cultivars with their allied species.

Saxifraga 'Ruby Wedding'

Saxifraga cortusifolia

Tremendous variation exists among the leaves of this species.

S. **'Ruby Wedding'** Collected in Japan under the number BSWJ4951, the beautiful bronzy purple palmate leaves are fleshy and overlaid with silvery markings. In late summer these are delightfully complemented by large panicles of white, pink-tinged flowers with the characteristic two elongated lower petals. 40cm.

Saxifraga epiphylla

This fascinating Asiatic species forms clumps of compact rosettes of kidney-shaped evergreen leaves; at the base of each is produced a new plantlet. This "piggy-back" characteristic has given rise to the Piggy series of cultivar names.

S. **'Precious Piggy'** Collected under the number BWJ7750 in China, silver markings adorn the thickly textured leaves.

S. **'Purple Piggy'** Incredible magenta-purple undersides to otherwise green leaves. White flowers are typical of the group.

Saxifraga fortunei

Although known in Europe since the 1860s, in recent years many cultivars have come from Japan, adding a whole new dimension to this genus. Bigger in all its parts than its alpine cousins, this herbaceous species is almost evergreen, forming a clump of attractive scalloped leaves above which rise tall panicles of delightful star-shaped flowers, but not until early to late autumn, which is quite unexpected. Although sometimes said to need lime-free soil, they are quite happy in my garden soil, which is definitely not acidic. However, the topsoil has been improved to provide a lovely, friable, moisture-retentive, thus typical "woodsy" loam. 60cm.

S. **'Black Ruby'** The exact colour of the foliage will be influenced by light levels; in adequate light it will be so dark as to be almost black, fading to dark red in midautumn as the ruby-red flowers appear. Remarkably these last until early winter. 20cm.

S. **'Mount Nachi'** These white-flowered forms are my favourites; they show up so well against the autumnal gloom. They contrast well against bristly, dark copper-red foliage. 25cm.

S. **'Rubrifolia'** An excellent vigorous plant with rich green leaves, flushed with red. The flower stems are bright red, supporting drifts of fluffy white flowers. 45cm.

S. **'Sugar Plum Fairy'** Sugary pink flowers rise above green leaves. 35cm.

S. **'Wada'** The largest in the group, with proportionally large, glossy green leaves topped by dense clouds of icy white flowers. 60cm.

Left: *Saxifraga 'Sugar Plum Fairy'*

Above: *Saxifraga 'Wada'*

Saxifraga hirsuta

Clouds of starry white flowers in early summer float above kidney-shaped green leaves with reddish undersides. 30cm.

Saxifraga nipponica

This rhizomatous species is notable for flowering earlier in the season, in midsummer. Up to 20 white flowers per stem. 40cm.

S. **'Pink Pagoda'** Pink-flowered Japanese selection.

Left: *Saxifraga hirsuta*

Above: *Saxifraga 'Pink Pagoda'*

Saxifraga stolonifera

This classic plant is known as mother of thousands, alluding to its tendency to spread by long, thin, bright red stolons that form a new rosette of kidney-shaped leaves where they subsequently touch the ground. Very easily grown and evergreen in mild climates, but not the hardiest of species. I love the white flowers with their distinctive longer lower lobes, and although it spreads, it is not so solid and heavy as to prevent other plants growing among them. Try it with small hostas or spiky *Ophiopogon* and *Liriope* or to take over when the arching stems of *Convallaria* are past their best.

S. **'Harvest Moon'** Delightful groundcover in mild gardens, with bright yellow to orange-red leaves darkening with age. The exact leaf colour will depend on the light levels. White flowers.

S. **'Hime'** Dwarf selection; even the flower spikes reach only 15cm tall in late summer and early autumn. The rounded leaves are daintily veined with pale cream, with pink flushing beneath, which visibly extends into the upper margins.

S. **'Hsitou Silver'** BSWJ1980 White flower spikes above pretty leaves which are strongly veined with silver.

S. **'Kinki Purple'** BSWJ4972 Gorgeous rich purple foliage from which emerge pyramidal spikes of ethereal white flowers, delicately suffused with pink, from early summer to early autumn. 30cm.

S. **'Maroon Beauty'** White flowers are held over maroon leaves marked with silver.

Saxifraga stolonifera

Scilla (Hyacinthaceae)

Spring would not be the same in the woodland garden without these exquisite little blue-flowered bulbs. Perhaps 80 species are distributed from Europe into Asia, Africa, and even across the Pacific. Basal tufts of narrow leaves erupt from tiny bulbs in early spring, followed by six-petalled starry to bell-shaped flowers on short stems. They will naturalise in drier areas of the woodland floor, flowering beneath the bare twigs of deciduous trees, following on from *Galanthus* to give a splash of blue among other spring bulbs. They can be tucked around the base of late risers provided they are not too damp when dormant. Growing to 20cm tall, most are small enough to be perfect for underplanting beneath shrubs in even the smallest garden. A woodland effect can be created without lots of trees, just layering the plants to make the most of every inch of garden.

It is indicative of their close relationship that *Scilla* and *Chionodoxa* will hybridise. ×*Chionoscilla allenii* is a hybrid between *Chionodoxa* (either *C. luciliae* or *C. siehei*) and *Scilla bifolia*. The offspring will be variable within the characteristics of their similar parents. Look for the clone ×*Chionoscilla allenii* 'Fra Angelico'.

Note that all parts of *Scilla* are highly toxic.

Scilla bifolia

Its wide distribution through Europe into Asia gives rise to several geographical variants as well as colour selections of garden origin. Just two leaves but up to eight flowers appear per stem.

'**Alba**' White flowers.

'**Praecox**' Deep purple-blue, early-flowering clone.

'**Rosea**' Pink flowers.

Scilla bithynica

Choose this species for damper sites and enjoy substantial heads of five to fifteen starry blue flowers, in varying shades. Naturalised in France and southeastern Europe.

'**Somerset Pearl**' Smoky, mother-of-pearl coloured flowers.

Scilla liliohyacinthus

A leafier species from France and Spain, producing loose pyramidal racemes of starry blue flowers. The foliage lasts for so much longer that a moist site is preferred.

'**Alba**' Scarce but dramatic white selection.

Scilla mischtschenkoana

What a mouthful. A lovely plant, though, usually represented by the clone 'Tubergeniana'. The first palest blue flowers open as they push through the soil early in the new year, elongating to clothe a 10cm stem.

Scilla siberica

Very much the archetypal *Scilla* with rich blue, flared, bell-shaped flowers. It naturalises freely, popping up in unlikely places but never to the point of being a nuisance. The leaves are a lovely deep green and are held tidily upright, even dying neatly so the

Scilla siberica and
S. siberica 'Alba'

foliage is never an irritation. From the Caucasus to Iran, several botanically distinct but aesthetically similar subspecies exist. *Scilla armena* is similar and worth planting, but rarely commercially available.

'**Alba**' Pure white.

'**Spring Beauty**' Deeply coloured, almost violet selection.

Scoliopus (Trilliaceae)

Woodlands do provide an excuse for acquiring an eclectic range of plants, and few are more strange than these! Closely related to *Trillium*, which explains why everything is arranged in threes (though the foliage reminds me of *Erythronium*), these need to be tucked into the woodland rock garden. They thrive in typical woodsy conditions where the soil retains just enough moisture through the summer.

Scoliopus bigelowii

This species is native to my personal plant-hunting mecca of Oregon. The flowers, excitingly early in late winter, are perched on slender 20cm stems on a level with the tops of the vertically held, brown-blotched leaves. As in *Trillium*, the "showy" part of the flower is three, almost horizontally held, bracts in the centre of which the true flower consists of a cluster of tiny petals and stamens. Unfortunately, they smell of bad meat, which causes the plant to be known as the stink pod. This attribute does have a use; it attracts the flies which pollinate it. The three bracts are quite unique, being striped with reddish brown to varying degrees.

Scoliopus hallii

The same principle but even smaller growing, with plain, lighter green leaves. Quicker to flower from seed. I love this quote from the renowned Scottish alpine grower Ian Young (from the Scottish Rock Garden Club's *Bulb Log Diary*, March 2003): "It is the sort of plant that is described as a 'connoisseur's plant' which means that you are either mad, sad or both to want to grow it." It is always such a relief to be reminded that I am not the only one.

Silene (Caryophyllaceae)

Various of the 500 or so species distributed around the world grow wild in shady woods, though the majority are sun-lovers. Campions are classic English wildflowers, of both hedgerows and coastal zones, but some of the best woodland species are from North America. It is interesting how common names can vary between continents. In parts of North America, these are referred to as catchflies, referring to the sticky sap which does just that. Whatever we call them, they are undemanding to grow and vary from delightful prostrate mounds to taller clumps. The species listed here all come from woodland habitats, but it tends to be open woodland rather than heavy shade. Sadly, many are scarce in their native habitat on both continents. The flowers all have five petals and are usually held in groups above the simple leaves.

Excess moisture in winter can cause *Silene* to damp off, particularly if the site is too shady, which will also result in weak, straggly growth.

Silene californica

A common name is pink, but this species is vivid scarlet. Native to the forests of the west coast of North America, this delightful plant makes a mound, with a taproot to maximise its access to water in its preferred drier conditions. Try it at the foot of a tree. Flowering in late spring to early summer, each of the five petals has a rather ragged edge, for a shaggy effect. 30cm. *Silene laciniata* is similar, but with even shaggier flowers. Both are an amazing colour.

Silene caroliniana

The origin of this one is obvious from the name, but the flowers from midspring to early summer are quite unique, pale pink in colour and 2.5cm wide, with each petal rounded and very simple. Forming a mound of stems to no more than 25cm, this species requires only poor, shallow soil, so is worth trying beneath even a mature tree. White and varying colour forms are known.

Silene dioica

Native European campion can form clumps as tall as 90cm with vivid reddish pink flowers and prefers cooler, moister positions. Several selections are available in Britain, with white or varying degrees of double flowers and, heaven-forbid, even with variegation.

'**Minikin**' Useful dwarf selection reaching little more than 35cm.

Silene schafta

From the Caucasus and Iran, this species is one for the woodland rock garden, sneaking its roots into rocky crevasses. The stems can reach 15cm long, ending in clusters of starlike flowers. These are usually bright pink but there are named colour forms.

'**Shell Pink**' Paler pink flowers.

Silene virginica

Similar in habit to *S. polypetala* but with lax stems to 50cm long and vivid, red, star-shaped flowers with narrow petals. Hybrids between these two species are being developed which have tremendous potential.

×*Sinocalycalycanthus* (Calycanthaceae)

In 1991, reciprocal crosses between *Sinocalycanthus chinensis* and *Calycanthus floridus* were performed by an undergraduate student at North Carolina State University. One of the four resulting progeny flowered for the first time, spectacularly, in 1996 and was named after its breeder, Richard Hartlage. Inspired by the success of 'Hartlage Wine', development work has continued, and although new to cultivation, there is every reason to believe that these hybrids will soon become highly desirable residents of the woodland glade.

×*Sinocalycalycanthus raulstonii*
A recently named, mouth-watering hybrid between *Sinocalycanthus* and *Calycanthus*.

    'Hartlage Wine' This hybrid displays the best qualities of both parents, producing dusky wine-red flowers which open widely to reveal a cream-coloured centre and subtle fragrance.

×Sinocalycalycanthus raulstonii 'Hartlage Wine'

×*Sinocalycalycanthus* 'Venus'
More complicated in its parentage, adding *Calycanthus occidentalis* to the mix, this gorgeous shrub produces large ivory-coloured buds which open into white flowers flushed with yellow and purple in the middle. The fragrant blooms are produced primarily in spring, but sporadic flowering will continue all summer.

Sinocalycanthus (Calycanthaceae)

A remarkable monotypic genus initially included in *Calycanthus* and certainly closely related. Found in eastern China in 1983, seed was sent to Britain from the Shanghai Botanic Garden, to flower in Roy Lancaster's garden for the first time in cultivation in 1989.

Sinocalycanthus chinensis

Enormous leaves make this deciduous plant stand out in any company, but the flowers are even better. Approximately 7cm across, they consist of two whorls, each of 10 tepals, in early summer. The outer ring is white, sometimes flushed pink, while the smaller inner tepals are pale yellow with white and maroon basal markings. Apparently tolerant of even heavy shade, the large leaves demand a moisture-retentive, humus-rich soil with wind protection. They are perfect therefore for a prominent spot in the woodland.

Soldanella (Primulaceae)

These are wonderful plants for the well-drained, but moisture-retentive soil of our woodland rock garden, coming as they do from the mountains of Europe. However, some are snowmelt or scree plants, so careful selection is crucial. Related to *Primula*, possessing a clump of basal leaves sprouting from a matted, rhizomatous root system, the nodding, bell-shaped flowers produced in early spring have characteristically tattered edges.

These are not the easiest of plants to grow successfully, though they are well worth the extra effort. They respond to regular dividing (after flowering) with renewed vigour. They have a reputation for being shy to flower, though this could be a physical problem caused by the flower buds (which are formed in late autumn) being damaged by insects, botrytis, or slugs over the winter.

Soldanella montana

Preferring acid soils, this pretty plant is widespread through the pine woods of the central European mountains. The lilac-coloured flowers are deeply fringed and hang from 15cm tall stems.

Soldanella villosa

From the Pyrénées, this is arguably the easiest species for the woodland, differing from *S. montana* by its hairiness and even more deeply fringed purple-blue flowers.

Spigelia (Loganiaceae)

This plant will stop all garden visitors in their tracks. Indian pink is strangely scarce, even in its native North America. Although the genus includes some 50 species from the Americas, just one is suitable for woodland culture, requiring moist, humus-rich soil and preferably warm summers. They appreciate humidity, so positioning adjacent to water (though not in overly wet soil) can help.

Spigelia was used to great effect medicinally by Native Americans, though it is extremely toxic.

Spigelia marilandica

Clump-forming perennial found wild in few locations outside Missouri, with spectacular flowers held in a one-sided spike at the top of 50cm leafy stems. Long, thin tubes of the most intense scarlet imaginable flare and divide at the mouths to give a five-pointed starlike effect of bright chartreuse. The contrast could hardly be more marked.

'Wisley Jester' The form available in Britain.

Spiranthes (Orchidaceae)

Forty-two species of more modest orchids than many, but captivating nonetheless, unusually prefer alkaline soil.

Spiranthes cernua var. *odorata* 'Chadd's Ford'

The species comes originally from eastern North America, but this named cultivar is the easiest variant to obtain because it has been commercially propagated by tissue culture (which is the best way to buy orchids anyway). Extremely robust and easy to grow for an orchid, it forms vigorous flower spikes to 50cm or so above a fleshy basal rosette of leaves, with numerous small, richly vanilla-scented, creamy white flowers from late summer to late autumn. It spreads rapidly by tuberous roots to form a handsome colony. They are subtle in their beauty so should not be hidden too far from the path. Wonderful in conjunction with autumn *Cyclamen* or *Saxifraga*, or surrounded by the kaleidoscopic fallen leaves of autumn.

Stachyurus (Stachyuraceae)

This small Asiatic genus of large, spreading deciduous shrubs flowers in early spring before the leaves unfurl. Individually small and cup-shaped, the flowers are held in long racemes, dangling from arching stems. Perfect for more open areas of the woodland, they enjoy moisture-retentive, humus-rich but well-drained soil, but they also appreci-

Stachyurus chinensis

ate the protection of their surroundings since they can be vulnerable to damage in early spring from late frost and chilly winds.

Stachyurus chinensis

Introduced from China by Wilson in 1908, this species produces 30 or more flowers in each raceme.

Stachyurus praecox

The leaves of this Japanese introduction from 1864 are broader, with 15 to 24 flowers per raceme, some two weeks earlier than those of *S. chinensis*.

    var. *matsuzakii* Chunkier plant, with stout pale green stems, large leaves, and squat flower racemes.

    'Rubriflorus' The flowers are delicately flushed with pink, particularly noticeable while still in bud.

Stachyurus cultivar

    'Magpie' Pretty leaves are broadly margined with cream. Typical flowers.

Left: *Stachyurus praecox* 'Rubriflorus'

Below: *Stachyurus* 'Magpie'

Thin out twiggy side growth to reveal the striated bark of *Staphylea bumalda*.

Opposite: *Staphylea holocarpa* 'Rosea'

Staphylea (Staphyleaceae)

This small genus from the northern hemisphere is not as widely known and grown as it deserves to be. Known as bladdernut due to the long, inflated seedpod containing several hard brown seeds, its flowers are pretty. Small white bells hang in clusters from midspring to early summer, just as the pinnate leaves are opening. When the yellow leaves of autumn drop, they reveal striated bark. Often suckering to form large multi-stemmed shrubs, these handsome plants are happy in more open areas of the woodland. If the shade is too heavy, they may become leggy with loss of flower. They are also tough enough to create the canopy for a small-scale woodland planting—perfect in a small garden. Happy in moisture-retentive soil, they will tolerate drier conditions once established.

Staphylea bumalda
Introduced from the Orient in 1812, this is an elegant plant with particularly stripy bark.

Staphylea colchica
Upright flower spikes with the fragrance of orange blossom distinguish this Caucasian species.
   'Hessei' Elusive form with red-purple–flushed flowers.

Staphylea holocarpa
Native to China and the Japanese Alps, *S. holocarpa* was introduced by Wilson in 1908. It is often the first to flower.
   'Rosea' One of my favourite of all small trees, the young leaves are flushed bronze but the flowers are exquisitely tinted pink. This selected form is far superior to the assortment of dirty flowers found so often in *S. holocarpa* var. *rosea*.

Staphylea pinnata

Usually five leaflets identify this species, though both seven and three are known. Native to central Europe, records of its cultivation go back to 1596.

Staphylea trifolia

This slightly hairy North American species dates back to 1640.

Stenanthium (Melanthiaceae)

What an unexpectedly lovely genus. Melanthiaceae is a subdivision of Liliaceae, which immediately tells us that this is bulbous. Easily grown on the woodland floor in rich, moisture-retentive soil, albeit with adequate drainage in winter, and summer shade, they ideally prefer acid soil, though this is not crucial if the structure is right.

Stenanthium gramineum

Leafy clumps of basal leaves are easily mistaken for a grass when out of flower. Flowers are white and bell-shaped with six narrow tepals and occur on tall stems from early summer to early autumn in several panicles, creating a rather shaggy plume. Found in southeastern North America, its two varieties vary in overall height. This statuesque plant looks fantastic towering above hostas and other great leaves, rubbing shoulders with the pink, airy spikes of *Phlox*, or surrounded by graceful ferns.

Stenanthium occidentale

This species is sufficiently different to have periodically been classified elsewhere. However, it has been concluded that the differences are not enough to justify that. Enjoying moist, shady crevices through a limited area of the North American western seaboard, the flowers are much more like lilies—small bells, daintily flared, and almost recurved at their mouths. They are yellowish green in colour, often flushed purple. The basal leaves are much wider in this species, more typical of a lily, definitely not like grass.

Streptopus (Convallariaceae)

Their close kinship to *Polygonatum* is clear to see; the greatest difference is that the petals of the bell-like flowers of *Streptopus* are joined only at the base, whereas in *Polygonatum* they are fused for the length of the bell, until it flares at the mouth. Typical woodland floor growing conditions suit them well, where they enjoy humus-rich soil in which their slender rhizomes can spread. The thin stems are not as delicate as they appear, but they amusingly zigzag, from one leaf node to the next, with a flower dangling on a long stalk from each of the upper leaf axils from late spring to midsummer.

Streptopus amplexifolius

Small, white bell-like flowers are often held in pairs, which give way to bright red berries. 70cm. The wide distribution from southern Europe to Japan and North America gives rise to several geographical variants. From China, *S. simplex* is similar, though its flowers tend to be larger and solitary.

var. *americanus* Glaucous leaf undersides.

Streptopus lanceolatus

(previously *S. roseus*) Widespread throughout North America, its delightful pale pink flowers are perhaps the prettiest of the genus. 60cm.

Streptopus ×oreopolus

(*S. amplexifolius* × *S. lanceolatus*) From a small area from New Hampshire to Newfoundland and originally thought to be a variant of *S. amplexifolius*, it is now treated as a sterile natural hybrid, with characteristics intermediate between its parents.

Streptopus streptopoides

The smallest grower has perhaps the largest leaves, which can hide the flowers beneath them. They are worth seeking out and appreciating more closely, though, reminding me of miniature *Lilium nepalense* flowers. Creamy yellow bells have rich ruby markings inside. Found from Siberia to North America, via Japan, there is further localised variation. 25cm.

var. *brevipes* The North American incarnation is even smaller, often found in conifer forests, so more tolerant of the drier areas of the woodland floor.

var. *japonicus* A little bigger in all its parts.

Strobilanthes (Acanthaceae)

With about 180 species, this large genus is interesting in this company; allied to *Acanthus*, which is definitely sun loving, those listed here grow naturally in wooded places in Asia, but not under the heaviest shade. The flowers are simplest described as bent-over trumpets, being hooded or pouch-like, clustered at the end of stout stems rising from leafy clumps. Lacking the rigidity and spikiness of many *Acanthus*, all parts of these plants are soft, covered in minute hairs; for this reason they dislike too much moisture and prefer drier, lighter areas of the woodland floor. Valuable particularly for their long display of pretty flowers late in the season, they can be positioned to soften more angular plants and to disguise the aging stems of Convallariaceae. Unfortunately there is nomenclature confusion here, particularly surrounding the concept that the plants widely known as *S. atropurpurea* should actually be called *S. wallichii*. Many sources describe this completely differently. There is also debate about hardiness. Definitely scope for experimentation and further research.

Strobilanthes attenuata

Easily grown, its prostrate habit to 25cm tall allows it to root in as the nodes touch the soil. Lots of violet-blue to purple flowers are freely borne over an extended period from midsummer until the autumn frosts. *Strobilanthes rankanensis* is similar in habit and flower colour.

Strobilanthes flexicaulis

Introduced from northern Taiwan under the collection number BSWJ354, this graceful, bushy plant grows to 1m by a little broader. Trumpet-shaped flowers are often prettily spotted over bluish purple and are held on more slender stems.

Strobilanthes nutans

Unexpectedly for a Nepalese epiphyte, this species is perfectly growable in normal garden conditions (certainly in zone 7) in shade beneath large shrubs, where it forms dense leafy clumps. In contrast to the others, flowers are white.

Strobilanthes wallichii

Potentially to 2m, it is the tallest of those listed here. Violet-blue to purple flowers.

Stylophorum (Papaveraceae)

These yellow poppy-like flowers add a brilliant splash of colour to the woodland floor where they appreciate the humus-rich soil. Avoid areas of deepest shade as leggy plants with less flowers will result; plant in sunny clearings and nice soil, and they will self-seed prolifically to the point of being a nuisance. Treat it mean, in a relatively dry site less conducive to germination.

Stylophorum lasiocarpum

Stylophorum diphyllum

The flowers in early to late spring of this widespread North American native remind me of the lovely yellow *Meconopsis*, but the leaves betray it as something different. Although deeply divided into five or seven lobes, they are much coarser and also hairy. The ever-resourceful Native Americans utilised the yellow sap of this one as a dye. 30cm.

Stylophorum lasiocarpum

This Chinese species is sturdier, with less divided leaves, but it has a local use as well: the red juice in the thick roots has medicinal properties. The early spring flowers are held in clusters above the leafy clump. Usually dazzling yellow, forms with more reddish flowers are also known.

Styrax (Styracaceae)

Their common name, snowbell, says it all, though that is also sometimes used to refer to *Halesia*—that shows the problem with common names. This is a large genus, distributed through the northern hemisphere with more than 100 species now known; numbers are swollen by the many successful recent expeditions to China. They make beautiful small trees, thriving in dappled shade on slightly acid, moisture-retentive, humus-rich, well-drained soils, seemingly dripping with white bell-shaped flowers in spring. Many of the new introductions have yet to be assessed for hardiness or to become widely available.

The young emerging leaves are vulnerable to late frost, though generally larger plants sprout again from dormant buds; young plants without this energy reserve can be damaged.

Styrax japonicus

The best known and to date arguably the showiest species hails from Japan and Korea, with small leaves and elegant habit. The lovely white bells are punctuated by prominent yellow stamens, produced in profusion in early summer.

'**Emerald Pagoda**' The late J. C. Raulston was interested in *Styrax*, developing a good collection at North Carolina University. He rated this as one of the best, collected from Korea, where it stood out among the native population. Larger in all its parts with good yellow autumn colour.

'**Fargesii**' Generally more substantial and tolerant, thriving in my garden while other forms struggle, to become one of my favourites. Larger flowers.

'**Pink Chimes**' Gorgeous Japanese selection with rich pink flowers. Not to be confused with Benibana Group, which includes pink-flowered seedlings of variable quality.

'**Snowfall**' More dense and rounded habit than other selections, displaying prolific, slightly fragrant, white flowers.

Styrax obassia

Introduced from Japan, Korea, and Manchuria in 1879, with upright habit, potentially to 10m. Large leaves with softly hairy undersides can partially obscure the flowers which are delightful and fragrant, earlier than *S. japonicus*. Exfoliating older bark maintains interest through the winter. *Styrax hemsleyanus* is similar but with less downy leaves and chocolate-coloured leaf buds.

×*Sycoparrotia* (Hamamelidaceae)

A bigeneric hybrid between *Parrotia persica* and *Sycopsis sinensis* raised in Switzerland in the 1950s, it is happy in all but the heaviest shade and tough enough to stand by itself and be underplanted.

×*Sycoparrotia semidecidua*
This forms a large semi-deciduous shrub of rather arching habit, with small leaves which are retained long into the autumn, finally turning a bright yellow in midwinter. The pinky yellow staminoid flowers shimmer as they catch the low winter sun once the shrub finally relinquishes its leaves.

Sycopsis (Hamamelidaceae)

This monotypic Asian genus introduced from China by Wilson in 1901 is an excellent woodland plant, its winter contribution being both aesthetic and useful.

Sycopsis sinensis
Eventually a large, bushy, evergreen shrub with small elliptic leaves. Fascinating dense clusters of early spring flowers have no petals, being composed of yellow stamens and red anthers.

Symphoricarpos (Caprifoliaceae)

Essentially an American genus, *Symphoricarpos* is perfectly adapted to a wide range of conditions in most climates, including all areas of the woodland. Undistinguished in leaf, flower, or form, they should be planted for their crop of berries that develop in autumn and last well into the winter, maintaining structure and interest when spirits sag. They form small deciduous bushes with slender stems and small ovate leaves. Straggly plants can be rejuvenated with hard pruning as necessary.

Symphoricarpos albus
Inevitably dubbed snowberry on account of the marble-sized white berries, it is widespread through eastern North America.

 var. *laevigatus* This western variant is larger in all its parts.

Symphoricarpos ×*chenaultii*
(*S. microphyllus* × *S. orbiculatus*) Small dense shrub producing copious berries of pinkish white, tinged purplish red where exposed.

'**Hancock**' The best form with a low-spreading habit. Excellent groundcover, even at the foot of big trees.

Symphoricarpos ×doorenbosii

Fantastic range of hybrids from an eminent Dutch horticulturalist, involving *S. albus* var. *laevigatus*, *S. ×chenaultii*, and *S. orbiculatus*, selected for their bumper crops of marble-sized berries.

'**Magic Berry**' Rose-pink berries.

'**Mother of Pearl**' Profusion of rose-flushed white berries.

'**White Hedge**' Stiff, upright habit. Pure white berries.

Symphoricarpos orbiculatus

The Indian currant is distinguished by its small, dark purplish pink berries. Taller growing to 2m.

'**Foliis Variegatis**' Small leaves are irregularly margined yellow. The best foliage colour will come in reasonable light.

Symphytum (Boraginaceae)

This European native, widely known as comfrey, is perfectly adapted for life on the woodland floor. I prefer other plants over this one, but it is tough and does make a dense, weed-suppressing groundcover, with underground rhizomes spreading to form rosettes of thick, almost felted, heart-shaped leaves. As always, a fine line exists between good groundcover and an invasive intruder. From these rosettes, flower spikes rise to varying heights. The flowers themselves are not the most spectacular, being clusters of narrow tubular bells in pastel colours. Care should be taken that the tallest species do not flop over and swamp smaller neighbours.

Symphytum asperum

Reaching 1.2m, *S. asperum* is a little reminiscent of many *Pulmonaria* in the way the flowers open pink, before maturing to blue. Beware of the similar *S. caucasicum*, which, although a purer blue colour, can be invasive.

Symphytum grandiflorum

As the name implies, this species has the largest flowers, which are yellowish in colour. It grows to 40cm tall and spreads fairly rapidly.

Symphytum orientale

Quite different from the archetypal groundcover, having pure white flowers, it is larger in all its parts. Particularly tolerant of dry shade, this is definitely worth planting if all else fails, though in harsher conditions it will spread less enthusiastically. 70cm.

Symphytum ×*uplandicum*

This hybrid has naturalised through much of Europe and is rather a thug. However, the variegated forms can be worth growing for their foliage. Cutting them hard to the ground regenerates lots of lush leaves without the flowers to distract the eye or set seed.

'**Axminster Gold**' Almost completely gold. Hard pruning maximises the foliar display at the acceptable price of floral performance.

'**Variegatum**' The standard pale yellow variegated selection.

Symphytum cultivars

'**Hidcote Blue**' This derivative of *S. grandiflorum* is not a bright blue; rather it is a subtle wash, shading across a creamy base colour.

'**Hidcote Pink**' A pink flushed selection.

'**Rubrum**' Thought to be a hybrid from *S. ibericum* and *S. officinale*, it has rather handsome blood-red flowers, though they are fairly small.

Syneilesis (Asteraceae)

Happily my enthusiasm was only temporarily tainted by *Symphytum*, because I just love this genus. If only one could capture the early days of this plant, rather than allowing it to grow up to maturity.

Syneilesis aconitifolia

Syneilesis aconitifolia

Recently introduced from China, the newly emerged eruptions of woolly leaves cannot fail to attract attention. They could be described in so many ways—primeval mushrooms perhaps, or my favourite description comes from an American nurseryman: shredded umbrellas after a hurricane. I cannot better that. Anything less allied to a daisy (this is the aster family after all) would be hard to imagine. Unfortunately, the flowers are a complete disappointment. I actually cut off the developing flower stalk to allow my plant to concentrate its energies on expanding, thus increasing the gorgeous colony.

Syneilesis palmata

This version, also from eastern Asia, is slightly less shredded though just as deeply divided, but it has wider lobes, giving the feeling of a little more substance. The indumentum on the silky, newly emerging shoots quickly gives way to more traditionally green leaves, though still with a lovely shape, deeply cut and slightly droopy at the edges.

Synthyris (Scrophulariaceae)

The woodland garden is such an exciting place to explore. Every meander can reveal a different treasure, and this genus is full of little gems. As many as 15 species are variations on a theme, heralding from western North America—such a rich oasis of woodland plants. They make tidy little clumps of roughly heart-shaped, glossy green leaves from which rise short, stout racemes of rich blue to violet, bell-like flowers, very early in the spring or even late winter. The flowers could be likened to squat and chunky grape hyacinths, perhaps, only prettier and much more desirable. Wonderful in company with snowdrops and aconites. Perfect for smaller scale woodland floors or a carefully selected location within a wider landscape.

Syneilesis palmata

Synthyris missurica

Synthyris missurica

Confined essentially to Washington, Oregon, and Idaho, this is the most widely available species, the benchmark with which others are compared. Although not exclusively a woodland plant, it grows extremely well in its partial shade with adequate summer moisture. Flower spikes are usually to 20cm, though as tall as 60cm is recorded.

> var. *stellata* Specific to an isolated area of the Columbia River Gorge in the American Northwest, this variant has more sharply toothed leaf margins.

Synthyris reniformis

With more kidney-shaped leaves, this species is similar to *S. missurica* but smaller. In the wild, it is often found in coniferous forests, so it is more tolerant of drier conditions. Similar in leaf shape is *S. schizantha*, which prefers moister places.

Tellima (Saxifragaceae)

Another genus closely allied to *Heuchera* and also native of western North America, when first discovered, it was thought to be a species of *Mitella*. It was subsequently classified on its own, and its close relationship with *Mitella* was recognised by devising an anagram for its name. With just one species, characteristics are as per *Heuchera*; clumps of more or less evergreen leaves will increase more rapidly on moisture-retentive soil, though drier sites are well tolerated.

Tellima grandiflora
Tiny flowers are held on tall, erect stems. Though yellow-flowered and green-leaved in the type form, some cultivars are also available. 40–80cm.

    'Forest Frost' Green veins dominate a paler, hairy leaf, the whole flushed with rose. The flowers, on tall spikes to 80cm, are also tinged with pink.

    'Purpurteppich' Arising from the *T. grandiflora* Rubra Group, this selection has rich, reddish purple foliage, particularly strongly coloured in winter. Short spikes of pink-stained flowers. 60cm.

Thalictrum (Ranunculaceae)

Well known as border plants, many of the 85 or so exquisite species are equally well suited to life on the woodland floor, with a number of new species being introduced to Western cultivation in recent years from China, Korea, and India. Several of these newer species are sufficiently difficult to obtain that it seems cruel to include them here. Though I cannot list them all, they are worth looking out for, though some experimentation may be required to ascertain their hardiness and cultural limitations. Though the family resemblance is clear (the flowers are all similar in structure, in shades of lilac and white and occasionally yellow), sufficient variation in stature makes it possible to find one for every scale of planting, including the woodland rock garden, though soil moisture and light levels will influence the heights of individuals.

Combine them with ferns for a dreamy feel or let them stand above the heavy leaves of glaucous hostas. The individual flowers are quite small, often lacking true petals and consisting of little more than a bunch of stamens; but they are held in great panicles, giving a fuzzy, out-of-focus effect, remaining in full glory for an unexpectedly long time considering their perceived fragility. All are herbaceous, form clumps of ferny foliage, and spread slowly by rhizomes to enjoy the typical woodland composition of humus-rich, moisture-retentive soil which drains adequately well in winter.

Thalictrum aquilegiifolium

Native to much of Europe, the often glaucous foliage resembles that of its namesake *Aquilegia*, rendering it a lovely and graceful species, perfectly at home in the woodland. The staminate flowers are held on tall stems in late spring to midsummer, occurring in a range of pinks, purples, and white. 150cm.

> **var. *album*** A variable wild white form.

> **'Thundercloud'** Highly desirable double-purple form.

Thalictrum chelidonii

This pretty Nepalese species has pink-lilac flowers; unusual for this genus, they have proper petals, creating an elegant bell-like effect. Small bulbils are held in the leaf axils.

Thalictrum clavatum

From southeastern North America, this natural woodlander is not widely available. It is shorter in stature with long-lasting, large pink or white flowers. 30cm.

Thalictrum filamentosum

Korea is richly endowed with *Thalictrum* species; this one is also found in China and Japan. Slender, erect stems rise to perhaps 60cm alongside single large leaves which emerge directly from the ground. The typically staminate white or purple flowers are borne in flat-topped panicles for many weeks through the summer.

> **var. *yakusimense*** Dwarf form rarely exceeding 20cm. Try it on the woodland rock garden.

The tiny, fluffy flowers of *Thalictrum filamentosum* make a wonderful foil for more dramatically coloured flowers, such as those of geranium.

Thalictrum ichangense var. minus

As foliage is very important to me, this unique Chinese dwarf form is appealing. The leaflets apparently perch on top of the stalks, but more importantly turn purple, overlaid with a silver pattern. The white, fluffy flowers from late spring to midsummer could be incidental, yet they beautifully enhance the effect.

Thalictrum kiusianum

A gorgeous, low-growing Japanese species, whose lack of height makes it suitable for the woodland rock garden. It will gently spread by underground rhizomes. Tiny flowers linger over the graceful leaves that resemble maidenhair fern, in a purple haze from early summer to early autumn. 10cm.

Thalictrum omeiense

The white staminate flowers are fairly typical, yet the features that make this species stand out, in addition to its fragrance, are the rich, purplish red sepals which encase the flowers in bud, making a delightful contrast. This species is tolerant of even heavy shade, provided the soil does not dry out in summer. 40cm.

Thalictrum punctatum

The fragrant flowers of this Korean species appear like tiny hedgehogs, whose pink spines are tipped with white in mid to late summer; they are perched on stocky, erect stems above ferny foliage. 60cm.

Thalictrum reniforme

The purple flowers of this species seem to be darkest in its Nepalese form, though it can grow rather tall at 150cm. However the hanging, cup-shaped flowers take up 30cm of that, blooming later than many, from midsummer to midautumn. The glaucous leaves are aromatic. Heavy shade is acceptable, provided adequate moisture supports the flowers through the summer.

Tiarella (Saxifragaceae)

With only seven or so species in this predominantly North American genus, recent popularity and breeding has seen a veritable explosion in the number of named cultivars—each supposedly more tempting than its predecessor. Most of these are hybrids, so they are not attributed to a particular species. Unless reconstructing a garden to a particular era, this is an occasion when I regretfully turn my back on the species in favour of the more glamorous modern hybrids. They will all do their job admirably; it comes down to personal taste and the preferred combination of foliage pattern and flower colour.

Closely related to *Heuchera*, *Tiarella* are a little more refined in their appearance with neater, pyramidal flower spikes to 25–30cm for many weeks through midspring to early summer and generally have more compact basal clumps of foliage. Excellent plants for the woodland floor, *Tiarella* provide year-round interest with palmate evergreen leaves, whose rich colours intensify with the onset of winter. I like the selections with deeply divided and lobed leaves; for me it adds an extra dimension to their attractiveness beyond the basic species, in which the leaves are more heart-shaped and only shallowly lobed. Since their appeal is year-round and they are tolerant (once established) of even dry shade, they can be planted wherever there is space or to associate with almost anything, whether it be autumn *Crocus* and *Cyclamen* or spring bulbs, or to bring colour to the quiet greenery of ferns in the extremes of summer or winter. They are versatile little plants.

Tiarella cordifolia

Noticeably stoloniferous, this species can colonise rapidly. It produces the best white flower spikes, so it is influential in many hybrids; these will spread more or less quickly according to how many of the stoloniferous genes they inherited.

> **'Oakleaf'** An early selection, but still one of the best. Light pink flowers are held above wonderfully shaped leaves which are richly flushed bronze in spring, later developing excellent burgundy colour through winter.
>
> **'Winterglow'** At its best in winter when the yellow leaves are marked with red blotches. These can look dramatic set against evergreen ferns for winter colour.

Tiarella polyphylla

Although the named clones are generally more ornamental, sometimes a species is required and this is perhaps the nicest. From eastern North America, the bloom time is particularly long, with pink or white spice-scented flowers from early spring until the first frosts. The pale green, maple-shaped leaves turn bronze-red in winter.

Tiarella wherryi

This species is very similar to *T. cordifolia* in leaf and flower, but importantly it is rhizomatous rather than stoloniferous, so it spreads only slowly. Therefore if the site is restricted, look for cultivars of this species or hybrids closely derived from it. The flowers tend to be white, tinged with pink.

> **'Bronze Beauty'** Reddish bronze leaves.

Tiarella cultivars

> **'Black Snowflake'** The concept of a black snowflake may sound a little strange, but the foliage of this cultivar is deeply cut and almost black as it opens. It can be effectively combined with any colour flower; place it with white and yellow for stark impact or deep purples for a moody effect.

Tiarella 'Mint Chocolate' evergreen foliage is attractive, even in winter.

Tiarella 'Pink Bouquet'

'**Mint Chocolate**' Toffee-coloured flower buds open to cream above beautifully marked (chocolate over mint green), maple-like, divided leaves.

'**Pink Bouquet**' Perhaps my favourite, with delightful deeper pink flower buds opening to silver-pink above beautifully shaped leaves. This hybrid has the best of both foliage and flower.

'**Skid's Variegated**' *Heuchera* foliage tends to come in shades of purple, so the truly variegated forms of *Tiarella* are distinctive, though considerably less vigorous as a result, needing a more conducive site. This selection has pink young growth, maturing to yellow through the summer, and then becoming orange-pink in winter as the temperature drops.

Tradescantia (Commelinaceae)

My late father was not a great gardener, but I do have strong memories of his long-suffering house plants. One of these was a tradescantia, which I, as an ignorant and impressionable five year old, thought was probably the most boring plant I knew. This clouded my judgment of this genus for many years, even after I discovered that some of the species were actually hardy (all of them come from the Americas). I have come to the conclusion that they work well on the woodland floor; the basal clump of straplike leaves is natural, almost grasslike, while the flowers are pretty enough to give some colour without being vulgarly ornamental. Flowers last only one day, but they emerge in daily succession from a pair of terminal leaflike bracts. After flowering, the plant can look untidy, so if it is in a visual part of the woodland, a haircut may be in order. If it is happily growing in a more wild area, it can be left alone. They are easily grown in light shade in moisture-retentive soil, where they will be at their peak from midsummer into autumn. These later performers take over from the ephemeral excitement of spring.

Tradescantia Andersoniana Group
The majority of modern hybrids are classified under the Andersoniana Group (sometimes known as *T.* ×*andersoniana*). These are derived from *T. virginiana* which has violet-blue flowers; three petals are arranged symmetrically to form a triangle. The hybrids are available in every shade imaginable from white through pink to lilac and blue. They will seed around and the cultivars will not breed true to colour.
> **'Bilberry Ice'** One of my favourite selections; white flowers, flushed with pink and stained with purple in the centre. 35cm.
> **'Concorde Grape'** Richest deep purple highlighted with vivid yellow stamens. 45cm.
> **'J. C. Weguelin'** Purest blue flowers. 45–60cm.
> **'Little White Doll'** Sparkling white flowers. 30–45cm.
> **'Osprey'** White with blue stamens that are prominent enough to appear as a blue centre to the flower. 60–90cm.
> **'Pauline'** Lilac-pink with a fluffy boss of stamens. 60cm.
> **'Red Grape'** Vivid magenta-pink. Nothing subtle about this one. 45cm.
> **'Zwanenburg Blue'** Deep violet-blue. 60cm.

Trautvetteria (Ranunculaceae)

This small genus enjoys moist areas of the woodland floor.

Trautvetteria caroliniensis
The large (up to 20 cm across), maple-like leaves can completely cover the ground, emerging in early spring from shallow rhizomes. High above them, clusters of tiny,

cream-coloured, fragrant staminate flowers (like *Thalictrum*) are perched on tall stems in mid to late summer. Technically, the species itself should be referred to as one of the two geographical variants described here. 80cm.

> **var. *japonica*** This Japanese version is generally the taller of the two, with slightly less deeply lobed foliage. The flower is nearer to white than cream.

> **var. *occidentalis*** This American form is probably the more common in cultivation and is generally the one meant when no varietal name is specified.

Tricyrtis (Convallariaceae)

Largely originating in Japan, less than 20 species are known, though disagreement exists regarding nomenclature. The classic woodland floor inhabitants revel in the humus-rich, moisture-retentive soil and shade. Generally clump-forming, the erect stems are clothed in alternate leaves, where the flowers develop in the upper leaf axils from late summer into early autumn. The flowers are quite complex in their structure, with three swollen nectaries in the centre, beyond which spread usually six petals. They appear late in the season and are a welcome sight when the time for new colour seems long past; many will continue until the first frosts of autumn. Once the stems have died down for the winter, treat them to a thick layer of mulch to help insulate the crowns through the winter, though they are surprisingly hardy. Ensure that adequate moisture is available to them in summer, but not to the extent that they waterlog in winter.

Some cultivars are more stiffly upright, making tidy clumps, while others are laxer and arch over, which can be delightful in an informal area, unless smaller neighbours become suppressed beneath their leafy stems. They add late summer colour when interplanted among ferns and daphne. Lots of choice hybrids and cultivars are available, many with exotically speckled flowers. Inevitably, as nurserymen look for innovative new plants, increasing numbers of variegated cultivars become available. But the flowers are complicated enough with their orchidlike shape and spots that foliage colour is just too much.

Tricyrtis formosana

Tricyrtis formosana

This Taiwanese species is one of the easiest to grow and worth planting in its own right. Stoloniferous, so ample colonies of semi-erect stems will be formed, topped with amazing spotted flowers held in a panicle above the leaves; this is unusual, as they are normally in the leaf axils. It is variable, in shades of white and pink, overlaid with dense purple speckling. 80cm.

> **'Dark Beauty'** The name says it all. Very dark flowers, freely produced; good robust habit. 90cm.

Tricyrtis hirta

Variable Japanese species with hairy stems and leaves, which can lack vigour in cultivation. I prefer some of the cultivars from it, selected for their better temperament.

'Miyazaki' Pale flowers finely spotted with deep purple. 60cm.

'Silver Blue' Blue spots almost merge to give the effect of a blue flower. Attractive arching stems are effective hanging over medium-sized hostas. 60cm.

Tricyrtis oshumiensis

Try this species trailing down over a rock in the woodland rock garden. The primrose-yellow flowers are accentuated by the broader petals. Due to its lax habit, it rarely exceeds 30cm in height.

Tricyrtis perfoliata

Another yellow with a lax habit, but the base colour is more golden and is overlaid with fine red spots—enough to add interest without disguising the fact that it is essentially a yellow flower. Spreading to 30–40cm, but reaching only 15cm tall.

Tricyrtis cultivars

'Empress' With major influence from *T. formosana*, this fantastic selection has large, darkly spotted flowers earlier than many, held sturdily above glossy leaves which clothe the 75cm stems right to the ground. Many others can look tatty at the base.

'Ivory Queen' Sturdy upright grower, the pure white flowers appear more substantial than many because the petals are broader. 45cm.

'Lilac Towers' On a white background, the dark purple spots are noticeably larger at the base of the petals. Yellow markings in the middle are also distinctive. 45cm.

'Moonlight Treasure' The yellow-flowered *Tricyrtis* seem to be harder to grow and are certainly less inclined to tidy growth. This superb new selection could be the answer. Clusters of two to five butter-yellow flowers crowd in seemingly every leaf axil, almost hiding the prettily marked foliage which is tough enough to resist all manner of less clement conditions.

'Tojen' Late-flowering clone with subtle, upward-facing flowers allowing full appreciation. The almost white flowers darken to violet at the petal edges. Arching habit limits physical height to 60cm.

Tricyrtis 'Tojen'

Trientalis (Primulaceae)

Just a few species of this diminutive woodlander are distributed from the Arctic across the northern temperate zone to Japan. They are rhizomatous and tuberous rooted, gently spreading across the woodland floor but never with enough substance to worry anything else. Scatter them around and let them run free; their starry white flowers will enhance any area, including those difficult sites around hostas and other late emergers who need plenty of space as the season progresses. A rosette of leaves will form on short, slender stems and from within this the delightful flowers will rise.

Trientalis borealis
This American species is the largest, growing potentially to 25cm tall. Anemone-like white flowers appear on slender stems, as if protected within the open whorl of large leaves.

Trientalis europaea
This European species is also found in Asia and is similar to *T. borealis*, but smaller in all its parts.

Trillium (Trilliaceae)

A firm favourite with all woodland aficionados, trilliums possess an oddly captivating simplicity; perhaps it is their reputation for confused naming and difficulty in establishment which draws us to them. Distributed widely across North America, but also present in Asia and the Himalayas, they grow from thickened rhizomes to produce a whorl of three leaves (everything is in threes). The flowers develop from this whorl in mid-spring and neatly divide the genus into two groups: those with pedicellate (with stalks) flowers and those with sessile (without stalks) flowers. The latter group occurs naturally only in North America, and many of them also have beautifully mottled foliage. Held singly, the flowers consist of three protective sepals and three petals, in shades of white to dusky red or yellow, arranged almost vertically in the sessile species and flat in a triangular formation, or even bell-shaped when hanging from a stalk.

Many of the white forms develop pink staining as they mature. The duration of their presence through the summer will be determined by moisture levels. If they dry out too soon, they will go dormant more quickly. Although they hate to desiccate (the cause of death of many bulbs dug unethically and illegally from the wild, and the reason for their difficulty in establishment), they equally resent waterlogged conditions in winter. The woodland floor is ideal, though some of the smaller species may be better suited to the woodland rock garden.

Many trilliums are confusingly similar and in cultivation highly promiscuous, rendering nomenclature a seemingly irresolvable minefield of uncertainty and mistaken identity. To keep the progeny of the species true to type, they should be planted in isolation. Otherwise, they will go forth and multiply with potentially interesting results. As a professional grower, I worry about names. It is important to me to supply plants which are correctly identified. Yet in a garden situation, this sometimes does not matter, so long as a plant thrives and is aesthetically pleasing. Indeed, cultivated hybrids are producing some irresistible smoky colours. The few genuine named cultivars are choice and frighteningly expensive, since they should be propagated only by division, which is a slow process.

Trillium albidum

This one is closely related to *T. chloropetalum*, but with sessile white flowers.

Trillium catesbyi

The stalked flowers are a delicate shade of pink with wavy edged petals that recurve at maturity. Unfortunately, they tend to hang among or below the leaves, which makes them difficult to admire, though the stems are quite tall. 50cm.

Trillium luteum hybrid

Trillium albidum

Trillium chloropetalum

Often considered the aristocrat of the genus, the upright, sessile flowers can have 9cm long petals, sitting on broad leaves to 25cm tall, for an extremely dramatic effect. It is worth searching out the forms with beautifully marked leaves. Unfortunately, this species is probably surrounded by the greatest amount of naming confusion. In simple terms, it comes in two flavours, var. *chloropetalum* and var. *giganteum*, with subtle differences between them. The flowers may be in assorted shades from white through cream to red-brown and garnet. Scented forms are known. *Trillium sessile* is similar.

Trillium cuneatum

This species is similar to *T. chloropetalum* but with smaller, sessile, brownish red flowers and particularly lovely foliage.

Trillium erectum

This tall, elegant plant has rich, mahogany-red stalked flowers that become flat and outward facing, making a wonderful display. 60cm.

> **f. *albiflorum*** When so many are so similar, it is confusing to have white forms of essentially red-flowered species. It makes it risky to use flower colour as an identifying feature.

Trillium flexipes

This highly ornamental species has outward-facing, stalked white flowers, rather like a white equivalent of *T. sulcatum*. 40cm. All *Trillium* species hybridise readily, but some spectacular coloured forms arise from crossing this one with *T. erectum*, with bicolours and subtly shaded flowers in hues of salmon, orange, pink, and red.

Trillium grandiflorum

Probably the most easily obtained species, and with good reason. This smaller-growing trillium is the provincial flower of Ontario, Canada. It carpets huge swathes of forest in eastern North America, surviving years of overcollecting, deer grazing, and loss of habitat to development. What a happy coincidence that the best and most floriferous species is also the easiest to grow. The stalked, large white flowers are held conspicuously above the leaves.

> **'Flore Pleno'** Semi-double.
> **f. *roseum*** Flushed with pink.
> **'Snowbunting'** Fully double form.

Trillium kurabayashii

This species is similar to *T. chloropetalum*, which adds to the confusion. Its sessile flowers are a little more brown than red—a subtle difference easier seen when the two plants are side by side for comparison.

Trillium luteum

Sweetly citrus-scented, yellow sessile flowers distinguish this species. (Occasional yellow forms are found in other species, so it is not a categorical identifying characteristic.) Leaves are gold and silver flecked. 20–40cm.

Trillium chloropetalum contrast with *Narcissus cyclamineus*

Trillium cuneatum

Trillium cuneatum in bloom

Trillium flexipes × *T. erectum*

Trillium grandiflorum

Trillium kurabayashii

Trillium luteum

Trillium ovatum

Similar to *T. grandiflorum*, the stalked, white flowers have more oval, less overlapping petals.

Trillium pusillum

This delightful tiny species needs the seclusion of the woodland rock garden to prevent it being overrun by larger plants. The often ruffle-edged, stalked white flowers are held above the proportionally lighter foliage, highlighted with bright yellow stamens. Pink-flushed forms are also known. 15cm.

Trillium rivale

Another miniature treasure for the woodland rock garden, its essentially white, stalked flowers are variable in colour, with some forms maturing to a rich, dusky pink. 10–15cm.

'**Purple Heart**' Spotted with rich purple.

Trillium rugelii

Thickly textured broad petals recurve to give a hanging Turk's-cap stalked flower. White with pink flushing from a maroon nose. *T. cernuum* is similar.

Trillium simile

Closely related to *T. erectum*, though the stalked flowers have broad white, thickly textured petals around a distinctive violet-coloured central boss. *Trillium cernuum* is similar.

Trillium sulcatum

Similar to *T. erectum*, this species is generally considered superior. The petals of the rich maroon stalked flowers tend to be broader, resulting in a more solidly triangular flower.

Trillium vaseyi

This most statuesque stalked species produces large, rich red flowers in great contrast to the bright pollen covering the long anthers. The flowers are surprisingly sweetly scented and appear to hang, though the arching stalks are quite rigid. A wonderful series of hybrids is available between this species and *T. rugelii*, all different but taking features from both parents. 60cm.

Triosteum (Caprifoliaceae)

I grow one species of this unusual herbaceous *Lonicera* relative for its gorgeous foliage alone, in a well-drained but humus-rich area of the woodland floor. None of the flowers in this genus warrant much excitement.

Triosteum pinnatifidum

Rare even in its native China and Japan, the slightly hairy, rich glossy green, opposite leaves remind me of the oak-leaved hydrangeas, but these have the added bonus of rich red central ribs. Growing to 60cm tall from a stout rootstock.

Uvularia (Convallariaceae)

Heralding from eastern North America, these delightful woodland floor dwellers are rhizomatous with slender, erect stems and simple leaves, forming tidy clumps. The yellow, nodding, bell-shaped flowers in early summer are made up of six petals which are often attractively twisted.

Uvularia grandiflora

The showiest of the genus, arching stems bow their heads with the weight of the bright yellow flowers clustered at their tips. Leafy clumps develop rapidly. 75cm.

    var. *pallida* Subtle primrose-yellow flowers.

Left: *Uvularia grandiflora*

Above: *Uvularia grandiflora var. pallida*

Uvularia perfoliata

The typical flowers are pale yellow, but the leaves are distinctive, with no leaf stalks; it almost looks as if the stem has pushed up through the leaf itself. 20–60cm.

Uvularia sessilifolia

This species creates a unique effect, since colonies tend to be less dense; this is more a case of single stems here and there so they rarely create a statement by themselves, but merely punctuate other plantings—among late-flowering small *Saxifraga* perhaps, or popping up among tiny ferns and hostas. Pale greeny yellow flowers are more tightly bell-like without the amusing twisted shagginess of the other two species. *Uvularia caroliniana* and *U. floridana* are sufficiently similar that they could almost be considered geographical variants.

Vancouveria (Berberidaceae)

This North American genus includes only three species, all similar in characteristics to the closely related *Epimedium*. Slender rhizomes creep across the woodland floor, forming basal clumps of heart-shaped leaves above which float panicles of light, airy flowers in early summer. A wide range of soil conditions are tolerated, but their health and vigour will reflect the fertility and moisture content of the medium. Prominent stamens and tiny petals give the individual flower the appearance of a shooting star. If the leaves look tatty coming out of winter, they can be removed. Admittedly less showy than many epimediums, they have an understated elegance when grown beneath shrubs or with the tall stems of Convallariaceae pushing up through them.

Vancouveria chrysantha

Bright yellow flowers are suspended over verdant, leathery evergreen foliage.

Vancouveria hexandra

Deciduous, this toughest member of the genus has white flowers.

Vancouveria planipetala

Glossy evergreen leaves prefer a little winter protection from larger adjacent evergreens. Ten to twenty-five, or even fifty, tiny white or purple-flushed flowers appear in a single spike.

Veratrum (Melanthiaceae)

These plants are irresistible for leafy people like me. There is little to compare with them as they erupt from the woodland floor in spring. I wish I could freeze the frame, to stop them at their leafy best, since the flowers are such an anticlimax. The large leaves are deeply pleated and strongly veined, lending a luxuriance to the woodland carpet. Such lush growth does need ample moisture in summer. They do not need to be planted in great drifts, and though they need plenty of room, they can be popped in here and there among the other woodland plants. They are most effective when mixed with spiky or feathery plants for maximum contrast—the tall stems of *Polygonatum*, fluffy *Astilbe*, or even lilies provide interest as these pass their glory time or combine with ferns for different textures.

All parts of this plant are toxic; cows grazing on it in its natural habitat would be poisoned. Supposedly, some Native Americans used it democratically to select their new chief. The candidate who survived the given dose was deemed the most effective ruler!

Veratrum album

Native to much of Europe, extending east through the Caucasus to China, Japan, and even Alaska, this is my favourite species because the midsummer flowers are actually worth having. These tower up to 2m, with plumes of white flowers. The North American *V. viride* is similar.

Veratrum mengtzeanum

This species is ideal where scale dictates a more restrained plant. Similar to *V. album*, except that the flower spikes reach to 100–150cm, with more modest leaves.

Veratrum nigrum

With a wide natural distribution similar to that of *V. album*, this widely available species is spectacular as those great leaves emerge; but the brownish black flowers do nothing for me. They even have an unpleasant smell, attracting flies. In a woodland, they add to the natural harmony, or you can simply cut them off.

Viburnum (Caprifoliaceae)

Valued by every gardener, more than 100 species of *Viburnum* are distributed primarily through the northern temperate zone. Variable in shape, size, and flowering time, some are deciduous, while others are evergreen; most are fragrant. Most viburnums hold their flowers in cymes, clusters in which the central flower opens first, the others in sequence, from the middle outwards. Certainly a plant for every eventuality, the difficulty is in identifying those which actually thrive in shady sites as opposed to survive. Many will grow perfectly well in shade, but with a tendency to become leggy with disappointing flowers, fruit, or autumn colour. Another issue is that some of those hailed for their autumn colour in North America do not fulfil their potential in much of Britain, due to the climate.

Most viburnums produce significantly more berries when more than one clone is planted. This can be achieved by growing them from seed; all seedlings will be genetically slightly different. Cuttings taken from one plant will all be genetically the same clone as the parent and will not achieve the desired results. Closely related species will often suffice, particularly in the case of the hybrids. *Phytophthora ramorum* (sudden oak death) can affect viburnums. Buy your plants from an inspected source and be vigilant for sudden die-back.

Viburnum acerifolium

This eastern North American native has trilobed leaves that resemble those of maples. Deciduous and suckering to 2m, white flowers in late spring to midsummer are followed by blue-black berries. Red or purple autumn colours are reminiscent of their namesake.

Viburnum ×burkwoodii
'Anne Russell'

Viburnum ×burkwoodii

(*V. carlesii* × *V. utile*) This range of hybrids initiated in 1924 are mostly semi-evergreen and more suited to shady environs than deciduous *V. carlesii*. However, they do inherit an exquisite fragrance, with typical flowers (pink in bud, opening white) produced early, from midwinter to late spring, according to location and season.

> **'Anne Russell'** One of my favourites, supposedly more compact and with a dense habit, it has still reached over 3m in 20 years in my garden. 'Chenaultii' and 'Fulbrook' are similar.
>
> **'Conoy'** This one definitely is dwarf, with tiny leaves and tight heads of almost pure white flowers. Great habit, little scent.
>
> **'Mohawk'** Back-crossed with *V. carlesii* and almost completely deciduous as a result. Red flower buds open white. Better in a slightly more open site.
>
> **'Park Farm Hybrid'** Much the standard to which others are compared. Lovely fragrance and flowers, but can be more untidy.

Viburnum davidii

This wonderful woodland shrub from China was introduced by Wilson in 1904. Low, evergreen mounds to 1.5m have elliptic, glossy leaves, indented with three conspicuous parallel veins. White flowers are followed by metallic blue fruits.

Viburnum nudum
'Pink Beauty'

Viburnum nudum

From eastern North America, with dark, glossy narrow leaves. Typical white flowers give rise to kaleidoscopic berries, transforming as they ripen from white through pink to blue, by which time the foliage has also changed colour for autumn, to rich purples. An incredible combination. 2m.

> **'Pink Beauty'** and **'Winterhur'** These cultivars maximise autumn colour and fruit.

Viburnum opulus

Native of Europe, North Africa, and northern Asia, its blooms resemble those of lace-cap hydrangea, having an outer ring of white sterile flowers surrounding inconspicuous fertile ones. Popular in cultivation, large-lobed leaves are somewhat maple-like. Great bunches of sticky berries are produced in autumn. Very tough and tolerant of all conditions. 2–4m.

> **'Aureum'** Golden yellow foliage. 2–3m.
>
> **'Compactum'** Dense compact habit; floriferous. 1.5m.
>
> **'Roseum'** (syn. 'Sterile') Sterile flowers form a globular head of bracts, hence the common name snowball tree. 2–3m.
>
> **'Xanthocarpum'** Golden yellow fruits become almost translucent. 2–3m.

Viburnum prunifolium

An inspired choice for structural planting a new area, it is tolerant of most conditions including drought. Use instead of cherry trees, to which it bears superficial resemblance. The eastern North American black haw bears shiny, bright green leaves on reddish stems and white spring flowers. Rich red to purple colours develop in autumn along with deceptively sweet and palatable damson-like fruit. Attractive bark. 5m or more. *Viburnum rufidulum* is similar, distinguished by unique rusty brown pubescence surrounding the buds.

Viburnum ×rhytidophylloides

(*V. lantana* × *V. rhytidophyllum*) Intermediate between its parents (though vastly superior to *V. lantana*, a British native hedgerow plant of minimal ornamental value), it makes a superb semi-evergreen shrub with dense flowerheads displayed well against the lustrous dark foliage. Red berries mature to shiny black. 3–4m.

> **'Alleghany'** and **'Willowwood'** Excellent American selections to look out for.

Viburnum rhytidophyllum

Viburnum rhytidophyllum

Large, upright, evergreen shrub with long, corrugated leathery leaves, rich green above and white felted beneath. Yellowish cream-coloured flowers are followed by red berries which ripen to shiny black. Very shade tolerant and brilliant for chalky soils. Another Wilson introduction from China. 3–4m.

> **'Roseum'** Rose-pink tinted flowers, particularly in bud.

Viburnum sargentii

Similar to *V. opulus*, but with larger leaves and corky bark. Purple (rather than yellow) anthers give a pinky tint to the lacecap-like flowers from a distance. 2m.

> **f.** *flavum* (syn. 'Fructuluteo') Yellow fruit.
>
> **'Onondaga'** Strong, upright plant, with maroon young leaves beautifully complemented by deep purplish red flower buds.

Viburnum tinus

This popular evergreen, known as laurustinus, gives winter protection but is also ornamental in its own right. Flowers are generally pink in bud, opening white and produced from early autumn through the winter into spring. Steely blue berries. Very tolerant of most conditions. 2–4m.

> **'Eve Price'** Classic compact form.
>
> **'French White'** Strong growing with deep green leaves and rich pink flower buds.
>
> **'Israel'** Waxy white flowers in stark contrast to the foliage.
>
> **'Lucidum'** Bigger in all its parts.
>
> **'Lucidum Variegatum'** Irregular creamy yellow variegation. Much hardier than the other variegated forms.
>
> **'Pink Prelude'** White flowers mature to pink.
>
> **SPIRIT ('Anvi')** Long-flowering recent compact selection. Tiny peach-pink buds are a display in themselves, before opening to star-shaped white flowers.
>
> **'Spring Bouquet'** Another recent addition, with rich reddish pink buds that open to pinky white flowers. Definitely different.

Viburnum trilobum

North American equivalent of *V. opulus*. 3-4m.

> **'Bailey Compact'** Compact form. 2m.
>
> **'Phillips'** Dwarf selection with fruit resembling cranberries.
>
> **REDWING ('JN Select')** Red-tinged new leaves and autumn colour.

Viburnum cultivar

> **'Pragense'** (*V. rhytidophyllum* × *V. utile*) Beautiful, hardy, and rapid hybrid bred in Prague in the 1950s. Foliage is reminiscent of *V. rhytidophyllum*, and clusters of pink buds open to white, spicily fragrant flowers in spring. 2–3m.

Vinca (Apocynaceae)

A genus of evergreen carpeting plants from Europe, North Africa, and Asia, they are extremely easily cultivated and tolerant of most conditions, including dry shade once established. Elliptic leaves clothe long trailing stems, which will be studded with starry blue or white flowers in spring. Their spread can be controlled by pruning new shoots if required.

A fungus, vinca stem blight (*Phomopsis livella*), can afflict them but is rarely terminal. In excessively wet conditions, large patches can turn brown and die out. Prune out the affected sections and it will recover if moisture levels subsequently recede.

Vinca difformis

The least hardy species, with distinctive pale violet-blue propeller-like flowers. Equivalent to *V. major* in size.

Greystone form White flowers.

'Jenny Pym' Delightful flowers are pink with a white base.

Vinca difformis

Vinca major

Larger leaves to 8cm long and blue-violet flowers. In the heaviest shade, they will produce a lovely leafy mass of stems but fewer flowers.

'Alba' White flowers.

'Maculata' Leaves with yellow central blotch.

var. *oxyloba* Narrow petalled, deeper purple flowers.

'Variegata' (syn. 'Elegantissima') Creamy margined leaves.

Vinca minor

The best suited species for serious woodland conditions, it has naturalised in Britain but is doubtfully native; in its wild form, lilac-blue flowers punctuate the green, leafy stems. However, over the years every combination of flower colour (shades of white to blue to purple) and foliage colour (white or yellow variegation) have been selected.

f. *alba* 'Gertrude Jekyll' Smaller form with white flowers.

'**Alba Variegata**' Yellow-edged leaves and white flowers.

'**Azurea Flore Pleno**' Double powder-blue flowers and green foliage.

'**Illumination**' Less rampant selection with green margins to bright yellow leaf centres. Blue-lavender flowers.

'**La Grave**' Collected by E. A. Bowles from a French churchyard in the 1920s, this is superior to most examples of 'Bowles Variety' though supposedly synonymous. Vigorous, with large azure-blue flowers.

'**Multiplex**' Double purple form, dark green foliage.

Viola (Violaceae)

With 500 or so species, it is difficult to know where to start with this genus of diminutive plants. Most gardeners are familiar with their endearing flowers, like upturned faces, in late winter and early spring, and their tufted clumps of kidney- to heart-shaped leaves. The task is simply to sort out those which will grow and flower well in the shade of the woodland floor. It is important to maintain habitats for these captivating little plants, as many provide vital food sources for rare and endangered butterfly larvae, such as *V. adunca* for the Oregon silverspot, while British violets host a number of fritillaries.

Some forms are prone to red spider mite, though I have avoided those known to be particularly susceptible.

Viola adunca
Distributed across North America, it is best grown in open woodland. Blue flowers.

Viola dissecta
This pretty little violet has unexpectedly dissected foliage and scented white flowers. It seeds around but never aggressively enough here to be a problem.

Viola labradorica
Caught in the middle of the Bermuda triangle of violet naming, this blue-flowered species does exist and is indeed suitable for woodland cultivation. However, it has been classified as *V. adunca* var. *minor* while the purple-flushed form sometimes available under this name is in fact *V. riviniana* Purpurea Group.

Viola odorata
Having spent many of my childhood holidays in Devon, the classic Devon violet of hedgerows (and gift shops) has immense sentimental value for me. This species is distributed across much of Europe down to North Africa, naturalising to the degree that it is no longer certain where its true natural boundaries lie. Adorable, with usually violet-coloured or white flowers in the wild, it forms little clumps or mats, spreading by stolons.

360

Viola odorata nestles among anemones and primroses.

var. *alba* Simple white flowers.
'**Katy**' Floriferous mid-pink.

Viola pedata

This North American native has prettily divided leaves and large lilac-purple flowers with a white throat and prominent orange stamens. It sets seed sparsely, however, which is both good and bad! Although it enjoys good drainage, it should not dry out in summer.

var. *alba* Exquisite but scarce wild white form.

'**Artist's Palette**' Dark upper petals and whitish lower ones, with a darker central stripe.

'**Bicolor**' Two-tone flowers—dark violet above light.

Viola riviniana

Distributed from Iceland south through Britain and Europe to North Africa. Flower colour varies from deep violet to pale mauve.

Purpurea Group Purple-flushed foliage, and violet-blue flowers with relatively narrow petals.

Viola sororia

Viola pedata

(syn. *V. papilionacea*) Comparatively large blue flowers adorn these pretty, moisture-tolerant woodlanders, but they can spread prodigiously. It appears to carpet by stolons, but it is in fact self-seeding. Two sets of flowers are formed. The problem set open at almost ground level, often with no petals to advertise their presence. These self-fertilise and set seed, distributing themselves around the periphery of the plant before you even realise it has happened. This can be highly desirable in a difficult area needing a dense, clean green groundcover, but be vigilant of more delicate treasures being steamrollered in their wake. The pretty yellow *V. glabella* has a similar tendency.

'**Albiflora**' White.

'**Freckles**' Pale blue flowers are heavily spotted with purple. Extremely vigorous.

Viola cultivars

Many selections have been made for differing colours. Those listed here are derived from *V. odorata* to maximise the exquisite fragrance.

'**Annie**' Small but prolific flowering in an unusual carmine colour.

'**Becky Groves**' Pale pink, splashed with a carmine centre.

'**Königen Charlotte**' (syn. *V.* 'Reine Charlotte') Deep purple-blue flowers unusually look skywards.

'**Pamela Zambra**' Vigorous, larger mid-purple.

Wisteria (Papilionaceae)

Wisterias are not remotely shade loving; they need an open site for the wood to ripen and set flower. This is not a problem, though; since they are climbers, they will wind their way up through the canopy of even a big tree and create quite a stir, with long racemes of pealike flowers in late spring to early summer, though these will be concentrated on the sunniest side.

Naming is a minefield. Many have been introduced to Western gardeners as new plants, but these are actually the same old favourites, just given fancy marketing names. However, there are named forms with subtle colour variations. It is difficult to distinguish them when out of flower, so if a particular colour is preferred, buy it in flower.

Seed-raised plants are the cheapest but should be avoided; they will take many years to produce flowers of potentially indifferent quality. Traditionally cultivars are grafted, but suckers can be a problem, sometimes taking over the plant. Some skilled nurserymen root the cuttings, and these are the best to buy since they will flower young but are on their own roots. Flowers are lost on many garden wisterias by overzealous pruning. When trained up into a tree, no pruning is possible, but neither is it necessary. Let nature take over and enjoy the results.

Wisteria brachybotrys

(syn. *W. venusta*) Distinctive vigorous Japanese species with silvery downy leaves. Individually larger flowers are held in squat racemes and are usually exquisitely scented. Violet is typical, though whites are common. A second flush of flowers may be enjoyed later in the summer if conditions suit.

Wisteria floribunda

This classic Japanese species introduced in 1830 produces traditional lavender-blue flowers, though white and pink forms are also available. (Stems twine in a clockwise direction.)

'**Multijuga**' (syn. *W. floribunda* f. *macrobotrys*) Distinctive, with long racemes—1.8m recorded in Japan.

Wisteria frutescens

Although the Oriental wisterias have a higher profile in Britain, this species from America was the first to be introduced to Europe back in 1724. Less vigorous (which can be to their advantage) and typically lilac-blue, darker and white forms are in cultivation. *Wisteria macrostachya* is closely related.

Wisteria sinensis

Introduced from a Canton garden in 1816, this Chinese species is potentially the biggest. Many selections in blues, pinks, and whites have been named. (Stems twine counterclockwise.)

Woodsia (Woodsiaceae)

Encompasses 14 species of small, tufted ferns, not all of which are hardy. Rather small and dainty, they are perfect tucked into a crevice in the woodland rock garden, where the roots will be kept cool and moist.

Woodsia obtusa

From Central America, it creeps slowly by rhizomes to make a compact mound, 45cm across, of deeply cut, lacy fronds. North American *W. oregana* is closely allied.

Woodsia polystichoides

This Japanese native was named for its superficial resemblance to *Polystichum*; pale lemon-coloured newly emerged fronds are frosted silver.

Where to See Woodland Plants

United States

The Arnold Arboretum of
Harvard University
125 Arborway
Jamaica Plain, MA 02130-3500
www.arboretum.harvard.edu

Atlanta Botanical Garden
1345 Piedmont Avenue Northeast
Atlanta, GA 30309
www.atlantabotanicalgarden.org

Bernheim Arboretum and
Research Forest
State Highway 245
P.O. Box 130
Clermont, KY 40110
www.bernheim.org

The Berry Botanic Garden
11505 Southwest Summerville Avenue
Portland, OR 97219
www.berrybot.org

The Bloedel Reserve
7571 Northeast Dolphin Drive
Bainbridge Island, WA 98110
www.bloedelreserve.org

Brooklyn Botanic Garden
1000 Washington Avenue
Brooklyn, NY 11225
www.bbg.org

Brookside Gardens
Wheaton Regional Park
1800 Glenallan Avenue
Wheaton, MD 20902
www.mc-mncppc.org/Parks/brookside

Chanticleer Foundation
786 Church Road
Wayne, PA 19087
www.chanticleergarden.org

Chicago Botanic Garden
1000 Lake Cook Road
Glencoe, IL 60022
www.chicagobotanic.org

Cornell Plantations
One Plantations Road
Ithaca, NY 14850
www.plantations.cornell.edu

Green Spring Gardens Park
4603 Green Spring Road
Alexandria, VA 22312
www.co.fairfax.va.us/parks

The Holden Arboretum
9500 Sperry Road
Kirtland, OH 44094-5172
www.holdenarb.org

Longwood Gardens
Route 1, P.O. Box 501
Kennett Square, PA 19348-0501
www.longwoodgardens.org

Missouri Botanical Garden
4344 Shaw Boulevard
St. Louis, MO 63110
www.mobot.org

The Morris Arboretum of the
University of Pennsylvania
100 Northwestern Avenue
Philadelphia, PA 19118
www.business-services.upenn.edu/
arboretum

The Morton Arboretum
4100 Illinois Route 53
Lisle, IL 60532-1293
www.mortonarb.org

New England Wild Flower Society
at Garden in the Woods
180 Hemenway Road
Framingham, MA 01701
www.newfs.org

Mount Cuba Center, Inc.
P.O. Box 3570
Greenville, DE 19807-0570
www.mtcubacenter.org

The New York Botanic Garden
Bronx River Parkway, Fordham Road
Bronx, NY 10458
www.nybg.org

North Carolina Botanical Garden
The University of North Carolina,
Totten Center
Chapel Hill, NC 27599-3375
www.ncbg.unc.edu

The J. C. Raulston Arboretum
North Carolina State University
Raleigh, NC 27695-7522
www.ncsu.edu/jcraulstonarboretum

Planting Fields Arboretum State
Historic Park
P.O. Box 58
Oyster Bay, NY 11771
www.plantingfields.org

The Polly Hill Arboretum
809 State Road
West Tisbury, MA 02575
www.pollyhillarboretum.org

The State Botanical Garden of Georgia
University of Georgia
2450 South Milledge Avenue
Athens, GA 30605
www.uga.edu/~botgarden

Washington Park Arboretum
University of Washington
Box 358010
Seattle, WA 98195-8010
http://depts.washington.edu/wpa

Winterthur Museum and Country Estate
Winterthur, DE 19735
www.winterthur.org

Yew Dell Gardens
P.O. Box 1334
5800 North Camden Lane
Crestwood, KY 40014
www.yewdellgardens.org

United Kingdom

The UK is richly endowed with gardens of all shapes and sizes; those listed here are just the tip of the iceberg. Informative tourist pamphlets are available, whilst the "Yellow Book" lists gardens open for charity under the National Garden Scheme, including some of the most beautiful private gardens in the country.

Aberglasney Gardens
Llangathen, Carmarthenshire,
SA32 8QH
www.aberglasney.org

The Beth Chatto Gardens
Elmstead Market, Colchester,
Essex CO7 7DB
www.bethchatto.co.uk

The Garden House
Buckland Monachorum,
Yelverton PL20 7LQ
www.thegardenhouse.org.uk

Greencombe Gardens
Porlock TA24 8NU
www.greencombe.org.uk

Sir Harold Hillier Gardens
Jermyns Lane, Ampfield, Romsey
Hampshire SO51 0QA
www.hillier.hants.gov.uk

Knightshayes Court
Bolham, Tiverton, Devon EX16 7RQ
www.nationaltrust.org.uk/main/w-vh/w-visits/w-findaplace/w-knightshayescourt

Marwood Hill Gardens
Barnstaple, North Devon EX31 4EB
www.marwoodhillgarden.co.uk

Royal Horticultural Society Garden,
Wisley, Woking, Surrey GU23 6QB
www.rhs.org.uk/WhatsOn/gardens/Wisley

Royal Botanic Garden Edinburgh
20A Inverleith Row
Edinburgh EH3 5LR
www.rbge.org.uk

Savill Garden
Crown Estate Office, The Great Park
Windsor, Berkshire SL4 2HT
www.savillgarden.co.uk

Westonbirt, The National Arboretum
Tetbury, Gloucestershire GL8 8QS
www.forestry.gov.uk/westonbirt

Where to Buy Woodland Plants

Many of these nurseries also have beautiful and informative display gardens.

North America

Asiatica Nursery
P.O. Box 270
Lewisberry, PA 17339
www.asiaticanursery.com

Foliage Gardens
2003 128th Avenue Southeast
Bellevue, WA 98005
www.foliagegardens.com

Greer Gardens, Inc.
1280 Goodpasture Island Road
Eugene, OR 97401-1794
www.greergardens.com

Gossler Farms Nursery
1200 Weaver Road
Springfield, OR 97478
www.gosslerfarms.com

Hillside Nursery
107 Skinner Road
Shelburne Falls, MA 01370
www.hillsidenursery.biz

Munchkin Nursery and Gardens
323 Woodside Drive Northwest
Depauw, IN 47115-9039
www.munchkinnursery.com

Naylor Creek Nursery
2610 West Valley Road
Chimacum, WA 98325
www.naylorcreek.com

Pacific Rim Native Plant Nursery
P.O. Box 413
Chilliwack, BC V2P 6J7, Canada
www.hillkeep.ca

Plant Delights Nursery, Inc.
9241 Sauls Road
Raleigh, NC 27603
www.plantdelights.com

Rosslyn Nursery
211 Burrs Lane
Dix Hills, NY 11746
www.roslynnursery.com

Trans-Pacific Nursery
20110 Canyon Road
Sheridan, OR 97378
www.worldplants.com

United Kingdom

The RHS Plant Finder, published annually, is an invaluable source of reference, listing every plant grown in the UK and where to buy it.

Ashwood Nurseries
Ashwood Lower Lane, Ashwood,
Kingswinford, West Midlands DY6 0AE
www.ashwood-nurseries.co.uk

Avon Bulbs
Burnt House Farm, Mid Lambrook,
South Petherton, Somerset TA13 5HE
www.avonbulbs.com

BlueBell Nursery
Annwell Lane, Smisby, Ashby de la
Zouch, Leicestershire LE65 2TA
www.bluebellnursery.com

Bowden Hostas
Sticklepath, Okehampton, Devon
EX20 2NL
www.bowdenhostas.com

Broadleigh Gardens
Bishops Hull, Taunton, Somerset
TA4 1AE
www.broadleighbulbs.co.uk

Buckland Plants
The School, Whinnieliggate,
Kirkcudbright DG6 4XP
www.bucklandplants.co.uk

Cotswold Garden Flowers
Sands Lane, Badsey, Worcestershire
WR11 7EZ
www.cgf.net

Crûg Farm Plants
Griffith's Crossing, Caernarfon,
Gwynedd LL55 1TU
www.crug-farm.co.uk

Edrom Nurseries
Coldingham, Eyemouth,
Berwickshire TD14 5TZ
www.edromnurseries.co.uk

Farmyard Nurseries
Llandysul, Dyfed SA44 4RL
www.farmyardnurseries.co.uk

Harveys Garden Plants
Great Green, Thurston, Bury St.
Edmunds, Suffolk IP31 3SJ
www.harveysgardenplants.co.uk

Junker's Nursery Ltd.
Lower Mead, West Hatch,
Taunton, Somerset TA3 5RN
www.junker.co.uk

Long Acre Plants
Charlton Musgrove,
Somerset BA9 8EX
www.longacreplants.co.uk

The Place for Plants
East Bergholt Place
East Bergholt
Suffolk CO7 6UP

Further Reading

Beckett, K. 1993. *Alpine Garden Society Encyclopaedia of Alpines.* Worcestershire, UK: AGS Publications.

Buffin, M. W. 2005. *Winter-Flowering Shrubs.* Portland, Oregon: Timber Press.

Cappiello, P., and D. Shadow. 2005. *Dogwoods: The Genus Cornus.* Portland, Oregon: Timber Press.

Case, F. W. and R. B. 1997. *Trilliums.* Portland, Oregon: Timber Press.

Darke, R. 2002. *The American Woodland Garden: Capturing the Spirit of the Deciduous Forest.* Portland, Oregon: Timber Press.

Dirr, M. 1997. *Dirr's Hardy Trees and Shrubs: An Illustrated Encyclopedia.* Portland, Oregon: Timber Press.

Gardiner, J. 2000. *Magnolias: A Gardener's Guide.* Portland, Oregon: Timber Press.

Grenfell, D., and M. Shadrack. 2004. *The Color Encyclopedia of Hostas.* Portland, Oregon: Timber Press.

Gusman, G. and L. 2002. *The Genus Arisaema: A Monograph for Botanists and Nature Lovers.* Portland, Oregon: Timber Press.

Le Hardÿ de Beaulieu, A. 2003. *An Illustrated Guide to Maples.* Portland, Oregon: Timber Press.

Hoshizaki, B. J., and R. C. Moran. 2001. *Fern Grower's Manual.* Portland, Oregon: Timber Press.

National Gardens Scheme. Gardens of England and Wales Open for Charity. http://www.ngs.org.uk/. Accessed February 2006.

Phillips, R., and M. Rix. 1989. *Bulbs.* Pan Garden Plants Series. London: Pan Books Ltd.

———. 1993. *Perennials* Vols. 1 and 2. Pan Garden Plants Series. London: Pan Books Ltd.

Royal Horticultural Society. Annual. *RHS Plant Finder.* London: Dorling Kindersley Ltd.

———. *RHS Plant Finder*, online version. http://www.rhs.org.uk/rhsplantfinder/plantfinder.asp. Accessed February 2006.

Schmid, W. G. 2002. *An Encyclopedia of Shade Perennials.* Portland, Oregon: Timber Press.

Stearn, W. T. 2002. *The Genus Epimedium.* Portland, Oregon: Timber Press.

Vertrees, J. D. 2001. *Japanese Maples* 3rd ed. Portland, Oregon: Timber Press.

Index

Photographs appear on page numbers designated in *italics*.
Page numbers in **bold face** indicate a descriptive entry in the Plant Directory.